Aspen Institute
Executive Seminar Program

Basic Readings

Aspen Institute Readings

Edited by
Martin Krasney

**with commentary
on texts and authors
by Sidney Hyman**

Aspen Institute for Humanistic Studies

Published in the United States of America in 1977
by the Aspen Institute for Humanistic Studies
717 Fifth Avenue, New York, N.Y. 10022

© 1977 by the Aspen Institute for Humanistic Studies
Book composition by Curt Chelin and Mark Woodworth, San Francisco, California
Typeface—Souvenir
Manufactured by Malloy Lithographing, Inc., Ann Arbor, Michigan

ISBN: 0—915436—48—5

Basic Books, Inc.—for "To Reveal One's True Feelings" by Mao Tse-tung from *Mao Tse-tung: The Man in the Leader* by Lucian Pye, c. 1976. Reprinted by permission of the publisher.

The Brookings Institution—for *Equality and Efficiency: The Big Trade-off* (selection, Chapter 4) by Arthur M. Okun, c. 1975. Reprinted by permission of the publisher.

Dell Books—for "Domestic Law and International Order" from *Soul On Ice* by Eldridge Cleaver, c. 1970. Reprinted by permission of the publisher.

Ganish & Co.—for *Indian Home Rule* by Mohandas Gandhi, c. 1921.

Harcourt Brace Jovanovich, Inc.—for "The Hollow Men" from *Collected Poems, 1909-1962* by T. S. Eliot, c. 1963. Reprinted by permission of the publisher. Also for *A Room of One's Own* (selection) by Virginia Woolf, c. 1963. Reprinted by permission of the publisher.

Harper & Row, Publishers, Inc.—for "Buddhist Economics" from *Small Is Beautiful: Economics As If People Mattered* by E. F. Schumacher, c. 1976, reprinted by permission of the publisher; for "The Blurring of 'Public' and 'Private'" from *The Future Executive: A Guide for Tomorrow's Managers* by Harlan Cleveland, c. 1972, reprinted by permission of the publisher and the author; for "Letter From Birmingham City Jail" from *Why We Can't Wait* by Martin Luther King, Jr., c. 1964, reprinted by permission of the publisher; and for *The Unseen Revolution: How Pension Fund Socialism Came to America* (selection, Chapters 1 and 5) by Peter F. Drucker, c. 1976, reprinted by permission of the publisher.

National Affairs, Inc.—for "The Corporation and Society in the 1970s" by Daniel Bell, *The Public Interest*, No. 24, Summer, c. 1971. Reprinted by permission of the author.

W. W. Norton & Company, Inc.—for *Business Civilization in Decline* (selection, Chapter 5) by Robert L. Heilbroner, c. 1976. Reprinted by permission of the publisher.

The Viking Press, Inc.—for "The Lives of a Cell" and "Ceti" from *The Lives of a Cell* by Lewis Thomas, c. 1976 by the Viking Press, Inc.

Acknowledgments

There have been invaluable suggestions on the content and structure of these readings from many persons close to the Aspen Institute, including most moderators and many alumni of the Aspen Institute Executive Seminar Program. Space does not permit a listing of all those to whom I am indebted, but several contributed so significantly that their names should be recorded here: Joe Slater for his continuing guidance and support; Harlan Cleveland, Michael Haltzel, Sidney Hyman, Lionel Landry, Robert McKay, Barbara Miller, Joseph and Kit Reed, and Charles Yost for their assistance in the identification and organization of the texts; and Barbara Anderson, David Brennan, Catherine McGowan and Gretchen Mueller for their help in preparations. Special thanks to Richard Kuhn and Linda Brandt for their conscientious supervision of the production and publication of the *Aspen Institute Readings*.

New York, December 1976   Martin Krasney

Man was not born to solve the problem of the universe, but rather to seek to lay bare the heart of the problem and then confine himself within the limits of what is amenable to understanding.

The question to ask is not whether we are perfectly agreed, but whether we are proceeding from a common basis of sentiment.

Johann Wolfgang von Goethe
(1749-1832)

Preface

The Aspen Institute Executive Seminar Program is designed to provide a significant personal and professional experience for business executives and leaders from other sectors of society, an opportunity to come together for reflective examination of the most fundamental issues facing humanity and of the great ideas expressed throughout history with regard to those issues. The readings which serve as the basis for the seminars point to both the continuity and the diversity of human introspection and action. They focus on the importance of independent personal exploration while reemphasizing the interconnectedness of human problems and opportunities.

The Executive Seminar Program texts are presented with the realization that value considerations, although we are not always conscious of them, underpin and pervade all human actions, from the interpersonal to the global. These texts underscore the belief that, in a just society, humanistic perspectives must prevail, that civilizations and persons must be conscious of the sources of their behavior and reflective about the ramifications. The readings imply that both vital individuals and vital institutions must be three-dimensionally oriented—drawing nourishment from the best traditions of the past, working with commitment on the concerns of the present, and responding hopefully to the challenges of the future.

While the readings constitute the heart of the Executive Seminar Program they do not represent its totality. They provide a point of departure for the reexamination of contemporary societal problems and for personal reassessment by each individual. This humanistic process is enhanced by the growth of mutual respect and regard which develops among seminar partipants in a physical setting that removes the individuals from their everyday world while involving them intimately with natural beauty.

The Aspen Institute for Humanistic Studies has developed considerably since Walter P. Paepcke's inspired act of faith following the Goethe Bicentennial in 1949. It has been broadened and deepened under the leadership for more than two decades of Robert O. Anderson. Now international in its mentality, governance, participants, and the location of its facilities, the Institute includes programs of Thought-Leading-To-Action in seven major areas of societal concern: Communications and Society; Education for a Changing Society; Environment and the Quality of Life; International Affairs; Justice, Society and the Individual; Pluralism and the Commonweal; and Science, Technology and Humanism. The Executive Seminar Program, which remains the core element of the Institute, has been established beginning in 1977 on a year-round basis and will offer its seminars for the first time in a number of sites outside Aspen. The year 1977 also marks the inception of a new seminar on the Corporation and Society for those who have completed the basic Executive Seminar.

J. E. Slater
President
Aspen Institute
  for Humanistic Studies

Martin Krasney
Executive Director
Aspen Institute
  Executive Seminar Program

Table of Contents

The word selection identifies readings which are excerpted rather than presented in their entirety.

PART THREE:
PROPERTY

Second Week

PART FOUR:
THE AMERICAN TESTAMENT

PART FIVE:
AGREEMENT, CONSENSUS, AND LIMITS OF DISSENT

PART SIX:
PARTICIPATION AND POWER:
THE MODERN CORPORATION AND SOCIETY

Fourth Day

Fifth Day

PART SEVEN:
INTERDEPENDENCE

Sixth Day

Commentary
on Texts
and Authors

by Sidney Hyman

Plato

Plato was born in 428 or 427 B.C. and died in 348 or 347 B.C. His family on both sides was one of the most distinguished in Athens. Legend traces his father's line of descent back to the god Poseidon. On his mother's side, the family was related to Solon, the celebrated Athenian lawgiver. After his mother was widowed, she married her uncle Tyrilamtes, a prominent supporter of Pericles, and Plato was probably reared in that home.

Plato's early life coincided with the disastrous years of the Peloponnesian War, the shattering of the Athenian empire, and the fierce struggle of the oligarchs and democrats in the year of anarchy, 404–403 B.C. He was too young to have learned anything from the experience of the Imperial Democracy of Pericles or the full tide of the "sophistic" movement. He was not a pupil of Socrates, but must have known him in boyhood, for his relatives Critias and Charmides were old friends of Socrates.

Plato reports that his early ambitions were political instead of philosophical. Following the establishment of the Tyranny of the Thirty in 404, in which his relatives were leaders, Plato was "invited to share in their doings." He initially held back until their policy was revealed, and then was repelled by their violence, particularly their attempt to implicate Socrates in an illegal execution. Though he hoped for better days when the democracy was restored, the condemnation of Socrates convinced him that he could no more collaborate with the democrats than with the oligarchs. Concluding that "public affairs at Athens were not carried on in accordance with the manners and practices of our fathers, nor was there any ready method by which I could make new friends," Plato abandoned his intention of devoting himself to politics.

After the execution of Socrates in 399 B.C., Plato reportedly went on a series of travels in Greece, Egypt, and Italy. During this time, he seems to have discovered his vocation in philosophy as he reflected on the life and teachings of Socrates. On his return to Athens in about 387, he founded the Academy. He had presumably already completed some of his dialogues by this time, particularly those celebrating the memory of Socrates. For the rest of his life, Plato presided over the Academy, making it the intellectual center of Greek life. In addition to philosophy, particular attention was given to science and law. "Problems" were propounded for solution by the joint research of the students, and the most important mathematical work of the fourth century was done by Plato's friends and pupils. The Academy was frequently called upon by the Greek cities and colonies to furnish advisers on legislative matters.

The Republic, written in Plato's mature years, provides an awesome richness of themes. The selection from Plato's *Republic* which opens the Executive Seminar, "The Allegory of the Cave," has intrigued students of philosophy over the ages. As the title indicates, *The Republic* is about the state, but it is also about justice, the human soul, education, human weakness and corruption, and the ultimate reality of philosophic knowledge. In Plato's vision of the ideal human community, a philosopher-king would play the central role, because reason—the ruler of the perfect soul—must form the basis of the perfect state.

The Republic provides a vivid description of the philosopher and his relation to the community and, at the same time, considers some of the fundamental questions of philosophy. Plato's literary artistry conveys poignantly the philosopher's all too human impulse to shrink from his mission of bringing order to the human community and to remain instead in the perpetual enjoyment of contemplative wisdom. It shows the scornful attitude of most men toward philosophy and the philosopher and concludes, sadly, that the best practical solution is for the philosopher to dwell apart from the common life. It shows how the philosopher may triumph over these obstacles and bring to others the "light"—the knowledge of reality—he himself has seen.

Through his dramatic dialogue, Plato provides a basic philosophic theme on the nature of knowledge and the nature of reality. He expounds the distinction between knowledge and opinion and between the primary reality of "ideas" and the secondary, reflected reality of "concrete experience."

Dostoevsky

"The Grand Inquisitor" is a self-contained story within *The Brothers Karamazov,* the last novel written by Fyodor Mikhailovich Dostoevsky (1821–1881). The extraordinary range of the novel itself is equaled only by the extraordinary nature of the author's own life. An epileptic with an irresponsible father who was murdered by his serfs, Dostoevsky was educated in Moscow and at the School of Military Engineers in St. Petersburg (Leningrad). Commissioned a lieutenant in the army in 1841. he left the service three years later to devote himself to literature.

Dostoevsky achieved immediate literary success by writing poignant stories of the humiliated and the injured, but his success was soon followed by a period of literary failure and a precarious economic existence. These difficult years were climaxed by his arrest for belonging to a socialist study group concerned with the desperate plight of the Russian masses under the feudal Czarist regime. He was tried and sentenced to a bogus execution: a coffin was readied, he was bound to the stake, last rites were offered, and then he was informed of a sudden reprieve and a sentence to imprisonment.

This experience permanently affected Dostoevsky, as did the prison sentence itself—four years of hard labor in Siberia, where he considered himself buried alive. His experiences intensified his epilepsy, but also opened his heart and mind to religious convictions, especially those of universal compassion and pity for human suffering. Upon being released from prison, Dostoevsky served as a private in the Russian army in Siberia, until, ten years after his mock execution, he was allowed to return to Russia's capital cities. There, he and his brother began a journal, dedicated to Christian nationalism, which regarded the Russian peasantry as a peculiar repository of Russian spiritual values.

His novels, including *The House of the Dead* (about the Siberian penal colony) and *The Insulted and the Injured*, were published in this new journal in serial form. The journal was a financial success, but the government, misunderstanding its purpose, suppressed it. Again, Dostoevsky was in financial difficulty. He tried to recoup his fortune at the gambling tables but only added to his losses and was forced to turn out stories at enormous speed in order to obtain money. Some of his best works, such as *Crime and Punishment*, were produced under these circumstances. Though he was plagued by epilepsy, poverty, and a gambling mania, the last twelve years of his life were richly creative—*The Idiot, The Possessed,* and *The Brothers Karamazov* were all written during this period. His literary success ultimately brought him financial solvency and comparatively easy circumstances.

Outside Russia, Dostoevsky's rise to fame was very slow. Compared with Gogol, Turgenev, and Tolstoy, he remained a rather obscure figure in the West. However, with the spiritual and historical crises of the twentieth century, Dostoevsky's writings became one of the chief sources of illumination on the condition of modern man. Philosophers and theologians, as well as literary critics and common readers, sought depth of understanding in his writings.

The Brothers Karamazov was the fulfillment of Dostoevsky's long-held ambition to write a major work that would discuss the "eternal questions" of human existence and deal with sin, suffering, and the "existence of God—the problem that has consciously and unconsciously tormented me all my life." The book, which he started in 1878, was to have been part of a cycle of five novels entitled *The Life of a Great Sinner*. But when he began to work, he decided to scale down his original plan to two novels. *The Brothers Karamazov* is only the first half of the author's intended work, for Dostoevsky died shortly after completing it. But critics and readers alike generally acclaim it as the greatest of Dostoevsky's novels.

The Brothers Karamazov is the story of a Russian family. The father, Fyodor Pavlovitch Karamazov, is a selfish sensualist, interested only in his own power and pleasure. He has three legitimate sons who embody three distinct types of character and perhaps different aspects of the Russian soul. The eldest son, Dimitri, is a military man, who is passionate, reckless, and sensual. The second son, Ivan, is an intellectual, educated in the thought and literature of the past and receptive to the philosophical currents of his own day, particularly nihilism. The youngest son, Alyosha, is a gentle, spiritual, and compassionate person, a novice at a local monastery. Fyodor also has a fourth son, Smerdyakov, the illegitimate offspring of an idiot girl. Smerdyakov, an epileptic, acts as a servant to Fyodor and plays an enigmatic but important role in the novel.

While the plot of the novel resembles a detective story about a shocking murder—a parricide—it is far more than an engrossing tale. Above all, it represents the conflict in the human heart between good and evil, faith and doubt, freedom and bondage. Gross sensuality and spiritual impulses accompany one another, often in the same person. Simple goodness of heart and profound spiritual potentialities are revealed in the roisterer and brawler. *The Brothers Karamazov* is regarded as one of the great spiritual documents of the modern age—a source of illumination and insight for present-day philosophers, theologians, and psychologists, and an instructive example for the contemporary writer of existentialist, psychological, and religious novels.

Genesis

It is characteristic of nearly all the books of the *Old Testament* that they were not completed by a single hand, but were gradually expanded to their present form through several stages of writings and compilations. The authors did not, as a rule, completely rewrite the material. Instead, they excerpted passages from preexisting documents that were suitable to their purposes and then incorporated them with additional material of their own. Sometimes, the excerpted passages formed long, complete narratives; sometimes they consisted of short passages taken alternatively from two older narratives and dovetailed by the author to make a continuous story. The points of juncture of older and more recent writings are often discernible, and the sources can frequently be disentangled.

The Hebrew traditions regarding Israel's origins and early history were probably first set down in writing in the 10th or 9th century B.C. by a Judean prophet who, because of his almost exclusive use of the sacred Hebrew name Yahweh or Jahveh, is identified by scholars with the abbreviation J. This writer, who possessed a singularly adroit and picturesque style and deep religious feeling and insight, relates man's creation from the dust, his first sin, and its consequences. Then he gives an account of the early growth of civilization, the flood, and the origins of different languages. Finally, in a series of vivid pictures, he tells the traditional story of the patriarchs, of Moses and the Exodus, and of the conquest of Canaan. Excerpts from *Genesis 3:1—20*, which appear as the second version of the creation of man, are generally ascribed to J.

Somewhat later another writer emerged. He is referred to as E because he preferred the name Elohim, representing a conception of God somewhat different from Yahweh. E, who apparently lived in the northern kingdom of Israel, recorded the traditions current in his region. His style resembles that of J, but there are small differences of expression and representation. Traces of E are found in *Genesis, Exodus, Numbers,* and *Joshua*. He covered essentially the same ground as J, often relating a parallel but somewhat different account of the same events.

After the fall of the northern kingdom in 722 B.C., a prophet of Judah known as JE selected extracts from J and E and combined them with additions of his own in a single narrative. JE treated history from the standpoint of the religious ideas of the prophets, and most of the best-known narratives of the patriarchal and Mosaic age belong to him.

Probably in the seventh century, during the reign of Josiah, the narrative of JE was enlarged by the addition of the discourses of *Deuteronomy.* This book voiced the religious ideals of the age and molded the phraseology by which those ideals were expressed in the later priestly sections of the *Old Testament.* These sections, known as P, were apparently the work of a school of priests who, after the destruction of the temple, began to codify the pre-Exilic ceremonial regulations of the Hebrews, combining these regulations with a narrative extending from the Creation to the settlement in Canaan.

The chief object of their work, which was completed during the century following the Restoration of 537 B.C., was to describe in detail the leading institutions of the theocracy and the origin of these institutions in the Mosaic age. Thus, P's picture of Hebrew history represents a priestly idealization rather than the actual past. The story of creation in *Genesis 1* and some of the passages in *Genesis 2* are generally ascribed to P. Though P's version of the story appears first in *The Bible,* it was probably added 400 to 500 years after the story of man's creation and fall contained in *Genesis 2* and *3.*

Mencius

In the pantheon of classical Chinese thought, the first is Confucius, who lived between 551 and 479 B.C. Next in rank is his follower Mencius, who lived between 371 and 289 B.C. The patterns of their lives were strikingly similar. Like Confucius, Mencius was born in what is now Shantung province and, according to legend, lost his father when he was about three years old. Also like Confucius, he lived during a period of political chaos, social and cultural disorganization, and intellectual conflict.

Mencius became a professional teacher, served briefly as an official in the state of Ch'i from 319 to 312 B.C., and traveled for 40 years from state to state, advocating reform. Mencius was more self-confident than Confucius: "If heaven wished peace and order for the world," he said, "who is there besides me to bring it about?" He was also more argumentative and dogmatic and relentlessly attacked opposing schools of thought while strenuously defending Confucius as a supreme sage and master. He finally became disappointed with his lack of impact and retired from active life.

Mencius's philosophy is the first in Chinese history to espouse a doctrine of the original goodness of human nature. Because he lived in an age of great disorder, he equated righteousness with love, saying that "love is man's mind and righteousness man's path. These two are to be the guiding principles in government." He frequently lectured the feudal rulers on their "neverland government" and vigorously advocated righteousness, as opposed to utility and profit. He wanted to overcome "the way of the desperate" (the way of force) by "the kingly way" (the way of moral power).

Following the teachings of Confucius, he maintained that only good men should rule. A ruler's right to govern comes from the mandate of heaven, which is revealed in the condition and sentiment of the people.

Mencius believed that, in a political state, "the people are most important, territory is secondary, and the ruler least important." Bad rulers are to be overthrown, by revolution if necessary, for they have lost heaven's mandate. For practical measures, he recommended the establishment of schools, permanent property for the people, agricultural reform, and the restoration of the ancient Nine-Square system, with eight families cultivating one square each but jointly cultivating the ninth for the state. He also advocated equal distribution of wealth, little punishment of infractions, and protection of the old and weak. His teachings, found in the *Book of Mencius* compiled after his death, are regarded as Orthodox Confucianism and have greatly influenced Chinese thought, especially Neo-Confucianism.

Hsun Tzu

Western scholars of Chinese intellectual history sometimes compare Confucius to Socrates, Mencius to Plato, and Hsun Tzu to Aristotle. Hsun Tzu, who lived from 298 to 238 B.C., witnessed the extinction of the Chou aristocracy and the emergence of the first centralized bureaucracy in China. His intellectual pursuits included linguistic theory, epistemology, logic, and the art of argument. He was also well-informed in practical political affairs and spent the greater part of his life as a regional administrator in the local government of central China.

Unlike Confucius and Mencius, Hsun Tzu expressed his ideas not merely through sayings and conversations recorded by disciples, but also through his own well-organized essays. Essentially, he preached a philosophy of culture. His most famous dictum is that "the nature of man is evil; his goodness is acquired only through training." Hsun Tzu maintained that human nature at birth consisted of instinctual desires which, left to themselves, were selfish, anarchic, and antisocial. As society exerted a gradual civilizing influence upon the individual, through teaching and training, the person became a disciplined and morally conscious human being. Of prime importance in this civilizing process were the *Li* (ceremonies, rules of social behavior, traditional mores) and music, which Hsun Tzu regarded as having profound moral significance.

Hsun Tzu's views of human nature put him in radical opposition to Mencius. Both thinkers agreed that all men are potentially capable of becoming sage and morally responsible, but, for Mencius, every man has the power to develop further the sparks of goodness which are already present at birth. For Hsun Tzu, every man could learn from society how to overcome his initially antisocial impulses. The differences between these two philosophers began a major controversy in Confucian thought.

Hsun Tzu also denied supernaturalism and proposed a sophisticated interpretation of popular religious observances and "superstitions." These, he said, were merely poetic fictions, useful for the common people as an orderly outlet for human emotions but not to be taken as true by educated men. Hsun Tzu thus inaugurated in Confucianism a rationalistic trend congenial to scientific thinking. At the same time, his warning that man should shun the investigation of natural phenomena in favor of humanistic studies suggests that he was decidedly hostile to scientific development.

John

The *Gospel of St. John* is the fourth and most recent Gospel of the *Bible*. The book takes its character from five qualities of John as a writer and philosopher: (1) a readiness to handle traditional material with a sovereign freedom, controlled and limited only by doctrinal conviction and great devotion; (2) a mystic's deep love for double meanings; (3) the influence of certain ideas and concepts unique to the text, such as *"logos,"* "the only begotten," "light of the world," and "eternal life"; (4) a continual striving to contemplate history in ways in which man's evolvement appears to be a successive revelation of God's will; and (5) a resort to allegory, in which truth is revealed symbolically through the ideas and lessons expressed by the story, rather than through the story's factual accuracy.

As is true of much of the *Old* and *New Testaments*, the origin and authorship of the *Gospel of St. John* has been the subject of dispute among Biblical scholars. The only agreement is that the author was a Christian of Judeo-Alexandrine background; a believer with apparently no personal reminiscences of the life, preachings, and death of Jesus; and a theologian far removed from a historical preoccupation, except that he retained certain major traditional facts.

Eliot

Thomas Stearns Eliot was born in St. Louis, Missouri, in 1888, the youngest of seven children of Henry Ware Eliot and Charlotte Chauncy Stearns Eliot, both of whom were descended from old New England families. In 1906, Eliot entered Harvard and in three years completed the work required for the B.A. degree. While an undergraduate, he was editor of the *Harvard Advocate,* in which several of his poems appeared. He entered graduate school as a student of philosophy, and in 1910 received the M.A. degree.

Eliot spent the next year studying philosophy and French literature, particularly poetry; then he returned to Harvard to resume his graduate work, supplementing the study of philosophy with the study of ancient languages, including Sanskrit. He remained at Harvard for three years, and in 1913-1914 he was an assistant in the Department of Philosophy. He went abroad from 1914 to 1915 on a traveling fellowship, first to Germany, where he spent part of the summer before the outbreak of the World War, then to England, where he continued the study of philosophy at Merton College, Oxford.

In the spring of 1915, Eliot married an Englishwoman, Vivienne Haigh. As a result of his marriage and congenial literary contacts, he decided to settle in England. After leaving Oxford, he taught for a year at the Highgate School near London, then changed his occupation to banking and for several years worked as a clerk in Lloyd's Bank, Ltd. Meanwhile, he had begun to write for several British and American periodicals, and he finally resigned from Lloyd's to devote all of his time to writing and editing.

Eliot's first published poems appeared in 1915 in *Poetry,* a magazine of verse of which Ezra Pound was foreign editor, and in *Catholic Anthology,* another periodical edited by Pound. Thereafter, Eliot contributed to a number of magazines and brought out several slender volumes of poetry. His work brought him into public notice by 1917 and won him the admiration of numerous critics and many of his fellow poets. His reputation was already well-established before the publication in 1922 of his noted epic poem, *The Wasteland,* which develops themes and attitudes similar to those of *The Hollow Men.*

Eliot's poetry, plays, and criticism over the next four decades won him a large public as well as a critical following. He received the Nobel Prize for Literature in 1948 and died in 1965, after becoming an Anglican and a British subject.

Freud

Sigmund Freud, the founder of psychoanalysis, was born in Moravia in 1855 and died in London in 1939. He lived in Vienna from 1859 to 1938, when he moved to London following the absorption of Austria by Nazi Germany. Originally, he felt no inclination toward medical practice, being more interested in purely scientific research. However, influenced by Goethe's essay *Die Natur,* he ultimately embarked on a medical curriculum and became a neurologist.

In 1884, a Viennese physician, Josef Breuer, told Freud about an extraordinary experience in which symptoms of hysteria were cured by having the patient recollect, in a state of hypnosis, the circumstances of the symptoms' origins and the accompanying emotions. This "cathartic" method of treatment, which was the starting point for what later became psychoanalysis, intrigued Freud. In 1885, he went to Paris to study under the great neurologist J. M. Charcot, whose moral support strengthened Freud's determination to continue his then-revolutionary study of hysteria from a psychological point of view. These studies met with almost unanimous disapproval from his colleagues.

In the next few years, Freud published several important works in neurology, particularly on aphasia and cerebral paralysis in children. His interest in clinical psychology continued as well, and in 1893 he persuaded Breuer to collaborate with him on a book, *Of the Studies of Hysteria.* In 1894, Freud took the decisive step of replacing hypnotism by the technique of free association as a means of resuscitating a patient's buried memories. This technique became the kernel of Freud's psychoanalytical method.

Freud gradually extended his investigations to abnormal psychology and evolved new concepts and methods for identifying and treating obsessions, phobias, addiction, psychosomatic illnesses, and the hallucinations of the insane. The stamp of "degeneracy" impressed upon neurotic behavior by other schools of medicine was altogether erased by Freud. More research convinced him that a person might exhibit neurotic symptoms as a result of certain environmental experiences and that there was no definite dividing line between the normal and abnormal.

Freud theorized that the adult mind retains all of the infantile psychic structures in an unconscious setting. Nothing is lost, and the unconscious forever tries to express itself. Infantile wishes and primitive impulses can always be demonstrated in adult behavior and on occasion are brought back to the conscious level when the individual finds it impossible to cope with the difficulties of the world of reality. A normal person also constantly revives repressed childhood fears and desires in dreams, whereas the neurotic or psychotic individual is one who regresses back into a sort of psychic infantilism in his or her conscious behavior. Thus, Freud contended that the behavior and emotions of the civilized adult result directly from his or her earliest childhood experiences and impressions.

Monod

Jacques L. Monod, the French molecular biologist, was born in 1910 and died in 1976. At the time of his death, he was director and head of the Department of Cellular Biochemistry at the Pasteur Institute in Paris. The Nobel Laureate for Medicine in 1965, Monod was an eminent researcher in the physiology, kinetics, and metabolism of bacterial growth; in the mechanism of the biosynthesis of enzymes; and in the regulation of cellular metabolism. Widely recognized and highly regarded as a statesman of science, Monod was the author of *Chance and Necessity,* published in 1970, and the essay "On Values in the Age of Science," which was prepared for the Fourteenth Nobel Symposium (1969) on "The Place of Value in a World of Facts."

Exodus

The *Book of Exodus* draws its name from the Greek word for the most prominent event of the history it narrates—the deliverance of Israel from Egypt. Strictly speaking, however, the title is applicable to only the first half of the book, the historical portion, and takes no account of the chapters which describe the law given on Mount Sinai, the covenant between God and the people of Israel, the furnishing of the tabernacle, and the Hebrew codes for religious, ritualistic, moral, and ethical behavior.

The point made earlier about the *Old Testament* in general applies in particular to *Exodus:* It is a composite work which has passed through the hands of many editors. The documents from which the book was compiled reflect the moods of several periods in the history of Israel, but they all present God, not Moses, as the source of law. Moses merely announces the law as revealed to him by God (indeed, the Hebrew word for prophet— *nuvhi*—means announcer). Because all law was viewed as derived from God, and because the Israelites were meant to comprise a theocracy in which God was king, the *Old Testament* contains no Hebrew word for "crime." Breaches of the law were regarded as sins, not crimes.

Mark

The name of St. Mark, the traditional author of the Second Gospel, suggests that he was of Hellenic origin. It is known that he was fluent in Greek, that he was a nephew or cousin of Barnabas of Cyprus, and that the house of his mother, Mary, was a center of Christian life in Jerusalem. The apostle Peter was apparently a familiar visitor there.

Mark was associated at first with the missionary work of Barnabas and Paul beyond Judea and Syria. On their behalf, he undertook certain practical administrative tasks at which he excelled. An obscure period followed during which Mark returned to Jerusalem, apparently because of a policy disagreement with Paul. He appeared once more in Paul's company in Rome, where he joined in the salutations to the Christians of Colossæ, and then as a Christian worker in Asia Minor.

After the death of Barnabas and Paul, Mark attached himself to Peter, the friend of his younger years in Jerusalem. Peter's words "Mark, my son" suggest a close spiritual tie between the older and the younger man. Mark apparently wrote his Gospel in Rome under the influence of Peter's preachings. It is sometimes asserted that he acted to some degree as Peter's interpreter, because of the apostle's imperfect mastery of Greek. Nothing is known of Mark's later life or of his death. Mark's role throughout his career was that of an administrative lieutenant to, successively, Barnabas, Paul, and Peter—which helps to explain the essential harmony of their messages in his writings.

Plutarch

Plutarch, the Greek biographer, was probably born during the reign of the Roman emperor Claudius in about 45 or 50 A.D. His native town was Chæronea in Greece, where his family had long been settled and was of good standing. After studies in Athens, he visited Egypt and later went to Rome on public business, perhaps for his native city. Whether he visited Italy more than once is uncertain, but his lectures in Rome attracted considerable public attention. Plutarch appears to have spent most of his life in the little town of Chæronea, which "he was loathe to make less by the withdrawal of even one inhabitant." He took part in public affairs, was *archon* in the town, served for many years as priest of Apollo, and was married and the father of at least five children. He died in Chæronea in 120 A.D.

Plutarch is primarily a moralist rather than a historian. He had little interest in policies and the concern of empires and cared much more about the personal character of leaders and the motives for individual actions— duty performed and rewarded; arrogance chastised; hasty anger corrected; and the triumph of humane, fair dealing and generous behavior in the world. He wrote during the last great era of Roman literature, the era of Tacitus, Pliny the Younger, Martial, Juvenal. His language was that of a man happy with himself and his surroundings. His natural cheerfulness seemed undiminished by recollections of years passed under the terrors of imperial wickedness.

Plutarch's *Lives* displays great learning and research and must have required many years of composition. Plutarch's diligence as a historian cannot be questioned, even if his accuracy is sometimes impeached. The author's sympathy with Doric characters and institutions is evident, as in his sketch of the legendary Lycurgus.

Montesquieu

Charles de Secondat, Baron de Montesquieu, was born in 1689 and died in 1755. He was known in his youth as M. de la Brede, after the Chateau of La Brede near Bordeaux, where he was born. His mother was the heiress of an English family in Gascon. The title Montesquieu came from his uncle, the lifelong "president" of the Parliament of Bordeaux, who left this important office, along with his title and a considerable fortune, to his nephew. In 1715, Montesquieu married Jeanne Laritque, a Protestant heiress. They appeared to have lived on good terms despite her lack of education.

Montesquieu was admitted to the presidency of the Bordeaux Parliament in 1714 and held that office for 12 years, during which time he contributed papers on philosophy, politics, and natural science to the Bordeaux Academy. He also wrote a series of pieces which unmercifully satirized the French social, political, ecclesiastical, and literary follies of the day. Presented in the form of letters written by two fictitious Persians of distinction traveling in Europe, the *Lettres Persanes* caused a scandalous uproar and proved a great popular success, passing through four editions within a single year.

In 1725, Montesquieu was elected a member of the French Academy, but an almost obsolete rule requiring residence in Paris was invoked to nullify his election. Thus, in 1726, Montesquieu sold his life tenure in his Bordeaux office, reserving the reversion for his son, and went to live in the capital. In January 1728, he was finally admitted to the Academy.

Almost immediately afterwards, he began a tour of Europe, traveling through Austria to Hungary and then to Italy, where he remained nearly a year. He then spent eighteen months in England and acquired a lifelong admiration for English characters and polity. He returned not to Paris but to La Brede, and there composed *Spirit of the Laws*. Because of his reputation as a jester, he thought it wise to soften the transition from the *Lettres Persanes* to *Spirit of the Laws* with a publication graver than the former and less elaborate than the latter. The intermediate book was *Considerations of the Causes of the Grandeur and the Dependence of the Romans*, published in 1734.

Before the publication of *Spirit of the Laws* in 1748, Montesquieu submitted his manuscript to a committee of the Academy, according to a common practice, to hear their opinion on his work. They unanimously advised the author not to publish the book, which has since been described as "one of the most important books ever written," and which may be almost certainly ranked as the greatest French book of the eighteenth century. Because of its moderate views on politics and religion, *Spirit of the Laws* was not well-received at first in France. But eventually, even Voltaire, Montesquieu's avowed enemy, was forced to acknowledge the freshness of its language and the greatness of its ideas.

Han Fei Tzu

Han Fei Tzu was born in 280 B.C. and died in 230 B.C. As a prince in the ruling house of Han province, he studied under the Confucianist Hsun Tzu and carried his teachings a step beyond where Hsun Tzu had stopped. Hsun Tzu had regretted the absence of a higher authority that could compel people to act in the ways of virtue; Han Fei Tzu converted this regret into a doctrine, which made him one of the foremost representatives of the legalist school of Chinese philosophy. As an envoy to Emperor Ch'in, the conqueror of China and founder of the Ch'in dynasty, Han Fei Tzu expounded the implications of his legalistic teachings for the rulings of the emperor. He apparently prospered for a while at the court of Ch'in, but eventually incurred the deadly enmity of other courtiers, including his old schoolmate, Li Ssu, who had become chief minister to the emperor. Han Fei Tzu was sent to prison, where he committed suicide.

Machiavelli

Niccolo Machiavelli was born in Florence in 1469, the descendant of an old Tuscan family. Little is known about his formal education, because Machiavelli's father was a lawyer, so it can be assumed that the son was well-educated. It is clear from his writings that Machiavelli was a humanist, that he discovered his ideals in Rome, and that he read Greek authors in Latin translations.

Machiavelli grew up under the rule of that member of the Medici dynasty to whom the Florentines gave the title Lorenzo the Magnificent. Lorenzo was a distinguished humanist and poet and a generous patron of artists and scholars. He has been credited with maintaining a sort of balance of power among the five major Italian city-states: Naples, Rome, Venice, Florence, and Milan. However, during the period of his rule (1469–1492), the five cities were engaged in continuous struggles and often open warfare with the lesser city-states, such as Genoa and Pisa. The balance was so precarious that a shrewd observer like Machiavelli could have no illusions about his city's having found a solution to the political conflict.

Lorenzo died in 1492. His successor, Piero, was exiled two years later, when the French army under Charles VIII appeared in Florence. Subsequently, the Dominican monk Savonarola tried to establish a theocracy in Florence, but failed and was burnt to death in 1498. Some months later, with the establishment of the Republic of Florence, Machiavelli was elected Secretary to the Second Chancery and given charge of foreign and military affairs. As tribute to the political confidence in which he was held by the Republic, Machiavelli was sent on 24 foreign missions, including four to the king of France, several to Rome, and one to Emperor Maximilian. When Pope Julius II drove the French from Italy, Florence was lost. Not even the new citizen army trained by Machiavelli could withstand the combined forces of the Pope's political prestige and his mercenary armies. One of the conditions of papal peace was the restoration of the Medici in Florence; and so Machiavelli, who had always been staunchly republican and anti-Medici, found himself, at the age of 43, a dejected liberal without a job and in danger of arrest.

He tried to make his peace with the Medici but to no avail. In Florence, everyone was suspect who had ever been identified with the liberal cause. Machiavelli was accused of being a republican conspirator and was arrested and tortured. But he was clearly innocent and was finally released. He fled some distance from Florence, and for the next 14 years importuned the Medici and the Pope for reinstatement to political office, which meant nothing less than a return to life for him.

Ironically, it was during this period of his disgrace that he reached the high point of his creativity. As he retreated more and more into his study, he produced *The Prince, The Art of Work, The Discourses, The History of Florence,* and a variety of plays, poetry, stories, and biographical sketches. The civil servant, the politician, the diplomat, and the military organizer had become a man of letters.

There was one final irony. In 1527, after the papal armies were defeated and Rome was sacked by the soldiers of Charles V, the popular party in Florence overthrew the Medici and for a short time restored democratic government. Machiavelli hurried back to Florence, eager to regain his post as Secretary, but *The Prince,* circulated in manuscript, had brought him new enemies. The governors feared his brilliance and wit. Mercifully, Machiavelli fell sick and never learned that the final vote of the Council was overwhelmingly against him. He died in 1532.

Hobbes

Thomas Hobbes, the English philosopher, was born in 1588 and died in 1679. His life spans one of the most turbulent epochs of English history: the struggle of the parliamentary forces against the rule of the Stuarts, the outbreak of the Civil War, the trial and execution of Charles I, the establishment of the Commonweal under Cromwell, the restoration of the throne of England to Charles II, and the rising tide of popular discontent that would culminate after Hobbes' death in the Glorious Revolution of 1688. Hobbes himself was to say that there was scarcely a day that he was not afraid for his life.

Hobbes entered Oxford at the age of 15 and received his bachelor's degree in 1608 at the age of 20. That same year, he was appointed a tutor to the son of William Cavendish (afterwards the second Earl of Devonshire). This began a lifelong connection with a great and powerful family. He traveled abroad with young Cavendish and remained by his side for several years until an adverse turn in the family fortune cost Hobbes his position. Years later, he returned to the patronage of the Cavendish family, this time as a tutor to the son of his previous pupil.

In the intervening years, Hobbes had written draft treatises on nature, on human nature, and on the body politic. In 1637, he returned from his travels abroad to an England seething with discontent. In November 1640, a succession of political events induced Hobbes to believe that he had become a marked man, destined perhaps for the Tower and a beheading. He fled to Europe and the group of scientists and academics he had befriended on earlier trips. He remained abroad for eleven years, living mainly in Paris.

The Civil War had broken out in 1642 and the Royalist cause began to decline after its defeat in a critical battle in 1644. This precipitated an exodus of the King's friends to Paris as refugees. The sight of these exiles caused Hobbes to despair of ever being able to return to his homeland. He was on the point of leaving Paris to take up permanent residence in the south of France when he was engaged "by the month" as a mathematics instructor to the young Prince of Wales (later Charles II) who had come to France from Jersey in 1646. This engagement lasted until 1648, when Charles went to Holland.

Thrown into the company of the exiled Royalists, Hobbes undertook the writing of a book describing his theory of civil government in relation to the political crisis in England. Published in 1651, the work was titled *The Leviathan, or, The Matter, Form and Power of the Commonwealth, Ecclesiastic and Civil.* Its author was simultaneously lauded and decried to excess. The enmity Hobbes felt in France left him no choice but to return in secret to London. There, the revolutionary government allowed him to pursue an anonymous private life. Not until the restoration of Charles II was Hobbes permitted to re-establish himself solidly as a public personality in England.

Locke

John Locke, who lived from 1632 to 1704, is probably the most representative thinker in the entire Anglo-American political tradition. He expressed with remarkable clarity and strength the political traditions and beliefs that were the stock in trade of liberty-loving Englishmen and Americans in the seventeenth and eighteenth centuries. Often called the theorist of the English revolution of 1688, he was also the primary source of the ideas which were drawn upon in the Declaration of Independence to justify the American Revolution of 1776.

John Locke was born in the west of England to a substantial middle-class family. His father was a small landowner and attorney from whom Locke received his early education. In 1652, he entered Christ Church, Oxford, beginning an association of some 30 years with that institution. Locke was extremely critical of the education he received at the university; he was impatient with the scholastic curriculum still in force and not always respectful of his teachers. However, he read a great deal, was stirred especially by the ideas of Descartes, and, years after receiving his degree, became a lecturer at the college. Locke's training was in medicine, although that was never his sole profession.

In 1665-1666, Locke first visited the Continent as secretary to Sir Walter Vane, on a mission to Brandenburg. At the same time, he began his close association with Anthony Ashley Cooper, the First Earl of Shapesbury and a prominent politician. Locke acted as family physician to the Coopers and also served as tutor to Cooper's son, the second Earl, who later became famous as one of the leading Deists of Europe. During the period of political unrest in England at the end of the 1670s, Locke's liberal notions got him into mild trouble at Oxford, and in late 1683, he went to Holland as a political exile. He remained abroad during the years of preparation for the ascent of William of Orange to the English throne and finally returned to his native land in 1689, in the expedition that brought Mary to join her husband William. From this time until his death in 1704, Locke lived in the country, except when called to London by his official duties as Commissioner of the Board of Trade and Plantations.

No one who lived in seventeenth-century Europe, and particularly in England, could fail to be affected by the revolutionary political upheavals and the vigorous new intellectual climate. There was less religious interest and more study of science and economics, a shift evident in the character of Locke's Christianity. Religious faith was certainly important in his thinking, yet it belonged to the Enlightenment rather than to the twilight of the Middle Ages. The old era had been full of passion and orthodoxy; the new era leaned toward reasonableness and simplification in dogma and toleration of dissent in practice. The old era assumed that man was naturally vicious or wicked; the new era was optimistic about man's nature and potentialities—an optimism spurred by Isaac Newton's *Mathematical Principles of Natural Philosophy* which, when it appeared in 1687, seemed to unlock the secrets of nature.

Locke's two essays on government were written while he was in exile in Holland. They were first published in 1690, to justify the Revolution of 1688 and the ascension of William and Mary to the throne. *The First Treatise on Civil Government* was directed against the theory of Sir Robert Filmore that monarchs ruled by divine right—a right supposedly transmitted from Adam. In *The Second Treatise,* Locke asserted the tradition that government is subordinate to law and must seek the popular welfare.

It was Locke's contention that, even before government existed, men were free, independent, and equal in the enjoyment of inalienable rights, chiefly life, liberty, and property. Among these, property received the most attention in *The Second Treatise.* In a striking modification of previous thinking on natural law, Locke identified property as a natural right, preceding civil society rather than being created. He believed that man created property merely by applying his labor to the gifts of nature, and that the protection of private property was the primary function of government. Locke's ideas of property were vital elements in his teachings and were clearly influenced by the emergence of the middle class and its self-serving notions about the functions of government.

Locke's general political philosophy spread throughout eighteenth-century Europe and provided the central source of ideas for the American Revolution and the Declaration of Independence. Locke also greatly influenced the thinking of Karl Marx and Friedrich Engels on what constituted property and how it was formed. Locke's thesis that property was created by the application of labor to raw materials was the seed of the "labor theory" of Marx and Engels.

Aristotle

Aristotle was born in 384 B.C. in Stagira, a small Greek colonial town east of modern Salonika, on the border of the kingdom of Macedonia. The place of his birth and the fact that his father was court physician to a previous king of Macedonia probably explains how he became the tutor, in about 342, to the young Prince Alexander. His parentage would also explain Aristotle's interest in biological studies, which he began to pursue in about 345, and on which he wrote and lectured after 335. His approach to other fields of study also reflected his medical background. For example, he classified state constitutions and political systems as a biologist would classify living types, by the structure and arrangements of their parts; and in the spirit of a doctor, he suggested methods of remedial treatment for the infirmities of the different constitutions.

Aristotle's life and work is usually considered in three sections. The first section, referred to as the "apprentice period," began in 367, when Aristotle went to Athens as a youth of 17 to study at Plato's Academy. Athens at that time had begun to renew something of the vigor of the Periclean Age of the previous century. Sparta, which had defeated and crushed Athens at the end of the Peloponnesian War in 404, was beginning to fail, while Athens had already formed a second Athenian confederation, less widespread than the one in the fifth century but more generous in the autonomy of the confederates. Athens was once again the mistress of the seas, the primary trade center and money market of Greece, and the cultural center of the Greek-speaking world.

The second section of Aristotle's life, the "journeyman period," lasted from 347 to 335 and was spent partly in the northwest corner of Asia and partly in Macedonia, where he served as tutor to the young Prince Alexander. The third, "master period," during which Aristotle lived again in Athens, lasted from 335 to Aristotle's death in 332, the year that Athenian control of the Aegean Sea ended with the battle of Amorgos.

During the master period, Aristotle founded his school in Athens, side by side with the Platonic Academy and Isocrates' School of Oratory. From this grove of academia on the eastern side of the city, one could see the Acropolis and the Parthenon. The grove included a gymnasium, with covered walks, or "peripapoi," which served as places of leisure and discussion for the students and instructors. Because the grove was dedicated to Apollo Lyzeius, the School of Aristotle came to be known as the Lyceum. Aristotle is said to have devoted his morning lectures to esoteric and philosophical subjects and the afternoon or evening lectures to more popular material, such as politics and rhetoric.

One of the themes which runs through Aristotle's thought is "evolution." This distinguishes his thought from that of Plato, who had been more interested in "being" than in "becoming" and had posited the static universe of the permanent truth of mathematics. The universe of Aristotle is, by comparison, dynamic: "The nature of each thing is a potentiality which improves through a process of development until a final perfection is reached.

The structure of Aristotle's *Politics*, which has exerted a deep and continuing influence on all subsequent political thought, is not homogeneous. It is a collection of several different essays assembled by Aristotle under a single title and includes some of the greatest political maxims ever set forth. Among them are the concepts that the state is the natural organization of man; that it exists for the common good of its members; that the law is the true sovereign of the state and that members of government are servants of the law; that there is a fundamental difference between the laws of monarchs and of tyrants; that the people have an inherent right, by virtue of their capacity of collective judgment, to elect their rulers and call them to account for their actions.

Rousseau

Jean Jacques Rousseau was born in Geneva, Switzerland, in 1712. His ancestors, converts to Calvinism, had taken refuge in Geneva in the middle of the sixteenth century. Rousseau's mother died a few days after his birth. His father, an affectionate but irritable man, looked after him until he was ten years old and provided most of his schooling, encouraging a precocious taste for Plutarch and novels.

At the age of ten, Rousseau began to be passed around among relatives. As a teenager, he entered into a series of apprenticeships, first as a notary and then as an engraver. Eventually, he made his way to Savoy, where he became involved in an odd relationship with an older and wealthy woman, Mademoiselle de Warins, first as her convert to Catholicism, and then as her lover. The young Rousseau alternately fled her embrace and returned to it, depending, it seems, on the state of his pocketbook.

In 1744, Rousseau went to Paris to seek his fortune. He devoted most of his energies to writing social comedies and musical critiques, but for years he had little success. However, he became acquainted with the rich and famous in Parisian society; and when his best friend, Denis Diderot, commissioned him to write an article on music for the *Encyclopedia*, he began to achieve some moderate fame.

Early in 1745, Rousseau had become involved with Therese le Vasseur, a servant in the hotel where he was staying. He kept her for the rest of his life, and they had five children, all of whom were sent to a foundling hospital. Later, after he became famous as a moralist, he was markedly sensitive about his abandoned children. The emotional burden of a guilt that he would not admit is said to have contributed to the insanity at the end of his life.

Rousseau's real celebrity dates from July 1759, when he was awarded first prize by the Academy of Dijon for an essay on whether the revival of the sciences and arts had helped to corrupt or to purify morals. All of his subsequent work, whether popular or unpopular, seemed to add to his fame. However, he continued to depend for his sustenance on women of means, one of whom was Mademoiselle d'Epiney. A passionate but unrequited love affair with a woman 20 years his junior led to a breach with Mademoiselle d'Epiney and with Diderot. It was then that Rousseau first gave obvious signs of the persecution mania from which he suffered, intermittently but with increasing severity, for the rest of his life.

Rousseau's *The Social Contract* appeared in April 1762. Its criticism of dogmatic Christianity and its political skepticism were offensive to the French authorities, and an order was issued for Rousseau's arrest. He was obliged to leave France and eventually took refuge in England, where he came under the protection and help of the English philosopher David Hume. In but a few years, however, the two famous men became embroiled in an open quarrel which excited and amused all of Europe. Finally, in May 1767, Rousseau, who was by this time more than a little mad, fled in panic from England to France, where the order for his arrest was still unrevoked. The French government left him in peace, however, and he spent much of his remaining years attempting to justify his conduct to the world. He died on the estate of Marquis Rene de Gierardis in 1778. His remains were moved to Paris to the Pantheon during the French Revolution.

Throughout his life, Rousseau was an outsider, a mystic, a vagabond, who never felt spiritually at home in society as it existed. He was the first and most eloquent of the great radical thinkers of the eighteenth century.

Rousseau never preached revolution, for he disapproved of violence and precipitous change and believed that victims of oppression are so debased by servitude that they are unfit for freedom and must come to it gradually, like invalids to food too rich for their weakened stomachs. His influence was revolutionary, however, because his denunciations of the evils of society were so passionate and so eloquent that he made the established order an object of hatred and contempt. His attitude toward Christianity was equivocal, for he was as much attracted by its moral and spiritual force as he was critical of some of its dogma and practices. No one of his time was more insistent and convincing that people are dominated by customs and prejudices, that faith is stronger than reason, and that freedom is the fruit of moral self-discipline, as slowly acquired as it is easily lost.

Tocqueville

Alexis de Tocqueville was born into the French aristocracy in 1805. From 1827 to 1832, he was a junior magistrate at Versailles. In 1831, he accepted, with his friend Gustave de Beaumont, a commission to examine the prisons and penitentiaries of the United States. This journey led to the publication of a study of the American prison system and also provided Tocqueville with material for his penetrating study of American society and politics, *Democracy in America.*

This work, the first part of which appeared in 1835 and the second in 1840, was a great critical success and won Tocqueville a seat in the French Academy. He also entered politics, and after an unsuccessful contest in 1831, he was elected to the Chamber of Deputies as an Independent in 1839. He remained a deputy, generally critical of governmental policies, until the fall of the monarchy in 1848. He was then elected to the 1848 Constituent Assembly, helped draft the Constitution of the Second Republic, and served for several months as Minister of Foreign Affairs.

Tocqueville withdrew from public life in 1851, after the ascendancy of Louis Napoleon, whom he had vigorously opposed. He spent his remaining years traveling and preparing his book *The Ancient Regime Before the Revolution,* which was published in 1856. He died at Cannes in 1859.

Woolf

Virginia Woolf is one of the most distinguished English critics and novelists of this century. Born in 1882, the daughter of Sir Leslie Stephen, she was married in 1912 to Leonard Woolf, with whom she established the Hogarth Press, the publisher of most of her work. She wrote a number of remarkable and highly acclaimed novels between 1915 and her death in 1941, including *The Voyage Out, Night and Day, Jacob's Room, Mrs. Dalloway, To the Lighthouse, Orlando, The Waves, The Years,* and *Between the Acts.*

The merit of Woolf's novels lies in her sensitive understanding of human needs and emotions, in the felicity with which she used words, and in her innovative style. Instead of writing novels in which the thoughts of the characters are deduced from what they say and do, Woolf chose a technique in which thought is so minutely revealed that words and actions lose much of their importance. Her acute perceptions and great skill in communicating them are also evident in her critical writings, which provide insightful observations about a broad range of authors.

A Room of One's Own, published in 1929, grew out of lectures Woolf delivered in 1928 at Newnham and Girton Colleges. Their major theme was her belief that a woman needed "money and a room of one's own" in order to write fiction.

She drowned near Lewes, Sussex, in 1941, an apparent suicide.

Marx and Engels

Karl Marx was born to a successful Prussian lawyer and his simple Hungarian wife in the Rhineland city of Trier in 1818. A reluctant student, Marx attended the universities at Bonn and Berlin before receiving a doctorate in philosophy from the notoriously undemanding University of Jena. He rejected the conservative profession of teaching for journalism and became an editor of the liberal Cologne newspaper *Rheinische Zeitung.*

When the paper was suppressed for its leftist views, Marx went with his new wife, the aristocratic Jenny von Westphalen, to Paris, which was the intellectual center of the Socialist movement. While working in Paris as a radical journalist and essayist for German-language publications, Marx met Friedrich Engels (1820-1895) and initiated a life-long friendship and professional partnership with him. Engels, the son of a German cotton manufacturer, was working at the time in one of his father's factories in England. Engels' *Position of the Working Classes in England* was the result of his personal observation of modern industrial organizations and their impact on workers.

In 1845, the Prussian government forced the ouster from France of the entire staff of the radical journal *Vorwärts.* Marx and Engels moved on to Brussels, where they wrote *German Ideology* (unpublished until 1932) and acquired a local German newspaper. To further their goals of "political agitation," the two young men joined The League of the Just, which evolved into the Communist League. Marx and Engels set forth its aims in *The Communist Manifesto* (1847).

After the outbreak of the February Revolution of 1848, Marx and Engels were expelled from Brussels. They moved briefly to France and then on to Cologne, where they founded another radical newspaper. Once again, their work was suppressed by the Prussians and Marx was arrested and tried for treason. He was sent into exile, first in France and then in England, where he lived the last 34 years of his life in the slums of Soho. His means of support came primarily from Engels.

Marx wrote sporadically for the *New York Tribune,* but spent most of his time in study at the British Museum. Despite personal infirmities and family tragedies, he produced *The Critique on Political Economy* in 1859 and the first volume of *Capital* eight years later. He organized the International Working Men's Association in 1864 and was active in it until its dissolution at a conference in Philadelphia in 1876. Marx perceived his main work as the completion of *Capital,* but continuing ill health conspired against him. Engels brought out the second and third volumes of the work after Marx's death in London in 1883.

Mao

Mao Tse-tung was born in 1893, an obscure peasant at a time when China was wracked by civil strife, enfeebled by official corruption and desperate poverty, and oppressed by the colonialist nations of the West. When he died in 1976, he had restored China to its ancient standing as a great nation of the world, and he was universally acknowledged as one of history's outstanding revolutionary leaders. In Chinese terms, he is often likened to Chin-shih-kuang, the first emperor, who unified China in 221 B.C.

Mao was one of the most complex, multifaceted personalities of the twentieth century: a patriot, a revolutionary, an evangelist, a military strategist, a poet, a philosopher, and a statesman. He was above all a moralist, in the tradition of Confucius, who deeply believed in human goodness and in the priority of human needs over economic accomplishment. He combined totalitarianism and humanitarianism, romantic idealism and shrewd pragmatism in a political philosophy which seemed perversely self-contradictory to Western observers. He said in 1957

> Within the ranks of our people, democracy stands in relation to centralism and freedom to discipline. They are two conflicting aspects of a single entity, contradictory as well as united, and we should not one-sidedly emphasize one to the detriment of the other.

Mao Tse-tung was born to an industrious and stern father and a warm-hearted Buddhist mother in the southern province of Hunan. He began working in the rice fields at the age of six and retained the simple, almost rough ways of the peasant throughout his life. Sent to school to learn arithmetic, Mao showed a proclivity for intellectual pursuits and, as a teenager, continued his education despite parental protests. At the provincial normal school in Changsha, where he studied from 1913 to 1918, he became involved in the radical nationalistic May 4th Movement; and in 1920, after he had become a teacher and editor, he established a small Communist group in Changsha. He served as the group's delegate to the Shanghai Conference, which established the Chinese Communist Party.

Initially, the party was allied with the ruling Nationalist Party of Sun Yat-sen; but General Chiang Kai-shek, who succeeded to the leadership of the government in 1925, turned on the Communists two years later and massacred thousands of the party's membership. The next seven years of the Chinese Communist Party were marked by underground political activity and constant infighting over policies and leadership. The intra-party conflict and government persecution culminated in the famous Long March, in which Mao led thousands of his followers on an exodus across China that lasted more than a year and covered over 6,000 miles of difficult terrain. The success of the Long March in eluding the Nationalist armies and gathering additional supporters gave the Communists a legend of invinci-bility, a guerrilla ethic, and a sense of purpose and unity. It also established Mao's leadership in the party.

Mao's ascension to political power in China was greatly assisted by the growth of hostilities between China and Japan. In 1936, General Chiang was forced to establish a unified front with the Communists against the Japanese invaders. During the next eight years, the Communist forces increased in size to a formidable army of one million; and by the end of the war with Japan, they were well-situated to engage the Nationalists in full-scale civil war. Chiang's army was plagued by corruption and incompetence and by war-weariness and animosity from the populace. The vast numerical and material advantages of the Nationalists were swiftly reduced, and on October 1, 1949, Mao, then 54, stood at the Gate of Heavenly Peace in Peking and proclaimed the People's Republic of China.

Over much of the next decade, China's development followed the orthodox Soviet model, with an emphasis on heavy industry, centralized planning, and military and technological advances. In 1957, however, Mao seemed to reject this formula for development in favor of the energy of the peasantry. He envisioned organizing the peasants into self-sacrificing servants of the state and party, vastly increasing agricultural production and the well-being of the Chinese people, and then pursuing industrial develop-ment through trade with the developed nations.

These ideas led to the first serious challenge to Mao's leadership in nearly three decades, but Mao adroitly countered the attack and ousted the incumbent Defense Minister, his principal critic. Mao's launching of the Cultural Revolution in 1965 was in many ways the culmination of his life's work and his ultimate revolt against the influence of Soviet elitism and bureaucracy. Just before the start of the Cultural Revolution, Mao made a statement which might be the summary of his life and aspirations: "Once class struggle is grasped, miracles are possible."

Schumacher

Born in Germany in 1913, E. F. Schumacher went to England as a Rhodes Scholar in 1930 to study economics at New College, Oxford. At the age of 22, he became an instructor of economics at Columbia University; but he was uncomfortable as a theorist without practical experience, and conse-quently undertook a succession of jobs in business, journalism, and farming. He returned to Oxford as a professor for several years during

World War II and then served as Economic Advisor to the British Control Commission in Germany from 1946 to 1950.

From 1950 to 1970, Schumacher was Economic Advisor to the British National Coal Board. He also founded and serves as chairman of the Intermediate Technology Development Group, which specializes in tailoring tools, small-scale machines, and methods of production for the needs of developing countries. He is president of the Soil Association, one of Britain's oldest organic farming organizations, and a director of the Scott Bader Company, a pioneering effort at common ownership and worker control.

Jefferson
and the Declaration of Independence

On June 7, 1776, Richard Henry Lee, following the instructions of the Virginia Convention, submitted three resolutions to the Second Continental Congress:

> RESOLVED, That these United Colonies are, and of right ought to be free and independent states, that they are absolved from all allegiance to the British Crown, and that all political connection between them and the State of Great Britain is, and ought to be totally dissolved.
>
> That it is expedient forthwith to take the most effectual measures for forming foreign Alliances.
>
> That a plan of confederation be prepared and transmitted to the respective Colonies for their consideration and approbation.

During the debate on Lee's motion, the delegates concluded that a French alliance would be more probable if the colonies made a formal declaration of their independence from Britain. A few days later, Congress appointed a committee consisting of Thomas Jefferson, John Adams, Benjamin Franklin, Roger Sherman, and Robert R. Livingston to prepare the document.

On June 28, the committee reported the draft of the declaration. It had been written almost entirely by Jefferson, who had incorporated changes and additions suggested by Adams and Franklin. Congress adopted Lee's initial resolution on July 2—this is sometimes called the "real" Declaration of Independence. During the next two days, the Congress drafted and slightly modified the text before adopting the Declaration of Independence on July 4, 1776.

At the time of the Declaration, Jefferson was already a man of considerable public accomplishment. He had served as a justice of the peace and as a representative for six years in the Virginia House of Burgesses before being sent to Philadelphia in 1775 as one of his state's delegates to the First Continental Congress. Although he never delivered a speech in that body, he quickly emerged as one of its leaders on the basis of his skills in committee work and his persuasiveness in conversation. His major essay, *A Summary View of the Rights of British Americans* (1774), enhanced his influence.

After writing the Declaration of Independence, Jefferson contributed several important state documents to his native Virginia: a revision of the statutory law to eradicate traces of "ancient or future aristocracy," a revision of the penal law making it more humanitarian, and a statute outlawing the importation of slaves. He served two terms as Governor of Virginia before returning to national politics, first as a delegate to the 1783 Congress under the Articles of Confederation, then as special envoy to Europe and U.S. Minister to France, and ultimately as Secretary of State in Washington's Administration.

Jefferson was elected Vice President under John Adams and was inaugurated in 1801 as the third President of the United States. He served a second term and might have won a third had he not followed Washington's example and retired. The principal public act of his final 17 years was the supervision of the establishment and design of the University of Virginia.

In regard to Jefferson's authorship of the Declaration of Independence John Adams commented in 1822 that "there is not an idea in it, but what had been hackneyed in Congress for two years before." Jefferson replied to this charge that it might well be true:

> Of that I am not to be the judge. Richard H. Lee charged it as copied from Locke's treatise on Government. . .I know only that I turned to neither book nor pamphlet while writing it. I did not consider it as any part of my charge to invent new ideas altogether and to offer no sentiment which had ever been expressed before.

Again, in a letter to Lee in 1825, Jefferson said that his inspiration in writing the Declaration had been

> . . .to place before mankind the common sense of the subject, in terms so plain and firm as to command their assent. . . . Neither aiming at originality of principles or sentiments, nor yet copied from any particular and previous writing, it was intended to be an expression of the American mind. . . . All its authority rests then on the harmonizing sentiments of the day, whether expressed in conversation, in letters, printed essays, or the elementary books of public right, as Aristotle, Cicero, Locke, Sidney, etc.

The Constitution of the United States

On September 17, 1787, the United States Constitution—the oldest written constitution still in effect today—was approved and signed in Philadelphia by the 39 delegates to the federal convention. The document has been hailed as the most successful code of governance in modern history. William Gladstone, prime minister of Great Britain at the height of the British

Empire, called the Constitution "the most wonderful work ever struck off at a given time by the brain and purpose of man."

Despite such encomiums, it should not be forgotten that the U.S. Constitution is also, as Clinton Rossiter puts it, "a bundle of compromises and a mosaic of second choices." The delegates to the convention had widely differing views about the form that a central government should take. Perhaps the convention's genius was its ability to frame a single document that men of different political principles could agree to accept, if not always with enthusiasm. Witness Franklin's remark at the end of the convention:

> [I] doubt. . . whether any other Convention we can obtain, may be able to make a better Constitution. . . . Thus I consent. . . to this Constitution because I expect no better, and because I am not sure, that it is not the best.

The language of the Constitution, as Rossiter says, is both "precise and vague." These two qualities, apparently contradictory, may be the secret of the document's long life. "The Constitution of the United States was not made merely for the generation that then existed," Henry Clay observed in 1850, "but for posterity—unlimited, undefined, endless, perpetual posterity." The founding fathers were well-aware that they were acting for future generations and that certain phrases in the Constitution would have to be left open for future interpretation. As Franklin D. Roosevelt said in his First Inaugural Address in 1933:

> Our Constitution is so simple and practical that it is possible always to meet extraordinary needs by changes in emphasis and arrangement without loss of essential form. That is why our constitutional system has proved itself the most superbly enduring political mechanism the modern world has produced.

The Constitution of the Confederate States of America (Preamble)

The secessionist Southern states adopted a provisional constitution on February 8, 1861, in Montgomery, Alabama. The permanent Constitution that was subsequently adopted resembled the Constitution of the United States in some respects and differed profoundly in others. It included some British features which reflected the influence of Alexander Stephens, the Vice President of the Confederacy. But the salient differences are found in the Preamble, which reflects the longstanding objections of the secessionist leaders to certain structural features of the federal Constitution which they considered the source of Northern abuses.

Lincoln

Abraham Lincoln, the sixteenth President of the United States, was born in a frontier log cabin in 1809 and died from an assassin's bullet in 1865, just days after General Robert E. Lee's surrender had concluded the divisive Civil War. His Gettysburg Address, delivered during the darkest hours of the war, is celebrated as one of the most eloquent and moving speeches in the English language.

After the Union victory at Gettysburg July 1-3, 1863, a national commission was established to create the National Soldiers' Cemetery at Gettysburg for the several thousand soldiers, of both sides, who gave their lives in the battle. The dedication ceremony was planned for November 19, and Edward Everett, former senator, former governor of Massachusetts, former president of Harvard, and a leading orator of the day, was chosen to give the major address. On November 2, President Lincoln was sent an invitation to attend and was requested to make "a few appropriate remarks" after Everett's speech.

Lincoln accepted, though many other matters weighed on his mind. He was in the midst of preparing his annual message to Congress, and the events of the war required his constant attention. Having prepared a first draft of the speech he would make, Lincoln left Washington for Gettysburg on November 18, at a time when his son Tad lay sick in bed. During the late afternoon train ride, the President seemed exceptionally weary. That night in his room, Lincoln wrote the final draft of his speech, showing it only to Secretary of State Seward.

Some 15,000 people were on Cemetery Hill for the ceremony when the President arrived. Everett spoke nearly two hours; then the Baltimore Glee Club sang an ode; finally Ward Hill Lamon, Lincoln's military attaché, presented the President. Lincoln delivered the Gettysburg Address in three minutes and afterward leaned over to Lamon and said, "Lamon, that speech won't scour. It is a flat failure [and] the people won't like it."

The following day Everett wrote Lincoln: "I should be glad if I could flatter myself that I came as near to the central idea of the occasion in two hours as you did in two minutes." Lincoln replied: "In our respective parts yesterday, you could not have been excused to make a short address, nor I a long one. I am pleased to know that, in your judgment, the little I did say was not entirely a failure."

The Federalist Papers

The Federalist Papers is the encompassing title for 85 newspaper essays written jointly by James Madison, Alexander Hamilton, and John Jay, as an attempt to persuade New York State legislators to accept the text of the new U.S. Constitution without amendment. The combination of the three men was the best in New York for a powerful intellectual defense of the Constitution.

Hamilton had been General Washington's personal secretary for four years and went on to become the first Secretary of the Treasury of the United States. He was the only New York delegate to the Constitutional Convention to sign the Constitution. Jay had served in the Continental Congress from its inception in 1774 and was later its president. He was the author of New York's first constitution and later became Chief Justice in New York and then the first Chief Justice of the United States. Madison, a Virginian, helped draft that state's new constitution during the revolution. He later served as private secretary to Governor Patrick Henry and as a delegate to the Continental Congress. With James Wilson of Pennsylvania, Madison was most responsible for the final form of the Constitution. In 1808, he was elected the fourth President of the United States.

The lasting effect of the *Federalist Papers* lay in their reasoned exposition of the meaning and benefits of the American invention of a federal system of concurrent democratic governments where national power acted on state power and both national and state power acted directly on the individual.

The authorship of particular numbers of the *Federalist Papers* has been disputed by some scholars, partly because of the haste with which Alexander Hamilton wrote down the names of the various authors on the eve of his fatal duel with Aaron Burr. But of *Federalist Ten*, which remains to this day one of the best known and most frequently quoted portions of the *Federalist Papers*, there is no doubt. It is entirely the work of Madison; the theme had been outlined by him in a long letter sent to Thomas Jefferson some months before the formal essay was written and published.

Federalist Ten is prophetic in its forecast of the nature of American party politics. It is also of particular interest in its appraisal of human nature and its frank acknowledgment that economic issues between the "haves" and "have-nots" are among the chief causes for political conflict.

Mill

John Stuart Mill, British philosopher and economist and a leading figure in the reform age of the nineteenth century, was born in London in 1806. He was educated exclusively by his father, James Mill, who was a strict disciplinarian and began the boy's education with Greek and arithmetic at the age of three. By the time he was eight, John Stuart Mill had read considerable history and much of Plato. From his earliest days he spent a great deal of time in his father's company and acquired many of his father's speculative opinions and methods of defending them. But he did not react passively or mechanically to what he was being taught. "One of the grandest objects of education," according to the elder Mill, "should be to generate a constant and anxious concern about evidence." The duty of collecting and weighing evidence for himself was constantly impressed upon the boy.

Mill's development as a political economist was marked by three stages, which he himself noted. First, in 1844, he published *Essays on Some Unsettled Questions in Political Economy,* which he had written several years earlier to propose solutions for perplexing technical problems in formal economics. In his second stage, the originality and independence of his thinking became more conspicuous as he struggled to write *Principles of Political Economy,* which was published in 1848. At about the same time, Mill made a thorough study of socialist writers and advocated the creation of peasant proprietorships as a remedy for the distress and disorder in Ireland. He declined to accept the proposition that property, devised originally to secure peace in primitive society, was necessarily sacred.

In his third stage as a political economist, Mill examined the questions of production and distribution. He was not satisfied with a system of distribution which condemned the working classes to a cramped and joyless existence. He rejected the socialist solution, however, and instead promoted his own innovative concept of a new economic foundation for industrial society.

During the seven years of his marriage to Harriet Taylor (1851 to 1858) Mill became increasingly absorbed in work for the East India Company and published less than in any other period of his life. In 1856, he became head of the examiner's office in the India House in London; and for two years, until the dissolution of the company in 1858, his official work kept him fully occupied. His retirement from official life was followed almost immediately by his wife's death at Avignon.

Mill spent most of the rest of his life at a villa in St. Veran near Avignon, returning to his Blackheath house only for a short period each year. During this time, he published a series of books on ethics and politics about which he had meditated and partly written in collaboration with his wife. His essay *On Liberty* appeared in 1859 with a touching dedication to her. In his *Thoughts on Parliamentary Reform* and *Consideration on Representative Government,* Mill systematized opinions already put forward in many earlier articles and essays. *Utilitarianism* was published in 1863.

In 1865, Mill stood as parliamentary candidate for Westminster, under stipulations strictly in accordance with his principles. He would not canvass or pay agents to canvass for him, nor would he engage to attend to the local business of the constituency. Mill was elected nonetheless and took an active part in the debates on the Reform Bills of 1866-1867. He was instrumental in compelling the government to make several important modifications in a bill preventing corrupt practices. In 1867, he was one of the founders, with Mrs. P. A. Taylor, Miss Emily Davis, and others, of the first women's suffrage society in Great Britain, and in 1869, he published *The Subjugation of Women,* the classic theoretical statement of the case for women's suffrage.

Mill died at Avignon in 1873. His autobiography and three essays on religion were published posthumously.

Sani

Ambassador Chaidir Anwar Sani of Indonesia has been in the diplomatic service of his country since 1950, serving in Paris, Egypt, the People's

Republic of China, and India. Between 1970 and 1972, he was Ambassador Extraordinary and Plenipotentiary to Belgium and Luxembourg and Head of the Indonesian Mission to the European Economic Community. Ambassador Sani has been Permanent Representative of the Indonesian Mission to the United Nations since 1972 and, in addition, was appointed Ambassador Extraordinary and Plenipotentiary to Trinidad and Tobago in 1974.

Thoreau

Henry David Thoreau, the American naturalist, philosopher, and writer, was born in Concord, Massachusetts, in 1817. In both his primary schooling and at Harvard College, Thoreau did not distinguish himself as a student, although he was an intelligent and receptive youngster and read widely. Upon graduating from Harvard, he and his brother set up a school in Concord which became notable for its progressive ideas. He later gave up teaching to become a lecturer and writer.

Thoreau's family was engaged in the business of pencil making, but Thoreau took part in the family business only when he was in need of ready cash. It was by the labor of his hands that Thoreau chiefly supported himself. He was convinced that the less work a man did for money beyond the absolute demands of necessity, the better he and his community would be. Thoreau would have preferred that the order of the week be reversed— six days for the expansion of mind and spirit, and one for commercially profitable labors. With Ralph Waldo Emerson, the chief friend and mentor of his life, Thoreau became one of the famous circle of Transcendentalists who sought spiritual truth behind all outward appearances.

In 1845, desirous of proving to himself and others that man could be independent of society, Thoreau retired to a hut of his own construction on a pine float above the shores of Walden pond near Concord. There he fed himself largely with foods that he gathered or grew. During his two years at Walden, he read considerably, wrote abundantly, thought actively and widely, and came to know the wildlife about him with extraordinary intimacy. *Walden—or Life in the Woods* (1854), which recalled his experience in the form of narrative essays, is regarded as one of the great books of American literature. The philosophy of *Walden* made it a bible for the English radicals who founded what became the British Labor Party.

In the great public controversy leading up to the Civil War, Thoreau was fiercely anti-slavery but was only slowly drawn into the Abolition movement. He distrusted all violence and dogmatism. Thus, when the national government required that his native state and he himself should become slave-catchers for the South, his deeply felt reaction was negative. Rather than pay federal taxes, used for what he regarded as immoral purposes, he went to jail. As a political moralist, Thoreau wrote two of the great works in the literature of civil liberty, *Life without Principle* and *Civil Disobedience*. His was a spiritual and intellectual radicalism as challenging in the twentieth century as it was before the Civil War. Thoreau died at the age of 45 in 1862.

Gandhi

Mohandas Karamchand Gandhi, the Hindu nationalist leader, was born in 1869 at Porbander in western India. At the age of 18, he was sent by his family to study law in London and remained there for more than three years, being admitted to the Bar in 1891. When he returned to India, he made little headway in his chosen profession until he was called to South Africa in 1893 by an Indian firm. There, he became aware at once of the disability under which the Indians were suffering in that country. Within a few years, he was drawn so completely into the struggle for political rights that he gave up what was a lucrative legal practice and undertook a drastic course in *brahma-charya,* or self-discipline, in order to devote his whole energies to public work.

From the time of the formation of the Natal Indian Congress in 1894, the agitation in South Africa grew stronger year by year. At one stage of the struggle, Gandhi and his friends, including several non-Indians, started a self-supporting colony called Tolstoi's Farm to free themselves for disciplined public activity without dependence on the ordinary life of the community. Gandhi became convinced that the good life was close to the soil, with a minimum of dependence on machines. He learned the arts of farming, cooking, nursing, sanitation, and teaching.

In the course of his struggle with the South African government, Gandhi, his wife, and his companions were arrested and imprisoned. The climax of the South African struggle came in 1913, when a series of repressive measures, culminating in a demand for government registration of every Indian seeking to live in the Transvaal, was met by repeated Indian resistance. Finally, a body of more than 2,000 Indians, many of them unlettered Kuli laborers, followed Gandhi over the frontier. The unfailing courtesy and restraint of the Indian leaders and followers greatly influenced public opinion, and a commission was appointed which favored the repeal of the registration act.

In 1914, feeling that he was no longer needed by the Indian community in South Africa, Gandhi returned to India. He was already convinced of the desirability of home rule, or *Fwarag* (self-rule), as it was usually called at that time; and he threw himself actively into the work of the Indian National Congress Party.

In South Africa, Gandhi had organized nonviolent resistance to the government with the conviction that war or revolution is always wrong, and that when changes cannot be achieved by persuasion and constitutional agitation alone, nonviolent forms of direct action must be attempted. During the first years of his residence in India, he and his friends organized a *Fattyagraha,* or "soul force," movement to seek remedies for social and political injustices. In 1919, after the promulgation of the Rowlatt Act, which gave the colonial government extraordinary powers to suppress widespread unrest in the Punjab, Gandhi called on his followers to withdraw from all government appointments and institutions, even schools and colleges, and undertake mass civil disobedience against the government.

Not all of his followers understood Gandhi's insistence on nonviolence; and when outbreaks of violence occurred, he cancelled the movement and underwent personal penance. Hundreds of people who had gathered in Amritsar to attend a prohibited political demonstration were shot down on April 19, 1919. Gandhi called the government "satanic," but confessed that he had committed a "Himalayan blunder" in failing to perceive that people were not yet sufficiently disciplined to remain nonviolent in the face of severe provocations. On three further occasions, the movement broke into violence, and Gandhi called off the public demonstrations despite the exasperation of many of his associates. Finally, in 1922, Gandhi was arrested and sentenced to six years' imprisonment.

He was released two years later, following an operation for appendicitis, but in the years to come, Gandhi was in and out of jail several more times. He came to use fasting as well as civil disobedience to call the attention of the world to the cause of Indian independence. Finally, at the conclusion of the Second World War, the new Labour government in Britain indicated its willingness to transfer power in India.

A new question arose: Was there to be one free India, or two? Gandhi withstood division of the subcontinent to the end, insisting that Hindus and Moslems were one people; but the tide of events was against him. In 1947, the leaders of the Indian Congress agreed to the division of India despite Gandhi's objections. The next months were marked by terrible violence between Hindus and Moslems in a struggle over boundaries and territory. Gandhi confessed that his lifelong teaching of nonviolence had not affected the people as he had hoped, but he fought on dauntlessly, still insisting that no matter what happened in Pakistan, all religious and racial communities must have equal rights in India. A small group of extremist Hindus concluded that, so long as Gandhi lived, India could never become a Hindu-dominated state. Accordingly, on January 30, 1948, ten days after Gandhi had concluded a fast for peace, he was fatally shot by a Hindu assassin.

King

Martin Luther King, Jr., was born in 1929 and died of an assassin's bullet in 1968. Though he had been carefully prepared for the tasks that gave distinction to his life, it was a personal decision by Mrs. Rosa Parks, an obscure black woman working as a domestic in Montgomery, Alabama, that helped catapult Dr. King into national and international prominence. In 1957, on her way home from a tiring day's work, Mrs. Parks found that she would have to stand up in the crowded rear of the bus. Instead, she sat down on an empty front seat which was reserved, under a Montgomery ordinance, for white people. She refused to obey the driver's order to move to the rear of the bus and was arrested.

As a reaction to that arrest, Dr. King, who was then serving as the clergyman of a black congregation in Montgomery, led the black community in an economic boycott that successfully broke the city's policy of bus segregation. The mass protest was noteworthy not only because it remained within the law and was successful, but also because the working-class blacks demonstrated a cohesiveness, determination, and fearlessness that had never before been conceded to blacks by Southern whites. Their example helped set the stage for a larger turn of events under the leadership of King.

Until the demonstrations in Montgomery, civil rights organizations, such as the National Association for the Advancement of Colored People (NAACP), had relied on the federal courts and Congress to overturn Southern segregation patterns. The legal struggle had gained the public schools decision of the Supreme Court in 1954 and a voting-rights bill from Congress in 1957. But Southern resistance to the Supreme Court decision had kept public school integration at a snail's pace, while physical intimidation at Southern polling booths kept black voting registration to token levels. The example of the Montgomery boycott led the thoughts of black activists away from the arena of the courtroom and legislature toward the use of more direct methods. The national center for black leadership also shifted away from the NAACP and settled on the Southern Christian Leadership Conference (SCLC), a loose coalition of Southern black clergymen that had formed around King during and immediately after the successful Montgomery struggle.

King's direct approach and assimilationist objectives had historical roots in the pre-Civil War abolitionists, in left-wing ghetto groups of the 1930s, in the youth-led Congress of Racial Equality (CORE), and in A. Philip Randolph's proposed March on Washington in March 1941, a march that was called off when Franklin D. Roosevelt agreed to create what became the Fair Employment Practices Committee. The new ingredient King injected into this tradition was a doctrine of nonviolent civil disobedience, combining Christian tenets with those of Thoreau and Gandhi. As applied to segregation in the South, King's doctrine meant something more than massive legal protests, such as the Montgomery boycott. It entailed the deliberate nonviolent breach of local segregation ordinances, either to force a legal test of their constitutionality or to force the enactment of federal legislation that would make them void.

In February 1960, the tenets of civil disobedience as taught by King became the foundation of the direct-action program launched by groups of black students, mostly of Southern middle-class background. A wave of black student sit-ins, stand-ins, kneel-ins, read-ins, and wait-ins ensued as part of an intensified drive to end racial segregation in such nongovernmental areas of Southern life as lunch counters, theaters, churches, beaches, and libraries. In October 1960, the student heads of the various demonstrations were brought together by Dr. King's Southern Christian Leadership Conference to form the Students' Nonviolent Coordinating Committee (SNCC). In late 1961, SNCC launched a program that went beyond the sit-ins. The objective of the new program was to prepare Southern blacks for full participation in electoral politics as an instrument for basic social change. Full-time workers were sent in to the rural communities of the South to induce black adults to register as voters.

These stepped-up efforts were met by stepped-up violence on the part of some Southern whites. In Mississippi, NAACP leader Medgar Evers was murdered. In Birmingham, four little black girls were killed when their church was dynamited. In Birmingham and Selma, civil rights demonstrators were hosed, clubbed, and set upon by unleashed dogs. On April 12, 1963, at the height of the unrest in Birmingham, eight Alabama clergymen representing different faiths issued a public statement addressed to Dr. King, who had been arrested and was then in a Birmingham jail. The clergymen urged the black community to withdraw support from the civil rights demonstrations and to look instead to the courts and to negotiations among local leaders for the redress of existing grievances. Dr. King's *Letter from Birmingham City Jail* was written in response to that public statement.

King, who was to be awarded the Nobel Peace Prize, later carried his nonviolent civil rights movement to Northern cities. But the continued frustrations experienced by blacks initiated rival movements which called for the separation of the races or for violent confrontation. The influence of Dr. King in the black community was on the decline when he was assassinated in Memphis by a white sniper.

Cleaver

Eldridge Cleaver's book *Soul on Ice* was written while he was serving a prison sentence in California for a felonious assault with a deadly weapon. The book, published when he was granted probation, was immediately acclaimed in literary circles. However, Cleaver himself burst into national prominence only after the August 1965 riots in the Watts section of Los Angeles.

The violence in Watts—and, later, in Newark—riveted national attention on racism outside the South, reminded established civil rights leaders, both black and white, of the deeper, more intractable sources of racism and poverty in the structure of American institutions and attitudes, and raised questions about whether those leaders could address these issues with the old concepts of nonviolence, massive resistance, and legalistic argument. The slogan "black power," articulated by Stokley Carmichael of SNCC, symbolized the turning of young black militants away from the integrationist and assimilationist spirit of the pre-1965 civil rights movement toward black self-sufficiency, self-defense, and freedom by any means, even if it meant toppling society's system of laws and values. While the student component of the civil rights movement had been largely drawn from blacks who were going to college, the new liberation movement reached down to embrace high school youth and drop-outs.

The fires of Watts were still burning when some black militant leaders began to point to a painful contradiction between our growing governmental commitment to protect the Vietnamese from the Viet Cong and the failure of the government to guarantee freedom and security to dispossessed citizens within America. Immediately after the Watts riot, some local blacks in Los Angeles formed a community-action group to monitor police conduct during arrests of blacks. In Oakland, other blacks carried the process a step further and instituted armed patrols, organized on an *ad hoc* basis and oriented to the single issue of police control.

The Black Panther party came into being through the Oakland liberation movement. Three leaders of the Black Panthers—Huey Newton, Bobby Seale, and Eldridge Cleaver—were to become national folk heroes who captured the imagination of a number of white radical student activists as well as young ghetto blacks. This was particularly true of Cleaver, the most articulate of the three. In time, Cleaver violated the terms of his parole from prison and escaped certain arrest by a secret flight out of the country. He found asylum, first in Cuba and then in Algiers, but after years spent in troubled exile, he voluntarily returned to the United States in 1975. His subsequent statements suggest that he has substantially mitigated his criticisms of the United States.

Roosevelt

Franklin Delano Roosevelt (1882-1945) was elected President of the United States four times and held that office during most of the Great Depression of the 1930s and almost the entirety of World War II. His policies for economic recovery substantially changed the relationship between the federal government and the nation's economy; his wartime leadership guided the United States and its allies in their victory against the Axis Powers. At the time of Roosevelt's death, he was involved in laying the foundation of the United Nations.

Roosevelt was born into an affluent and genteel household and raised as a gentleman, conscious of his social status and his responsibilities to those less fortunate than he. He was educated at Groton, Harvard, and Columbia Law School, but passed the New York Bar examination without completing his LL.B. degree. After a brief stint as a Wall Street lawyer, Roosevelt won a seat in the New York Senate. His support of Woodrow Wilson for President in 1912 won him an appointment as Assistant Secretary of the Navy. In 1920, Roosevelt was the vice-presidential candidate on the Democratic ticket, which lost to Republican Warren Harding. After his defeat, Roosevelt worked briefly as a banker, but gave it up when he was stricken suddenly with poliomyelitis in August 1921.

Despite his paralysis, he remained indefatigably involved in Democratic politics. He nominated Governor Alfred E. Smith of New York for President at the 1924 and 1928 conventions. When Smith won the nomination in 1928, he convinced Roosevelt to run for the governorship of New York. Roosevelt won by 25,000 votes and was overwhelmingly reelected in 1930. After a bitter battle with his old mentor, Smith, Roosevelt won the 1932 Democratic nomination for President and undertook a campaign against the incumbent, Herbert Hoover. The growing depression was the only issue of importance, and Roosevelt won decisively on a New Deal platform of recovery and reform.

Perhaps the most lasting result of Roosevelt's domestic New Deal was the general acceptance of the idea that the federal government is a positive instrument to promote the general welfare. In 1940, Roosevelt said:

> Democracy can thrive only when it enlists the devotion of... the common people. Democracy can hold that devotion only when it adequately respects their dignity by so ordering society as to assure to the masses of men and women reasonable security and hope... for themselves and for their children.

In his annual message to Congress on January 11, 1944, Roosevelt introduced his Economic Bill of Rights, adding economic security to Jefferson's political ideals of liberty, equality, and self-government.

Cleveland

Harlan Cleveland is a political scientist and public executive whose career has spanned the worlds of government, journalism, and education. He was a Rhodes Scholar in the late 1930s and served in the 1940s, first, as an economic warfare specialist and, then, in Italy and China as a United Nations relief operator. Subsequently, he was an administrator of the Marshall Plan, Executive Editor and Publisher of *The Reporter* Magazine, and dean of the Maxwell School of Public Administration at Syracuse University. He returned to government service in 1961 as Assistant Secretary of State for International Organization Affairs and was appointed United States Ambassador to NATO in 1965. From 1969 to 1974, he was President of the University of Hawaii. Since 1974, he has been Director of the Aspen Institute Program in International Affairs.

The range of his writings—including *The Overseas Americans, The Obligations of Power, NATO: The Transatlantic Bargain, The Future Executive, China Diary*, and, in 1976, *The Third Try at World Order*—reflects his broad experience and his capacity, amid day-to-day challenges, to see clearly and to see himself seeing.

Brandeis

Louis Dembitz Brandeis, United States jurist and public advocate for the interests of consumers, labor unions, and investors, was born in Louisville, Kentucky, in 1856. He attended the public schools of Louisville and the university in Dresden, Germany, before entering Harvard Law School, from which he was graduated at the head of his class in 1877.

After less than a year of law practice in St. Louis, Missouri, Brandeis returned to Boston, where he maintained an active practice until his appointment to the Supreme Court in 1916.

Brandeis came to be known as "The People's Attorney," because he represented interests that had not commonly enjoyed such formidable advocacy. He often took these responsibilities on the condition that he receive no compensation. In this way he was able, as a private citizen, to indulge his passion for public service and, more importantly, to devise constructive solutions that would transcend the narrow constraints of client and class. When the controversial affairs of the Equitable Life Assurance Society of New York precipitated widespread alarm in 1905, Brandeis became unpaid counsel for the new Policy Holders Protective Committee. His investigations and reports anticipated, in some respects, the findings and recommendations from the legislative committee appointed in New York under State Senator William W. Armstrong.

During the period 1907-1914, Brandeis served as counsel for a number of states fighting the opponents of state laws which prescribed maximum hours of labor and minimum wages. He devised what came to be known and copied as the "Brandeis Brief": legal propositions were set forth simply and the bulk of the argument was a massive collection of economic facts, historical experience, and expert opinion to support the reasonableness of the legislation under challenge. Brandeis' volume of essays, *Other People's Money and How the Bankers Use It*, published in 1914, was a study of the power exercised by investment bankers over United States industry. The book was a frontal assault on monopoly and interlocking directorates and influenced the enactment in 1914 of the Clayton Act and the Federal Trade Commission Act.

In politics, as in his law practice, Brandeis preserved his independence. Until his appointment to the Supreme Court in 1916, he had never held public office. Although he made a series of public speeches in 1912 on behalf of Senator Robert M. La Follette's nomination as Republican candidate for the Presidency, the failure of this movement left Brandeis a choice between Theodore Roosevelt as the Progressive candidate and Woodrow Wilson as the Democratic candidate. Without hesitation, Brandeis gave his support to Wilson, whose antitrust philosophy of enforced competition was far more congenial to him than Roosevelt's proposal of regulated monopoly. The first meeting between Brandeis and Wilson in August 1912 provided Wilson with an underpinning of fact and a framework of reform that toughened his policy toward big business.

The meeting was also the basis for an enduring friendship between the two men, and on January 28, 1916, President Wilson nominated Brandeis as an Associate Justice of the Supreme Court. After bitter opposition, the Senate by a vote of 47 to 22 confirmed the nomination. He was the first Jew to sit on the Supreme Court.

Brandeis' masterful judicial opinions reflected his distinctive methods and the coherence of his beliefs. He was solicitous of a viable federal system, with scope provided to the states for legislative experiments. He objected vigorously to any suppression of radical or unpopular sentiments, except where the propagation of these views created a proximate danger of unlawful action. On most important issues, Brandeis was in league, often in the minority, with his colleague Justice Oliver Wendell Holmes. Their outlooks were by no means identical, however. Holmes was content to support legislative experiments because of the prevailing skepticism in judging measures of social reform; Brandeis strove to understand and to explain sympathetically the needs and aspirations embodied in reformist measures.

During the period of the New Deal, many of the earlier dissenting positions Holmes and Brandeis had taken came to be accepted by the Court. While Brandeis supported the constitutional validity of most New Deal legislation, he did not do so indiscriminately. For example, he joined in the decisions holding the National Industrial Recovery Act to be unconstitutional. Brandeis retired from the Court in 1939 and died in Washington, D.C., in 1941.

Okun

Since 1969, Arthur F. Okun has been a Senior Fellow of the Brookings Institution in Washington, D.C. and a coeditor (with George L. Perry) of the Brookings Papers on Economic Activities. He was a member for fifteen years of the Yale University Economics Department and served in the Johnson Administration as Senior Economist and Chairman of the Council of Economic Advisers.

Equality and Efficiency is an expanded version of the Godkin Lectures presented by Okun at the John F. Kennedy School of Government at Harvard University in 1974. His other publications include two books, *The Political Economy of Prosperity* and *The Battle against Unemployment,* and numerous articles on economic forecasting and fiscal and monetary policies.

Drucker

Peter F. Drucker is widely acknowledged as one of the most respected management consultants today. Born in Vienna in 1909 and educated in Austria and England, he emigrated to the United States in 1937 and was naturalized in 1943. In 1929, he became a newspaper correspondent and an economist for an international bank in London. In the United States, he worked as an economist for a group of British banks and insurance companies before joining the faculty of Bennington College from 1942-1949 as a Professor of Politics and Philosophy.

Subsequent academic appointments include Professor of Management at New York University's Graduate Business School and Clark Professor of Social Science at the Claremont Graduate School in California.

Drucker's books include *The New Society; The Effective Executive; The Practice of Management; America's Next 20 Years; Landmarks of Tomorrow; Managing for Results; The Age of Discontinuity; Management: Tasks, Responsibilities, Practices;* and two volumes of essays, *Technology, Management and Society* and *Men, Ideas and Politics.*

Bell

At the end of the decade of the 1950s, Daniel Bell coined the phrase "post-industrial society" to describe the new social structure evolving in the Western World in the second half of the twentieth century. The term quickly entered the language of social parlance around the world. This was not the only time that Bell has given new ideas and a new vocabulary to the social sciences. As a professor of sociology at Columbia University and now at Harvard, as a contributing editor to *Fortune,* as an editor of *The Public Interest,* and as the chairman of the Commission on the Year 2000 of the American Academy of Arts and Sciences, Daniel Bell has written countless articles and books—including *The End of Ideology, The Radical Rights, Towards the Year 2000, The Coming of Post-Industrial Society,* and *The Cultural Contradiction of Capitalism*—which have consistently generated intellectual excitement and controversy. He has been particularly forceful in formulating a major post-Marxist theory of social change.

Heilbroner

Robert L. Heilbroner, like Peter F. Drucker and Daniel Bell, has combined an academic career with writing. He is now Norman Thomas Professor of Economics at the New School for Social Research in New York. The range of his interests is reflected in the titles of his major books: *The Worldly Philosophers, The Future as History, The Quest for Wealth,* and *An Inquiry Into the Human Prospect.* In *Business Civilization in Decline,* Professor Heilbroner deals with the challenges that will assault modern-day capitalism and the changes it will undergo. He foresees our present business society making way for another system: "a tightly controlled society where the traditional pillars of capitalism—private property and the market—have been amended beyond recognition."

Thomas

Dr. Lewis Thomas, physician, educator, medical administrator, and currently president of the Sloan-Kettering Cancer Center, received the National Book Award in 1975 for his book *The Lives of a Cell.* Dr. Thomas has served in academia for the past several decades. Between 1954 and 1969, he was, successively, Chairman of the Department of Pathology,

Chairman of the Department of Medicine, and Dean of the Medical School at New York University. From 1969-1973, he served as Chairman of the Department of Pathology and Dean of the School of Medicine at Yale. Dr. Thomas is a Fellow of the American Academy of Arts and Science, and in 1975, he received the Distinguished Achievement Award for Modern Medicine.

Commager

Henry Steele Commager, professor of history at Amherst College, has been one of America's foremost historians for more than four decades. His wise and perceptive books on virtually all aspects of American history have brought home to Americans the meaning and worth of their collective experience—how they got where they are, and how they should best go forward into the future. Commager's mastery of facts, combined with his profound love of country, make him one of the most compelling contemporary critics of American life. The World Affairs Council of Philadelphia commissioned Commager's *Declaration of INTERdependence* as part of their observation of the Bicentennial Era (1976-1989). The document has been endorsed by 130 members of Congress as a subject for public study.

Chardin

Teilhard de Chardin was born in France in 1881, the fourth child in a family of twelve. He was prepared for the priesthood at a Jesuit college and was ordained in 1912. Although Chardin's writings were in the field of paleontology, the implications of his ideas for Catholic theology led to his censorship by his superiors in the Church. Pope Pius XII was approached about prosecuting Chardin on a charge of heresy, but Pius reportedly turned the matter aside, saying, "One Galileo in 2,000 years is enough." Chardin's *The Phenomenon of Man,* published in France in 1955, the year of his death, is credited with contributing to the ferment that led to the Second Vatican Council.

Justice:
The Individual
and Society

First Week — First Day

Plato, *The Republic,* Book VII (selection) *
Fyodor Dostoevsky, *Grand Inquisitor*

* The word selection identifies readings which are excerpted rather than presented in their entirety.

The Republic

by Plato

BOOK VII

AND NOW, I said, let me show in a figure how far our nature is enlightened or unenlightened:—Behold! human beings living in an underground den, which has a mouth open towards the light and reaching all along the den; here they have been from their childhood, and have their legs and necks chained so that they can not move, and can only see before them, being prevented by the chains from turning round their heads. Above and behind them a fire is blazing at a distance, and between the fire and the prisoners there is a raised way; and you will see, if you look, a low wall built along the way, like the screen which marionette players have in front of them, over which they show the puppets.

I see.

And do you see, I said, men passing along the wall carrying all sorts of vessels, and statues and figures of animals made of wood and stone and various materials, which appear over the wall? Some of them are talking, others silent.

You have shown me a strange image, and they are strange prisoners.

Like ourselves, I replied; and they see only their own shadows, or the shadows of one another, which the fire throws on the opposite wall of the cave?

True, he said; how could they see anything but the shadows if they were never allowed to move their heads?

And of the objects which are being carried in like manner they would only see the shadows?

Yes, he said.

And if they were able to converse with one another, would they not suppose that they were naming what was actually before them?

Very true.

And suppose further that the prison had an echo which came from the other side, would they not be sure to fancy when one of the passers-by spoke that the voice which they heard came from the passing shadow?

No question, he replied.

To them, I said, the truth would be literally nothing but the shadows of the images.

That is certain.

And now look again, and see what will naturally follow if the prisoners are released and disabused of their error. At first, when any of them is liberated and compelled suddenly to stand up and turn his neck round and walk and look towards the light, he will suffer sharp pains; the glare will distress him, and he will be unable to see the realities of which in his former state he had seen the shadows; and then conceive some one saying to him, that what he saw before was an illusion, but that now, when he is approaching nearer to being and his eye is turned towards more real existence, he has a clearer vision,—what will be his reply? And you may further imagine that his instructor is pointing to the objects as they pass and requiring him to name them,—will he not be perplexed? Will he not fancy that the shadows which he formerly saw are truer than the objects which are now shown to him?

Far truer.

And if he is compelled to look straight at the light, will he not have a pain in his eyes which will make him turn away to take refuge in the objects of vision which he can see, and which he will conceive to be in reality clearer than the things which are now being shown to him?

True, he said.

And suppose once more, that he is reluctantly dragged up a steep and narrow ascent, and held fast until he is forced into the presence of the sun himself, is he not likely to be pained and irritated? When he approaches the light his eyes will be dazzled, and he will not be able to see anything at all of what are now called realities.

Not all in a moment, he said.

He will require to grow accustomed to the sight of the upper world. And first he will see the shadows best, next the reflections of men and other objects in the water, and then the objects themselves; then he will gaze upon the light of the moon and the stars and the spangled heaven; and he will see the sky and the stars by night better than the sun or the light of the sun by day?

Certainly.

Last of all he will be able to see the sun, and not mere reflections of him in the water, but he will see him in his own proper place, and not in another; and he will contemplate him as he is.

Certainly.

He will then proceed to argue that this is he who gives the season and the years, and is the guardian of all that is in the visible world, and in a certain way the cause of all things which he and his fellows have been accustomed to behold?

Clearly, he said, he would first see the sun and then reason about him.

And when he remembered his old habitation, and the wisdom of the den and his fellow-prisoners, do you not suppose that he would felicitate himself on the change, and pity them?

Certainly, he would.

And if they were in the habit of conferring honors among themselves on those who were quickest to observe the passing shadows and to remark which of them went before, and which followed after, and which were together; and who were therefore best able to draw conclusions as to the future, do you think that he would care for such honors and glories, or envy the possessors of them? Would he not say with Homer,

Better to be the poor servant of a poor master,

and to endure anything, rather than think as they do and live after their manner?

Yes, he said, I think that he would rather suffer anything than entertain these false notions and live in this miserable manner.

Imagine once more, I said, such an one coming suddenly out of the sun to be replaced in his old situation; would he not be certain to have his eyes full of darkness?

To be sure, he said.

And if there were a contest, and he had to compete in measuring the shadows with the prisoners who had never moved out of the den, while his sight was still weak, and before his eyes had become steady (and the time which would be needed to acquire this new habit of sight might be very considerable), would he not be ridiculous? Men would say of him that up he went and down he came without his eyes; and that it was better not even to think of ascending; and if any one tried to loose another and lead him up to the light, let them only catch the offender, and they would put him to death.

No question, he said.

This entire allegory, I said, you may now append, dear Glaucon, to the previous argument; the prison-house is the world of sight, the light of the fire is the sun, and you will not misapprehend me if you interpret the journey upwards to be the ascent of the soul into the intellectual world according to my poor belief, which, at your desire, I have expressed—whether rightly or wrongly God knows. But, whether true or false, my opinion is that in the world of knowledge the idea of good appears last of all, and is seen only with an effort; and, when seen, is also inferred to be the universal author of all things beautiful and right, parent of light and of the lord of light in this visible world, and the immediate source of reason and truth in the intellectual; and that this is the power upon which he who would act rationally either in public or private life must have his eye fixed.

I agree, he said, as far as I am able to understand you.

Moreover, I said, you must not wonder that those who attain to this beatific vision are unwilling to descend to human affairs; for their souls are ever hastening into the upper world where they desire to dwell; which desire of theirs is very natural, if our allegory may be trusted.

Yes, very natural.

And is there anything surprising in one who passes from divine contemplations to the evil state of man, misbehaving himself in a ridiculous manner; if, while his eyes are blinking and before he has become accustomed to the surrounding darkness, he is compelled to fight in courts of law, or in other places, about the images or the shadows of images of justice, and is endeavoring to meet the conceptions of those who have never yet seen absolute justice?

Anything but surprising, he replied.

Any one who has common sense will remember that the bewilderments of the eyes are of two kinds, and arise from two causes, either from coming out of the light or from going into the light, which is true of the mind's eye, quite as much as of the bodily eye; and he who remembers this when he sees any one whose vision is perplexed and weak, will not be too ready to laugh; he will first ask whether that soul of man has come out of the brighter life, and is unable to see because unaccustomed to the dark, or having turned from darkness to the day is dazzled by excess of light. And he will count the one happy in his condition and state of being, and he will pity the other; or, if he have a mind to laugh at the soul which comes from below into the light, there will be more reason in this than in the laugh which greets him who returns from above out of the light into the den.

That, he said, is a very just distinction.

But then, if I am right, certain professors of education must be wrong when they say that they can put a knowledge into the soul which was not there before, like sight into blind eyes.

They undoubtedly say this, he replied.

Whereas, our argument shows that the power and capacity of learning exists in the soul already; and that just as the eye was unable to turn from darkness to light without the whole body, so too the instrument of knowledge can only by the movement of the whole soul be turned from the world of becoming into that of being, and learn by degrees to endure the sight of being, and of the brightest and best of being, or in other words, of the good.

Very true.

And must there not be some art which will effect conversion in the easiest and quickest manner; not implanting the faculty of sight, for that exists already, but has been turned in the wrong direction, and is looking away from the truth?

Yes, he said, such an art may be presumed.

And whereas the other so-called virtues of the soul seem to be akin to bodily qualities, for even when they are not originally innate they can be implanted later by habit and exercise, the virtue of wisdom more than anything else contains a divine element which always remains, and by this conversion is rendered useful and profitable; or, on the other hand, hurtful and useless. Did you never observe the narrow intelligence flashing from the keen eye of a clever rogue—how eager he is, how clearly his paltry soul sees the way to his end; he is the reverse of blind, but his keen eye-sight is forced into the service of evil, and he is mischievous in proportion to his cleverness?

Very true, he said.

But what if there had been a circumcision of such natures in the days of their youth; and they had been severed from those sensual pleasures, such as eating and drinking, which, like leaden weights, were attached to them at their birth, and which drag them down and turn the vision of their souls upon the things that are below—if, I say, they had been released from these impediments and turned in the opposite direction, the very same faculty in them would have seen the truth as keenly as they see what their eyes are turned to now.

Very likely.

Yes, I said; and there is another thing which is likely, or rather a necessary interference from what has preceded, that neither the uneducated and uninformed of the truth, nor yet those who never make an end of their education, will be able ministers of State; not the former, because they have no single aim of duty which is the rule of all their actions, private as well as public; nor the latter, because they will not act at all except upon compulsion, fancying that they are already dwelling apart in the islands of the blest.

Very true, he replied.

Then, I said, the business of us who are the founders of the State will be to compel the best minds to attain that knowledge which we have already shown to be the greatest of all—they must continue to ascend until they arrive at the good; but when they have ascended and seen enough we must not allow them to do as they do now.

What do you mean?

I mean that they remain in the upper world: but this must not be allowed; they must be made to descend again among the prisoners in the den, and partake of their labors and honors, whether they are worth having or not.

But is not this unjust? he said; ought we to give them a worse life, when they might have a better?

You have again forgotten, my friend, I said, the intention of the legislator, who did not aim at making any one class in the State happy above the rest; the happiness was to be in the whole State, and he held the citizens together by persuasion and necessity, making them benefactors of the State, and therefore benefactors of one another; to this end he created them, not to please themselves, but to be his instruments in binding up the State.

True, he said, I had forgotten.

Observe, Glaucon, that there will be no injustice in compelling our philosophers to have a care and providence of others; we shall explain to them that in other States, men of their class are not obliged to share in the toils of politics: and this is reasonable, for they grow up at their own sweet will, and the government would rather not have them. Being self-taught, they can not be expected to show any gratitude for a culture which they have never received. But we have brought you into the world to be rulers of the hive, kings of yourselves and of the other citizens, and have educated you far better and more perfectly than they have been educated, and you are better able to share in the double duty. Wherefore each of you, when his turn comes, must go down to the general underground abode, and get the habit of seeing in the dark. When you have acquired the habit, you will see ten thousand times better than the inhabitants of the den, and you will know what the several images are, and what they represent, because you have seen the beautiful and just and good in their truth. And thus our State, which is also yours, will be a reality, and not a dream only, and will be administered in a spirit unlike that of other States, in which men fight with one another about shadows only and are distracted in the struggle for power, which in their eyes is a great good. Whereas the truth is that the State in which the rulers are most reluctant to govern is always the best and most quietly governed, and the State in which they are most eager, the worst.

Quite true, he replied.

And will our pupils, when they hear this, refuse to take their turn at the toils of State, when they are allowed to spend the greater part of their time with one another in the heavenly light?

Impossible, he answered; for they are just men, and the commands which we impose upon them are just; there can be no doubt that every one of them will take office as a stern necessity, and not after the fashion of our present rulers of State.

Yes, my friend, I said; and there lies the point. You must contrive for your future rulers another and a better life than that of a ruler, and then you may have a well-ordered State; for only in the State which offers this, will they rule who are truly rich, not in silver and gold, but in virtue and wisdom, which are the true blessings of life. Whereas if they go to the administration of public affairs, poor and hungering after their own private advantage, thinking that hence they are to snatch the chief good, order there can never be; for they will be fighting about office, and the civil and domestic broils which thus arise will be the ruin of the rulers themselves and of the whole State.

Most true, he replied.

And the only life which looks down upon the life of political ambition is that of true philosophy. Do you know of any other?

Indeed, I do not, he said.

And those who govern ought not to be lovers of the task? For, if they are, there will be rival lovers, and they will fight.

No question.

Who then are those whom we shall compel to be guardians? Surely they will be the men who are wisest about affairs of State, and by whom the State is best administered, and who at the same time have other honors and another and a better life than that of politics?

They are the men, and I will choose them, he replied. . . .

The Grand Inquisitor

by Fyodor Dostoevsky

Do you know, Alyosha—don't laugh! I made a poem about a year ago. If you can waste another ten minutes on me, I'll tell it to you."

"You wrote a poem?"

"Oh, no, I didn't write it," laughed Ivan, "and I've never written two lines of poetry in my life. But I made up this poem in prose and I remembered it. I was carried away when I made it up. You will be my first reader—that is, listener. Why should an author forego even one listener?" smiled Ivan. "Shall I tell it to you?"

"I am all attention," said Alyosha.

"My poem is called 'The Grand Inquisitor'; it's a ridiculous thing, but I want to tell it to you."...

"My story is laid in Spain, in Seville, in the most terrible time of the Inquisition, when fires were lighted every day to the glory of God, and 'in the splendid AUTO DA FE the wicked heretics were burnt.'...

"In His infinite mercy He came once more among men in that human shape in which He walked among men for three years fifteen centuries ago. He came down to the 'hot pavement' of the southern town in which on the day before almost a hundred heretics had, AD MAJOREM GLORIAM DEI, been burnt by the cardinal, the Grand Inquisitor, in a magnificent AUTO DA FE, in the presence of the king, the court, the knights, the cardinals, the most charming ladies of the court, and the whole population of Seville.

"He came softly, unobserved, and yet, strange to say, every one recognized Him. That might be one of the best passages in the poem. I mean, why they recognized Him. The people are irresistibly drawn to Him, they surround Him, they flock about Him, follow Him. He moves silently in their midst with a gentle smile of infinite compassion. The sun of love burns in His heart, light and power shine from His eyes, and their radiance, shed on the people, stirs their hearts with responsive love. He holds out His hands to them, blesses them, and a healing virtue comes from contact with Him, even with His garments. An old man in the crowd, blind from childhood, cries out, 'O Lord, heal me and I shall see Thee!' and, as it were, scales fall from his eyes and the blind man sees Him. The crowd weeps and kisses the earth under His feet. Children throw flowers before Him, sing, and cry hosannah. 'It is He—it is He!' all repeat. 'It must be He, it can be no one but Him!' He stops at the steps of the Seville cathedral at the moment when the weeping mourners are bringing in a little open white coffin. In it lies a child of seven, the only daughter of a prominent citizen. The dead child lies hidden in flowers. 'He will raise your child,' the crowd shouts to the weeping mother. The priest, coming to meet the coffin, looks perplexed, and frowns, but the mother of the dead child throws herself at His feet with a wail. 'If it is Thou, raise my child!' she cries, holding out her hands to Him. The procession halts, the coffin is laid on the steps at His feet. He looks with compassion, and His lips once more softly pronounce, 'Maiden, arise!' and the maiden arises. The little girl sits up in the coffin and looks round, smiling with wide-open wondering eyes, holding a bunch of white roses they had put in her hand.

"There are cries, sobs, confusion among the people, and at that moment the cardinal himself, the Grand Inquisitor, passes by the cathedral. He is an old man, almost ninety, tall and erect, with a withered face and sunken eyes, in which there is still a gleam of light. He is not dressed in his gorgeous cardinal's robes, as he was the day before, when he was burning the enemies of the Roman Church—at that moment he was wearing his coarse, old, monk's cassock. At a distance behind him comes his gloomy assistants and slaves and the 'holy guard.' He stops at the sight of the crowd and watches it from a distance. He sees everything; he sees them set the coffin down at His feet, sees the child rise up, and his face darkens. He knits his thick grey brows and his eyes gleam with a sinister fire. He holds out his finger and bids the guards take Him. And such is his power, so completely are the people cowed into submission and trembling obedience to him, that the crowd immediately makes way for the guards, and in the midst of death-like silence they lay hands on Him and lead Him away. The crowd instantly bows down to the earth, like one man, before the old inquisitor. He blesses the people in silence and passes on.

"The guards lead their prisoner to the close, gloomy vaulted prison in the ancient palace of the Holy Inquisition and shut Him in it. The day passes and is followed by the dark, burning 'breathless' night of Seville. The air is 'fragrant with laurel and lemon.' In the pitch darkness the iron door of the prison is suddenly opened and the Grand Inquisitor himself comes in with a light in his hand. He is alone: the door is closed at once behind him. He stands in the doorway and for a minute or two gazes in His face. At last he goes up slowly, sets the light on the table and speaks.

The Grand Inquisitor Speaks to the Prisoner

" 'Is it Thou? Thou?' but receiving no answer, he adds at once, 'Don't answer, be silent. What canst Thou say indeed? I know too well what Thou wouldst say. And Thou hast no right to add anything to what Thou hadst said of old. Why, then, art Thou come to hinder us? For Thou has come to hinder us, and Thou knowest that. But dost Thou know what will be tomorrow? I know not who Thou art and care not to know whether it is Thou or only a semblance of Him, but tomorrow I shall condemn Thee and burn Thee at the stake as the worst of Heretics. And the very people who have today kissed Thy feet, tomorrow at the faintest sign from me will rush to heap up the embers of Thy fire. Knowest Thou that? Yes, maybe Thou knowest it,' he added with thoughtful penetration, never for a moment taking his eyes off the Prisoner."

"I don't quite understand, Ivan. What does it mean?" Alyosha, who had been listening in silence, said with a smile. "Is it simply a wild fantasy, or a mistake on the part of the old man—some impossible QUID PRO QUO?"

Take it as the last," said Ivan, laughing, "if you are so corrupted by modern realism and can't stand anything fantastic. If you like it to be a case of mistaken identity, let it be so. It is true," he went on, laughing, "the old man was ninety, and he might well be crazy over his set idea. He might have been struck by the appearance of the Prisoner. It might, in fact, be simply his ravings, the delusion of an old man of ninety, overexcited by the AUTO DA FE of a hundred heretics the day before. But does it matter to us after all whether it was a mistake of identity or a wild fantasy? All that matters is that the old man should speak out, should speak openly of what he has thought in silence for ninety years."

"And the Prisoner too is silent? Does He look at him and not say a word?"

"That's inevitable in any case," Ivan laughed again. "The old man has told Him He hasn't the right to add anything to what He has said of old. One may say it is the most fundamental feature of Roman Catholicism, in my opinion at least. 'All has been given by Thee to the Pope,' they say, 'and all, therefore, is still in the Pope's hands, and there is no need for Thee to come now at all. Thou must not meddle for the time, at least.' That's how they speak and write too—the Jesuits, at any rate. I have read it myself in the works of their theologians."

" 'Hast Thou the right to reveal to us one of the mysteries of that world from which Thou hast come?' my old man asks Him, and answers the question for Him. 'No, Thou hast not; that Thou mayest not add to what has been said of old, and mayest not take from men the freedom which Thou didst exalt when Thou wast on earth. Whatsoever Thou revealest anew will encroach on men's freedom of faith; for it will be manifest as a miracle, and the freedom of their faith was dearer to Thee than anything in those days fifteen hundred years ago. Didst Thou not often say then, "I will make you free"? But now Thou hast seen these "free" men,' the old man adds suddenly, with a pensive smile. 'Yes, we've paid dearly for it,' he goes on, looking sternly at Him, 'but at last we have completed that work in Thy name. For fifteen centuries we have been wrestling with Thy freedom, but now it is ended and over for good? Thou lookest meekly at me and deignest not even to be wroth with me. But let me tell Thee that now, today, people are more persuaded than ever that they have perfect freedom, yet they have brought their freedom to us and laid it humbly at our feet. But that has been our doing. Was this what Thou didst? Was this Thy freedom?' "

"I don't understand again," Alyosha broke in. "Is he ironical, is he jesting?"

"Not a bit of it! He claims it as a merit for himself and his Church that at last they have vanquished freedom and have done so to make men happy."

" 'For now' (he is speaking of the Inquisition, of course) 'for the first time it has become possible to think of the happiness of men. Man was created a rebel; and how can rebels be happy? Thou wast warned,' he says to Him. 'Thou hast had no lack of admonitions, and warnings, but Thou didst not listen to those warnings; Thou didst reject the only way by which men might be made happy. But, fortunately, departing Thou didst hand on the work to us. Thou hast promised, Thou hast established by Thy word, Thou hast given to us the right to bind and to unbind, and now, of course, Thou canst not think of taking it away. Why, then, hast Thou come to hinder us?' "

"And what's the meaning of 'no lack of admonitions and warnings'?" asked Alyosha.

"Why, that's the chief part of what the old man must say."

The Three Temptations Foreshadowed the Whole Subsequent History of Mankind

" 'The wise and dread Spirit, the spirit of self-destruction and non-existence,' the old man goes on, 'the great spirit talked with Thee in the wilderness, and we are told in the books that he "tempted" Thee. Is that so? And could anything truer be said than what he revealed to Thee in three questions and what Thou didst reject, and what in the books is called "the temptation"? And yet if there has ever been on earth a real stupendous miracle, it took place on that day, on the day of the three temptations. The statement of those three questions was itself the miracle. If it were possible to imagine simply for the sake of argument that those three questions of the dread spirit had perished utterly from the books, and that we had to restore them and to invent them anew, and to do so had gathered together all the wise men of the earth—rulers, chief priests, learned men, philosophers, poets—and had set them the task to invent three questions, such as would not only fit the question, but express in three words, three human phrases, the whole future history of the world and of humanity—dost Thou believe that all the wisdom of the earth united could have invented anything in depth and force equal to the three questions which were actually put to Thee then by the wise and mighty spirit in the wilderness? From those questions alone, from the miracle of their statements, we can see that we have here to do not with the fleeting human intelligence, but with the absolute and eternal. For in those three questions the whole subsequent history of mankind is, as it were, brought together into one whole, and foretold, and in them are united all the unsolved historical contradictions of human nature. At the time it could not be so clear, since the future was unknown; but now that fifteen hundred years have passed, we see that everything in those three questions was so justly divined and foretold, and has been so truly fulfilled, that nothing can be added to them or taken from them.

The First Temptation: The Problem of Bread

" 'Judge Thyself who was right—Thou or he who questioned Thee then? Remember the first question; its meaning, in other words, was this: "Thou wouldst go into the world, and art going with empty hands, with some promise of freedom which men in their simplicity and their natural unruliness cannot even understand, which they fear and dread—for nothing has ever been more insupportable for a man and a human society than freedom. But seest Thou these stones in this parched and barren wilderness? Turn them into bread, and mankind will run after Thee like a flock of sheep, grateful and obedient, though for ever trembling, lest Thou withdraw Thy hand and deny them Thy bread." But Thou wouldst not deprive man of freedom and didst reject the offer, thinking, what is that freedom worth, if obedience is bought with bread? Thou didst reply that man lives not by bread alone. But dost Thou know that for the sake of that earthly bread the spirit of the earth will rise up against Thee, and all will follow him, crying, "Who can compare with this beast? He has given us fire from heaven!" Dost Thou know that the ages will pass, and humanity will proclaim by the lips of their sages that there is no crime, and therefore no sin; there is only hunger? "Feed men, and then ask of them virtue!" That's what they'll write on the banner, which they will raise against Thee, and with which they will destroy Thy temple. Where Thy temple stood will rise a new building; the terrible tower of Babel will be built again, and though, like the one of old, it will not be finished, yet Thou mightest have prevented that new tower and have cut short the sufferings of men for a thousand years; for they will come back to us after a thousand years of agony with their tower. They will seek us again, hidden underground in the catacombs, for we shall be again persecuted and tortured. They will find us and cry to us, "Feed us, for those who have promised us fire from heaven haven't given it!" And then we shall finish building their tower, for he finishes the building who feeds them. And we alone shall feed them in Thy name, declaring falsely that it is in Thy name. Oh, never, never can they feed themselves without us! No science will give them bread so long as they remain free. In the end they will lay their freedom at our feet, and say to us, "Make us your slaves, but feed us." They will understand themselves, at last, that freedom and bread enough for all are inconceivable together, for never, never will they be able to share between them! They will be convinced, too, that they can never be free, for they are weak, vicious, worthless and rebellious.

" 'Thou didst promise them the bread of Heaven, but, I repeat again, can it compare with earthly bread in the eyes of the weak, ever sinful and ignoble race of man? And if for the sake of the bread of Heaven thousands and tens of thousands shall follow Thee, what is to become of the millions and tens of thousands of millions of creatures who will not have the strength to forego the earthly bread for the sake of the heavenly? Or dost Thou care only for the tens of thousands of the great and strong, while the millions, numerous as the sands of the sea, who are weak but love Thee, must exist only for the sake of the great and strong? No, we care for the weak too. They are sinful and rebellious, but in the end they too will become obedient. They will marvel at us and look on us as gods, because we are ready to endure the freedom which they have found so dreadful to rule over them—so awful it will seem to them to be free. But we shall tell them that we are Thy servants and rule them in Thy name. We shall deceive them again, for we will not let Thee come to us again. That deception will be our suffering, for we shall be forced to lie.

" 'This is the significance of the first question in the wilderness, and this is what Thou hast rejected for the sake of that freedom which Thou hast exalted above everything. Yet in this question lies hid the great secret of this world.

" 'Choosing "bread," Thou wouldst have satisfied the universal and everlasting craving of humanity—to find some one to worship.

" 'So long as man remains free he strives for nothing so incessantly and so painfully as to find some one to worship. But man seeks to worship what is established beyond dispute, so that all men would agree at once to worship it. For these pitiful creatures are concerned not only to find what one or the other can worship, but to find something that all would believe in and worship; what is essential is that all may be TOGETHER in it. This craving for COMMUNITY of worship is the chief misery of every man individually and of all humanity from the beginning of time. For the sake of common worship they've slain each other with the sword. They have set up gods and challenged one another, "Put away your gods and come and worship ours, or we will kill you and your gods!" And so it will be to the end of the world, even when gods disappear from the earth; they will fall down before idols just the same. Thou didst know, Thou couldst not but have known, this fundamental secret of human nature, but Thou didst reject the one infallible banner which was offered Thee to make all men bow down to Thee alone—the banner of earthly bread; and Thou hast rejected it for the sake of freedom and the bread of Heaven.

The Second Temptation: The Problem of Conscience

" 'Behold what Thou didst further. And all again in the name of freedom! I tell Thee that man is tormented by no greater anxiety than to find some one quickly to whom he can hand over that gift of freedom with which the ill-fated creature is born. But only one who can appease their conscience can take over their freedom. In bread there was offered Thee an invincible banner; give bread, and man will worship Thee, for nothing is more certain than bread. But if some one else gains possession of his conscience—oh! then he will cast away Thy bread and follow after him who has ensnared his conscience. In that Thou wast right. For the secret of man's being is not only to live but to have something to live for. Without a stable conception of the object of life, man would not consent to go on living, and would rather destroy himself than remain on earth, though he had bread in abundance. That is true.

" 'But what happened?

" 'Instead of taking men's freedom from them, Thou didst make it greater than ever! Didst Thou forget that man prefers peace, and even death, to freedom of choice in the knowledge of good and evil? Nothing is more seductive for man than his freedom of conscience, but nothing is a greater cause of suffering. And behold, instead of giving a firm foundation for setting the conscience of man at rest for ever, Thou didst choose all that is exceptional, vague and enigmatic; Thou didst choose what was utterly beyond the strength of men, acting as though Thou didst not love them at all—Thou who didst come to give Thy life for them. Instead of taking possession of men's freedom, Thou didst increase it, and burdened the spiritual kingdom of mankind with its sufferings for ever. Thou didst desire man's free love, that he should follow Thee freely, enticed and taken captive by Thee. In place of the rigid ancient law, man must hereafter with free heart decide for himself what is good and what is evil, having only Thy image before him as his guide. But didst Thou not know he would at last reject even Thy image and Thy truth, if he is weighed down with the fearful burden of free choice? They will cry aloud at last that the truth is not in Thee, for they could not have been left in greater confusion and suffering than Thou hast caused, laying upon them so many cares and unanswerable problems.

" 'So that, in truth, Thou didst Thyself lay the foundation for the destruction of Thy kingdom, and no one is more to blame for it. Yet what was offered Thee? There are three powers, three powers alone, able to conquer and to hold captive for ever the conscience of these impotent rebels for their happiness—those forces are miracle, mystery and authority. Thou hast rejected all three and hast set the example for doing so. When the wise and dread spirit set Thee on the pinnacle of the temple and said to Thee, "If Thou wouldst know whether Thou art the Son of God then cast Thyself down, for it is written: the angels shall hold him up lest he fall and bruise himself, and Thou shalt know then whether Thou art the Son of God and shalt prove then how great is Thy faith in Thy father." But Thou didst refuse and wouldst not cast Thyself down. Oh! of course, Thou didst proudly and well like God; but the weak, unruly race of men, are they gods? Oh, Thou didst know then that in taking one step, in making one movement to cast Thyself down, Thou wouldst be tempting God and have lost all Thy faith in Him, and wouldst have been dashed to pieces against that earth which Thou didst come to save. And the wise spirit that tempted Thee would have rejoiced. But I ask again, are there many like Thee? And couldst Thou believe for one moment that men, too, could face such a temptation? Is the nature of men such, that they can reject miracle, and at the great moments of their life, the moments of their deepest, most agonizing spiritual difficulties, cling only to the free verdict of the heart?

" 'Oh, Thou didst know that Thy deed would be recorded in books, would be handed down to remote times and the utmost ends of the earth, and Thou didst hope that man, following Thee, would cling to God and not ask for a miracle. But Thou didst not know that when man rejects miracle he rejects God too; for man seeks not so much God as the miraculous. And as man cannot bear to be without the miraculous, he will create new miracles of his own for himself, and will worship deeds of sorcery and witchcraft, though he might be a hundred times over a rebel, heretic, and infidel. Thou didst not come down from the Cross when they shouted to Thee, mocking and reviling Thee, "Come down from the cross, and we will believe that Thou art He." Thou dist not come down, for again Thou wouldst not enslave man by a miracle, and didst crave faith given freely, not based on miracle. Thou didst crave for free love and not the base raptures of the slave before the might that has overawed him for ever.

" 'But Thou didst think too highly of men therein, for they are slaves, of course, though rebellious by nature. Look around and judge; fifteen centuries have passed, look upon them. Whom hast Thou raised up to Thyself? I swear, man is weaker and baser by nature than Thou hast believed him! Can he, can he do what Thou didst? By showing him so much respect, Thou didst, as it were, cease to feel for him, for Thou didst ask far too much from him—Thou who hast loved him more than Thyself! Respecting him less, Thou wouldst have asked less of him. That would have been more like love. for his burden would have been lighter. He is weak and vile. What though he is everywhere now rebelling against our power, and proud of his rebellion? It is the pride of a child and a schoolboy. They are little children rioting and barring out the teacher at school. But their childish delight will end; it will cost them dear. They will cast down temples and drench the earth with blood. But they will see at last, the foolish children, that, though they are rebels, they are impotent rebels, unable to keep up their own rebellion. Bathed in their foolish tears, they will recognize at last that He who created them rebels must have meant to mock at them. They will say this in despair, and their utterance will be a blasphemy which will make them more unhappy still, for man's nature cannot bear blasphemy, and in the end always avenges it on itself. And so unrest, confusion and unhappiness—that is the present lot of man after Thou didst bear so much for their freedom!

" 'Thy great prophet tells in vision and in image, that he saw all those who took part in the first resurrection and that there were of each tribe twelve thousand. But if there were so many of them, they must have been not men but gods. They had borne Thy cross, they had endured scores of years in the barren, hungry wilderness, living upon locusts and roots—and Thou mayest indeed point with pride at those children of freedom, of free love, of free and splendid sacrifice for Thy name. But remember that they were only some thousands; and what of the rest? And how are the other weak ones to blame, because they could not endure what the strong have endured? How is the weak soul to blame that it is unable to receive such terrible gifts? Canst Thou have simply come to the elect and for the elect? But if so, it is a mystery and we cannot understand it. And if it is a mystery, we too have a right to preach a mystery, and to teach them that it's not the free judgment of their hearts, not love that matters, but a mystery which they must follow blindly, even against their conscience. So we have done. We have corrected Thy work and have founded it upon MIRACLE, MYSTERY and AUTHORITY. And men rejoiced that they were again led like sheep, and that the terrible gift that had brought them such suffering, was, at last, lifted from their hearts.

" 'Were we right teaching them this?

" 'Speak!

" 'Did we not love mankind, so meekly acknowledging their feebleness, lovingly lightening their burden, and permitting their weak nature even sin with our sanction? Why hast Thou come now to hinder us? And why dost Thou look silently and searchingly at me with Thy mild eyes? Be angry. I don't want Thy love, for I love Thee not. And what use is it for me to hide anything from Thee? Don't I know to Whom I am speaking? All that I can say is known to Thee already. And is it for me to conceal from Thee our mystery? Perhaps it is Thy will to hear it from my lips.

The Third Temptation: The Problem of Unity

" 'Listen, then. We are not working with Thee, but with HIM— that is our mystery. It's long—eight centuries—since we have been on HIS side and not on Thine. Just eight centuries ago, we took from him what Thou didst reject with scorn, that last gift he offered Thee, showing Thee all the kingdoms of the earth. We took from him Rome and the sword of Caesar, and proclaimed ourselves sole rulers of the earth, though hitherto we have not been able to complete our work. But whose fault is that? Oh, the work is only beginning, but it has begun. It has long to await completion and the earth has yet much to suffer, but we shall triumph and shall be Caesars, and then we shall plan the universal happiness of man. But Thou mightest have taken even the sword of Caesar.

" 'Why didst Thou reject that last gift?

" 'Hadst Thou accepted that last counsel of the mighty spirit, Thou wouldst have accomplished all that man seeks on earth—that is, some one to worship, some one to keep his conscience, and some means of uniting all in one unanimous and harmonious antheap, for the craving for universal unity is the third and last anguish of men. Mankind as a whole has always striven to organize a universal state. There have been many great nations with great histories, but the more highly they were developed the more unhappy they were, for they felt more acutely than other people the craving for worldwide union. The great conquerors, Timours and Genghis-Khans, whirled like hurricanes over the face of the earth striving to subdue its people, and they too were but the unconscious expression of the same craving for universal unity. Hadst Thou taken the world and Caesar's purple, Thou wouldst have founded the universal state and have given universal peace. For who can rule men if not he who holds their conscience and their bread in his hands?

" 'We have taken the sword of Caesar, and in taking it, of course, have rejected Thee and followed HIM.

" 'Oh, ages are yet to come of the confusion of free thought, of their science and cannibalism. For having begun to build their tower of Babel without us, they will end, of course, with cannibalism. But then the beast will crawl to us and lick our feet and spatter them with tears of blood. And we shall sit upon the beast and raise the cup, and on it will be written, "Mystery." But then, and only then, the reign of peace and happiness will come for men.

" 'Thou art proud of Thine elect, but Thou hast only the elect, while we give rest to all. And besides, how many of those elect, those mighty ones who could become elect, have grown weary waiting for Thee, and have transferred and will transfer the powers of their spirit and the warmth of their heart to the other camp, and end by raising their FREE banner against Thee. Thou didst Thyself lift up that banner. But with us all will be happy and will no more rebel or destroy one another as under Thy freedom.

" 'Oh, we shall persuade them that they will only become free when they renounce their freedom to us and submit to us. And shall we be right or shall we be lying? They will be convinced that we are right, for they will remember the horrors of slavery and confusion to which Thy freedom brought them. Freedom, free thought and science, will lead them into such straits and will bring them face to face with such marvels and insoluble mysteries, that some of them, the fierce and rebellious, will destroy themselves, others, rebellious but weak, will destroy one another, while the rest, weak and unhappy, will crawl fawning to our feet and whine to us: "Yes, you were right, you alone possess His mystery, and we come back to you, save us from ourselves!"

Summary: The Inquisitor's Utopia

" 'Receiving bread from us, they will see clearly that we take the bread made by their hands from them, to give it to them, without any miracle. They will see that we do not change the stones to bread, but in truth they will be more thankful for taking it from our hands than for the bread itself! For they will remember only too well that in old days, without our help, even the bread they made turned to stones in their hands, while since they have come back to us, the very stones have turned to bread in their hands. Too, too well they know the value of complete submission! And until men know that, they will be unhappy. Who is most to blame for their not knowing it, speak? Who scattered the flock and sent it astray on unknown paths? But the flock will come together again and will submit once more, and then it will be once for all. Then we shall give them the quiet humble happiness of weak creatures such as they are by nature. Oh, we shall persuade them at last not to be proud, for Thou didst lift them up and thereby taught them to be proud. We shall show them that they are weak, that they are only pitiful children, but that childlike happiness is the sweetest of all. They will become timid and will look to us and huddle close to us and will be awe-stricken before us, and will be proud at our being so powerful and clever, that we have been able to subdue such a turbulent flock of thousands of millions. They will tremble impotently before our wrath, their minds will grow fearful, they will be quick to shed tears like women and children, but they will be just as ready at a sign from us to pass to laughter and rejoicing, to happy mirth and childish song. Yes, we shall set them to work, but in their leisure hours we shall make their life like a child's game, with children's songs and innocent dance. Oh, we shall allow them even sin, they are weak and helpless, and they will love us like children because we allow them to sin. We shall tell them that every sin will be expiated, if it is done with our permission, that we allow them to sin because we love them, and the punishment for these sins we take upon ourselves. And we shall take it upon ourselves, and they will adore us as their saviours who have taken on themselves their sins before God. And they will have no secrets from us. We shall allow or forbid them to live with their wives and mistresses, to have or not to have children—according to whether they have been obedient or disobedient—and they will submit to us gladly and cheerfully. The most painful secrets of their conscience, all, all they will bring to us, and we shall have an answer for all. And they will be glad to believe our answer, for it will save them from the great anxiety and terrible agony they endure at present in making a free decision for themselves. And all will be happy, all the millions of creatures except the hundred thousand who rule over them. For only we, we who guard the mystery, shall be unhappy.

" 'There will be thousands of millions of happy babes, and a hundred thousand sufferers who have taken upon themselves the curse of the knowledge of good and evil. Peacefully they will die, peacefully they will expire in Thy name, and beyond the grave they will find nothing but death. But we shall keep the secret, and for their happiness we shall allure them with the reward of heaven and eternity. Though if there were anything in the other world, it certainly would not be for such as they.

" 'It is prophesied that Thou wilt come again in victory, Thou wilt come with Thy chosen, the proud and strong, but we will say that they have only saved themselves, but we have saved all. We are told that the harlot who sits upon the beast, and holds in her hands the MYSTERY, shall be put to shame, that the weak will rise up again, and will rend her royal purple and will strip naked her loathsome body. But then I will stand up and point out to Thee the thousand millions of happy children who have known no sin. And we who have taken their sins upon us for their happiness will stand up before Thee and say: "Judge us if Thou canst and darest." Know that I fear Thee not. Know that I too have been in the wilderness, I too have lived on roots and locusts, I too prized the freedom with which Thou hast blessed men, and I too was striving to stand among Thy elect, among the strong and powerful, thirsting "to make up the number." But I awakened and would not serve madness. I turned back and joined the ranks of those WHO HAVE CORRECTED THY WORK. I left the proud and went back to the humble, for the happiness of the humble. What I say to Thee will come to pass, and our dominion will be built up. I repeat, tomorrow Thou shalt see that obedient flock who at a sign from me will hasten to heap up the hot cinders about the pile on which I shall burn Thee for coming to hinder us. For if any one has ever deserved our fires, it is Thou. Tomorrow I shall burn Thee. DIXI.' "

Ivan stopped. He was carried away as he talked and spoke with excitement; when he had finished, he suddenly smiled.

Alyosha had listened in silence; toward the end he was greatly moved and seemed several times on the point of interrupting, but restrained himself. Now his words came with a rush.

"But...that's absurd!" he cried, flushing. "Your poem is in praise of Jesus, not in blame of Him—as you meant it to be. And who will believe you about freedom? Is that the way to understand it? That's not the idea of it in the Orthodox Church...That's Rome, and not even the whole of Rome, it's false—those are the worst of the Catholics, the Inquisitors, the Jesuits!... And there could not be such a fantastic creature as your Inquisitor. What are these sins of mankind they take on themselves? Who are these keepers of the mystery who have taken some curse upon themselves for the happiness of mankind? When have they been seen? We know the Jesuits, they are spoken ill of, but surely they are not what you describe? They are not that at all, not at all.... They are simply the Romish army for the earthly sovereignty of the world in the future, with the Pontiff of Rome for Emperor...that's their ideal, but there's no sort of mystery or lofty melancholy about it... It's simple lust of power, of filthy earthly gain, of domination—something like a universal serfdom with them as masters—that's all they stand for. They don't even believe in God perhaps. Your suffering Inquisitor is a mere fantasy."

"Stay, stay," laughed Ivan, "how hot you are! A fantasy you say, let it be so! Of course it's a fantasy. But allow me to say: do you really think that the Roman Catholic movement of the last centuries is actually nothing but the lust of power, of filthy earthly gain? Is that Father Paissy's teaching?"

"No, no, on the contrary, Father Paissy did once say something the same as you. . .but of course it's not the same, not a bit the same," Alyosha hastily corrected himself.

"A precious admission, in spite of your 'not a bit the same.' I ask you why your Jesuits and Inquisitors have united simply for vile material gain? Why can there not be among them one martyr oppressed by great sorrow and loving humanity? You see, only suppose that there was one such man among all those who desire nothing but filthy material gain—if there's only one like my old Inquisitor, who had himself eaten roots in the desert and made frenzied efforts to subdue his flesh to make himself free and perfect. But yet all his life he loved humanity, and suddenly his eyes were opened, and he saw that is no great moral blessedness to attain perfection and freedom, if at the same time one gains the conviction that billions of God's creatures have been created as a mockery, that they will never be capable of using their freedom, that these poor rebels can never turn into giants to complete the tower, that it was not for such geese that the great idealist dreamt his dream of harmony. Seeing all that he turned back and joined—the clever people. Surely that could have happened?"

"Joined whom, what clever people?" cried Alyosha, completely carried away. "They have no such great cleverness and no mysteries and secrets. . . Perhaps nothing but Atheism, that's all their secret. Your Inquisitor does not believe in God, that's his secret!"

"What if it is so! At last you have guessed it. It's perfectly true that that's the whole secret, but isn't that suffering, at least for a man like that, who has wasted his whole life in the desert and yet could not shake off his incurable love of humanity? In his old age he reached the clear conviction that nothing but the advice of the great dread spirit could build up any tolerable sort of life for the feeble, unruly 'incomplete, empirical creatures created in jest.' And so, convinced of this, he sees that he must follow the council of the wise spirit, the dread spirit of death and destruction, and therefore accept lying and deception, and lead men consciously to death and destruction, and yet deceive them all the way so that they may not notice where they are being led, that the poor blind creatures may at least on the way think themselves happy. And note, the deception is in the name of Him in Whose ideal the old man had so fervently believed all his life long. Is not that tragic? And if only one such stood at the head of the whole army 'filled with the lust of power only for the sake of filthy gain'—would not one such be enough to make a tragedy? More than that, one such standing at the head of enough to create the actual leading idea of the Roman Church with all its armies and Jesuits, its highest idea. I tell you frankly that I firmly believe that there has always been such a man among those who stood at the head of the movement. Who knows, there may have been some such even among the Roman Popes. Who knows, perhaps the spirit of that accursed old man who loves mankind so obstinately in his own way, is to be found even now in a whole multitude of such old men, existing not by chance but by agreement, as a secret league formed along ago for the guarding of the mystery, to guard it from the weak and unhappy, so as to make them happy. No doubt it is so, and so it must be indeed. I fancy that even among the Masons there's something of the same mystery at the bottom, and that that's why the Catholics so detest the Masons as their rivals breaking up the unity of the idea, while it is so essential that there should be one flock and one shepherd . . . But from the way I defend my idea I might be an author impatient of your criticism. Enough of it."

"You are perhaps a Mason yourself!" broke suddenly from Alyosha. "You don't believe in God," he added, speaking this time very sorrowfully. He fancied besides that this brother was looking at him ironically. "How does your poem end?" he asked, suddenly looking down. "Or was it the end?"

"I meant it to end like this:

"When the Inquisitor ceased speaking he waited some time for his Prisoner to answer him. His silence weighed down upon him. He saw the Prisoner had listened intently all the time, looking gently in his face and evidently not wishing to reply. The old man longed for Him to say something, however bitter and terrible. But He suddenly approached the old man in silence and softly kissed him on his bloodless aged lips. That was all His answer. The old man shuddered. His lips moved. He went to the door, opened it, and said to Him: 'Go, and come no more . . . Come not at all, never, never!' And he let Him out into the dark alleys of the town. The Prisoner went away."

"And the old man?"

"The kiss glows in his heart, but the old man adheres to his idea."

First Week — Second Day

Old Testament, Genesis 1-2, 3:1-20

Mencius, "Human Nature"

Hsun Tzu, "Man's Nature is Evil"

New Testament, John 1:1-14

T. S. Eliot, "The Hollow Men"

Sigmund Freud, *The Future of an Illusion,* Chapter 1 (selection)

Jacques Monod, "On Values in the Age of Science"

The Old Testament
Genesis

Chapter 1

IN the beginning God created the heaven and the earth.

2 And the earth was without form, and void; and darkness *was* upon the face of the deep. And the Spirit of God moved upon the face of the waters.

3 And God said, Let there be light: and there was light.

4 And God saw the light, that *it was* good: and God divided the light from the darkness.

5 And God called the light Day, and the darkness he called Night. And the evening and the morning were the first day.

6 ¶ And God said, Let there be a firmament in the midst of the waters, and let it divide the waters from the waters.

7 And God made the firmament, and divided the waters which *were* under the firmament from the waters which *were* above the firmament: and it was so.

8 And God called the firmament Heaven. And the evening and the morning were the second day.

9 ¶ And God said, Let the waters under the heaven be gathered together unto one place, and let the dry *land* appear: and it was so.

10 And God called the dry *land* Earth; and the gathering together of the waters called he Seas: and God saw that *it was* good.

11 And God said, Let the earth bring forth grass, the herb yielding seed, *and* the fruit tree yielding fruit after his kind, whose seed *is* in itself, upon the earth: and it was so.

12 And the earth brought forth grass, *and* herb yielding seed after his kind, and the tree yielding fruit, whose seed *was* in itself, after his kind: and God saw that *it was* good.

13 And the evening and the morning were the third day.

14 ¶ And God said, Let there be lights in the firmament of the heaven to divide the day from the night; and let them be for signs, and for

seasons, and for days, and years:

15 And let them be for lights in the firmament of the heaven to give light upon the earth: and it was so.

16 And God made two great lights; the greater light to rule the day, and the lesser light to rule the night: *he made* the stars also.

17 And God set them in the firmament of the heaven to give light upon the earth,

18 And to rule over the day and over the night, and to divide the light from the darkness: and God saw that *it was* good.

19 And the evening and the morning were the fourth day.

20 And God said, Let the waters bring forth abundantly the moving creature that hath life, and fowl *that* may fly above the earth in the open firmament of heaven.

21 And God created great whales, and every living creature that moveth, which the waters brought forth abundantly, after their kind, and every winged fowl after his kind: and God saw that *it was* good.

22 And God blessed them, saying, Be fruitful, and multiply, and fill the waters in the seas, and let fowl multiply in the earth.

23 And the evening and the morning were the fifth day.

24 ¶ And God said, Let the earth bring forth the living creature after his kind, cattle, and creeping thing, and beast of the earth after his kind: and it was so.

25 And God made the beast of the earth after his kind, and cattle after their kind, and every thing that creepeth upon the earth after his kind: and God saw that *it was* good.

26 ¶ And God said, Let us make man in our image, after our likeness: and let them have dominion over the fish of the sea, and over the fowl of the air, and over the cattle, and over all the earth, and over every creeping thing that creepeth upon the earth.

27 So God created man in his *own* image, in the image of God created he him; male and female created he them.

28 And God blessed them, and God said unto them, Be fruitful, and multiply, and replenish the earth, and subdue it: and have dominion over the fish of the sea, and over the fowl of the air, and over every living thing that moveth upon the earth.

29 ¶ And God said, Behold, I have given you every herb bearing seed, which *is* upon the face of all the earth, and every tree, in the which *is* the fruit of a tree yielding seed; to you it shall be for meat.

30 And to every beast of the earth, and to every fowl of the air, and to every thing that creepeth upon the earth, wherein *there is* life, *I have given* every green herb for meat: and it was so.

31 And God saw every thing that he had made, and, behold, *it was* very good. And the evening and the morning were the sixth day.

Chapter 2

THUS the heavens and the earth were finished, and all the host of them.

2 And on the seventh day God ended his work which he had made; and he rested on the seventh day from all his work which he had made.

3 And God blessed the seventh day, and sanctified it: because that in it he had rested from all his work which God created and made.

4 ¶ These *are* the generations of the heavens and of the earth when

they were created, in the day that the Lord God made the earth and the heavens,

5 And every plant of the field before it was in the earth, and every herb of the field before it grew: for the Lord God had not caused it to rain upon the earth, and *there was* not a man to till the ground.

6 But there went up a mist from the earth, and watered the whole face of the ground.

7 And the Lord God formed man *of* the dust of the ground, and breathed into his nostrils the breath of life; and man became a living soul.

8 ¶ And the Lord God planted a garden eastward in Eden; and there he put the man whom he had formed.

9 And out of the ground made the Lord God to grow every tree that is pleasant to the sight, and good for food; the tree of life also in the midst of the garden, and the tree of knowledge of good and evil.

10 And a river went out of Eden to water the garden; and from thence it was parted, and became into four heads.

11 The name of the first *is* Pison: that *is* it which compasseth the whole land of Havilah, where *there is* gold;

12 And the gold of that land *is* good: there *is* bdellium and the onyx stone.

13 And the name of the second river *is* Gihon: the same *is* it that compasseth the whole land of Ethiopia.

14 And the name of the third river *is* Hiddekel: that *is* it which goeth toward the east of Assyria. And the fourth river *is* Euphrates.

15 And the Lord God took the man, and put him into the garden of Eden to dress it and to keep it.

16 And the Lord God commanded the man, saying, Of every tree of the garden thou mayest freely eat:

17 But of the tree of the knowledge of good and evil, thou shalt not eat of it: for in the day that thou eatest thereof thou shalt surely die.

18 ¶ And the Lord God said, *It is* not good that the man should be alone; I will make him an help meet for him.

19 And out of the ground the Lord God formed every beast of the field, and every fowl of the air; and brought *them* unto Adam to see what he would call them: and whatsoever Adam called every living creature, that *was* the name thereof.

20 And Adam gave names to all cattle, and to the fowl of the air, and to every beast of the field; but for Adam there was not found an help meet for him.

21 And the Lord God caused a deep sleep to fall upon Adam, and he slept: and he took one of his ribs, and closed up the flesh instead thereof;

22 And the rib, which the Lord God had taken from man, made he a woman, and brought her unto the man.

23 And Adam said, This *is* now bone of my bones, and flesh of my flesh: she shall be called Woman, because she was taken out of Man.

24 Therefore shall a man leave his father and his mother, and shall cleave unto his wife: and they shall be one flesh.

25 And they were both naked, the man and his wife, and were not ashamed.

Chapter 3

NOW the serpent was more subtil than any beast of the field which the Lord God had made. And he said unto the woman, Yea, hath God said, Ye shall not eat of every tree of the garden?

2 And the woman said unto the serpent, We may eat of the fruit of the trees of the garden:

3 But of the fruit of the tree which *is* in the midst of the garden, God hath said, Ye shall not eat of it, neither shall ye touch it, lest ye die.

4 And the serpent said unto the woman, Ye shall not surely die:

5 For God doth know that in the day ye eat thereof, then your eyes shall be opened, and ye shall be as gods, knowing good and evil.

6 And when the woman saw that the tree *was* good for food, and that it *was* pleasant to the eyes, and a tree to be desired to make *one* wise, she took of the fruit thereof, and did eat, and gave also unto her husband with her; and he did eat.

7 And the eyes of them both were opened, and they knew that they *were* naked; and they sewed fig leaves together, and made themselves aprons.

8 And they heard the voice of the Lord God walking in the garden in the cool of the day: and Adam and his wife hid themselves from the presence of the Lord God amongst the trees of the garden.

9 And the Lord God called unto Adam, and said unto him, Where *art* thou?

10 And he said, I heard thy voice in the garden, and I was afraid, because I *was* naked; and I hid myself.

11 And he said, Who told thee that thou *wast* naked? Hast thou eaten of the tree, whereof I commanded thee that thou shouldest not eat?

12 And the man said, The woman whom thou gavest *to be* with me, she gave me of the tree, and I did eat.

13 And the Lord God said unto the woman, What *is* this *that* thou hast done? And the woman said, The serpent beguiled me, and I did eat.

14 And the Lord God said unto the serpent, Because thou hast done this, thou *art* cursed above all cattle, and above every beast of the field; upon thy belly shalt thou go, and dust shalt thou eat all the days of thy life:

15 And I will put enmity between thee and the woman, and between thy seed and her seed; it shall bruise thy head, and thou shalt bruise his heel.

16 Unto the woman he said, I will greatly multiply thy sorrow and thy conception; in sorrow thou shalt bring forth children; and thy desire *shall be* to thy husband, and he shall rule over thee.

17 And unto Adam he said, Because thou hast hearkened unto the voice of thy wife, and hast eaten of the tree, of which I commanded thee, saying, Thou shalt not eat of it: cursed *is* the ground for thy sake; in sorrow shalt thou eat *of* it all the days of thy life;

18 Thorns also and thistles shall it bring forth to thee; and thou shalt eat the herb of the field;

19 In the sweat of thy face shalt thou eat bread, till thou return unto the ground; for out of it wast thou taken: for dust thou *art,* and unto dust shalt thou return.

20 And Adam called his wife's name Eve; because she was the mother of all living.

Human Nature

by Mencius

K AO TZU[1] said: "The nature of man may be likened to the willow tree, whereas righteousness may be likened to wooden cups and wicker baskets. To turn man's nature into humanity and righteousness is like turning a willow tree into cups and baskets." Mencius replied: "Sir, can you follow the nature of the willow tree, and make the cups and baskets? Or must you violate its nature to make the cups and baskets? If you must violate the nature of the willow tree to turn it into cups and baskets, then don't you mean you must also violate the nature of man to turn it into humanity and righteousness? Your words, alas, would incite everyone in the world to regard humanity and righteousness as a curse!"

Kao Tzu said: "The nature of man may be likened to a swift current of water: you lead it eastward and it will flow to the east; you lead it westward and it will flow to the west. Human nature is neither disposed to good nor to evil, just as water is neither disposed to east nor west." Mencius replied: "It is true that water is neither disposed to east nor west, but is it neither disposed to flowing upward nor downward? The tendency of human nature to do good is like that of water to flow downward. There is no man who does not tend to do good; there is no water that does not flow downward. Now you may strike water and make it splash over your forehead, or you may even force it up in the hills. But is this in the nature of water? It is of course due to the force of circumstances. Similarly, man may be brought to do evil, and that is because the same is done to his nature."

Kao Tzu said: "Nature is what is born in us." Mencius asked: " 'Nature is what is born in us'—is it not the same as saying white is white?" "Yes," said Kao Tzu. Mencius asked: "Then the whiteness of a white feather is the same as the whiteness of white snow, and the whiteness of white snow the same as the whiteness of white jade?" "Yes," Kao Tzu replied. Mencius asked: "Well, then, the nature of a dog is the same as the nature of a cow,

73

and the nature of a cow the same as the nature of a man, is it not?"[2]

Kao Tzu said: "The appetite for food and sex is part of our nature. Humanity comes from within and not from without, whereas righteousness comes from without and not from within." Mencius asked: "What do you mean when you say that humanity comes from within while righteousness comes from without?" Kao Tzu replied: "When I see anyone who is old I regard him as old. This regard for age is not a part of me. Just as when I see anyone who is white I regard him as white, because I can observe the whiteness externally. For this reason I say righteousness comes from without." Mencius said: "Granted there is no difference between regarding the white horse as white and the white man as white. But is there no difference between one's regard for age in an old horse and one's regard for age in an old man, I wonder? Moreover, is it old age itself or our respectful regard for old age that constitutes a point of righteousness?" Kao Tzu persisted: "My own brother I love; the brother of a man of Ch'in I do not love. Here the sanction for the feeling rests in me, and therefore I call it (i.e., humanity) internal. An old man of Ch'u I regard as old, just as an old man among my own people I regard as old. Here the sanction for the feeling lies in old age, and therefore I call it (i.e., righteousness) external." Mencius answered him: "We love the Ch'in people's roast as much as we love our own roast. Here we have a similar situation with respect to things. Would you say, then, that this love of roast is also something external?"

The disciple Kung-tu Tzu said: "Kao Tzu says that human nature is neither good nor bad. Some say that human nature can be turned to be good or bad. Thus when [sage-kings] Wen and Wu were in power the people loved virtue; when [wicked kings] Yu and Li were in power the people indulged in violence. Some say that some natures are good and some are bad. Thus even while [the sage] Yao was sovereign there was the bad man Hsiang, even a bad father like Ku-sou had a good son like [the sage-king] Shun, and even with [the wicked] Chou for nephew and king there were the men of virtue Ch'i, the Viscount of Wei, and the Prince Pi-kan. Now, you say that human nature is good. Are the others then all wrong?" Mencius replied: "When left to follow its natural feelings human nature will do good. This is why I say it is good. If it becomes evil, it is not the fault of man's original capability. The sense of mercy is found in all men; the sense of shame is found in all men; the sense of respect is found in all men; the sense of right and wrong is found in all men. The sense of mercy constitutes humanity; the sense of shame constitutes righteousness; the sense of respect constitutes decorum [li]; the sense of right and wrong constitutes wisdom. Humanity, righteousness, decorum, and wisdom are not something instilled into us from without; they are inherent in our nature. Only we give them no thought. Therefore it is said: 'Seek and you will find them, neglect and you will lose them.' Some have these virtues to a much greater degree than others—twice, five times, and incalculably more—and that is because those others have not developed to the fullest extent their original capability. It is said in the *Book of Odes*:

Heaven so produced the teeming multitudes that
For everything there is its principle.
The people will keep to the constant principles,
And all will love a beautiful character.

"Confucius said, regarding this poem: 'The writer of this poem understands indeed the nature of the Way! For wherever there are things and affairs there must be their principles. As the people keep to the constant principles, they will come to love a beautiful character.' "

Mencius said: "All men have a sense of commiseration. The ancient kings had this commiserating heart and hence a commiserating government. When a commiserating government is conducted from a commiserating heart, one can rule the whole empire as if one were turning it on one's palm. Why I say all men have a sense of commiseration is this: Here is a man who suddenly notices a child about to fall into a well. Invariably he will feel a sense of alarm and compassion. And this is not for the purpose of gaining the favor of the child's parents, or seeking the approbation of his neighbors and friends, or for fear of blame should he fail to rescue it. Thus we see that no man is without a sense of compassion, or a sense of shame, or a sense of courtesy, or a sense of right and wrong. The sense of compassion is the beginning of humanity; the sense of shame is the beginning of righteousness; the sense of courtesy is the beginning of decorum; the sense of right and wrong is the beginning of wisdom. Every man has within himself these four beginnings; just as he has four limbs. Since everyone has these four beginnings within him, the man who considers himself incapable of exercising them is destroying himself. If he considers his sovereign incapable of exercising them, he is likewise destroying his sovereign. Let every man but attend to expanding and developing these four beginnings that are in our very being, and they will issue forth like a conflagration being kindled and a spring being opened up. If they can be fully developed, these virtues are capable of safeguarding all within the four seas; if allowed to remain undeveloped, they will not suffice even for serving one's parents."

Mencius said: "Man's innate ability is the ability possessed by him that is not acquired through learning. Man's innate knowledge is the knowledge possessed by him that is not the result of reflective thinking. Every child knows enough to love his parents, and when he is growing up he knows enough to respect his elder brothers. The love for one's parents is really humanity and the respect for one's elders is really righteousness—all that is necessary is to have these natural feelings applied to all men."

---

[1] Kao Tzu was a critic and possibly a former pupil of Mencius. In general, Kao Tzu held human nature to be neutral, while Mencius insisted it was good.

[2] Evidently Mencius here considers he has achieved a *reductio ad absurdum* of Kao Tzu's original proposition. The point of Mencius' complaint is that Kao Tzu has failed to distinguish between the nature of man and the nature of any other being, which Mencius insists must be made.

Man's Nature is Evil

by Hsun Tzu

MAN's nature is evil; goodness is the result of conscious activity. The nature of man is such that he is born with a fondness for profit. If he indulges this fondness, it will lead him into wrangling and strife, and all sense of courtesy and humility will disappear. He is born with feelings of envy and hate, and if he indulges these, they will lead him into violence and crime, and all sense of loyalty and good faith will disappear. Man is born with the desires of the eyes and ears, with a fondness for beautiful sights and sounds. If he indulges these, they will lead him into license and wantonness, and all ritual principles and correct forms will be lost. Hence, any man who follows his nature and indulges his emotions will inevitably become involved in wrangling and strife, will violate the forms and rules of society, and will end as a criminal. Therefore, man must first be transformed by the instructions of a teacher and guided by ritual principles, and only then will he be able to observe the dictates of courtesy and humility, obey the forms and rules of society, and achieve order. It is obvious from this, then, that man's nature is evil, and that his goodness is the result of conscious activity.

A warped piece of wood must wait until it has been laid against the straightening board, steamed, and forced into shape before it can become straight; a piece of blunt metal must wait until it has been whetted on a grindstone before it can become sharp. Similarly, since man's nature is evil, it must wait for the instructions of a teacher before it can become upright, and for the guidance of ritual principles before it can become orderly. If men have no teachers to instruct them, they will be inclined towards evil and not upright; and if they have no ritual principles to guide them, they will be perverse and violent and lack order. In ancient times the sage kings realized that man's nature is evil, and that therefore he inclines toward evil and violence and is not upright or orderly. Accordingly they created ritual principles and laid down certain regulations in order to reform man's emotional nature and make it upright, in order to train and transform it and guide it in the proper channels. In this way they caused all men to become orderly and to conform to the Way. Hence, today any man who takes to heart the instructions of his teacher, applies himself to his studies, and abides by ritual principles may become a gentleman, but anyone who gives free rein to his emotional nature, is content to indulge his passions, and disregards ritual principles becomes a petty man. It is obvious from this, therefore, that man's nature is evil, and that his goodness is the result of conscious activity.

Mencius states that man is capable of learning because his nature is good, but I say that this is wrong. It indicates that he has not really understood man's nature nor distinguished properly between the basic nature and conscious activity. The nature is that which is given by Heaven; you cannot learn it, you cannot acquire it by effort. Ritual principles, on the other hand, are created by sages; you cǎn learn to apply them, you can work to bring them to completion. That part of man which cannot be learned or acquired by learning and brought to completion by effort is called conscious activity. This is the difference between nature and conscious activity.

It is a part of man's nature that his eyes can see and his ears can hear. But the faculty of clear sight can never exist separately from the eye, nor can the faculty of keen hearing exist separately from the ear. It is obvious, then, that you cannot acquire clear sight and keen hearing by study. Mencius states that man's nature is good, and that all evil arises because he loses his original nature. Such a view, I believe, is erroneous. It is the way with man's nature that as soon as he is born he begins to depart from his original naivete and simplicity, and therefore he must inevitably lose what Mencius regards as his original nature. It is obvious from this, then, that the nature of man is evil.

Those who maintain that the nature is good praise and approve whatever has not departed from the original simplicity and naivete of the child. That is, they consider that beauty belongs to the original simplicity and naivete and goodness to the original mind in the same way that clear sight is inseparable from the eye and keen hearing from the ear. Hence, they maintain that the nature possesses goodness in the same way that the eye possesses clear vision or the ear keenness of hearing. Now it is the nature of man that when he is hungry he will desire satisfaction, when he is cold he will desire warmth, and when he is weary he will desire rest. This is his emotional nature. And yet a man, although he is hungry, will not dare to be the first to eat if he is in the presence of his elders, because he knows that he should yield to them, and although he is weary, he will not dare to demand rest because he knows that he should relieve others of the burden of labor. For a son to yield to his father or a younger brother to yield to his elder brother, for a son to relieve his father of work or a younger brother to relieve his elder brother—acts such as these are all contrary to man's nature and run counter to his emotions. And yet they represent the way of filial piety and the proper forms enjoined by ritual principles. Hence, if men follow their emotional nature, there will be no courtesy or humility; courtesy and humility in fact run counter to man's emotional nature. From this it is obvious, then, that man's nature is evil, and that his goodness is the result of conscious activity.

Someone may ask: if man's nature is evil, then where do ritual principles come from? I would reply: all ritual principles are produced by the conscious activity of the sages; essentially they are not products of man's nature. A potter molds clay and makes a vessel, but the vessel is the product of the conscious activity of the potter, not essentially a product of his human nature. A carpenter carves a piece of wood and makes a utensil, but the utensil is the product of the conscious activity of the carpenter, not essentially a product of his human nature. The sage gathers together his thoughts and ideas, experiments with various forms of conscious activity, and so produces ritual principles and sets forth laws and regulations. Hence, these ritual principles and laws are the products of the conscious activity of the sage, not essentially products of human nature.

Phenomena such as the eye's fondness for beautiful forms, the ear's fondness for beautiful sounds, the mouth's fondness for delicious flavors, the mind's fondness for profit, or the body's fondness for pleasure and ease — these are all products of the emotional nature of man. They are instinctive and spontaneous; man does not have to do anything to produce them. But that which does not come into being instinctively but must wait for some activity to bring it into being is called the product of conscious activity. These are the products of the nature and of conscious activity respectively, and the proof that they are not the same. Therefore, the sage transforms his nature and initiates conscious activity; from this conscious activity he produces ritual principles, and when they have been produced he sets up rules and regulations. Hence, ritual principles and rules are produced by the sage. In respect to human nature the sage is the same as all other men and does not surpass them; it is only in his conscious activity that he differs from and surpasses other men.

It is man's emotional nature to love profit and desire gain. Suppose now that a man has some wealth to be divided. If he indulges his emotional nature, loving profit and desiring gain, then he will quarrel and wrangle even with his own brothers over the division. But if he has been transformed by the proper forms of ritual principle, then he will be capable of yielding even to a complete stranger. Hence, to indulge the emotional nature leads to the quarreling of brothers, but to be transformed by ritual principles makes a man capable of yielding to strangers.

Every man who desires to do good does so precisely because his nature is evil. A man whose accomplishments are meager longs for greatness; an ugly man longs for beauty; a man in cramped quarters longs for spaciousness; a poor man longs for wealth; a humble man longs for eminence. Whatever a man lacks in himself he will seek outside. But if a man is already rich, he will not long for wealth, and if he is already eminent, he will not long for greater power. What a man already possesses in himself he will not bother to look for outside. From this we can see that men desire to do good precisely because their nature is evil. Ritual principles are certainly not a part of man's original nature.

Therefore, he forces himself to study and to seek to possess them. An understanding of ritual principles is not a part of man's original nature and therefore he ponders and plans and thereby seeks to understand them. Hence, man in the state in which he is born neither possesses nor understands ritual principles. If he does not possess ritual principles, his behaviour will be chaotic, and if he does not understand them, he will be wild and irresponsible. In fact, therefore, man in the state in which he is born possesses this tendency towards chaos and irresponsibility. From this it is obvious, then, that man's nature is evil, and that his goodness is the result of conscious activity.

Mencius states that man's nature is good, but I say that this view is wrong. All men in the world, past and present, agree in defining goodness as that which is upright, reasonable, and orderly, and evil as that which is prejudiced, irresponsible, and chaotic. This is the distinction between good and evil. Now suppose that man's nature was in fact intrinsically upright, reasonable, and orderly—then what need would there be for sage kings and ritual principles? The existence of sage kings and ritual principles could certainly add nothing to the situation. But because man's nature is in fact evil, this is not so. Therefore, in ancient times the sages, realizing that man's nature is evil, that it is prejudiced and not upright, irresponsible and lacking in order, for this reason established the authority of the ruler to control it, elucidated ritual principles to transform it, set up laws and standards to correct it, and meted out strict punishments to restrain it. As a result, all the world achieved order and conformed to goodness. Such is the orderly government of the sage kings and the transforming power of ritual principles. Now let someone try doing away with the authority of the ruler, ignoring the transforming power of ritual principles, rejecting the order that comes from laws and standards, and dispensing with the restrictive power of punishments, and then watch and see how the people of the world treat each other. He will find that the powerful impose upon the weak and rob them, the many terrorize the few and extort from them, and in no time the whole world will be given up to chaos and mutual destruction. It is obvious from this, then, that man's nature is evil, and that his goodness is the result of conscious activity.

Those who are good at discussing antiquity must demonstrate the validity of what they say in terms of modern times; those who are good at discussing Heaven must show proofs from the human world. In discussions of all kinds, men value what is in accord with the facts and what can be proved valid. Hence if a man sits on his mat propounding some theory, he should be able to stand right up and put it into practice, and show that it can be extended over a wide area with equal validity. Now Mencius states that man's nature is good, but this is neither in accord with the facts, nor can it be proved to be valid. One may sit down and propound such a theory, but he cannot stand up and put it into practice, nor can he extend it over a wide area with any success at all. How, then, could it be anything but erroneous?

If the nature of man were good, we could dispense with sage kings and forget about ritual principles. But if it is evil, then we must go along with the sage kings and honor ritual principles. The straightening board is made because of the warped wood; the plumb line is employed because things are crooked; rulers are set up and ritual principles elucidated because the nature of man is evil. From this it is obvious, then, that man's nature is evil, and that his goodness is the result of conscious activity. A straight piece of wood does not have to wait for the straightening board to become straight; it is straight by nature. But a warped piece of wood must wait until it has been laid against the straightening board, steamed, and forced into shape before it can become straight, because by nature it is warped. Similarly, since man's nature is evil, he must wait for the ordering power of the sage kings and the transforming power of ritual principles; only then can he achieve order and conform to goodness. From this it is obvious, then, that man's nature is evil, and that his goodness is the result of conscious activity.

Someone may ask whether ritual principles and concerted conscious activity are not themselves a part of man's nature, so that for that reason the sage is capable of producing them. But I would answer that this is not so. A potter may mold clay and produce an earthen pot, but surely molding pots out of clay is not a part of the potter's human nature. The sage stands in the same relation to ritual principles as the potter to the things he molds and produces. How, then, could ritual principles and concerted conscious activity be a part of man's basic human nature?

As far as human nature goes, the sages Yao and Shun possessed the same nature as the tyrant Chieh or Robber Chih, and the gentleman possesses the same nature as the petty man. Would you still maintain, then, that ritual principles and concerted conscious activity are a part of man's nature? If you do so, then what reason is there to pay any particular honor to Yao, Shun, or the gentleman? The reason people honor Yao, Shun, and the gentleman is that they are able to transform their nature, apply themselves to conscious activity, and produce ritual principles as the potter to the things he molds and produces. Looking at it this way, how could ritual principles and concerted conscious activity be a part of man's nature? The reason people despise Chieh, Robber Chih, or the petty man is that they give free rein to their nature, follow their emotions, and are content to indulge their passions, so that their conduct is marked by greed and contentiousness. Therefore, it is clear that man's nature is evil, and that his goodness is the result of conscious activity.

The New Testament

The Gospel according to Saint John

Chapter 1

IN the beginning was the Word, and the Word was with God, and the Word was God.

2 The same was in the beginning with God.

3 All things were made by him; and without him was not any thing made that was made.

4 In him was life; and the life was the light of men.

5 And the light shineth in darkness; and the darkness comprehended it not.

6 ¶ There was a man sent from God, whose name *was* John.

7 The same came for a witness, to bear witness of the Light, that all *men* through him might believe.

8 He was not that Light, but *was sent* to bear witness of that Light.

9 *That* was the true Light, which lighteth every man that cometh into the world.

10 He was in the world, and the world was made by him, and the world knew him not.

11 He came unto his own, and his own received him not.

12 But as many as received him, to them gave he power to become the sons of God, *even* to them that believe on his name:

13 Which were born, not of blood, nor of the will of the flesh, nor of the will of man, but of God.

14 And the Word was made flesh, and dwelt among us, (and we beheld his glory, the glory as of the only begotten of the Father) full of grace and truth.

The Hollow Men

by T. S. Eliot

Mistah Kurtz— he dead.
*   A penny for the Old Guy.*

I

We are the hollow men
We are the stuffed men
Leaning together
Headpiece filled with straw. Alas!
Our dried voices, when
We whisper together
Are quiet and meaningless
As wind in dry grass
Or rats' feet over broken glass
In our dry cellar

Shape without form, shade without color,
Paralyzed force, gesture without motion;

Those who have crossed
With direct eyes, to death's other Kingdom
Remember us—if at all—not as lost
Violent souls, but only
As the hollow men
The stuffed men.

II

Eyes I dare not meet in dreams
In death's dream kingdom

These do not appear:
There, the eyes are
Sunlight on a broken column
There, is a tree swinging
And voices are
In the wind's singing
More distant and more solemn
Than a fading star.

Let me be no nearer
In death's dream kingdom
Let me also wear
Such deliberate disguises
Rat's coat, crowskin, crossed staves
In a field
Behaving as the wind behaves
No nearer—

Not that final meeting
In the twilight kingdom

III

This is the dead land
This is cactus land
Here the stone images
Are raised, here they receive
The supplication of a dead man's hand
Under the twinkle of a fading star.

Is it like this
In death's other kingdom
Waking alone
At the hour when we are
Trembling with tenderness
Lips that would kiss
Form prayers to broken stone.

IV

The eyes are not here
There are no eyes here
In this valley of dying stars
In this hollow valley
This broken jaw of our lost kingdoms

In this last of meeting places
We grope together
And avoid speech
Gathered on this beach of the tumid river

Sightless, unless
The eyes reappear
As the perpetual star
Multifoliate rose
Of death's twilight kingdom
The hope only
Of empty men.

V

Here we go round the prickly pear
Prickly pear prickly pear
Here we go round the prickly pear
At five o'clock in the morning.

Between the idea
And the reality
Between the motion
And the act
Falls the Shadow
                    For Thine is the Kingdom

Between the conception
And the creation
Between the emotion
And the response
Falls the Shadow
                            Life is very long

Between the desire
And the spasm
Between the potency
And the existence
Between the essence
And the descent
Falls the Shadow
                    For Thine is the Kingdom

For Thine is
Life is
For Thine is the

This is the way the world ends
This is the way the world ends
This is the way the world ends
Not with a bang but a whimper.

The Future of an Illusion

by Sigmund Freud

Chapter I

WHEN one has lived for quite a long time in a particular civilization and has often tried to discover what its origins were and along what path it has developed, one sometimes also feels tempted to take a glance in the other direction and to ask what further fate lies before it and what transformations it is destined to undergo. But one soon finds that the value of such an enquiry is diminished from the outset by several factors. Above all, because there are only a few people who can survey human activity in its full compass. Most people have been obliged to restrict themselves to a single, or a few, field of it. But the less a man knows about the past and the present the more insecure must prove to be his judgement of the future. And there is the further difficulty that precisely in a judgement of this kind the subjective expectations of the individual play a part which it is difficult to assess; and these turn out to be dependent on purely personal factors in his own experience, on the greater or lesser optimism of his attitude to life, as it has been dictated for him by his temperament or by his success or failure. Finally, the curious fact makes itself felt that in general people experience their present naively, as it were, without being able to form an estimate of its contents; they have first to put themselves at a distance from it—the present, that is to say, must have become the past—before it can yield points of vantage from which to judge the future.

Thus anyone who gives way to the temptation to deliver an opinion on the probable future of our civilization will do well to remind himself of the difficulties I have just pointed out, as well as of the uncertainty that attaches quite generally to any prophecy. It follows from this, so far as I am concerned, that I shall make a hasty retreat before a task that is too great, and shall promptly seek out the small tract of territory which has claimed my attention hitherto, as soon as I have determined its position in the general scheme of things.

Human civilization, by which I mean all those respects in which human life has raised itself above its animal status and differs from the life of beasts —and I scorn to distinguish between culture and civilization—, presents, as we know, two aspects to the observer. It includes on the one hand all the knowledge and capacity that men have acquired in order to control the forces of nature and extract its wealth for the satisfaction of human needs, and, on the other hand, all the regulations necessary in order to adjust the relations of men to one another and especially the distribution of the available wealth. The two trends of civilization are not independent of each other: firstly, because the mutual relations of men are profoundly influenced by the amount of instinctual satisfaction which the existing wealth makes possible; secondly, because an individual man can himself come to function as wealth in relation to another one, in so far as the other person makes use of his capacity for work, or chooses him as a sexual object; and thirdly, moreover, because every individual is virtually an enemy of civilization, though civilization is supposed to be an object of universal human interest. It is remarkable that, little as men are able to exist in isolation, they should nevertheless feel as a heavy burden the sacrifices which civilization expects of them in order to make a communal life possible. Thus civilization has to be defended against the individual, and its regulations, institutions and commands are directed to that task. They aim not only at effecting a certain distribution of wealth but at maintaining that distribution; indeed, they have to protect everything that contributes to the conquest of nature and the production of wealth against men's hostile impulses. Human creations are easily destroyed, and science and technology, which have built them up, can also be used for their annihilation.

One thus gets an impression that civilization is something which was imposed on a resisting majority by a minority which understood how to obtain possession of the means to power and coercion. It is, of course, natural to assume that these difficulties are not inherent in the nature of civilization itself but are determined by the imperfections of the cultural forms which have so far been developed. And in fact it is not difficult to indicate those defects. While mankind has made continual advances in its control over nature and may expect to make still greater ones, it is not possible to establish with certainty that a similar advance has been made in the management of human affairs; and probably at all periods, just as now once again, many people have asked themselves whether what little civilization has thus acquired is indeed worth defending at all. One would think that a re-ordering of human relations should be possible, which would remove the sources of dissatisfaction with civilization by renouncing coercion and the suppression of the instincts, so that, undisturbed by internal discord, men might devote themselves to the acquisition of wealth and its enjoyment. That would be the golden age, but it is questionable if such a state of affairs can be realized. It seems rather that every civilization must be built up on coercion and renunciation of instinct; it does not even seem certain that if coercion were to cease the majority of human beings would be prepared to undertake to perform the work necessary for acquiring new wealth. One has, I think, to reckon with the fact that there are present in all men destructive, and therefore anti-social and anti-cultural, trends and that in a great number of people these are strong enough to determine their behaviour in human society.

This psychological fact has a decisive importance for our judgement of human civilization. Whereas we might at first think that its essence lies in controlling nature for the purpose of acquiring wealth and that the dangers which threaten it could be eliminated through a suitable distribution of that wealth among men, it now seems that the emphasis has moved over from the material to the mental. The decisive question is whether and to what extent it is possible to lessen the burden of the instinctual sacrifices imposed on men, to reconcile men to those which must necessarily remain and to provide a compensation for them. It is just as impossible to do without control of the mass by a minority as it is to dispense with coercion in the work of civilization. For masses are lazy and unintelligent; they have no love for instinctual renunciation, and they are not to be convinced by argument of its inevitability; and the individuals composing them support one another in giving free rein to their indiscipline. It is only through the influence of individuals who can set an example and whom masses recognize as their leaders that they can be induced to perform the work and undergo the renunciations on which the existence of civilization depends. All is well if these leaders are persons who possess superior insight into the necessities of life and who have risen to the height of mastering their own instinctual wishes. But there is a danger that in order not to lose their influence they may give way to the mass more than it gives way to them, and it therefore seems necessary that they shall be independent of the mass by having means to power at their disposal. To put it briefly, there are two widespread human characteristics which are responsible for the fact that the regulations of civilization can only be maintained by a certain degree of coercion—namely, that men are not spontaneously fond of work and that arguments are of no avail against their passions.

I know the objections which will be raised against these assertions. It will be said that the characteristic of human masses depicted here, which is supposed to prove that coercion cannot be dispensed with in the work of civilization, is itself only the result of defects in the cultural regulations, owing to which men have become embittered, revengeful and inaccessible. New generations, who have been brought up in kindness and taught to have a high opinion of reason, and who have experienced the benefits of civilization at an early age, will have a different attitude to it. They will feel it as a possession of their very own and will be ready for its sake to make the sacrifices as regards work and instinctual satisfaction that are necessary for its preservation. They will be able to do without coercion and will differ little from their leaders. If no culture has so far produced human masses of such a quality, it is because no culture has yet devised regulations which will influence men in this way, and in particular from childhood onwards.

It may be doubted whether it is possible at all, or at any rate as yet, at the present stage of our control over nature, to set up cultural regulations of this kind. It may be asked where the number of superior, unswerving and disinterested leaders are to come from who are to act as educators of the future generations, and it may be alarming to think of the enormous amount of coercion that will be required before these intentions can be carried out. The grandeur of the plan and its importance for the future of human civilization cannot be disputed. It is securely based on the psychological discovery that man is equipped with the most varied instinctual dispositions, whose ultimate course is determined by the experiences of early childhood. But for the same reason the limitations of man's capacity for education set bounds to the effectiveness of such a transformation in his culture. One may question whether, and in what degree, it would be possible for a different cultural environment to do away with the two characteristics of human masses which make the guidance of human affairs so difficult. The experiment has not yet been made. Probably a certain percentage of mankind (owing to a pathological disposition or an excess of instinctual strength) will always remain asocial; but if it were feasible merely to reduce the majority that is hostile towards civilization to-day into a minority, a great deal would have been accomplished—perhaps all that *can* be accomplished.

On Values
in the Age of Science

by Jacques Monod

IN THE PRESENT PAPER I wish to summarize the following simple and radical theme: the traditional concepts which provided the ethical foundation of human societies from time immemorial, all consisted of imaginary ontogenies, none of which remains tenable in the face of scientific enquiry. Modern societies, technically based on science, still attempt to withhold the traditional views, or some modernized version of them. This contradiction creates intolerable tensions under which these societies will collapse, unless a radically new foundation for their value system can be defined, accepted and respected.

The most significant, the most profound, the most disturbing (and to man the most frightening) consequence of the development of Science lies not in the industrial and technical revolution, but in the agonizing reappraisal, which Science forces upon Man, of his deepest rooted concepts of himself and of his relationship to the universe.

The urge, the anguish to understand the meaning of his own existence, the demand to rationalize and justify it within some coherent framework has been, and still is, one of the most powerful motivations in the human mind. This profound urge which has given rise to all the myths and religions of humanity and to the great philosophical concepts, also is, of course, at the root of the discovery of the scientific method. But while the myths, religions and philosophies did bring positive answers to the problem of meaning, and while it was believed for a long time that Science would bring the final, definitive solution, we now realize, at last, that the problem of meaning is the one to which no scientific answer ever could be provided.

Science, in its development, has gradually attacked and dissolved to the core the very foundations of the various value systems which, from prehistoric times, had served as ethical framework for human societies. I believe that most social anthropologists would agree with the statement that the structure of virtually all ancient or primitive myths, as well as of more advanced religions, is essentially ontogenic. Primitive myths provide histories which almost invariably refer to one or several god-like heroes, whose sagas both account for the foundation of the group and imperatively govern its social structure and traditions, that is, its basic ethical system. The great religions may be regarded as generalizations, attempting to embrace the whole of Mankind in a similar, except much wider, interpretative ontogeny, whose recognized function is to provide a transcendent and therefore permanent and indisputable basis for a system of values. Most of the great philosophical systems, from Plato to Hegel and Marx may also be regarded as attempts to establish on an ontogenic basis an untouchable, irrefutable basis for a system of values, in turn serving as foundation of the social system.

Whether an ethical structure is justified by reference to a founder-hero, to a universal god, to an absolute idea, to the "laws" of history, or to some "natural" foundation for human rights, all such systems, from the concepts of Australian aborigines, to the ideas of Rousseau or Marx, share one essential characteristic: namely that values and ethics are not a matter of human choice. Whether they are supposed to stand on divine, or "natural" foundations, they are beyond the realm of human freedom. Reason or faith may serve to identify and recognize values, but not to define or alter them. To Man, Ethics and values do not belong; he belongs to them.

It is indeed easy to see the psychological purpose and the social function of raising these concepts on to so high a pedestal as to put them beyond human reach and make them untouchable. The psychological purpose is to abate and perhaps satiate the hunger for meaning; for the meaning of such absolute realities as life and death. The social function is one of stability: no social structure could survive whose very foundations could be questioned, denied or dismissed by anyone at any time. The foundations of a value system therefore must appear not only unquestionable, but as it were, inaccessible.

The invention of Myths and Religions, the construction of vast philosophical systems, thus may be regarded as the price that Man had to pay for surviving as a highly social animal. As is well known, of course, other social animals, such as bees, ants or termites, have had recourse to a much more reliable method of insuring the stability of their social institutions: namely genetic determination of behavior through proper embryological wiring of their nervous system. Man, in fact, is the only highly social animal whose code of conduct is largely transmitted culturally rather than genetically. Hence the fact that human societies have histories, while animal societies could only claim a paleontology.

Genetically coded traits are not immune to change, as we know. They are however off limits and beyond reach to the species itself. Once stabilized by selection, they may survive, unchanged, for hundreds of thousands or millions of years. In spite of all the efforts of priests, statesmen and philosophers, cultural codes are not untouchable. They have changed through prehistoric and historic times, at a rate that no biological, genetic evolution could have approached. In spite of all these changes, however, one concept remained, up to recent times, invariant: namely that SOME immutable foundation of the value system did exist, and could be found or recognized.

It is this concept, the most essential within any ethical system, the cornerstone of any social structure, the sole (even though unreliable) substitute for genetic coding, that science now has destroyed, reduced to absurdity, relegated to the state of nonsensical wishful thinking.

Many may not agree with this last, somewhat radical statement. There has been, as we all know, an enormous amount of benevolent, systematically optimistic talking and writing about Science, presenting it as an exclusively constructive and creative activity. The phenomenal destructive potential of the scientific method has largely been ignored, in part I believe, not from ignorance but from fear of facing it. (I am referring of course exclusively to the destruction of ideas or concepts, not to the Bomb.) That the ideas or concepts that Science has proved to be untenable indeed were wrong or meaningless from an objective point of view does not imply that they were subjectively meaningless and served no function. The reverse is obviously true. Let us however see, briefly, how and how far, the traditional concepts which lent "meaning" to man's existence, have all become more and more untenable in the context of modern science.

The core of the matter may, I believe, be put as follows: In virtually all the mythic, religious or philosophic systems, Man's existence receives its meaning from being supposed part of some general purpose which accounts for the whole of nature and creation. The "purpose" may be naively attributed to a mythic founder-hero, or more grandiosely (albeit less poetically) to some abstract divine intention; or it may be assumed that the "laws of nature" are such that the universe in its evolution, could not fail to produce Man and history, inevitably leading eventually to the classless society. The structure and the social function of these systems, diverse as they are, remain the same. They all assume between Man and the Universe, between Cosmology and History an unbroken continuity, a profound immanent alliance, wherein Man and Nature together serve the universal purpose or the inevitable outcome of the whole of creation. Such views necessarily imply also the assumption of a certain identity of essence between Man and Nature. And since the essence of Man, as he cannot fail to experience it, is his own consciousness, his subjective knowledge of himself and of his own dialectical thought-process, the same "essence" is attributed to Nature itself. These assumptions of course are most precisely and clearly expressed in primitive animist Myths. But the initial, basic animist assumption, the interpretative projection into Nature itself of Man's conscious essence is equally basic to certain modern Philosophies. The most revealing example may be Dialectical Materialism whose cornerstone (even though actually a late addition to an already largely erected edifice of social philosophy) according to Engels is the recognition that the three "dialectical laws" of Hegel are the general laws of Nature itself.

That the fundamentally very same assumption had to be introduced into their system of the world by Engels and Marx as well as by Indian Tribesmen, would prove, if necessary, how essential to Man it always has appeared, and still does, to discover in Nature his own "meaning" and in himself the "meaning" of Nature.

It is precisely this initial assumption, this idea perhaps as old as Man, of a twofold relationship based on a community of purpose between Nature and Himself, that Science has utterly destroyed. This it has done in two ways.

To begin with, the adoption of the scientific method, defining "true" knowledge as having no possible source other than the objective confrontation of logic and observation, eliminates IPSO FACTO the animist assumption of the existence of some kind of subjectivity in nature. The absolute OBJECTIVITY of Nature is the basic postulate of the scientific method, initially grounded in the formulation of the concept of Inertia, by Galileo and Descartes, which eliminated once and for all the teleological physics and astronomy of Aristotle. The church would have been wise to condemn Galileo for this ominous discovery, rather than for his defence of the Copernican system.

This basic postulate, however, was for a long time used mostly in the physical sciences. The enormous complexity of living beings, and more than anything else, the fact that in their structure, development and behavior one can immediately see their obviously purposeful "essence," appeared to estrange them, and Man, from the physical world. Indeed how could a postulate of objectivity apply to the interpretation of such evidently intentional creatures? As more was learnt of the structure and physiology of living beings, this apparently valid objection to the Cartesian views appeared to make them less and less tenable.

Thus, the animist assumption was eliminated from the study of physical phenomena, while it could, and did, remain in Biology in one form or other of vitalism. Vitalism indeed can take many aspects, some subtle enough to pass as expressing an objective approach. The formulation of the theory of evolution, first by Buffon and Lamarck, then much more forcibly and demonstratively by Darwin, did not interrupt this current of thought. In some ways it reinforced it: evolution in the biosphere appeared to testify to the existence of some ascending driving force, necessarily and unfailingly leading from the physical to the biological world, and through it to its crowning achievement, Man himself.

This idea, which in fact reinstated in an apparently "scientific" form the old animist alliance, is not only clearly present in Engels and Teilhard de Chardin. It in fact subtends much of XIXth Century "progressist" positivism. The theory of selection as the one driving force of evolution, due to Darwin's genius, should have cautioned against this kind of wishful thinking. Actually, while evolution was enthusiastically accepted by progressists of all kinds, and furiously rejected by all types of reactionaries, the theory of selection was neither fully understood, nor widely accepted. The main reason was that, while the concept of "survival of the fittest" was easy enough to comprehend, it could not fail to shock the moral code of heirs to the American and French Revolutions. Moreover Darwin had not, and could not have, formulated with any precision the mechanism of the initial events wherein lay the ultimate source of evolution, these "sports" which, of course, had to precede selection. Indeed Darwin himself did not reject Lamarckian adaptationism, which to many appeared as a "natural," easily acceptable mechanism, and of course pleased the progressists much better.

It remained for modern Biology, beginning with classical genetics, and blossoming into Molecular Biology, to discover the ultimate source of both stability and evolution in the Biosphere, and thus blow to its last shreds the myth of the old alliance.

I may perhaps be allowed to simply summarize without proof or illustration, the main conclusions of Modern Biology which are relevant to this discussion:

1. The one universal and essential characteristic of living beings is the conservativity of the chemical structure (DNA) wherein the genetic code is written.

2. Evolution is not an inherent tendency of living beings. Quite the reverse: their whole structure is intensely conservative, mostly resisting successfully any alteration.

3. The ultimate and only sources of true novelty in the biosphere are random perturbations within the conservative machinery. Perturbations such as any physical object shall inevitably be subject to. These perturbations affect SINGLE molecules, and are, therefore, fundamentally unpredictable and uncontrollable.

It should perhaps be pointed out that the concept of a strictly random source for Evolution does not stem from or express ignorance of the intimate mechanism itself. Quite the reverse: it is because the nature of these mechanisms is clearly understood that one is led to the conclusion that they only be purely random in origin. Thus the appearance of life itself and, within the biosphere, the emergency of Man, can only be conceived as the result of a huge Monte-Carlo game, where our number eventually did come out, when it might as well not have appeared and, in any case, the unfathomable cosmos around us could not have cared less.

From these conclusions there is no escape, nor any prospect whatever that they might be radically altered as a result of future scientific progress. One hardly needs to insist on the absolute incompatibility between this scientific view of Man and his origin and the traditional concepts upon which values, ethics and societies were founded. The scientific approach reveals to Man that he is an accident, almost a stranger in the universe, and reduces the "old alliance" between him and the rest of creation to a tenuous and fragile thread. None of the gracious or frightening myths that he had dreamed, none of the hopes he had tenaciously entertained, none of the certainties that had formed the structure of his moral and social life for thousands of years, can stand anymore.

Science, as it emerged and developed, has shaped the modern world, given modern nations their technology and power. Yet these societies have failed to accept, hardly have they understood the most profound message of science. They still teach and preach some more or less modernized version of traditional systems of values, blatantly incompatible with what scientific culture they have. The western, liberal-capitalist countries still pay lip service to a nauseating mixture of Judeo-Christian religiosity, "Natural" Human Rights, pedestrian utilitarianism and XIXth Century progressism. The Marxist countries still throw up a stupefying smoke-screen of nonsensical Historicism and Dialectical materialism.

They all lie and they know it. No intelligent and cultivated person, in any of these societies can really believe in the validity of these dogma. More sensitive, more impatient, the youth perceives the lies and revolts against them, forcefully revealing the intolerable contradictions within modern societies. Let us not live with the illusion that it always was more or less so, in previous times. Primitives do believe in the Myths which guide their whole life; Medieval societies did believe in Paradise, Hell and Sin; French revolutionists did believe in Natural Human Rights; Lenin and Trotsky had absolute confidence in Historical Materialism and in its formal promise of a classless society, free of contradictions.

No society can survive without a moral code based on values understood, accepted, respected by the majority of its members. We have none of this kind anymore. Could modern societies indefinitely master and control the huge powers which they owe to science on the criterion of a vague humanism admixed with a sort of hopeful materialistic Hedonism? Could they, on this basis, resolve their intolerable tensions? Or shall they collapse under the strain?

I believe they will, except perhaps at the price of a profound reappraisal of human values, of their true nature, of their source; beginning with the recognition of Man's strangeness in the cosmos, of his absolute loneliness. Then he may realize that there is, that there can be outside or beyond himself no source, no criterion, divine, historical or natural for his values. That he alone creates, defines and shapes them. This is to say that, in order to reconstruct the foundations of a system of values upon which social, political and personal life might be based in the age of Science, we must start from an absolute TABULA RASA; we must go further and deeper than Nietzsche's prophetic "Gott ist tod," for, not only is God dead, but also his various romantic, historicist and progressist substitutes. Nor can we, as Nietzsche did, followed by some of the modern French existentialists, proclaim the "absolute" freedom of Man. No biologist could accept such a view; we know that we are made up of the same amino acids and nucleotides, and that we carry the same genetic code as any bacterium, plant, or fish. We would have to be blind not to recognize our close similarity, not only structural, but behavioral, to our first cousins, the great apes. And we had better listen attentively to the ethologists pointing out, as does Professor Lorenz, that many genetically determined behavioral attitudes of mammals, birds, or fishes, could be described as obeying strictly certain commandments of the Decalogue. One need not look for a transcendent basis for the categorical imperative: its biological source is clear enough in many instances.

This profound, demanding, biological heritage is part of Man's essence. It would be just as foolish to disregard it, as it would also be to deny that his "essence" also partakes of another realm, which transcends the physical and even the biological, I mean the kingdom of ideas and knowledge, the "Noosphere," to use Teilhard's word. The noosphere exists as a partially autonomous realm, because, in the Hominid family, a form of communication was developed, which is unique to that particular family. Undoubtedly selected and developed, primitively, for its survival value, it must have also (by introducing new selective pressures), influenced the physical evolution of Man, I mean the development of his cortex which it is reasonable to consider as "prewired" for the acquisition of language. Thus language is, simultaneously, inseparably, a physiological trait and a cultural development, and partakes most intimately of the dual nature of man's essence.

It has recently becomes fashionable, in certain French philosophic circles, to deny any meaning, any value, to the concept of a human "essence." No biologist could consider such a statement as anything but sheer nonsense. The concept of a human essence signifies, to my mind, the most important, the most fascinating of all problems, embracing genetic, embryological and physiological questions as well as cultural, linguistic, psychological and aesthetic aspects.

A rational reconstruction of our values system will have to take all these aspects into account, and be prepared for evolution and alteration, as our insight into Man's essence becomes more profound. But it must be fully understood and recognized that even in the age of Science, moral philosophy coud not rely simply on some sort of biological essentialism, for no value system, no Ethics, could ever be based on a purely objective analysis of Man as he is. By definition, by function, a value system, an Ethics must define an "ought," not an "is," a high ideal, a goal to be pursued WHICH CANNOT BE MAN HIMSELF. No ethical system can be purely utilitarian: this is a psychological error, a contradiction in terms, a denial of the very function of Ethics.

It follows that, in the age of Science, when none of the traditional transcendent assumptions is tenable anymore, whose function it had been to define a superhuman goal or command, we must do the same, except for the fundamental departure that we will know and proclaim our choice to be deliberate; that is, in fact and intention, axiomatic. I believe it can be done, that such a system could be taught, understood, and would be respected to the very extent that it defined the loftiest values as measure and criterion of all values, of social and personal Ethics.

And what other ultimate values to choose then, than those creations, born from Men, yet transcending their creators, as existing in the Kingdom of ideas, richer and wider in content than any single man nor even all men at any one time, can perceive? I mean of course the great, ever unfinished, monument of creation and knowledge, that is, of Art and Science.

Ethics and values have, since Man started enquiring into the meaning of his own existence, always been based on some essential relationship assumed to exist between him and the universe. We now know that the only authentic relationship goes through that abstract kingdom, the noosphere; that man, the stranger in the cosmos, can conquer the universe only through knowledge. Art and Science express two complementary aspects of human knowledge, one synthetic and partially subjective, the other analytic and strictly objective. A society that would accept these transcendent values as the ultimate standard of all, more immediate, human values, and designed itself deliberately to serve them, would have to defend intellectual, political, and economic freedom; to foster education, both extensive and intensive, as its primary task; and it would also have to develop the welfare state, not as an end in itself, but as a means towards more freedom, creativity and knowledge, that is, towards serving Man in his most unique and precious essence.

The Social Contract

First Week — Third Day

Old Testament, Exodus 3, 5, 6:1-8, 19, 20

New Testament, Mark 12:28-32

Plutarch, "Lycurgus"

Charles de Sécondat, Baron de Montesquieu, *The Spirit of the Laws*, Book XI, Chapters 1-6

Afternoon session:
Governance and Human Rights

The Old Testament
Exodus

Chapter 3

NOW Moses kept the flock of Jethro his father in law, the priest of Midian: and he led the flock to the backside of the desert, and came to the mountain of God, *even* to Horeb.

2 And the angel of the Lord appeared unto him in a flame of fire out of the midst of a bush: and he looked, and, behold, the bush burned with fire, and the bush *was* not consumed.

3 And Moses said, I will now turn aside, and see this great sight, why the bush is not burnt.

4 And when the Lord saw that he turned aside to see, God called unto him out of the midst of the bush, and said, Moses, Moses. And he said, Here *am* I.

5 And he said, Draw not nigh hither: put off thy shoes from off they feet, for the place whereon thou standest *is* holy ground.

6 Moreover he said, I *am* the God of thy father, the God of Abraham, the God of Isaac, and the God of Jacob. And Moses hid his face; for he was afraid to look upon God.

7 ¶ And the Lord said, I have surely seen the affliction of my people which *are* in Egypt, and have heard their cry by reason of their taskmasters; for I know their sorrows;

8 And I am come down to deliver them out of the hand of the Egyptians, and to bring them up out of that land unto a good land and a large, unto a land flowing with milk and honey; unto the place of the Canaanites, and the Hittites, and the Amorites, and the Perizzites, and the Hivites, and the Jebusites.

9 Now therefore, behold, the cry of the children of Israel is come unto me: and I have also seen the oppression wherewith the Egyptians oppress them.

10 Come now therefore, and I will send thee unto Pharaoh, that thou mayest bring forth my people the children of Israel out of Egypt.

11 ¶ And Moses said unto God, Who *am* I, that I should go unto Phar-

aoh, and that I should bring forth the children of Israel out of Egypt?

12 And he said, Certainly I will be with thee; and this *shall be* a token unto thee, that I have sent thee: When thou hast brought forth the people out of Egypt, ye shall serve God upon this mountain.

13 And Moses said unto God, Behold, *when* I come unto the children of Israel, and shall say unto them, The God of your fathers hath sent me unto you; and they shall say to me, What *is* his name? what shall I say unto them?

14 And God said unto Moses, I AM THAT I AM: and he said, Thus shalt thou say unto the children of Israel, I AM hath sent me unto you.

15 And God said moreover unto Moses, Thus shalt thou say unto the children of Israel, The Lord God of your fathers, the God of Abraham, the God of Isaac, and the God of Jacob, hath sent me unto you: this *is* my name for *ever*, and this *is* my memorial unto all generations.

16 Go, and gather the elders of Israel together, and say unto them, The Lord God of your fathers, the God of Abraham, of Isaac, and of Jacob, appeared to me, saying, I have surely visited you, and *seen* that which is done to you in Egypt:

17 And I have said, I will bring you up out of the affliction of Egypt unto the land of the Canaanites, and the Hittites, and the Amorites, and the Perizzites, and the Hivites, and the Jebusites, unto a land flowing with milk and honey.

18 And they shall hearken to thy voice: and thou shalt come, thou and the elders of Israel, unto the king of Egypt, and ye shall say unto him, The Lord God of the Hebrews hath met with us: and now let us go, we be-seech thee, three days' journey into the wilderness, that we may sacrifice to the Lord our God.

19 ¶ And I am sure that the king of Egypt will not let you go, no, not by a mighty hand.

20 And I will stretch out my hand, and smite Egypt with all my wonders which I will do in the midst thereof: and after that he will let you go.

21 And I will give this people favour in the sight of the Egyptians: and it shall come to pass, that, when ye go, ye shall not go empty:

22 But every woman shall borrow of her neighbour, and of her that sojourneth in her house, jewels of silver, and jewels of gold, and raiment: and ye shall put *them* upon your sons, and upon your daughters; and ye shall spoil the Egyptians.

Chapter 5

AND afterward Moses and Aaron went in, and told Pharaoh, Thus saith the Lord God of Israel, Let my people go, that they may hold a feast unto me in the wilderness.

2 And Pharaoh said, Who *is* the Lord, that I should obey his voice to let Israel go? I know not the Lord, neither will I let Israel go.

3 And they said, The God of the Hebrews hath met with us: let us go, we pray thee, three days' journey into the desert, and sacrifice unto the Lord our God; lest he fall upon us with pestilence, or with the sword.

4 And the king of Egypt said unto them, Wherefore do ye, Moses and Aaron, let the people from their works? get you unto your burdens.

5 And Pharaoh said, Behold, the people of the land are *now* many, and ye make them rest from their burdens.

6 And Pharaoh commanded the

same day the taskmasters of the people, and their officers, saying,

7 Ye shall no more give the people straw to make brick, as heretofore: let them go and gather straw for themselves.

8 And the tale of the bricks, which they did make heretofore, ye shall lay upon them; ye shall not diminish *ought* thereof: for they *be* idle; therefore they cry, saying, Let us go *and* sacrifice to our God.

9 Let there more work be laid upon the men, that they may labour therein; and let them not regard vain words.

10 ¶ And the taskmasters of the people went out, and their officers, and they spake to the people, saying, Thus saith Pharaoh, I will not give you straw.

11 Go ye, get you straw where ye can find it: yet not ought of your work shall be diminished.

12 So the people were scattered abroad throughout all the land of Egypt to gather stubble instead of straw.

13 And the taskmasters hasted *them,* saying, Fulfil your works, *your* daily tasks, as when there was straw.

14 And the officers of the children of Israel, which Pharaoh's taskmasters had set over them, were beaten, *and* demanded, Wherefore have ye not fulfilled your task in making brick both yesterday and to day, as heretofore?

15 ¶ Then the officers of the children of Israel came and cried unto Pharaoh, saying, Wherefore dealest thou thus with thy servants?

16 There is no straw given unto thy servants, and they say to us, Make brick: and, behold, thy servants *are* beaten; but the fault *is* in thine own people.

17 But he said, Ye *are* idle, *ye are* idle: therefore ye say, Let us go *and* do sacrifice to the Lord.

18 Go therefore now, *and* work; for there shall no straw be given you, yet shall ye deliver the tale of bricks.

19 And the officers of the children of Israel did see *that* they *were* in evil *case,* after it was said, Ye shall not minish *ought* from your bricks of your daily task.

20 ¶ And they met Moses and Aaron, who stood in the way, as they came forth from Pharaoh:

21 And they said unto them, The Lord look upon you, and judge; because ye have made our savour to be abhorred in the eyes of Pharaoh, and in the eyes of his servants, to put a sword in their hand to slay us.

22 And Moses returned unto the Lord, and said, Lord, wherefore hast thou *so* evil entreated this people? why *is* it *that* thou hast sent me?

23 For since I came to Pharaoh to speak in thy name, he hath done evil to this people; neither hast thou delivered thy people at all.

Chapter 6

THEN the Lord said unto Moses, Now shalt thou see what I will do to Pharaoh: for with a strong hand shall he let them go, and with a strong hand shall he drive them out of his land.

2 And God spake unto Moses, and said unto him, I *am* the Lord:

3 And I appeared unto Abraham, unto Isaac, and unto Jacob, by *the name of* God Almighty, but by my name JEHOVAH was I not known to them.

4 And I have also established my covenant with them, to give them the land of Canaan, the land of their pilgrimage, wherein they were

strangers.

5 And I have also heard the groaning of the children of Israel, whom the Egyptians keep in bondage; and I have remembered my covenant.

6 Wherefore say unto the children of Israel, I *am* the Lord, and I will bring you out from under the burdens of the Egyptians, and I will rid you out of their bondage, and I will redeem you with a stretched out arm, and with great judgments:

7 And I will take you to me for a people, and I will be to you a God: and ye shall know that I *am* the Lord your God, which bringeth you out from under the burdens of the Egyptians.

8 And I will bring you in unto the land, concerning the which I did swear to give it to Abraham, to Isaac, and to Jacob; and I will give it you for an heritage: I *am* the Lord. . . .

Chapter 19

IN the third month, when the children of Israel were gone forth out of the land of Egypt, the same day came they *into* the wilderness of Sinai.

2 For they were departed from Rephidim, and were come *to* the desert of Sinai, and had pitched in the wilderness; and there Israel camped before the mount.

3 And Moses went up unto God, and the Lord called unto him out of the mountain, saying, Thus shalt thou say to the house of Jacob, and tell the children of Israel;

4 Ye have seen what I did unto the Egyptians, and *how* I bare you on eagles' wings, and brought you unto myself.

5 Now therefore, if ye will obey my voice indeed, and keep my covenant, then ye shall be a peculiar treasure unto me above all people:

for all the earth *is* mine:

6 And ye shall be unto me a kingdom of priests, and an holy nation. These *are* the words which thou shalt speak unto the children of Israel.

7 ¶ And Moses came and called for the elders of the people, and laid before their faces all these words which the Lord commanded him.

8 And all the people answered together, and said, All that the Lord hath spoken we will do. And Moses returned the words of the people unto the Lord.

9 And the Lord said unto Moses, Lo, I come unto thee in a thick cloud, that the people may hear when I speak with thee, and believe thee for ever. And Moses told the words of the people unto the Lord.

10 ¶ And the Lord said unto Moses, Go unto the people, and sanctify them to day and to morrow, and let them wash their clothes.

11 And be ready against the third day: for the third day the Lord will come down in the sight of all the people upon mount Sinai.

12 And thou shalt set bounds unto the people round about, saying, Take heed to yourselves, *that ye* go *not* up into the mount, or touch the border of it: whosoever toucheth the mount shall be surely put to death:

13 There shall not an hand touch it, but he shall surely be stoned, or shot through; whether *it be* beast or man, it shall not live: when the trumpet soundeth long, they shall come up to the mount.

14 ¶ And Moses went down from the mount unto the people, and sanctified the people; and they washed their clothes.

15 And he said unto the people, Be ready against the third day: come not at *your* wives.

16 ¶ And it came to pass on the third day in the morning, that there were thunders and lightnings, and a thick cloud upon the mount, and the voice of the trumpet exceeding loud; so that all the people that *was* in the camp trembled.

17 And Moses brought forth the people out of the camp to meet with God; and they stood at the nether part of the mount.

18 And mount Sinai was altogether on a smoke, because the Lord descended upon it in fire: and the smoke thereof ascended as the smoke of a furnace, and the whole mount quaked greatly.

19 And when the voice of the trumpet sounded long, and waxed louder and louder, Moses spake, and God answered him by a voice.

20 And the Lord came down upon mount Sinai, on the top of the mount: and the Lord called Moses *up* to the top of the mount; and Moses went up.

21 And the Lord said unto Moses, Go down, charge the people, lest they break through unto the Lord to gaze, and many of them perish.

22 And let the priests also, which come near to the Lord, sanctify themselves, lest the Lord break forth upon them.

23 And Moses said unto the Lord, The people cannot come up to mount Sinai: for thou chargedst us, saying, Set bounds about the mount, and sanctify it.

24 And the Lord said unto him, Away, get thee down, and thou shalt come up, thou, and Aaron with thee: but let not the priests and the people break through to come up unto the Lord, lest he break forth upon them.

25 So Moses went down unto the people, and spake unto them.

Chapter 20

AND God spake all these words, saying,

2 I *am* the Lord thy God, which have brought thee out of the land of Egypt, out of the house of bondage.

3 Thou shalt have no other gods before me.

4 Thou shalt not make unto thee any graven image, or any likeness *of any thing* that *is* in heaven above, or that *is* in the earth beneath, or that *is* in the water under the earth:

Thou shalt not bow down thyself to them, nor serve them: for I the Lord thy God *am* a jealous God, visiting the iniquity of the fathers upon the children unto the third and fourth *generation* of them that hate me;

6 And shewing mercy unto thousands of them that love me, and keep my commandments.

7 Thou shalt not take the name of the Lord thy God in vain; for the Lord will not hold him guiltless that taketh his name in vain.

8 Remember the sabbath day, to keep it holy.

9 Six days shalt thou labour, and do all thy work:

10 But the seventh day *is* the sabbath of the Lord thy God: *in it* thou shalt not do any work, thou, nor thy son, nor thy daughter, thy manservant, nor thy maidservant, nor thy cattle, nor thy stranger that *is* within thy gates:

11 For *in* six days the Lord made heaven and earth, the sea, and all that in them *is*, and rested the seventh day: wherefore the Lord blessed the sabbath day, and hallowed it.

12 ¶ Honour thy father and thy mother: that thy days may be long

upon the land which the Lord thy God giveth thee.

13 Thou shalt not kill.

14 Thou shalt not commit adultery.

15 Thou shalt not steal.

16 Thou shalt not bear false witness against thy neighbour.

17 Thou shalt not covet thy neighbour's house, thou shalt not covet thy neighbour's wife, nor his manservant, nor his maidservant, nor his ox, nor his ass, nor any thing that is thy neighbour's.

18 ¶ And all the people saw the thunderings, and the lightnings, and the noise of the trumpet, and the mountain smoking: and when the people saw it, they removed, and stood afar off.

19 And they said unto Moses, Speak thou with us, and we will hear: but let not God speak with us, lest we die.

20 And Moses said unto the people, Fear not: for God is come to prove you, and that his fear may be before your faces, that ye sin not.

21 And the people stood afar off, and Moses drew near unto the thick darkness where God was.

22 ¶ And the Lord said unto Moses, Thus thou shalt say unto the children of Israel, Ye have seen that I have talked with you from heaven.

23 Ye shall not make with me gods of silver, neither shall ye make unto you gods of gold.

24 ¶ An altar of earth thou shalt make unto me, and shalt sacrifice thereon thy burnt offerings, and thy peace offerings, thy sheep, and thine oxen: in all places where I record my name I will come unto thee, and I will bless thee.

25 And if thou wilt make me an altar of stone, thou shalt not build it of hewn stone: for if thou lift up thy tool upon it, thou hast polluted it.

26 Neither shalt thou go up by steps unto mine altar, that thy nakedness be not discovered thereon. . . .

The New Testament

The Gospel according to Saint Mark

Chapter 12

AND one of the scribes came, and having heard them reasoning together, and perceiving that he had answered them well, asked him, Which is the first commandment of all?

29 And Jesus answered him, The first of all the commandments *is*, Hear, O Israel; The Lord our God is one Lord:

30 And thou shalt love the Lord thy God with all thy heart, and with all thy soul, and with all thy mind, and with all thy strength: this *is* the first commandment.

31 And the second *is* like, *namely* this, Thou shalt love thy neighbour as thyself. There is none other commandment greater than these. . . .

Lycurgus

by Plutarch

THERE is so much uncertainty in the accounts which historians have left us of Lycurgus, the lawgiver of Sparta, that scarcely anything is asserted by one of them which is not called into question or contradicted by the rest. Their sentiments are quite different as to the family he came of, the voyages he undertook, the place and manner of his death, but most of all when they speak of the laws he made and the commonwealth which he founded. They cannot, by any means, be brought to an agreement as to the very age in which he lived; for some of them say that he flourished in the time of Iphitus, and that they two jointly contrived the ordinance for the cessation of arms during the solemnity of the Olympic games. Of this opinion was Aristotle; and for confirmation of it, he alleges an inscription upon one of the copper quoits used in those sports, upon which the name of Lycurgus continued uneffaced to his time. But Eratosthenes and Apollodorus and other chronologers, computing the time by the successions of the Spartan kings, pretend to demonstrate that he was much more ancient than the institution of the Olympic games. Timæus conjectures that there were two of this name, and in diverse times, but that the one of them being much more famous than the other, men gave to him the glory of the exploits of both; the elder of the two, according to him, was not long after Homer; and some are so particular as to say that he had seen him. But that he was of great antiquity may be gathered from a passage in Xenophon, where he makes him contemporary with the Heraclidæ. By descent, indeed, the very last kings of Sparta were Heraclidæ too; but he seems in that place to speak of the first and more immediate successors of Hercules. But notwithstanding this confusion and obscurity, we shall endeavour to compose the history of his life, adhering to those statements which are least contradicted, and depending upon those authors who are most worthy of credit.

The poet Simonides will have it that Lycurgus was the son of Prytanis, and not of Eunomus; but in this opinion he is singular, for all the rest deduce the genealogy of them both as follows: —

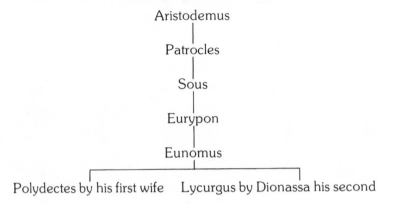

Aristodemus

Patrocles

Sous

Eurypon

Eunomus

Polydectes by his first wife   Lycurgus by Dionassa his second

Dieuchidas says he was the sixth from Patrocles and the eleventh from Hercules. Be this as it will, Sous certainly was the most renowned of all his ancestors, under whose conduct the Spartans made slaves of the Helots, and added to their dominions, by conquest, a good part of Arcadia. There goes a story of this King Sous, that, being besieged by the Clitorians in a dry and stony place so that he could come at no water, he was at last constrained to agree with them upon these terms, that he would restore to them all his conquests, provided that himself and all his men should drink of the nearest spring. After the usual oaths and ratifications, he called his soldiers together, and offered to him that would forbear drinking his kingdom for a reward; and when not a man of them was able to forbear, in short, when they had all drunk their fill, at last comes King Sous himself to the spring, and, having sprinkled his face only, without swallowing one drop, marches off in the face of his enemies, refusing to yield up his conquests, because himself and all his men had not, according to the articles, drunk of their water.

Although he was justly had in admiration on this account, yet his family was not surnamed from him, but from his son Eurypon (of whom they were called Eurypontids); the reason of which was that Eurypon relaxed the rigour of the monarchy, seeking favour and popularity with the many. They, after this first step, grew bolder; and the succeeding kings partly incurred hatred with their people by trying to use force, or, for popularity's sake and through weakness, gave way; and anarchy and confusion long prevailed in Sparta, causing, moreover, the death of the father of Lycurgus. For as he was endeavouring to quell a riot, he was stabbed with a butcher's knife, and left the title of king to his eldest son, Polydectes.

He, too, dying soon after, the right of succession (as every one thought) rested in Lycurgus; and reign he did, until it was found that the queen, his sister-in-law, was with child; upon which he immediately declared that the kingdom belonged to her issue, provided it were male, and that he himself exercised the regal jurisdiction only as his guardian; the Spartan name for which office is *prodicus*. Soon after, an overture was made to him by the queen, that she would herself in some way destroy the infant, upon condition that he would marry her when he came to the crown. Abhorring the woman's wickedness, he nevertheless did not reject her proposal, but, making show of closing with her, despatched the messenger with thanks and expressions of joy, but dissuaded her earnestly from procuring herself to miscarry, which would impair her health, if not endanger her life; he himself, he said, would see to it, that the child, as soon as born, should be taken out of the way.

By such artifices having drawn on the woman to the time of her lying-in, as soon as he heard that she was in labour, he sent persons to be by and observe all that passed, with orders that if it were a girl they should deliver it to the women, but if a boy, should bring it to him wheresoever he were, and whatsoever doing. It so fell out that when he was at supper with the principal magistrates the queen was brought to bed of a boy, who was soon after presented to him as he was at the table; he, taking him into his arms, said to those about him, "Men of Sparta, here is a king born unto us"; this said, he laid him down in the king's place, and named him Charilaus, that is, the joy of the people; because that all were transported with joy and with wonder at his noble and just spirit.

His reign had lasted only eight months, but he was honoured on other accounts by the citizens, and there were more who obeyed him because of his eminent virtues, than because he was regent to the king and had the royal power in his hands. Some, however, envied and sought to impede his growing influence while he was still young; chiefly the kindred and friends of the queen-mother, who pretended to have been dealt with injuriously. Her brother Leonidas, in a warm debate which fell out betwixt him and Lycurgus, went so far as to tell him to his face that he was well assured that ere long he should see him king; suggesting suspicions and preparing the way for an accusation of him, as though he had made away with his nephew, if the child should chance to fail, though by a natural death. Words of the like import were designedly cast abroad by the queen-mother and her adherents.

Troubled at this, and not knowing what it might come to, he thought it his wisest course to avoid their envy by a voluntary exile, and to travel from place to place until his nephew came to marriageable years, and, by having a son, had secured the succession; setting sail, therefore, with this resolution, he first arrived at Crete, where, having considered their several forms of government, and got an acquaintance with the principal men among them, some of their laws he very much approved of, and resolved to make use of them in his own country; a good part he rejected as useless. Among the persons there the most renowned for their learning and their wisdom in state matters was one Thales, whom Lycurgus, by importunities and assurances of friendship, persuaded to go over to Lacedæmon; where, though by his outward appearance and his own profession he seemed to be no other than a lyric poet, in reality he performed the part of one of the ablest lawgivers in the world. The very songs which he composed were exhortations to obedience and concord, and the very measure and cadence of the verse, conveying impressions of order and tranquillity, had so great an influence on the minds of the listeners, that they were insensibly softened and civilised, insomuch that they renounced their private feuds and animosities, and were reunited in a common admiration of virtue. So that it may truly be said that Thales prepared the way for the discipline introduced by Lycurgus.

From Crete he sailed to Asia, with design, as is said, to examine the difference betwixt the manners and rules of life of the Cretans, which were very sober and temperate, and those of the Ionians, a people of sumptuous and delicate habits, and so to form a judgment; just as physicians do by comparing healthy and diseased bodies. Here he had the first sight of Homer's works, in the hands, we may suppose, of the posterity of Creophylus; and, having observed that the few loose expressions and actions of ill example which are to be found in his poems were much outweighed by serious lessons of state and rules of morality, he set himself eagerly to transcribe and digest them into order, as thinking they would be of good use in his own country. They had, indeed, already obtained some slight repute among the Greeks, and scattered portions, as chance conveyed them, were in the hands of individuals; but Lycurgus first made them really known.

The Egyptians say that he took a voyage into Egypt, and that, being much taken with their way of separating the soldiery from the rest of the nation. he transferred it from them to Sparta, a removal from contact with those employed in low and mechanical occupations giving high refinement and beauty to the state. Some Greek writers also record this. But as for his voyages into Spain, Africa and the Indies, and his conferences there with the Gymnosophists, the whole relation, as far as I can find, rests on the single credit of the Spartan Aristocrates, the son of Hipparchus.

Lycurgus was much missed at Sparta, and often sent for, "for kings indeed we have," they said, "who wear the marks and assume the titles of royalty, but as for the qualities of their minds, they have nothing by which they are to be distinguished from their subjects"; adding, that in him alone was the true foundation of sovereignty to be seen, a nature made to rule, and a genius to gain obedience. Nor were the kings themselves averse to see him back, for they looked upon his presence as a bulwark against the insolence of the people.

Things being in this posture as his return, he applied himself, without loss of time, to a thorough reformation, and resolved to change the whole face of the commonwealth; for what could a few particular laws and a partial alteration avail? He must act as wise physicians do, in the case of one who labours under a complication of diseases, by force of medicines reduce and exhaust him, change his whole temperament, and then set him upon a totally new regimen of diet.

Having thus projected things, away he goes to Delphi to consult Apollo there; which having done, and offered his sacrifice, he returned with that renowned oracle, in which he is called beloved of God, and rather God than man; that his prayers were heard, that his laws should be the best, and the commonwealth which observed them the most famous in the world. Encouraged by these things he set himself to bring over to his side the leading men of Sparta, exhorting them to give him a helping hand in his great undertaking; he broke it first to his particular friends, and then by degrees gained others, and animated them all to put his design in execution.

When things were ripe for action, he gave orders to thirty of the principal men of Sparta to be ready armed at the market-place by break of day, to the end that he might strike a terror into the opposite party. Hermippus hath set down the names of twenty of the most eminent of them; but the name of him whom Lycurgus most confided in, and who was of most use to him, both in making his laws and putting them in execution was Arthmiadas. Things growing to a tumult, King Charilaus, apprehending that it was a conspiracy against his person, took sanctuary in the temple of Minerva of the Brazen House; but, being soon after undeceived, and having taken an oath of them that they had no designs against him, he quitted his refuge, and himself also entered into the confederacy with them; of so gentle and flexible a disposition he was, to which Archelaus, his brother-king, alluded, when, hearing him extolled for his goodness, he said, "Who can say he is anything but good? He is so even to the bad."

Amongst the many changes and alterations which Lycurgus made, the first and of greatest importance was the establishment of the senate, which having a power equal to the king's in matters of great consequence, and, as Plato expresses it, allaying and qualifying the fiery genius of the royal office, gave steadiness and safety to the commonwealth. For the state, which before had no firm basis to stand upon, but leaned one while towards an absolute monarchy, when the kings had the upper hand, and another while towards a pure democracy, when the people had the better, found in this establishment of the senate a central weight, like ballast in a ship, which always kept things in a just equilibrium; the twenty-eight always adhering to the kings so far as to resist democracy, and on the other hand, supporting the people against the establishment of absolute monarchy.

As for the determinate number of twenty-eight, Aristotle states, that it so fell out because two of the original associates, for want of course, fell off from the enterprise; but Sphærus assures us that there were but twenty-eight of the confederates at first; perhaps there is some mystery in the number, which consists of seven multiplied by four, and is the first of perfect numbers after six, being, as that is, equal to all its parts. For my part, I believe Lycurgus fixed upon the number of twenty-eight, that, the two kings being reckoned amongst them, they might be thirty in all. So eagerly set was he upon this establishment, that he took the trouble to obtain an oracle about it from Delphi, the Rhetra, which runs thus: "After that you have built a temple to Jupiter Helianius, and to Minerva Hellania, and after that you have *phyle'd* the people into *phyles*, and *obe'd* them into *obes*, you shall establish a council of thirty elders, the leaders included, and shall, from time to time, *apellazein* the people betwixt Babyca and Cnacion, there propound and put to the vote. The commons have the final voice and decision." By *phyles* and *obes* are meant the divisions of the people; by the *leaders,* the two kings; *apellazein,* referring to the Pythian Apollo, signifies to assemble; Babyca and Cnacion they now call Œnus; Aristotle says Cnacion is a river, and Babyca a bridge.

Betwixt this Babyca and Cnacion, their assemblies were held, for they had no councilhouse or building to meet in. Lycurgus was of opinion that ornaments were so far from advantaging them in their counsels, that they were rather an hindrance, by diverting their attention from the business before them to statues and pictures, and roofs curiously fretted, the usual embellishments of such places amongst the other Greeks.

The people then being thus assembled in the open air, it was not allowed to any one of their order to give his advice, but only either to ratify or reject what should be propounded to them by the king or senate. But because it fell out afterwards that the people, by adding or omitting words, distorted and perverted the sense of propositions, Kings Polydorus and Theopompus inserted into the Rhetra, or grand covenant, the following clause: "That if the people decide crookedly it should be lawful for the elders and leaders to dissolve"; that is to say, refuse ratification, and dismiss the people as depravers and perverters of their counsel. It passed among the people, by their management, as being equally authentic with the rest of the Rhetra, as appears by these verses of Tyrtæus, —

> *These oracles they from Apollo heard,*
> *And brought from Pytho home the perfect word:*
> *The heaven-appointed kings, who love the land,*
> *Shall foremost in the nation's council stand;*
> *The elders next to them; the commons last;*
> *Let a straight* Rhetra *among all be passed.*

Although Lycurgus had, in this manner, used all the qualifications possible in the constitution of his commonwealth, yet those who succeeded him found the oligarchical element still too strong and dominant, and to check its high temper and its violence, put, as Plato says, a bit in its mouth, which was the power of the ephori, estblished an hundred and thirty years after the death of Lycurgus. Elatus and his colleagues were the first who had this dignity conferred upon them in the reign of King Theopompus, who, when his queen upbraided him one day that he would leave the regal power to his children less than he had received it from his ancestors, said in answer, "No, greater; for it will last longer." For, indeed, their prerogative being thus reduced within reasonable bounds, the Spartan kings were at once freed from all further jealousies and consequent danger, and never experienced the calamities of their neighbours at Messene and Argos, who, by maintaining their prerogative too strictly, for want of yielding a little to the populace, lost it all.

Indeed, whosoever shall look at the sedition and misgovernment which befell these bordering nations to whom they were as near related in blood as in situation, will find in them the best reason to admire the wisdom and foresight of Lycurgus. For these three states, in their first rise, were equal, or, if there were any odds, they lay on the side of the Messenians and Argives, who, in the first allotment, were thought to have been luckier than the Spartans; yet was their happiness of but small continuance, partly the tyrannical temper of their kings and partly the ungovernableness of the people quickly bringing upon them such disorders, and so complete an overthrow of all existing institutions, as clearly to show how truly divine a blessing the Spartans had had in that wise lawgiver who gave their government its happy balance and temper. But of this I shall say more in its due place.

After the creation of the thirty senators, his next task, and, indeed, the most hazardous he ever undertook, was the making a new division of their lands. For there was an extreme inequality amongst them, and their state was overloaded with a multitude of indigent and necessitous persons, while its whole wealth had centred upon a very few. To the end, therefore, that he might expel from the state arrogance and envy, luxury and crime, and those yet more inveterate diseases of want and superfluity, he obtained of them to renounce their properties, and to consent to a new division of the land, and that they should live all together on an equal footing; merit to be their only road to eminence, and the disgrace of evil, and credit of worthy acts, their one measure of difference between man and man.

Upon their consent to these proposals, proceeding at once to put them into execution, he divided the country of Laconia in general into thirty thousand equal shares, and the part attached to the city of Sparta into nine thousand; these he distributed among the Spartans, as he did the others to the country citizens. Some authors say that he made but six thousand lots for the citizens of Sparta, and that King Polydorus added three thousand more. Others say that Polydorus doubled the number Lycurgus had made, which, according to them, was but four thousand five hundred. A lot was so much as to yield, one year with another, about seventy bushels of grain for the master of the family, and twelve for his wife, with a suitable proportion of oil and wine. And this he thought sufficient to keep their bodies in good health and strength; superfluities they were better without. It is reported, that, as he returned from a journey shortly after the division of the lands, in harvest time, the ground being newly reaped, seeing the stacks all standing equal and alike, he smiled, and said to those about him, "Methinks all Laconia looks like one family estate just divided among a number of brothers."

Not contented with this, he resolved to make a division of their movables too, that there might be no odious distinction or inequality left amongst them; but finding that it would be very dangerous to go about it openly, he took another course, and defeated their avarice by the following stratagem:

he commanded that all gold and silver coin should be called in, and that only a sort of money made of iron should be current, a great weight and quantity of which was very little worth; so that to lay up twenty or thirty pounds there was required a pretty large closet, and, to remove it, nothing less than a yoke of oxen. With the diffusion of this money, at once a number of vices were banished from Lacedæmon; for who would rob another of such a coin? Who would unjustly detain or take by force, or accept as a bribe, a thing which it was not easy to hide, nor a credit to have, nor indeed of any use to cut in pieces? For when it was just red hot, they quenched it in vinegar, and by that means spoilt it, and made it almost incapable of being worked.

In the next place he declared an outlawry of all needless and superfluous arts; but here he might almost have spared his proclamation; for they of themselves would have gone after the gold and silver, the money which remained being not so proper payment for curious work; for, being of iron, it was scarcely portable, neither, if they should take the means to export it, would it pass amongst the other Greeks, who ridiculed it. So there was now no more means of purchasing foreign goods and small wares; merchants sent no shiploads into Laconian ports; no rhetoric-master, no itinerant fortune-teller, no harlot-monger, or gold or silversmith, engraver, or jeweller, set foot in a country which had no money; so that luxury, deprived little by little of that which fed and fomented it, wasted to nothing and died away of itself. For the rich had no advantage here over the poor, as their wealth and abundance had no road to come abroad by but were shut up at home doing nothing. And in this way they became excellent artists in common, necessary things; bedsteads, chairs, and tables, and such like staple utensils in a family, were admirably well made there; their cup, particularly, was very much in fashion, and eagerly bought up by soldiers, as Critias reports; for its colour was such as to prevent water, drunk upon necessity and disagreeable to look at, from being noticed; and the shape of it was such that the mud stuck to the sides, so that only the purer part came to the drinker's mouth. For this, also, they had to thank their lawgiver, who, by relieving the artisans of the trouble of making useless things, set them to show their skill in giving beauty to those of daily and indispensable use.

The third and most masterly stroke of this great lawgiver, by which he struck a yet more effectual blow against luxury and the desire of riches, was the ordinance he made, that they should all eat in common, of the same bread and same meat, and of kinds that were specified, and should not spend their lives at home, laid on costly couches at splendid tables, delivering themselves up into the hands of their tradesmen and cooks, to fatten them in corners, like greedy brutes, and to ruin not their minds only but their bodies which, enfeebled by indulgence and excess, would stand in need of long sleep, warm bathing, freedom from work, and, in a word, of as much care and attendance as if they were continually sick.

It was certainly an extraordinary thing to have brought about such a result as this, but a greater yet to have taken away from wealth, as Theophrastus observes, not merely the property of being coveted, but its very nature of being wealth. For the rich, being obliged to go to the same table with the poor, could not make use of or enjoy their abundance, nor so much as please their vanity by looking at or displaying it. So that the common proverb, that Plutus, the god of riches, is blind, was nowhere in all the world literally verified but in Sparta. There, indeed, he was not only blind, but like a picture, without either life or motion. Nor were they allowed to take food at home first, and then attend the public tables, for every one had an eye upon those who did not eat and drink like the rest, and reproached them with being dainty and effeminate.

This last ordinance in particular exasperated the wealthier men. They collected in a body against Lycurgus, and from ill words came to throwing stones, so that at length he was forced to run out of the market-place, and make to sanctuary to save his life; by good-hap he outran all, excepting one Alcander, a young man otherwise not ill accomplished, but hasty and violent, who came up so close to him, that when he turned to see who was so near him, he struck him upon the face with his stick, and put out one of his eyes. Lycurgus, so far from being daunted and discouraged by this accident, stopped short and showed his disfigured face and eye beat out to his countrymen; they, dismayed and ashamed at the sight, delivered Alcander into his hands to be punished, and escorted him home, with expressions of great concern for his ill-usage.

Lycurgus, having thanked them for their care of his person, dismissed them all, excepting only Alcander; and, taking him with him into his house, neither did nor said anything severely to him, but, dismissing those whose place it was, bade Alcander to wait upon him at table. The young man, who was of an ingenuous temper, without murmuring did as he was commanded; and being thus admitted to live with Lycurgus, he had an opportunity to observe in him, besides his gentleness and calmness of temper, an extraordinary sobriety and an indefatigable industry, and so, from an enemy, became one of his most zealous admirers, and told his friends and relations that Lycurgus was not that morose and ill-natured man they had formerly taken him for, but the one mild and gentle character of the world. And thus did Lycurgus, for chastisement of his fault, make of a wild and passionate young man one of the discreetest citizens of Sparta.

In memory of this accident, Lycurgus built a temple to Minerva, surnamed Optiletis; *optilus* being the Doric of these parts for *ophthalmus*, the eye. Some authors, however, of whom Dioscorides is one (who wrote a treatise on the commonwealth of Sparta), say that he was wounded, indeed, but did not lose his eye with the blow; and that he built the temple in gratitude for the cure. Be this as it will, certain it is, that, after this misadventure, the Lacedæmonians made it a rule never to carry so much as a staff into their public assemblies.

But to return to their public repasts;—these had several names in Greek; the Cretans called them *andria*, because the men only came to them. The Lacedæmonians called them *phiditia*, that is, by changing *l* into *d*, the same as *philitia*, love feasts, because that, by eating and drinking together, they had opportunity of making friends. Or perhaps from *phido*, parsimony, because they were so many schools of sobriety; or perhaps the first letter is an addition, and the word at first was *editia,* from *edode,* eating. They met by companies of fifteen, more or less, and each of them stood bound to bring in monthly a bushel of meal, eight gallons of wine, five pounds of cheese, two pounds and a half of figs, and some very small sum of money to buy flesh or fish with. Besides this, when any of them made sacrifice to the gods, they always sent a dole to the common hall; and, likewise, when any of them had been ahunting, he sent thither a part of the venison he had killed; for these two occasions were the only excuses allowed for supping at home. The custom of eating together was observed strictly for a great while afterwards; insomuch that King Agis himself, after having vanquished the Athenians, sending for his commons at his return home, because he desired to eat privately with his queen, was refused them by the polemarchs; which refusal when he resented so much as to omit next day the sacrifice due for a war happily ended, they made him pay a fine.

They used to send their children to these tables as to schools of temperance; here they were instructed in state affairs by listening to experienced statesmen; here they learned to converse with pleasantry, to make jests without scurrility and take them without ill humour. In this point of good breeding, the Lacedæmonians excelled particularly, but if any man were uneasy under it, upon the least hint given, there was no more to be said to him. It was customary also for the eldest man in the company to say to each of them, as they came in, "Through this" (Pointing to the door), "no words go out."

When any one had a desire to be admitted into any one of these little societies, he was to go through the following probation: each man in the company took a little ball of soft bread, which a waiter carried round upon his head; those that liked the person to be chosen dropped their ball into the basin without altering its figure, and those who disliked him pressed it betwixt their fingers, and made it flat; and this signified as much as a negative vote. And if there were but one of these flattened pieces in the basin, the suitor was rejected, so desirous were they that all the members of the company should be agreeable to each other. The basin was called *caddichus,* and the rejected candidate had a name thence derived. Their most famous dish was the black broth, which was so much valued that the elderly men fed only upon that, leaving what flesh there was to the younger.

They say that a certain king of Pontus, having heard much of this black broth of theirs, sent for a Lacedæmonian cook on purpose to make him some, but had no sooner tasted it than he found it extremely bad, which the cook observing, told him, "Sir, to make this broth relish, you should have bathed yourself first in the river Eurotas."

After drinking moderately, every man went to his home without lights, for the use of them was, on all occasions, forbid, to the end that they might accustom themselves to march boldly in the dark. Such was the common fashion of their meals.

Lycurgus would never reduce his laws into writing; nay, there is a

Rhetra expressly to forbid it. For he thought that the most material points, and such as most directly tended to the public welfare, being imprinted on the hearts of their youth by a good discipline, would be sure to remain, and would find a stronger security, than any compulsion would be, in the principles of action formed in them by their best lawgiver, education. And as for things of lesser importance, as pecuniary contracts, and such like, the forms of which have to be changed as occasion requires, he thought it the best way to prescribe no positive rule or inviolable usage in such cases, willing that their manner and form should be altered according to the circumstances of time, and determinations of men of sound judgment. Every end and object of law and enactment it was his design education should effect.

One, then, of the Rhetras was, that their laws should not be written; another is particularly levelled against luxury and expensiveness, for by it it was ordained that the ceilings of their houses should only be wrought by the axe, and their gates and doors smoothed only by the saw. Epaminondas's famous dictum about his own table, that "Treason and a dinner like this do not keep company together," may be said to have been anticipated by Lycurgus. Luxury and a house of this kind could not well be companions. For a man might have a less than ordinary share of sense that would furnish such plain and common rooms with silver-footed couches and purple coverlets and gold and silver plate. Doubtless he had good reason to think that they would proportion their beds to their houses, and their coverlets to their beds, and the rest of their goods and furniture to these. It is reported that King Leotychides, the first of that name, was so little used to the sight of any other kind of work, that, being entertained at Corinth in a stately room, he was much surprised to see the timber and ceiling so finely carved and panelled, and asked his host whether the trees grew so in his country.

A third ordinance or Rhetra was, that they should not make war often, or long, with the same enemy, lest that they should train and instruct them in war, by habituating them to defend themselves. And this is what Agesilaus was much blamed for, a long time after; it being thought, that, by his continual incursions into Bœtia, he made the Thebans a match for the Lacedæmonians; and therefore Antalcidas, seeing him wounded one day, said to him, that he was very well paid for taking such pains to make the Thebans good soldiers, whether they would or no. These laws were called the Rhetras, to intimate that they were divine sanctions and revelations.

In regard to the good education of their youth (which, as I said before, he thought the most important and noblest work of a lawgiver), he went so far back as to take into consideration their very conception and birth, by regulating their marriages. For Aristotle is wrong in saying, that, after he had tried all ways to reduce the women to more modesty and sobriety, he was at last forced to leave them as they were, because that in the absence of their husbands, who spent the best part of their lives in the wars, their wives, whom they were obliged to leave absolute mistresses at home, took great liberties and assumed the superiority; and were treated with overmuch respect and called by the title of lady or queen. The truth is, he took in their case, also, all the care that was possible; he ordered the maidens to exercise themselves with wrestling, running, throwing the quoit, and casting the dart, to the end that the fruit they conceived might, in strong and healthy bodies, take firmer root and find better growth, and withal that they, with this greater vigour, might be the more able to undergo the pains of child-bearing.

And to the end he might take away their overgreat tenderness and fear of exposure to the air, and all acquired womanishness, he ordered that the young women should go naked in the processions, as well as the young men, and dance, too, in that condition, at certain solemn feasts, singing certain songs, whilst the young men stood around, seeing and hearing them. On these occasions they now and then made, by jests, a befitting reflection upon those who had misbehaved themselves in the wars; and again sang encomiums upon those who had done any gallant action, and by these means inspired the younger sort with an emulation of their glory. Those that were thus commended went away proud, elated, and gratified with their honour among the maidens; and those who were rallied were as sensibly touched with it as if they had been formally reprimanded; and so much the more, because the kings and the elders, as well as the rest of the city, saw and heard all that passed. Nor was there anything shameful in this nakedness of the young women; modesty attended them, and all wantonness was excluded. It taught them simplicity and a care for good health, and gave them some taste of higher feelings, admitted as they thus were to the field of noble action and glory. Hence it was natural for them to think and speak as Gorgo, for example, the wife of Leonidas, is said to have done, when some foreign lady, as it would seem, told her that the women of Lacedæmon were the only women in the world who could rule men; "With good reason," she said, "for we are the only women who bring forth men."

These public processions of the maidens, and their appearing naked in their exercises and dancings, were incitements to marriage, operating upon the young with the rigour and certainty, as Plato says, of love, if not of mathematics. But besides all this, to promote it yet more effectually, those who continued bachelors were in a degree disfranchised by law; for they were excluded from the sight of those public processions in which the young men and maidens danced naked, and, in winter-time, the officers compelled them to march naked themselves round the market-place, singing as they went a certain song to their own disgrace, that they justly suffered this punishment for disobeying the laws. Moreover, they were denied that respect and observance which the younger men paid their elders; and no man, for example, found fault with what was said to Dercyllidas, though so eminent a commander; upon whose approach one day, a young man, instead of rising, retained his seat, remarking, "No child of yours will make room for me."

In their marriages, the husband carried off his bride by a sort of force; nor were their brides ever small and of tender years, but in their full bloom and ripeness. After this, she who superintended the wedding comes and clips the hair of the bride close round her head, dresses her up in man's clothes, and leaves her upon a mattress in the dark; afterwards comes the bridegroom, in his everyday clothes, sober and composed, as having supped at the common table, and, entering privately into the room where the bride lies, unties her virgin zone, and takes her to himself; and, after staying some time together, he returns composedly to his own apartment, to sleep as usual with the other young men.

And so he continues to do, spending his days, and, indeed, his nights, with them, visiting his bride in fear and shame, and with circumspection, when he thought he should not be observed; she, also, on her part, using her wit to help and find favourable opportunities for their meeting, when company was out of the way. In this manner they lived a long time, insomuch that they sometimes had children by their wives before ever they saw their faces by daylight. Their interviews, being thus difficult and rare, served not only for continual exercise of their self-control, but brought them together with their bodies healthy and vigorous, and their affections fresh and lively, unsated and undulled by easy access and long continuance with each other; while their partings were always early enough to leave behind unextinguished in each of them some remaining fire of longing and mutual delight.

After guarding marriage with this modesty and reserve, he was equally careful to banish empty and womanish jealousy. For this object, excluding all licentious disorders, he made it, nevertheless, honourable for men to give the use of their wives to those whom they should think fit, that so they might have children by them; ridiculing those in whose opinion such favours are so unfit for participation as to fight and shed blood and go to war about it. Lycurgus allowed a man who was advanced in years and had a young wife to recommend some virtuous and approved young man, that she might have a child by him, who might inherit the good qualities of the father, and be a son to himself.

On the other side, an honest man who had love for a married woman upon account of her modesty and the well-favouredness of her children, might, without formality, beg her company of her husband, that he might raise, as it were, from this plot of good ground, worthy and well-allied children for themself. And indeed, Lycurgus was of a persuasion that children were not so much the property of their parents as of the whole commonwealth, and, therefore, would not have his citizens begot by the first-comers, but by the best men that could be found; the laws of other nations seemed to him very absurd and inconsistent, where people would be so solicitous for their dogs and horses as to exert interest and to pay money to procure fine breeding, and yet kept their wives shut up, to be made mothers only by themselves, who might be foolish, infirm, or diseased; as if it were not apparent that children of a bad breed would prove their bad qualities first upon those who kept and were rearing them, and well-born children, in like manner, their good qualities.

These regulations, founded on natural and social grounds, were certainly so far from that scandalous liberty which was afterwards charged upon their women, that they knew not what adultery meant. It is told, for instance, of Geradas, a very ancient Spartan, that, being asked by a stranger what punishment their law had appointed for adulterers, he answered, "There are no adulterers in our country." "But," replied the stranger, "suppose there were?" "Then," answered he, "the offender would have to give the plaintiff a bull with a neck so long as that he might drink from the top of Taygetus of the Eurotas river below it." The man, surprised at this, said, "Why, 'tis impossible to find such a bull." Geradas smilingly replied, " 'Tis as possible as to find an adulterer in Sparta." So much I had to say of their marriages.

Nor was it in the power of the father to dispose of the child as he thought fit; he was obliged to carry it before certain triers at a place called Lesche; these were some of the elders of the tribe to which the child belonged; their business it was carefully to view the infant, and, if they found it stout and well made, they gave order for its rearing, and allotted to it one of the nine thousand shares of land above mentioned for its maintenance, but, if they found it puny and ill-shaped, ordered it to be taken to what was called the Apothetæ, a sort of chasm under Taygetus; as thinking it neither for the good of the child itself, nor for the public interest, that it should be brought up, if it did not, from the very outset, appear made to be healthy and vigorous.

Upon the same account, the women did not bathe the new-born children with water, as is the custom in all other countries, but with wine, to prove the temper and complexion of their bodies; from a notion they had that epileptic and weakly children faint and waste away upon their being thus bathed, while, on the contrary, those of a strong and vigorous habit acquire firmness and get a temper by it, like steel.

There was much care and art, too, used by the nurses; they had no swaddling bands; the children grew up free and unconstrained in limb and form, and not dainty and fanciful about their food; not afraid in the dark, or of being left alone; and without peevishness, or ill-humour, or crying. Upon this account, Spartan nurses were often bought up, or hired by people of other countries; and it is recorded that she who suckled Alcibiades was a Spartan; who, however, if fortunate in his nurse, was not so in his preceptor; his guardian, Pericles, as Plato tells us, chose a servant for that office called Zopyrus, no better than any common slave.

Lycurgus was of another mind; he would not have masters bought out of the market for his young Spartans, nor such as should sell their pains; nor was it lawful, indeed, for the father himself to breed up the children after his own fancy; but as soon as they were seven years old they had to be enrolled in certain companies and classes, where they all lived under the same order and discipline, doing their exercises and taking their play together. Of these, he who showed the most conduct and courage was made captain; they had their eyes always upon him, obeyed his orders, and underwent patiently whatsoever punishment he inflicted; so that the whole course of their education was one continued exercise of a ready and perfect obedience. The old men, too, were spectators of their performances, and often raised quarrels and disputes among them, to have a good opportunity of finding out their different characters, and of seeing which would be valiant, which a coward, when they should come to more dangerous encounters. Reading and writing they gave them, just enough to serve their turn; their chief care was to make them good subjects, and to teach them to endure pain and conquer in battle. To this end, as they grew in years, their discipline was proportionately increased; their heads were close-clipped, they were accustomed to go barefoot, and for the most part to play naked.

After they were twelve years old, they were no longer allowed to wear any undergarment; they had one coat to serve them a year; their bodies were hard and dry, with but little acquaintance of baths and unguents; these human indulgences they were allowed only some few particular days in the year. They lodged together in little bands upon beds made of the rushes which grew by the banks of the river Eurotas, which they were to break off with their hands without a knife; if it were winter, they mingled some thistle-down with their rushes, which it was thought had the property of giving warmth. By the time they were come to this age there was not any of the more hopeful boys who had not a lover to bear him company. The old men, too, had an eye upon them, coming often to the grounds to hear and see them contend either in wit or strength with one another, and this as seriously and with as much concern as if they were their fathers, their tutors, or their magistrates; so that there scarcely was any time or place without some one present to put them in mind of their duty, and punish them if they had neglected it.

Besides all this, there was always one of the best and honestest men in the city appointed to undertake the charge and governance of them; he again arranged them into their several bands, and set over each of them for their captain the most temperate and boldest of those they called Irens, who were usually twenty years old, two years out of the boys; and the oldest of the boys, again, were Mell-Irens, as much as to say, who would shortly be men. This young man, therefore, was their captain when they fought and their master at home, using them for the offices of his house; sending the eldest of them to fetch wood, and the weaker and less able to gather salads and herbs, and these they must either go without or steal; which they did by creeping into the gardens, or conveying themselves cunningly and closely into the eating-houses; if they were taken in the act, they were whipped without mercy, for thieving so ill and awkwardly. They stole, too, all other meat they could lay their hands on, looking out and watching all opportunities, when people were asleep or more careless than usual. If they were caught, they were not only punished with whipping, but hunger, too, being reduced to their ordinary allowance, which was but very slender, and so contrived on purpose, that they might set about to help themselves, and be forced to exercise their energy and address.

This was the principal design of their hard fare; there was another not inconsiderable, that they might grow taller; for the vital spirits, not being overburdened and oppressed by too great a quantity of nourishment;

which necessarily discharges itself into thickness and breadth, do, by their natural lightness, rise; and the body, giving and yielding because it is pliant, grows in height. The same thing seems, also, to conduce to beauty of shape; a dry and lean habit is a better subject for nature's configuration, which the gross and over-fed are too heavy to submit to properly. Just as we find that women who take physic whilst they are with child, bear leaner and smaller but better-shaped and prettier children; the material they come of having been pliable and easily moulded. The reason, however, I leave others to determine.

To return from whence we have digressed. So seriously did the Lacedæmonian children go about their stealing, that a youth, having stolen a young fox and hid it under his coat, suffered it to tear out his very bowels with its teeth and claws and died upon the place, rather than let it be seen. What is practised to this very day in Lacedæmon is enough to gain credit to this story, for I myself have seen several of the youths endure whipping to death at the foot of the altar of Diana surnamed Orthia.

The Iren, or under-master, used to stay a little with them after supper, and one of them he bade to sing a song, to another he put a question which required an advised and deliberate answer; for example, Who was the best man in the city? What he thought of such an action of such a man? They used them thus early to pass a right judgment upon persons and things, and to inform themselves of the abilities or defects of their countrymen. If they had not an answer ready to the question, Who was a good or who an ill-reputed citizen, they were looked upon as of a dull and careless disposition, and to have little or no sense of virtue and honour; besides this, they were to give a good reason for what they said, and in as few words and as comprehensive as might be; he that failed of this, or answered not to the purpose, had his thumb bit by the master. Sometimes the Iren did this in the presence of the old men and magistrates, that they might see whether he punished them justly and in due measure or not, and when he did amiss, they would not reprove him before the boys, but, when they were gone, he was called to an account and underwent correction, if he had run far into either of the extremes of indulgence or severity.

Their lovers and favourers, too, had a share in the young boy's honour or disgrace; and there goes a story that one of them was fined by the magistrate, because the lad whom he loved cried out effeminately as he was fighting. And though this sort of love was so approved among them, that the most virtuous matrons would make professions of it to young girls, yet rivalry did not exist, and if several men's fancies met in one person, it was rather the beginning of an intimate friendship, whilst they all jointly conspired to render the object of their affection as accomplished as possible.

They taught them, also, to speak with a natural and graceful raillery, and to comprehend much matter of thought in few words. For Lycurgus, who ordered, as we saw, that a great piece of money should be but of an inconsiderable value, on the contrary would allow no discourse to be current which did not contain in few words a great deal of useful and curious sense; children in Sparta, by a habit of long silence, came to give just and sententious answers; for, indeed, as loose and incontinent livers are seldom fathers of many children, so loose and incontinent talkers seldom originate many sensible words. King Agis, when some Athenian laughed at their short swords, and said that the jugglers on the stage swallowed them with ease, answered him, "We find them long enough to reach our enemies with"; and as their swords were short and sharp, so, it seems to me, were their sayings. They reach the point and arrest the attention of the hearers better than any.

Lycurgus himself seems to have been short and sententious, if we may trust the anecdotes of him; as appears by his answer to one who by all means would set up a democracy in Lacedæmon. "Begin, friend," said he, "and set it up in your family." Another asked him why he allowed of such mean and trivial sacrifices to the gods. He replied, "That we may always have something to offer to them." Being asked what sort of martial exercises or combats he approved of, he answered, "All sorts, except that in which you stretch out your hands." Similar answers, addressed to his countrymen by letter, are ascribed to him; as, being consulted how they might best oppose an invasion of their enemies, he returned this answer, "By continuing poor, and not coveting each man to be greater than his fellow." Being consulted again whether it were requisite to enclose the city with a wall, he sent them word, "The city is well fortified which hath a wall of men instead of brick." But whether these letters are counterfeit or not is not easy to determine.

Of their dislike to talkativeness, the following apophthegms are evidence. King Leonidas said to one who held him in discourse upon some useful matter, but not in due time and place, "Much to the purpose, Sir, elsewhere." King Charilaus, the nephew of Lycurgus, being asked why his uncle had made so few laws, required, "Men of few words require but few laws." When one, named Hecatæus the sophist, because that, being invited to the public table, he had not spoken one word all supper-time, Archidamidas answered in his vindication, "He who knows how to speak, knows also when."

The sharp and yet not ungraceful retorts which I mentioned may be instanced as follows. Demaratus, being asked in a troublesome manner by an importunate fellow, Who was the best man in Lacedæmon?, answered at last, "He, Sir, that is the least like you." Some, in company where Agis was, much extolled the Eleans for their just and honourable management of the Olympic games; "Indeed," said Agis, "they are highly to be commended if they can do justice one day in five years." Theopompus answered a stranger who talked much of his affection to the Lacedæmonians, and said that his countrymen called him Philolacon (a lover of the Lacedæmonians), that it had been more for his honour if they had called him Philopolites (a lover of his own countrymen). And Plistoanax, the son of Pausanias, when an orator of Athens said the Lacedæmonians had no learning, told him, "You say true, Sir; we alone of all the Greeks have learned none of your bad qualities." One asked Archidamidas what number there might be of the Spartans, he answered: "Enough, Sir, to keep out wicked men."

We may see their character, too, in their very jests. For they did not throw them out at random, but the very wit of them was grounded upon something or other worth thinking about. For instance, one, being asked to go hear a man who exactly counterfeited the voice of a nightingale, answered, "Sir, I have heard the nightingale itself." Another, having read the following inscription upon a tomb—

> *Seeking to quench a cruel tyranny,*
> *They, at Selinus, did in battle die,*

said, it served them right; for instead of trying to quench the tyranny, they should have let it burn out. A lad, being offered some game-cocks that would die upon the spot, said that he cared not for cocks that would die, but for such that would live and kill others. Another, seeing people easing themselves on seats, said, "God forbid I should sit where I could not get up to salute my elders." In short, their answers were so sententious and pertinent, that one said well that intellectual much more truly than athletic exercise was the Spartan characteristic.

Nor was their instruction in music and verse less carefully attended to than their habits of grace and good-breeding in conversation. And their very songs had a life and spirit in them that inflamed and possessed men's minds with an enthusiasm and ardour for action; the style of them was plain and without affectation; the subject always serious and moral; most usually, it was in praise of such men as had died in defence of their country, or in derision of those that had been cowards; the former they declared happy and glorified; the life of the latter they described as most miserable and abject. There were also vaunts of what they would do, and boasts of what they had done, varying with the various ages, as, for example, they had three choirs in their solemn festivals, the first of the old men, the second of the young men, and the last of the children; the old men began thus:—

> *We once were young, and brave, and strong;*

the young men answered them, singing:—

> *And we're so now, come on and try;*

the children came last and said:—

> *But we'll be strongest by and by.*

Indeed, if we will take the pains to consider their compositions, some of which were still extant in our days, and the airs on the flute to which they marched when going to battle, we shall find that Terpander and Pindar had reason to say that musing and valour were allied. The first says of Lacedaemon—

> *The spear and song in her do meet,*
> *And Justice walks about her street;*

And Pindar—

> *Councils of wise elders here,*
> *And the young men's conquering spear,*
> *And dance, and song, and joy appear;*

both describing the Spartans as no less musical than warlike; in the words of one of their own poets—

> *With the iron stern and sharp,*
> *Comes the playing on the harp.*

For, indeed, before they engaged in battle, the king first did sacrifice to the Muses, in all likelihood to put them in mind of the manner of their education, and of the judgment that would be passed upon their actions, and thereby to animate them to the performance of exploits that should deserve a record. At such times, too, the Lacedaemonians abated a little the severity of their manners in favour of their young men, suffering them to curl and adorn their hair, and to have costly arms and fine clothes; and were well pleased to see them, like proud horses, neighing and pressing to the course. And, therefore, as soon as they came to be well-grown, they took a great deal of care of their hair, to have it parted and trimmed, especially against a day of battle, pursuant to a saying recorded of their lawgiver, that a large head of hair added beauty to a good face, and terror to an ugly one.

When they were in the field, their exercises were generally more moderate, their fare not so hard, nor so strict a hand held over them by their officers, so that they were the only people in the world to whom war gave a repose. When their army was drawn up in battle array, and the enemy near, the king sacrificed a goat, commanded the soldiers to set their garlands upon their heads, and the pipers to play the tune of the hymn to Castor, and himself began the paean of advance. It was at once a magnificent and a terrible sight to see them march on to the tune of their flutes, without any disorder in their ranks, any discomposure in their minds, or change in their countenances, calmly and cheerfully moving with the music to the deadly fight. Men, in this temper, were not likely to be possessed with fear or any transport of fury, but with the deliberate valour of hope and assurance, as if some divinity were attending and conducting them.

The king had always about his person some one who had been crowned in the Olympic games; and upon this account a Lacedaemonian is said to have refused a considerable present, which was offered to him upon condition that he would not come into the lists; and when he had with much to-do thrown his antagonist, some of the spectators saying to him, "And now, Sir Lacedaemonian, what are you the better for your victory?" he answered, smiling, "I shall fight next the king."

After they had routed an enemy, they pursued him till they were well assured of the victory, and then they sounded a retreat, thinking it base and unworthy of a Grecian people to cut men in pieces, who had given up and abandoned all resistance. This manner of dealing with their enemies did not only show magnanimity, but was politic too; for, knowing that they killed only those who made resistance, and gave quarter to the rest, men generally thought it their best way to consult their safety by flight.

Hippius the sophist says that Lycurgus himself was a great soldier and an experienced commander. Philostephanus attributes to him the first division of the cavalry into troops of fifties in a square body; but Demetrius the Phalerian says quite the contrary, and that he made all his laws in a continued peace. And, indeed, the Olympic holy truce, or cessation of arms, that was procured by his means and management, inclines me to think him a kind-natured man, and one that loved quietness and peace. Notwithstanding all this Hermippus tells us that he had no hand in the ordinance, that Iphitus made it, and Lycurgus came only as a spectator, and that by mere accident too. Being there, he heard as it were a man's voice behind him, blaming and wondering at him that he did not encourage his countrymen to resort to the assembly, and, turning about and seeing no man, concluded that it was a voice from heaven, and upon this immediately went to Iphitus and assisted him in ordering the ceremonies of that feast, which, by his means, were better established, and with more repute than before.

To return to the Lacedæmonians. Their discipline continued still after they were full-grown men. No one was allowed to live after his own fancy; but the city was a sort of camp, in which every man had his share of provisions and business set out, and looked upon himself not so much born to serve his own ends as the interest of his country. Therefore if they were commanded nothing else, they went to see the boys perform their exercises, to teach them something useful or to learn it themselves of those who knew better. And indeed one of the greatest and highest blessings Lycurgus procured his people was the abundance of leisure which proceeded from his forbidding to them the exercise of any mean and mechanical trade. Of the moneymaking that depends on troublesome going about and seeing people and doing business, they had no need at all in a state where wealth obtained no honour or respect. The Helots tilled their ground for them, and paid them yearly in kind the appointed quantity, without any trouble of theirs. To this purpose there goes a story of a Lacedæmonian who, happening to be at Athens when the courts were sitting, was told of a citizen that had been fined for living an idle life, and was being escorted home in much distress of mind by his condoling friends; the Lacedæmonian was much surprised at it and desired his friend to show him the man who was condemned for living like a freeman. So much beneath them did they esteem the frivolous devotion of time and attention to the mechanical arts and to money-making.

It need not be said that upon the prohibition of gold and silver all lawsuits immediately ceased, for there was now neither avarice nor poverty amongst them, but equality, where every one's wants were supplied, and independence, because those wants were so small. All their time, except when they were in the field, was taken up by the choral dances and the festivals, in hunting, and in attendance on the exercise-grounds and the places of public conversation.

Those who were under thirty years of age were not allowed to go into the market-place, but had the necessaries of their family supplied by the care of their relations and lovers; nor was it for the credit of elderly men to be seen too often in the market-place; it was esteemed more suitable for them to frequent the exercise-grounds and places of conversation, where they spent their leisure rationally in conversation, not on money-making and market-prices, but for the most part in passing judgment on some action worth considering; extolling the good, and censuring those who were otherwise, and that in a light and sportive manner, conveying, without too much gravity, lessons of advice and improvement. Nor was Lycurgus himself unduly austere; it was he who dedicated, says Sosibius, the little statue of Laughter. Mirth, introduced seasonably at their suppers and places of common entertainment, was to serve as a sort of sweet-meat to accompany their strict and hard life. To conclude, he bred up his citizens in such a way that they neither would nor could live by themselves; they were to make themselves one with the public good, and, clustering like bees around their commander, be by their zeal and public spirit carried all but out of themselves, and devoted wholly to their country.

What their sentiments were will better appear by a few of their sayings. Pædaretus, not being admitted into the list of the three hundred, returned home with a joyful face, well pleased to find that there were in Sparta three hundred better men than himself. And Polycratidas, being sent with some others ambassador to the lieutenants of the king of Persia, being asked by them whether they came in a private or in a public character, answered, "In a public, if we succeed; if not, in a private character." Argileonis, asking some who came from Amphipolis if her son Brasidas died courageously and as became a Spartan, on their beginning to praise him to a high degree, and saying there was not such another left in Sparta, answered, "Do not say so; Brasidas was a good and brave man, but there are in Sparta many better than he."

The senate, as I said before, consisted of those who were Lycurgus's chief aiders and assistants in his plans. The vacancies he ordered to be supplied out of the best and most deserving men past sixty years old, and we need not wonder if there was much striving for it; for what more glorious competition could there be amongst men, than one in which it was not contested who was swiftest among the swift or strongest of the strong, but who of many wise and good was wisest and best, and fittest to be intrusted for ever after, as the reward of his merits, with the supreme authority of the commonwealth, and with power over the lives, franchises, and highest interests of all his countrymen?

The manner of their election was as follows: The people being called together, some selected persons were locked up in a room near the place of election, so contrived that they could neither see nor be seen, but could only hear the noise of the assembly without; for they decided this, as most other affairs of moment, by the shouts of the people. This done, the competitors were not brought in and presented all together, but one after another by lot, and passed in order through the assembly without speaking a word. Those who were locked up had writing-tables with them, in which they recorded and marked each shout by its loudness, without knowing in favour of which candidate each of them was made, but merely that they came first, second, third, and so forth. He who was found to have the most and loudest acclamations was declared senator duly elected.

Upon this he had a garland set upon his head, and went in procession to all the temples to give thanks to the gods; a great number of young men followed him with applauses, and women, also, singing verses in his honour, and extolling the virtue and happiness of his life. As he went round the city in this manner, each of his relations and friends set a table before him, saying, "The city honours you with this banquet"; but he, instead of accepting, passed round to the common table where he formerly used to eat, and was served as before, excepting that now he had a second allowance, which he took and put by. By the time supper was ended, the women who were of kin to him had come about the door; and he, beckoning to her whom he most esteemed, presented to her the portion he had saved, saying, that it had been a mark of esteem to him, and was so now to her; upon which she was triumphantly waited upon home by the women.

Touching burials, Lycurgus made very wise regulations; for first of all, to cut off all superstition, he allowed them to bury their dead within the city, and even round about their temples, to the end that their youth might be accustomed to such spectacles, and not be afraid to see a dead body, or imagine that to touch a corpse or to tread upon a grave would defile a man. In the next place, he commanded them to put nothing into the ground with them, except, if they pleased, a few olive leaves, and the scarlet cloth that they were wrapped in. He would not suffer the names to be inscribed, except only of men who fell in the wars, or women who died in a sacred office. The time, too, appointed for mourning, was very short, eleven days; on the twelfth, they were to do sacrifice to Ceres, and leave it off; so that we may see, that as he cut off all superfluity, so in things necessary there was nothing so small and trivial which did not express some homage of virtue or scorn of vice.

He filled Lacedæmon all through with proofs and examples of good conduct; with the constant sight of which from their youth up the people would hardly fail to be gradually formed and advanced in virtue. And this was the reason why he forbade them to travel abroad, and go about acquainting themselves with foreign rules of morality, the habits of ill-educated people, and different views of government. Withal he banished from Lacedæmon all strangers who would not give a very good reason for their coming thither; not because he was afraid lest they should inform themselves of and imitate his manner of government (as Thucydides says), or learn anything to their good; but rather lest they should introduce something contrary to good manners. With strange people, strange words must be admitted; these novelties produce novelties in thought; and on these follow views and feelings whose discordant character destroys the harmony of the state. He was as careful to save his city from the infection of foreign bad habits, as men usually are to prevent the introduction of a pestilence.

Hitherto I, for my part, see no sign of injustice or want of equity in the laws of Lycurgus, though some who admit them to be well contrived to make good soldiers, pronounce them defective in point of justice. The Cryptia, perhaps (if it were one of Lycurgus's ordinances, as Aristotle says it was), gave both him and Plato, too, this opinion alike of the lawgiver and his government. By this ordinance, the magistrates despatched privately some of the ablest of the young men into the country, from time to time, armed only with their daggers, and taking a little necessary provision with them; in the daytime, they hid themselves in out-of-the-way places, and there lay close, but in the night issued out into the highways, and killed all the Helots they could light upon; sometimes they set upon them by day, as they were at work in the fields, and murdered them. As, also, Thucydides, in his history of the Peloponnesian war, tells us, that a good number of them, after being singled out for their bravery by the Spartans, garlanded, as enfranchised persons, and led about to all the temples in token of honours, shortly after disappeared all of a sudden, being about the number of two thousand; and no man either then or since could give an account how they came by their deaths. And Aristotle, in particular, adds, that the ephori, so soon as they were entered into their office, used to declare war against them, that they might be massacred without a breach of religion.

It is confessed on all hands, that the Spartans dealt with them very hardly; for it was a common thing to force them in that condition into their public halls, that the children might see what a sight a drunken man is; they made them to dance low dances, and sing ridiculous songs, forbidding them expressly to meddle with any of a better kind. And accordingly, when the Thebans made their invasion into Laconia, and took a great number of the Helots, they could by no means persuade them to sing the verses of Terpander, Alcman, or Spendon, "For," said they, "the masters do not like it." So that it was truly observed by one, that in Sparta he who was free was most so, and he that was a slave there, the greatest slave in the world. For my part, I am of opinion that these outrages and cruelties began to be exercised in Sparta at a later time, especially after the great earthquake, when the Helots made a general insurrection, and, joining with the Messenians, laid the country waste, and brought the greatest danger upon the city. For I cannot persuade myself to ascribe to Lycurgus so wicked and barbarous a course, judging of him from the gentleness of his disposition and justice upon all other occasions; to which the oracle also testified.

When he perceived that his more important institutions had taken root in the minds of his countrymen, that custom had rendered them familiar and easy, that his commonwealth was now grown up and able to go alone, then, as Plato somewhere tells us, the Maker of the world, when first he saw it existing and beginning its motion, felt joy, even so Lycurgus, viewing with joy and satisfaction the greatness and beauty of his political structure, now fairly at work and in motion, conceived the thought to make it immortal too, and, as far as human forecast could reach, to deliver it down unchangeable to posterity. He called an extraordinary assembly of all the people, and told them that he now thought everything reasonably well established, both for the happiness and the virtue of the state; but that there was one thing still behind, of the greatest importance, which he thought not fit to impart until he had consulted the oracle; in the meantime, his desire was that they would observe the laws without any the least alteration until his return, and then he would do as the god should direct him. They all consented readily, and bade him hasten his journey; but, before he departed, he administered an oath to the two kings, the senate, and the whole commons, to abide by and maintain the established form of polity until Lycurgus should be come back.

This done, he set out for Delphi, and, having sacrificed to Apollo, asked him whether the laws he had established were good, and sufficient for a people's happiness and virtue. The oracle answered that the laws were excellent, and that the people, while it observed them, should live in the height of renown. Lycurgus took the oracle in writing, and sent it over to Sparta; and, having sacrificed the second time to Apollo, and taken leave of his friends and his son, he resolved that the Spartans should not be released from the oath they had taken, and that he would, of his own act, close his life where he was.

He was now about that age in which life was still tolerable, and yet might be quitted without regret. Everything, moreover, about him was in a sufficiently prosperous condition. He therefore made an end of himself by a total abstinence from food, thinking it a statesman's duty to make his very death, if possible, an act of service to the state, and even in the end of his life to give some example of virtue and effect some useful purpose. He would, on the one hand, crown and consummate his own happiness by a death suitable to so honourable a life, and on the other hand, would secure to his countrymen the enjoyment of the advantages he had spent his life in obtaining for them, since they had solemnly sworn the maintenance of his institutions until his return.

Nor was he deceived in his expectations, for the city of Lacedæmon continued the chief city of all Greece for the space of five hundred years, in strict observance of Lycurgus's laws; in all which time there was no manner of alteration made, during the reign of fourteen kings down to the time of Agis, the son of Archidamus. For the new creation of the ephori, though thought to be in favour of the people, was so far from diminishing, that it very much heightened, the aristocratical character of the government.

In the time of Agis, gold and silver first flowed into Sparta, and with them all those mischiefs which attend the immoderate desire of riches. Lysander promoted this disorder; for by bringing in rich spoils from the wars, although himself incorrupt, he yet by this means filled his country with avarice and luxury, and subverted the laws and ordinances of Lycurgus; so long as which were in force, the aspect presented by Sparta was rather that of a rule of life followed by one wise and temperate man, than of the political government of a nation. And as the poets feign of Hercules, that, with his lion's skin and his club, he went over the world, punishing lawless and cruel tyrants, so may it be said of the Lacedæmonians, that, with a common staff and a coarse coat, they gained the willing and joyful obedience of Greece, through whose whole extent they suppressed unjust usurpations and despotisms, arbitrated in war, and composed civil dissensions; and this often without so much as taking down one buckler, but barely by sending some one single deputy to whose direction all at once submitted, like bees swarming and taking their places around their prince. Such a fund of order and equity, enough and to spare for others, existed in their state.

And therefore I cannot but wonder at those who say that the Spartans were good subjects, but bad governors, and for proof of it allege a saying of King Theopompus, who when one said that Sparta held up so long because their kings could command so well, replied, "Nay, rather because the people know so well how to obey." For people do not obey, unless rulers know how to command; obedience is a lesson taught by commanders. A true leader himself creates the obedience of his own followers; as it is the last attainment in the art of riding to make a horse gentle and tractable, so it is of the science of government, to inspire men with a willingness to obey. The Lacedæmonians inspired men not with a mere willingness, but with an absolute desire to be their subjects. For they did not send petitions to them for ships or money, or a supply of armed men, but only for a Spartan commander; and, having obtained one, used him with honour and reverence; so the Sicilians behaved to Gylippus, the Chalcidians to Brasidas, and all the Greeks in Asia to Lysander, Callicratidas, and Agesilaus; they styled them the composers and chasteners of each people or prince they were sent to, and had their eyes always fixed upon the city of Sparta itself, as the perfect model of good manners and wise government.

The rest seemed as scholars, they the masters of Greece; and to this Stratonicus pleasantly alluded, when in jest he pretended to make a law that the Athenians should conduct religious processions and the mysteries, the Eleans should preside at the Olympic games, and, if either did amiss, the Lacedæmonians be beaten. Antisthenes, too, one of the scholars of Socrates, said, in earnest, of the Thebans, when they were elated by their victory at Leuctra, that they looked like schoolboys who had beaten their master.

However, it was not the design of Lycurgus that his city should govern a great many others; he thought rather that the happiness of a state, as a private man, consisted chiefly in the exercise of virtue, and in the concord of the inhabitants; his aim, therefore, in all his arrangements, was to make and keep them free-minded, self-dependent, and temperate. And therefore all those who have written well on politics, as Plato, Diogenes, and Zeno, have taken Lycurgus for their model, leaving behind them, however, mere projects and words; whereas Lycurgus was the author, not in writing but in reality, of a government which none else could so much as copy; and while men in general have treated the individual philosophic character as unattainable, he, by the example of a complete philosophic state, raised himself high above all other lawgivers of Greece. And so Aristotle says they did him less honour at Lacedæmon after his death than he deserved, although he has a temple there, and they offer sacrifices yearly to him as to a god.

It is reported that when his bones were brought home to Sparta his tomb was struck with lightning, an accident which befell no eminent person but himself and Euripides, who was buried at Arethusa in Macedonia; and it may serve that poet's admirers as a testimony in his favour, that he had in this the same fate with that holy man and favourite of the gods. Some say Lycurgus died in Cirrha; Apollothemis says, after he had come to Elis; Timæus and Aristoxenus, that he ended his life in Crete; Aristoxenus adds that his tomb is shown by the Cretans in the district of Pergamus, near the strangers' road. He left an only son, Antiorus, on whose death without issue his family became extinct. But his relations and friends kept up an annual commemoration of him down to a long time after; and the days of the meeting were called Lycurgides. Aristocrates, the son of Hipparchus, says that he died in Crete, and that his Cretan friends, in accordance with his own request, when they had burned his body, scattered the ashes into the sea; for fear lest, if his relics should be transported to Lacedæmon, the people might pretend to be released from their oaths, and make innovations in the government. Thus much may suffice for the life and actions of Lycurgus.

The Spirit of Laws

by Charles de Secondat, Baron de Montesquieu

Book XI
Of the Laws Which Establish Political Liberty,
with regard to the Constitution

1. *A general Idea.* I make a distinction between the laws that establish political liberty, as it relates to the constitution, and those by which it is established, as it relates to the citizen. The former shall be the subject of this book; the latter I shall examine in the next.

2. *Different Significations of the word Liberty.* There is no word that admits of more various significations, and has made more varied impressions on the human mind, than that of *liberty*. Some have taken it as a means of deposing a person on whom they had conferred a tyrannical authority; others for the power of choosing a superior whom they are obliged to obey; others for the right of bearing arms, and of being thereby enabled to use violence; others, in fine, for the privilege of being governed by a native of their own country, or by their own laws.[1] A certain nation for a long time thought liberty consisted in the privilege of wearing a long beard.[2] Some have annexed this name to one form of government exclusive of others: those who had a republican state applied it to this species of polity; those who liked a monarchical state gave it to monarchy.[3] Thus they have all applied the name of liberty to the government most suitable to their own customs and inclinations: and as in republics the people have not so constant and so present a view of the causes of their misery, and as the magistrates seem to act only in conformity to the laws, hence liberty is generally said to reside in republics, and to be banished from monarchies. In fine, as in democracies the people seem to act almost as they please, this sort of government has been deemed the most free, and the power of the people has been confounded with their liberty.

3. *In what Liberty consists.* It is true that in democracies the people seem to act as they please; but political liberty does not consist in an un-limited freedom. In governments, that is, in societies directed by laws, liberty can consist only in the power of doing what we ought to will, and in not being constrained to do what we ought not to will.

We must have continually present to our minds the difference between independence and liberty. Liberty is a right of doing whatever the laws per-mit, and if a citizen could do what they forbid he would be no longer pos-sessed of liberty, because all his fellow-citizens would have the same power.

4. *The same Subject continued.* Democratic and aristocratic states are not in their own nature free. Political liberty is to be found only in moderate governments; and even in these it is not always found. It is there only when there is no abuse of power. But constant experience shows us that every man invested with power is apt to abuse it, and to carry his authority as far as it will go. Is it not strange, though true, to say that virtue itself has need of limits?

To prevent this abuse, it is necessary from the very nature of things that power should be a check to power. A government may be so consti-tuted, as no man shall be compelled to do things to which the law does not oblige him, nor forced to abstain from things which the law permits.

5. *Of the End or View of different Governments.* Though all govern-ments have the same general end, which is that of preservation, yet each has another particular object. Increase of dominion was the object of Rome; war, that of Sparta; religion, that of the Jewish laws; commerce, that of Marseilles; public tranquillity, that of the laws of China;[4] navigation, that of the laws of Rhodes; natural liberty, that of the policy of the Savages; in general, the pleasures of the prince, that of despotic states; that of monarch-ies, the prince's and the kingdom's glory; the independence of individuals is the end aimed at by the laws of Poland, thence results the oppression of the whole.[5]

One nation there is also in the world that has for the direct end of its constitution political liberty. We shall presently examine the principles on which this liberty is founded; if they are sound, liberty will appear in its highest perfection.

To discover political liberty in a constitution, no great labour is requisite. If we are capable of seeing it where it exists, it is soon found, and we need not go far in search of it.

6. *Of the Constitution of England.* In every government there are three sorts of power: the legislative; the executive in respect to things dependent on the law of nations; and the executive in regard to matters that depend on the civil law.

By virtue of the first, the prince or magistrate enacts temporary or perpetual laws, and amends or abrogates those that have been already enacted. By the second, he makes peace or war, sends or receives em-bassies, establishes the public security, and provides against invasions. By the third, he punishes criminals, or determines the disputes that arise between individuals. The latter we shall call the judiciary power, and the other simply the executive power of the state.

The political liberty of the subject is a tranquillity of mind arising from the opinion each person has of his safety. In order to have this liberty, it is requisite the government be so constituted as one man need not be afraid of another.

When the legislative and executive powers are united in the same persons, or in the same body of magistrates, there can be no liberty; because apprehensions may arise, lest the same monarch or senate should enact tyrannical laws, to execute them in a tyrannical manner.

Again, there is no liberty, if the judiciary power be not separated from the legislative and executive. Were it joined with the legislative, the life and liberty of the subject would be exposed to arbitrary control; for the judge would be then the legislator. Were it joined to the executive power, the judge might behave with violence and oppression.

There would be an end of everything, were the same man or the same body, whether of the nobles or of the people, to exercise those three powers, that of enacting laws, that of executing the public resolutions, and of trying the causes of individuals.

Most kingdoms in Europe enjoy a moderate government because the prince who is invested with the two first powers leaves the third to his subjects. In Turkey, where these three powers are united in the Sultan's person, the subjects groan under the most dreadful oppression.

In the republics of Italy, where these three powers are united, there is less liberty than in our monarchies. Hence their government is obliged to have recourse to as violent methods for its support as even that of the Turks; witness the state inquisitors,[6] and the lion's mouth into which every informer may at all hours throw his written accusations.

In what a situation must the poor subject be in those republics! The same body of magistrates are possessed, as executors of the laws, of the whole power they have given themselves in quality of legislators. They may plunder the state by their general determinations; and as they have likewise the judiciary power in their hands, every private citizen may be ruined by their particular decisions.

The whole power is here united in one body; and though there is no external pomp that indicates a despotic sway, yet the people feel the effects of it every moment.

Hence it is that many of the princes of Europe, whose aim has been levelled at arbitrary power, have constantly set out with uniting in their own persons all the branches of magistracy, and all the great offices of state.

I allow indeed that the mere hereditary aristocracy of the Italian republics does not exactly answer to the despotic power of the Eastern princes. The number of magistrates sometimes moderates the power of the magistracy; the whole body of the nobles do not always concur in the same design; and different tribunals are erected, that temper each other. Thus at Venice the legislative power is in the *council*, the executive in the *pregadi*, and the judiciary in the *quarantia*. But the mischief is, that these different tribunals are composed of magistrates all belonging to the same body; which constitutes almost one and the same power.

The judiciary power ought not to be given to a standing senate; it should be exercised by persons taken from the body of the people[7] at certain times of the year, and consistently with a form and manner prescribed by law, in order to erect a tribunal that should last only so long as necessity requires.

By this method the judicial power, so terrible to mankind, not being annexed to any particular state or profession, becomes, as it were, invisible. People have not then the judges continually present to their view; they fear the office, but not the magistrate.

In accusations of a deep and criminal nature, it is proper the person accused should have the privilege of choosing, in some measure, his judges, in concurrence with the law; or at least he should have a right to except against so great a number that the remaining part may be deemed his own choice.

The other two powers may be given rather to magistrates or permanent bodies, because they are not exercised on any private subject; one being no more than the general will of the state, and the other the execution of that general will.

But though the tribunals ought not to be fixed, the judgments ought; and to such a degree as to be ever conformable to the letter of the law. Were they to be the private opinion of the judge, people would then live in society, without exactly knowing the nature of their obligations.

The judges ought likewise to be of the same rank as the accused, or, in other words, his peers; to the end that he may not imagine he is fallen into the hands of persons inclined to treat him with rigour.

If the legislature leaves the executive power in possession of a right to imprison those subjects who can give security for their good behaviour, there is an end of liberty; unless they are taken up, in order to answer without delay to a capital crime, in which case they are really free, being subject only to the power of the law.

But should the legislature think itself in danger by some secret conspiracy against the state, or by a correspondence with a foreign enemy, it might authorise the executive power, for a short and limited time, to imprison suspected persons, who in that case would lose their liberty only for a while, to preserve it for ever.

And this is the only reasonable method that can be substituted to the tyrannical magistracy of the Ephori, and to the state inquisitors of Venice, who are also despotic.

As in a country of liberty, every man who is supposed a free agent ought to be his own governor; the legislative power should reside in the whole body of the people. But since this is impossible in large states, and in small ones is subject to many inconveniences, it is fit the people should transact by their representatives what they cannot transact by themselves.

The inhabitants of a particular town are much better acquainted with its wants and interests than with those of other places; and are better judges of the capacity of their neighbors than of that of the rest of their countrymen. The members, therefore, of the legislature should not be chosen from the general body of the nation; but it is proper that in every considerable place a representative should be elected by the inhabitants.

The great advantage of representatives is, their capacity of discussing public affairs. For this the people collectively are extremely unfit, which is one of the chief inconveniences of a democracy.

It is not at all necessary that the representatives who have received a general instruction from their constituents should wait to be directed on each particular affair, as is practised in the diets of Germany. True it is that by this way of proceeding the speeches of the deputies might with greater propriety be called the voice of the nation; but, on the other hand, this would occasion infinite delays; would give each deputy a power of controlling the assembly; and, on the most urgent and pressing occasions, the wheels of government might be stopped by the caprice of a single person.

When the deputies, as Mr. Sidney well observes, represent a body of people, as in Holland, they ought to be accountable to their constituents; but it is a different thing in England, where they are deputed by boroughs.

All the inhabitants of the several districts ought to have a right of voting at the election of a representative, except such as are in so mean a situation as to be deemed to have no will of their own.

One great fault there was in most of the ancient republics, that the people had a right to active resolutions, such as require some execution, a thing of which they are absolutely incapable. They ought to have no share in the government but for the choosing of representatives, which is within their reach. For though few can tell the exact degree of men's capacities, yet there are none but are capable of knowing in general whether the person they choose is better qualified than most of his neighbours.

Neither ought the representative body to be chosen for the executive part of government, for which it is not so fit; but for the enacting of laws, or to see whether the laws in being are duly executed, a thing suited to their abilities, and which none indeed but themselves can properly perform.

In such a state there are always persons distinguished by their birth, riches, or honours: but were they to be confounded with the common people, and to have only the weight of a single vote like the rest, the common liberty would be their slavery, and they would have no interest in supporting it, as most of the popular resolutions would be against them. The share they have, therefore, in the legislature ought to be proportioned to their other advantages in the state; which happens only when they form a body that has a right to check the licentiousness of the people, as the people have a right to oppose any encroachment of theirs.

The legislative power is therefore committed to the body of the nobles, and to that which represents the people, each having their assemblies and deliberations apart, each their separate views and interests.

Of the three powers above mentioned, the judiciary is in some measure next to nothing: there remain, therefore, only two; and as these have need of a regulating power to moderate them, the part of the legislative body composed of the nobility is extremely proper for this purpose.

The body of the nobility ought to be hereditary. In the first place it is so in its own nature; and in the next there must be a considerable interest to preserve its privileges—privileges that in themselves are obnoxious to popular envy, and of course in a free state are always in danger.

But as a hereditary power might be tempted to pursue its own particular interests, and forget those of the people, it is proper that where a singular advantage may be gained by corrupting the nobility, as in the laws relating to the supplies, they should have no other share in the legislation than the power of rejecting, and not that of resolving.

By the *power of resolving* I mean the right of ordaining by their own authority, or of amending what has been ordained by others. By the *power of rejecting* I would be understood to mean the right of annulling a resolution taken by another; which was the power of the tribunes at Rome. And though the person possessed of the privilege of rejecting may likewise have the right of approving, yet this approbation passes for no more than a declaration that he intends to make no use of his privilege of rejecting, and is derived from that very privilege.

The executive power ought to be in the hands of a monarch, because this branch of government, having need of despatch, is better administered by one than by many: on the other hand, whatever depends on the legislative power is oftentimes better regulated by many than by a single person.

But if there were no monarch, and the executive power should be committed to a certain number of persons selected from the legislative body, there would be an end then of liberty; by reason the two powers would be united, as the same persons would sometimes possess, and would be always able to possess, a share in both.

Were the legislative body to be a considerable time without meeting, this would likewise put an end to liberty. For of two things one would naturally follow: either that there would be no longer any legislative resolutions, and then the state would fall into anarchy; or that these resolutions would be taken by the executive power, which would render it absolute.

It would be needless for the legislative body to continue always assembled. This would be troublesome to the representatives, and, moreover, would cut out too much work for the executive power, so as to take off its attention to its office, and oblige it to think only of defending its own prerogatives, and the right it has to execute.

Again, were the legislative body to be always assembled, it might happen to be kept up only by filling the places of the deceased members with new representatives; and in that case, if the legislative body were once corrupted, the evil would be past all remedy. When different legislative bodies succeed one another, the people who have a bad opinion of that which is actually sitting may reasonably entertain some hopes of the next: but were it to be always the same body, the people upon seeing it once corrupted would no longer expect any good from its laws; and of course they would either become desperate or fall into a state of indolence.

The legislative body should not meet of itself. For a body is supposed to have no will but when it is met; and besides, were it not to meet unanimously, it would be impossible to determine which was really the legislative body; the part assembled, or the other. And if it had a right to prorogue itself, it might happen never to be prorogued; which would be extremely dangerous, in case it should ever attempt to encroach on the executive power. Besides, there are seasons, some more proper than others, for assembling the legislative body: it is fit, therefore, that the executive power should regulate the time of meeting, as well as the duration of those assemblies, according to the circumstances and exigencies of a state known to itself.

Were the executive power not to have a right of restraining the encroachments of the legislative body, the latter would become despotic; for as it might arrogate to itself what authority it pleased, it would soon destroy all the other powers.

But it is not proper, on the other hand, that the legislative power should have a right to stay the executive. For as the execution has its natural limits, it is useless to confine it; besides, the executive power is generally employed in momentary operations. The power, therefore, of the Roman tribunes was faulty, as it put a stop not only to the legislation, but likewise to the executive part of government; which was attended with infinite mischief.

But if the legislative power in a free state has no right to stay the executive, it has a right and ought to have the means of examining in what manner its laws have been executed; an advantage which this government has over that of Crete and Sparta, where the Cosmi and the Ephori gave no account of their administration.

But whatever may be the issue of that examination, the legislative body ought not to have a power of arraigning the person, nor, of course, the conduct, of him who is entrusted with the executive power. His person should be sacred, because as it is necessary for the good of the state to prevent the legislative body from rendering themselves arbitrary, the moment he is accused or tried there is an end of liberty.

In this case the state would be no longer a monarchy, but a kind of republic, though not a free government. But as the person entrusted with the executive power cannot abuse it without bad counsellors, and such as have the laws as ministers, though the laws protect them as subjects, these men may be examined and punished—an advantage which this government has over that of Gnidus, where the law allowed of no such thing as calling the Amymones[8] to an account, even after their administration;[9] and therefore the people could never obtain any satisfaction for the injuries done them.

Though, in general, the judiciary power ought not to be united with any part of the legislative, yet this is liable to three exceptions, founded on the particular interest of the party accused.

The great are always obnoxious to popular envy; and were they to be judged by the people, they might be in danger from their judges, and would, moreover, be deprived of the privilege which the meanest subject is possessed of in a free state, of being tried by his peers. The nobility, for this reason, ought not to be cited before the ordinary courts of judicature, but before that part of the legislature which is composed of their own body.

It is possible that the law, which is clearsighted in one sense, and blind in another, might, in some cases, be too severe. But as we have already observed, the national judges are no more than the mouth that pronounces the words of the law, mere passive beings, incapable of moderating either its force or rigour. That part, therefore, of the legislative body, which we have just now observed to be a necessary tribunal on another occasion, is also a necessary tribunal in this; it belongs to its supreme authority to moderate the law in favour of the law itself, by mitigating the sentence.

It might also happen that a subject entrusted with the administration of public affairs may infringe the rights of the people, and be guilty of crimes which the ordinary magistrates either could not or would not punish. But, in general, the legislative power cannot try causes; and much less can it try this particular case, where it represents the party aggrieved, which is the people. It can only, therefore, impeach. But before what court shall it bring its impeachment? Must it go and demean itself before the ordinary tribunals, which are its inferiors, and, being composed, moreover, of men who are chosen from the people as well as itself, will naturally be swayed by the authority of so powerful an accuser? No: in order to preserve the dignity of the people, and the security of the subject, the legislative part which represents the people must bring in its charge before the legislative part which represents the nobility, who have neither the same interests nor the same passions.

Here is an advantage which this government has over most of the ancient republics, where this abuse prevailed, that the people were at the same time both judge and accuser.

The executive power, pursuant of what has been already said, ought to have a share in the legislature by the power of rejecting, otherwise it would soon be stripped of its prerogative. But should the legislative power usurp a share of the executive, the latter would be equally undone.

If the prince were to have a part in the legislature by the power of resolving, liberty would be lost. But as it is necessary he should have a share in the legislature for the support of his own prerogative, this share must consist in the power of rejecting.

The change of government at Rome was owing to this, that neither the senate, who had one part of the executive power, nor the magistrates, who were entrusted with the other, had the right of rejecting, which was entirely lodged in the people.

Here then is the fundamental constitution of the government we are treating of. The legislative body being composed of two parts, they check one another by the mutual privilege of rejecting. They are both restrained by the executive power, as the executive is by the legislative.

These three powers should naturally form a state of repose or inaction. But as there is a necessity for movement in the course of human affairs, they are forced to move, but still in concert.

As the executive power has no other part in the legislative than the privilege of rejecting, it can have no share in the public debates. It is not even necessary that it should propose, because as it may always disapprove of the resolutions that shall be taken, it may likewise reject the decisions on those proposals which were made against its will.

In some ancient commonwealths, where public debates were carried on by the people in a body, it was natural for the executive power to propose and debate in conjunction with the people, otherwise their resolutions must have been attended with a strange confusion.

Were the executive power to determine the raising of public money, otherwise than by giving its consent, liberty would be at an end; because it would become legislative in the most important point of legislation.

If the legislative power was to settle the subsidies, not from year to year, but for ever, it would run the risk of losing its liberty, because the executive power would be no longer dependent; and when once it was possessed of such a perpetual right, it would be a matter of indifference whether it held it of itself or of another. The same may be said if it should come to a resolution of entrusting, not an annual, but a perpetual command of the fleets and armies to the executive power.

To prevent the executive power from being able to oppress, it is requisite that the armies with which it is entrusted should consist of the people, and have the same spirit as the people, as was the case at Rome till the time of Marius. To obtain this end, there are only two ways, either that the persons employed in the army should have sufficient property to answer for their conduct to their fellow-subjects, and be enlisted only for a year, as was customary at Rome: or if there should be a standing army, composed chiefly of the most despicable part of the nation, the legislative power should have a right to disband them as soon as it pleased; the soldiers should live in common with the rest of the people; and no separate camp, barracks, or fortress should be suffered.

When once an army is established, it ought not to depend immediately on the legislative, but on the executive, power; and this from the very nature of the thing, its business consisting more in action than in deliberation.

It is natural for mankind to set a higher value upon courage than timidity, on activity than prudence, on strength than counsel. Hence the army will ever despise a senate, and respect their own officers. They will naturally slight the orders sent them by a body of men whom they look upon as cowards, and therefore unworthy to command them. So that as soon as the troops depend entirely on the legislative body, it becomes a military government; and if the contrary has ever happened, it has been owing to some extraordinary circumstances. It is because the army was always kept divided; it is because it was composed of several bodies that depended each on a particular province; it is because the capital towns were strong places, defended by their natural situation, and not garrisoned with regular troops. Holland, for instance, is still safer than Venice; she might drown or starve the revolted troops; for as they are not quartered in towns capable of furnishing them with necessary subsistence, this subsistence is of course precarious.

In perusing the admirable treatise of Tacitus, *On the Manners of the Germans,* we find it is from that nation the English have borrowed the idea of their political government. This beautiful system was invented first in the woods.

As all human things have an end, the state we are speaking of will lose its liberty, will perish. Have not Rome, Sparta, and Carthage perished? It will perish when the legislative power shall be more corrupt than the executive.

It is not my business to examine whether the English actually enjoy this liberty or not. Sufficient it is for my purpose to observe that it is established by their laws; and I inquire no further.

Neither do I pretend by this to undervalue other governments, nor to say that this extreme political liberty ought to give uneasiness to those who have only a moderate share of it. How should I have any such design, I who think that even the highest refinement of reason is not always desirable, and that mankind generally find their account better in mediums than in extremes?

Harrington, in his *Oceana,* has also inquired into the utmost degree of liberty to which the constitution of a state may be carried. But of him indeed it may be said that for want of knowing the nature of real liberty he busied himself in pursuit of an imaginary one; and that he built a Chalcedon, though he had a Byzantium before his eyes.

---

[1] "I have copied," says Cicero, "Scævola's edict, which permits the Greeks to terminate their difference among themselves according to their own laws; this makes them consider themselves a free people."

[2] The Russians could not bear that Czar Peter shuld make them cut it off.

[3] The Cappadocians refused the condition of a republican state, which was offered them by the Romans.

[4] The natural end of a state that has no foreign enemies, or that thinks itself secured against them by barriers.

[5] Inconvenience of the *Liberum veto.*

[6] At Venice.

[7] As at Athens.

[8] These were magistrates chosen annually by the people. See Stephen of Byzantium.

[9] It was lawful to accuse the Roman magistrates after the expiration of their several offices.

First Week — Fourth Day

Han Fei Tzu, *Basic Writings* (selection)

Niccolo Machiavelli, *The Prince*,
Chapters 14-18, 25

Thomas Hobbes, *Leviathan*,
Chapters 13-14, 15 (selection)

John Locke,
Concerning Civil Government, Chapter VIII

Basic Writings

by Han Fei Tzu

The Way of the Ruler

THE Way is the beginning of all beings and the measure of right and wrong. Therefore the unenlightened ruler holds fast to the beginning in order to understand the wellspring of all beings, and minds the measure in order to know the source of good and bad. He waits, empty and still, letting names define themselves and affairs reach their own settlement. Being empty, he can comprehend the true aspect of fullness; being still, he can correct the mover. Those whose duty it is to speak will come forward to name themselves; those whose duty it is to act will produce results. When names and results match, the ruler need do nothing more and the true aspect of all things will be revealed.

Hence it is said: The ruler must not reveal his desires; for if he reveals his desires his ministers will put on the mask that pleases him. He must not reveal his will; for if he does so his ministers will show a different face. So it is said: Discard likes and dislikes and the ministers will show their true form; discard wisdom and wile and the ministers will watch their step. Hence, though the ruler is wise, he hatches no schemes from his wisdom, but causes all men to know their place. Though he has worth, he does not display it in his deeds, but observes the motives of his ministers. Though he is brave, he does not flaunt his bravery in shows of indignation, but allows his subordinates to display their valor to the full. Thus, though he discards wisdom, his rule is enlightened; though he discards worth, he achieves merit; and though he discards bravery, his state grows powerful. When the ministers stick to their posts, the hundred officials have their regular duties, and the ruler employs each according to his particular ability, this is known as the state of manifold constancy.

Hence it is said: "So still he seems to dwell nowhere at all; so empty no one can seek him out." The enlightened ruler reposes in nonaction above, and below his ministers tremble with fear.

This is the way of the enlightened ruler: he causes the wise to bring forth all their schemes, and he decides his affairs accordingly; hence his own wisdom is never exhausted. He causes the worthy to display their talents, and he employs them accordingly; hence his own worth never comes to an end. Where there are accomplishments, the ruler takes credit for their worth; where there are errors, the ministers are held responsible for the blame; hence the ruler's name never suffers. Thus, though the ruler is not worthy himself, he is the leader of the worthy; though he is not wise himself, he is the corrector of the wise. The ministers have the labor; the ruler enjoys the success. This is called the maxim of the worthy ruler. . . .

The ruler of men stands in danger of being blocked in five ways. When the ministers shut out their ruler, this is one kind of block. When they get control of the wealth and resources of the state, this is a second kind of block. When they are free to issue orders as they please, this is a third kind. When they are able to do righteous deeds in their own name, this is a fourth kind. When they are able to build up their own cliques, this is a fifth kind. If the ministers shut out the ruler, then he loses the effectiveness of his position. If they control wealth and resources, he loses the means of dispensing bounty to others. If they issue orders as they please, he loses the means of command. If they are able to carry out righteous deeds in their own name, he loses his claim to enlightenment. And if they can build up cliques of their own, he loses his supporters. All these are rights that should be exercised by the ruler alone; they should never pass into the hands of his ministers.

The way of the ruler of men is to treasure stillness and reserve. Without handling affairs himself, he can recognize clumsiness or skill in others; without laying plans of his own, he knows what will bring fortune or misfortune. Hence he need speak no word, but good answers will be given him; he need exact no promises, but good works will increase. When proposals have been brought before him, he takes careful note of their content; when undertakings are well on their way, he takes careful note of the result; and from the degree to which proposals and results tally, rewards and punishments are born. Thus the ruler assigns undertakings to his various ministers on the basis of the words they speak, and assesses their accomplishments according to the way they have carried out the undertaking. When accomplishments match the undertaking, and the undertaking matches what was said about it, then he rewards the man; when these things do not match, he punishes the man. It is the way of the enlightened ruler never to allow his ministers to speak words that cannot be matched by results.

The enlightened ruler in bestowing rewards is as benign as the seasonable rain; the dew of his bounty profits all men. But in doling out punishment he is as terrible as the thunder; even the holy sages cannot assuage him. The enlightened ruler is never overliberal in his rewards, never overlenient in his punishments. If his rewards are too liberal, then ministers who have won merit in the past will grow lax in their duties; and if his punishments are too lenient, then evil ministers will find it easy to do wrong. Thus if a man has truly won merit, no matter how humble and far removed he may be, he must be rewarded; and if he has truly committed error, no matter how close and dear to the ruler he may be, he must be punished. If those who are humble and far removed can be sure of reward, and those close and dear to the ruler can be sure of punishment, then the former will not stint in their efforts and the latter will not grow proud. . . .

Eminence in Learning

When the scholars of today discuss good government, many of them say, "Give land to the poor and destitute so that those who have no means of livelihood may be provided for." Now if men start out with equal opportunities and yet there are a few who, without the help of unusually good harvests or outside income, are able to keep themselves well supplied, it must be due either to hard work or to frugal living. If men start out with equal opportunities and yet there are a few who, without having suffered from some calamity like famine or sickness, still sink into poverty and destitution, it must be due either to laziness or to extravagant living. The lazy and extravagant grow poor; the diligent and frugal get rich. Now if the ruler levies money from the rich in order to give alms to the poor, he is robbing the diligent and frugal and indulging the lazy and extravagant. If he expects by such means to induce the people to work industriously and spend with caution, he will be disappointed.

Now suppose there is a man who on principle refuses to enter a city that is in danger, to take part in a military campaign, or in fact to change so much as a hair of his shin, though it might bring the greatest benefit to the world.[1] The rulers of the time are sure to honor him, admiring his wisdom, praising his conduct, and regarding him as a man who despises material things and values his life. Now the ruler hands out good fields and large houses and offers titles and stipends in order to encourage the people to risk their lives in his service. But if he honors and praises a man who despises material things and values life above everything else, and at the same time expects the people to risk their lives and serve him to the death, he will be disapointed.

Then there are other men who collect books, study rhetoric, gather bands of disciples, and devote themselves to literature, learning, and debate. The rulers of the time are sure to treat them with respect, saying, "It is the way of the former kings to honor worthy men." The farmers are the ones who must pay taxes to the officials, and yet the ruler patronizes scholars—thus the farmer's taxes grow heavier and heavier, while the scholars enjoy increasing reward. If the ruler hopes, in spite of this, that the people will work industriously and spend little time talking, he will be disappointed. . . .

When a sage rules the state, he does not depend on people's doing good of themselves; he sees to it that they are not allowed to do what is bad. If he depends on people's doing good of themselves, then within his borders he can count less than ten instances of success. But if he sees to it that they are not allowed to do what is bad, then the whole state can be brought to a uniform level of order. Those who rule must employ measures that will be effective with the majority and discard those that will be effective with only a few. Therefore they devote themselves not to virtue but to law.

If you depend on arrow shafts' becoming straight of themselves, you will never produce one arrow in a hundred generations. If you depend on pieces of wood's becoming round of themselves, you will never get a cart-wheel in a thousand years. If in a hundred generations you never find such a thing as an arrow shaft that makes itself straight or a piece of wood that makes itself round, then how is it that people all manage to ride around in carriages and shoot down birds? Because the tools of straightening and bending are used. And even if, without the application of such tools, there were an arrow shaft that made itself straight or a piece of wood that made itself round, a good craftsman would not prize it. Why? Because it is not only one man who wants to ride, and not just one shot that the archer wants to make. And even if, without depending upon rewards and punishments, there were a man who became good of himself, the enlightened ruler would not prize him. Why? Because the laws of the state must not be ignored, and it is more than one man who must be governed. Therefore a ruler who understands policy does not pursue fortuitous goodness, but follows the way of certain success. . . .

---

[1] A reference to the followers of Yang Chu. Cf. *Mencius* VIIA, 26: "Mencius said, 'The principle of Yang Tzu was "each one for himself." Though he might have benefited the whole world by plucking out a single hair, he would not have done it.' "

The Prince

by Niccolo Machiavelli

The Duties of a Prince with Regard to the Militia

A PRINCE should therefore have no other aim or thought, nor take up any other thing for his study, but war and its organisation and discipline, for that is the only art that is necessary to one who commands, and it is of such virtue that it not only maintains those who are born princes, but often enables men of private fortune to attain to that rank. And one sees, on the other hand, that when princes think more of luxury than of arms, they lose their state. The chief cause of the loss of states, is the contempt of this art, and the way to acquire them is to be well versed in the same.

Francesco Sforza, through being well armed, became, from private status, Duke of Milan; his sons, through wishing to avoid the fatigue and hardships of war, from dukes became private persons. For among other evils caused by being disarmed, it renders you contemptible; which is one of those disgraceful things which a prince must guard against, as will be explained later. Because there is no comparison whatever between an armed and a disarmed man; it is not reasonable to suppose that one who is armed will obey willingly one who is unarmed; or that any unarmed man will remain safe among armed servants. For one being disdainful and the other suspicious, it is not possible for them to act well together. And therefore a prince who is ignorant of military matters, besides the other misfortunes already mentioned, cannot be esteemed by his soldiers, nor have confidence in them.

He ought, therefore, never to let his thoughts stray from the exercise of war; and in peace he ought to practise it more than in war, which he can do in two ways: by action and by study. As to action, he must,

155

besides keeping his men well disciplined and exercised, engage continually in hunting, and thus accustom his body to hardships; and meanwhile learn the nature of the land, how steep the mountains are, how the valleys debouch, where the plains lie, and understand the nature of rivers and swamps. To all this he should devote great attention. This knowledge is useful in two ways. In the first place, one learns to know one's country, and can the better see how to defend it. Then by means of the knowledge and experience gained in one locality, one can easily understand any other that it may be necessary to observe; for the hills and valleys, plains and rivers of Tuscany, for instance, have a certain resemblance to those of other provinces, so that from a knowledge of the country in one province one can easily arrive at a knowledge of others. And that prince who is lacking in this skill is wanting in the first essentials of a leader; for it is this which teaches how to find the enemy, take up quarters, lead armies, plan battles and lay siege to towns with advantage.

Philopœmen, prince of the Achaei, among other praises bestowed on him by writers, is lauded because in times of peace he thought of nothing but the methods of warfare, and when he was in the country with his friends, he often stopped and asked them: If the enemy were on that hill and we found ourselves here with our army, which of us would have the advantage; How could we safely approach him maintaining our order? If we wished to retire, what ought we to do? If they retired, how should we follow them? And he put before them as they went along all the contingencies that might happen to any army, heard their opinion, gave his own, fortifying it by argument; so that thanks to these constant reflections there could never happen any incident when actually leading his armies for which he was not prepared.

But as to exercise for the mind, the prince ought to read history and study the actions of eminent men, see how they acted in warfare, examine the causes of their victories and defeats in order to imitate the former and avoid the latter, and above all, do as some men have done in the past, who have imitated some one, who has been much praised and glorified, and have always kept his deeds and actions before them, as they say Alexander the Great imitated Achilles, Cæsar Alexander, and Scipio Cyrus. And whoever reads the life of Cyrus written by Xenophon, will perceive in the life of Scipio how gloriously he imitated the former, and how, in chastity, affability, humanity, and liberality Scipio conformed to those qualities of Cyrus as described by Xenophon.

A wise prince should follow similar methods and never remain idle in peaceful times, but industriously make good use of them, so that when fortune changes she may find him prepared to resist her blows, and to prevail in adversity.

15
Of the Things for Which Men, and Especially Princes, Are Praised or Blamed

It now remains to be seen what are the methods and rules for a prince as regards his subjects and friends. And as I know that many have written of this, I fear that my writing about it may be deemed presumptuous, differing as I do, especially in this matter, from the opinions of others. But my intention being to write something of use to those who understand, it appears to me more proper to go to the real truth of the matter than to its imagination; and many have imagined republics and principalities which have never been seen or known to exist in reality; for how we live is so far removed from how we ought to live, that he who abandons what is done for what ought to be done, will rather learn to bring about his own ruin than his preservation. A man who wishes to make a profession of goodness in everything must necessarily come to grief among so many who are not good. Therefore it is necessary for a prince, who wishes to maintain himself, to learn how not to be good, and to use this knowledge and not use it, according to the necessity of the case.

Leaving on one side, then, those things which concern only an imaginary prince, and speaking of those that are real, I state that all men, and especially princes, who are placed at a greater height, are reputed for certain qualities which bring them either praise or blame. Thus one is considered liberal, another *misero* or miserly (using a Tuscan term, seeing that *avaro* with us still means one who is rapaciously acquisitive and *misero* one who makes grudging use of his own); one a free giver, another rapacious; one cruel, another merciful; one a breaker of his word, another trustworthy; one effeminate and pusillanimous, another fierce and high-spirited; one humane, another haughty; one lascivious, another chaste; one frank, another astute; one hard, another easy; one serious, another frivolous; one religious, another an unbeliever, and so on. I know that every one will admit that it would be highly praiseworthy in a prince to possess all the above-named qualities that are reputed good, but as they cannot all be possessed or observed, human conditions not permitting of it, it is necessary that he should be prudent enough to avoid the scandal of those vices which would lose him the state, and guard himself if possible against those which will not lose it him, but if not able to, he can indulge them with less scruple. And yet he must not mind incurring the scandal of those vices, without which it would be difficult to save the state, for if one considers well, it will be found that some things which seem virtues would, if followed, lead to one's ruin, and some others which appear vices result in one's greater security and well being.

16
Of Liberality and Niggardliness

Beginning now with the first qualities above named, I say that it would be well to be considered liberal; nevertheless liberality such as the world understands it will injure you, because if used virtuously and in the proper way, it will not be known, and you will incur the disgrace of the contrary vice. But one who wishes to obtain the reputation of liberality among men, must not omit every kind of sumptuous display, and to such an extent that a prince of this character will consume by such means all his resources, and will be at last compelled, if he wishes to maintain his name for liberality, to impose heavy taxes on his people, become extortionate, and do everything possible to obtain money. This will make his subjects begin to hate him, and he will be little esteemed being poor, so that having by this liberality injured many and benefited but few, he will feel the first little disturbance and be endangered by every peril. If he recognizes this and wishes to change his system, he incurs at once the charge of niggardliness.

A prince, therefore, not being able to exercise this virtue of liberality without risk if it be known, must not, if he be prudent, object to be called miserly. In course of time he will be thought more liberal, when it is seen that by his parsimony his revenue is sufficient, that he can defend himself against those who make war on him, and undertake enterprises without burdening his people, so that he is really liberal to all those from whom he does not take, who are infinite in number, and niggardly to all to whom he does not give, who are few. In our times we have seen nothing great done except by those who have been esteemed niggardly; the others have all been ruined. Pope Julius II, although he had made use of a reputation for liberality in order to attain the papacy, did not seek to retain it afterwards, so that he might be able to wage war. The present King of France has carried on so many wars without imposing an extraordinary tax, because his extra expenses were covered by the parsimony he had so long practised. The present King of Spain, if he had been thought liberal, would not have engaged in and been successful in so many enterprises.

For these reasons a prince must care little for the reputation of being a miser, if he wishes to avoid robbing his subjects, if he wishes to be able to defend himself, to avoid becoming poor and contemptible, and not to be forced to become rapacious; this niggardliness is one of those vices which enable him to reign. If it is said that Caesar attained the empire through liberality, and that many others have reached the highest positions through being liberal or being thought so, I would reply that you are either a prince already or else on the way to become one. In the first case, this liberality is harmful; in the second, it is certainly necessary to be considered liberal. Cæsar was one of those who wished to attain the mastery over Rome, but if after attaining it he had lived and had not moderated his expenses, he would have destroyed that empire. And should any one reply that there have been many princes, who have done great things with their armies, who have been thought extremely liberal, I would answer by saying that the prince may either spend his own wealth and that of his subjects or the wealth of others. In the first case he must be sparing, but for the rest he must not neglect to be very liberal. The liberality is very necessary to a prince who marches with his armies, and lives by plunder, sack and ransom, and is dealing with the wealth of others, for without it he would not be followed by his soldiers. And you may be very generous indeed with what is not the property of yourself or your subjects, as were Cyrus, Cæsar, and Alexander; for spending the wealth of others will not diminish your reputation, but increase it, only spending your own resources will injure you. There is nothing which destroys itself so much as liberality, for by using it you lose the power of using it, and become either poor and despicable, or, to escape poverty, rapacious and hated. And of all things that a prince must guard against, the most important are being despicable or hated, and liberality will lead you to one or the other of these conditions. It is, therefore, wiser to have the name of miser, which produces disgrace without hatred, than to incur of necessity the name of being rapacious, which produces both disgrace and hatred.

17
Of Cruelty and Clemency, and Whether It Is Better to Be Loved or Feared

Proceeding to the other qualities before named, I say that every prince must desire to be considered merciful and not cruel. He must, however, take care not to misuse this mercifulness. Cesare Borgia was considered cruel, but his cruelty had brought order to the Romagna, united it, and reduced it to peace and fealty. If this is considered well, it will be seen that he was really much more merciful than the Florentine people, who, to avoid the name of cruelty, allowed Pistoia to be destroyed. A prince, therefore, must not mind incurring the charge of cruelty for the purpose of keeping his subjects united and faithful; for, with a very few examples, he will be more merciful than those who, from excess of tenderness, allow disorders to arise, from whence spring bloodshed and rapine; for these as a rule injure the whole community, while the executions carried out by the prince injure only individuals. And of all princes, it is impossible for a new prince to escape the reputation of cruelty, new states being always full of dangers. Wherefore Virgil through the mouth of Dido says:

> *Res dura, et regni novitas me talia cogunt*
> *Moliri, et late fines custode tueri.*

Nevertheless, he must be cautious in believing and acting, and must not be afraid of his own shadow, and must proceed in a temperate manner with prudence and humanity, so that too much confidence does not render him incautious, and too much diffidence does not render him intolerant.

From this arises the question whether it is better to be loved more than feared, or feared more than loved. The reply is, that one ought to be both feared and loved, but as it is difficult for the two to go together, it is much safer to be feared than loved, if one of the two has to be wanting. For it may be said of men in general that they are ungrateful, voluble, dissemblers, anxious to avoid danger, and covetous of gain; as long as you benefit them, they are entirely yours; they offer you their blood, their goods, their life, and their children, as I have before said, when the necessity is remote; but when it approaches, they revolt. And the prince who has relied solely on their words, without making other preparations, is ruined; for the friendship which is gained by purchase and not through grandeur and nobility of spirit is bought but not secured, and at a pinch is not to be expended in your service. And men have less scruple in offending one who makes himself loved than one who makes himself feared; for love is held by a chain of obligation which, men being selfish, is broken whenever it serves their purpose; but fear is maintained by a dread of punishment which never fails.

Still, a prince should make himself feared in such a way that if he does not gain love, he at any rate avoids hatred; for fear and the absence of hatred may well go together, and will be always attained by one who abstains from interfering with the property of his citizens and subjects or with their women. And when he is obliged to take the life of any one, let him do so when there is a proper justification and manifest reason for it; but above all he must abstain from taking the property of others, for men forget more easily the death of their father than the loss of their patrimony. Then also pretexts for seizing property are never wanting, and one who begins to live by rapine will always find some reason for taking the goods of others, whereas causes for taking life are rarer and more fleeting.

But when the prince is with his army and has a large number of soldiers under his control, then it is extremely necessary that he should not mind being thought cruel; for without this reputation he could not keep any army united or disposed to any duty. Among the noteworthy actions of Hannibal is numbered this, that although he had an enormous army, composed of men of all nations and fighting in foreign countries, there never arose any dissension either among them or against the prince, either in good fortune or in bad. This could not be due to anything but his inhuman cruelty, which together with his infinite other virtues, made him always venerated and terrible in the sight of his soldiers, and without it his other virtues would not have sufficed to produce that effect. Thoughtless writers admire on the one hand his actions, and on the other blame the principal cause of them.

And that it is true that his other virtues would not have sufficed may be seen from the case of Scipio (famous not only in regard to his own times, but all times of which memory remains), whose armies rebelled against him in Spain, which arose from nothing but his excessive kindness, which allowed more licence to the soldiers than was consonant with military discipline. He was reproached with this in the senate by Fabius Maximus, who called him a corrupter of the Roman militia. Locri having been destroyed by one of Scipio's officers was not revenged by him, nor was the insolence of that officer punished, simply by reason of his easy nature; so much so, that some one wishing to excuse him in the senate said that there were many men who knew rather how not to err, than how to correct the errors of others. This disposition would in time have tarnished the fame and glory of Scipio had he persevered in it under the empire, but living under the rule of the senate this harmful quality was not only concealed but became a glory to him.

I conclude, therefore, with regard to being feared and loved, that men love at their own free will, but fear at the will of the prince, and that a wise prince must rely on what is in his power and not on what is in the power of others, and he must only contrive to avoid incurring hatred, as has been explained.

18
In What Way Princes Must Keep Faith

How laudable it is for a prince to keep good faith and live with integrity, and not with astuteness, every one knows. Still the experience of our times shows those princes to have done great things who have had little regard for good faith, and have been able by astuteness to confuse men's brains, and who have ultimately overcome those who have made loyalty their foundation.

You must know, then, that there are two methods of fighting, the one by law, the other by force: the first method is that of men, the second of beasts; but as the first method is often insufficient, one must have recourse to the second. It is therefore necessary for a prince to know well how to use both the beast and the man. This was covertly taught to rulers by ancient writers, who relate how Achilles and many others of those ancient princes were given to Chiron the centaur to be brought up and educated under his discipline. The parable of this semi-animal, semi-human teacher is meant to indicate that a prince must know how to use both natures, and that the one without the other is not durable.

A prince being thus obliged to know well how to act as a beast must imitate the fox and the lion, for the lion cannot protect himself from traps, and the fox cannot defend himself from wolves. One must therefore be a fox to recognize traps, and a lion to frighten wolves. Those that wish to be only lions do not understand this. Therefore, a prudent ruler ought not to keep faith when by so doing it would be against his interest, and when the reasons which made him bind himself no longer exist. If men were all good, this precept would not be a good one; but as they are bad, and would not observe their faith with you, so you are not bound to keep faith with them. Nor have legitimate grounds ever failed a prince who wished to show colourable excuse for the non-fulfilment of his promise. Of this one could furnish an infinite number of modern examples, and show how many times peace has been broken, and how many promises rendered worthless, by the faithlessness of princes, and those that have been best able to imitate the fox have succeeded the best. But it is necessary to be able to disguise this character well, and to be a great feigner and dissembler; and men are so simple and so ready to obey present necessities, that one who deceives will always find those who allow themselves to be deceived.

I will only mention one modern instance. Alexander VI did nothing else but deceive men, he thought of nothing else, and found the occasion for it; no man was ever more able to give assurances, or affirmed things with stronger oaths, and no man observed them less; however, he always succeeded in his deceptions, as he well knew this aspect of things.

It is not, therefore, necessary for a prince to have all the above-named qualities, but it is very necessary to seem to have them. I would even be bold to say that to possess them and always to observe them is dangerous, but to appear to possess them is useful. Thus it is well to seem merciful, faithful, humane, sincere, religious, and also to be so; but you must have the mind so disposed that when it is needful to be otherwise you may be able to change to the opposite qualities. And it must be understood that a prince, and especially a new prince, cannot observe all those things which are considered good in men, being often obliged in order to maintain the state, to act against faith, against charity, against humanity, and against religion. And, therefore, he must have a mind disposed to adapt itself according to the wind, and as the variations of fortune dictate, and, as I said before, not deviate from what is good, if possible, but be able to do ēvil if constrained.

A prince must take great care that nothing goes out of his mouth which is not full of the above-named five qualities, and, to see and hear him, he should seem to be all mercy, faith, integrity, humanity, and religion. And nothing is more necessary than to seem to have this last quality, for men in general judge more by the eyes than by the hands, for every one can see, but very few have to feel. Everybody sees what you appear to be, few feel what you are, and those few will not dare to oppose themselves to the many, who have the majesty of the state to defend them; and in the actions of men, and especially of princes, from which there is no appeal, the end justifies the means. Let a prince therefore aim at conquering and maintaining the state, and the means will always be judged honourable and praised by every one, for the vulgar is always taken by appearances and the issue of the event; and the world consists only of the vulgar, and the few who are not vulgar are isolated when the many have a rallying point in the prince. A certain prince of the present time, whom it is well not to name, never does anything but preach peace and good faith, but he is really a great enemy to both, and either of them, had he observed them, would have lost him state or reputation on many occasions.

25
How Much Fortune Can Do in
Human Affairs and How It May Be Opposed

It is not unknown to me how many have been and are of opinion that worldly events are so governed by fortune and by God, that men cannot by their prudence change them, and that on the contrary there is no remedy whatever, and for this they may judge it to be useless to toil much about them, but let things be ruled by chance. This opinion has been more held in our day, from the great changes that have been seen, and are daily seen, beyond every human conjecture. When I think about them, at times I am partly inclined to share this opinion. Nevertheless, that our free will may not be altogether extinguished, I think it may be true that fortune is the ruler of half our actions, but that she allows the other half or thereabouts to be governed by us. I would compare her to an impetuous river that, when turbulent, inundates the plains, casts down trees and buildings, removes earth from this side and places it on the other; every one flees before it, and everything yields to its fury without being able to oppose it; and yet though it is of such a kind, still when it is quiet, men can make provisions against it by dykes and banks, so that when it rises it will either go into a canal or its rush will not be so wild and angerous. So it is with fortune, which shows her power where no measures have been taken to resist her, and directs her fury where she knows that no dykes or barriers have been made to hold her. And if you regard Italy, which has been the seat of these changes, and which has given the impulse to them, you will see her to be a country without dykes or banks of any kind. If she had been protected by proper measures, like Germany, Spain, and France, this inundation would not have caused the great changes that it has, or would not have happened at all.

This must suffice as regards opposition to fortune in general. But limiting myself more to particular cases, I would point out how one sees a certain prince to-day fortunate and to-morrow ruined, without seeing that he has changed in character or otherwise. I believe this arises in the first place from the causes that we have already discussed at length; that is to say, because the prince who bases himself entirely on fortune is ruined when fortune changes. I also believe that he is happy whose mode of procedure accords with the needs of the times, and similarly he is unfortunate whose mode of procedure is opposed to the times. For one sees that men in those things which lead them to the aim that each one has in view, namely, glory and riches, proceed in various ways; one with circumspection, another with impetuosity, one by violence, another by cunning, one with patience, another with the reverse; and each by these diverse ways may arrive at his aim. One sees also two cautious men, one of whom succeeds in his designs, and the other not, and in the same way two men succeed equally by different methods, one being cautious, the other impetuous, which arises only from the nature of the times, which does or does not conform to their method of procedure. From this it results, as I have said, that two men, acting differently, attain the same effect, and of two others acting in the same way, one attains his goal and not the other. On this depend also the changes in prosperity, for if it happens that time and circumstances are favourable to one who acts with caution and prudence he will be successful, but if time and circumstances change he will be ruined, because he does not change his mode of procedure. No man is found so prudent as to be able to adapt himself to this, either because he cannot deviate from that to which his nature disposes him, or else because having always prospered by walking in one path, he cannot persuade himself that it is well to leave it; and therefore, the cautious man, when it is time to act suddenly, does not know how to do so and is consequently ruined; for if one could change one's nature with time and circumstances, fortune would never change.

Pope Julius II acted impetuously in everything he did and found the times and conditions so in conformity with that mode of procedure, that he always obtained a good result. Consider the first war that he made against Bologna while Messer Giovanni Bentivogli was still living. The Venetians were not pleased with it, neither was the King of Spain, France was conferring with him over the enterprise, notwithstanding which, owing to his fierce and impetuous disposition, he engaged personally in the expedition. This move caused both Spain and the Venetians to halt and hesitate, the latter through fear, the former through the desire to recover the entire kingdom of Naples. On the other hand, he engaged with him the King of France, because seeing him make this move and desiring his friendship in order to put down the Venetians, that king judged that he could not refuse him his troops without manifest injury. Thus Julius by his impetuous move achieved what no other pontiff with the utmost human prudence would have succeeded in doing, because, if he had waited till all arrangements had been made and everything settled before leaving Rome, as any other pontiff would have done, it would never have succeeded. For the King of France would have found a thousand excuses, and the others would have inspired him with a thousand fears. I will omit his other actions, which were all of this kind and which all succeeded well, and the shortness of his life did not suffer him to experience the contrary, for had times followed in which it was necessary to act with caution, his ruin would have resulted, for he would never have deviated from these methods to which his nature disposed him.

I conclude then that fortune varying and men remaining fixed in their ways, they are successful so long as these ways conform to circumstances, but when they are opposed then they are unsuccessful. I certainly think that it is better to be impetuous than cautious, for fortune is a woman, and it is necessary, if you wish to master her, to conquer her by force; and it can be seen that she lets herself be overcome by the bold rather than by those who proceed coldly. And therefore, like a woman, she is always a friend to the young, because they are less cautious, fiercer, and master her with greater audacity.

Leviathan

by Thomas Hobbes

Chapter XIII
Of the Natural Condition of Mankind as
concerning their Felicity and Misery

NATURE hath made men so equal in the faculties of body and mind as that, though there be found one man sometimes manifestly stronger in body or of quicker mind than another, yet when all is reckoned together the difference between man and man is not so considerable as that one man can thereupon claim to himself any benefit to which another may not pretend as well as he. For as to the strength of body, the weakest has strength enough to kill the strongest, either by secret machination or by confederacy with others that are in the same danger with himself.

And as to the faculties of the mind, setting aside the arts grounded upon words, and especially that skill of proceeding upon general and infallible rules, called *science*, which very few have and but in few things, as being not a native faculty born with us, nor attained, as prudence, while we look after somewhat else, I find yet a greater equality amongst men than that of strength. For prudence is but experience, which equal time equally bestows on all men in those things they equally apply themselves unto. That which may perhaps make such equality incredible is but a vain conceit of one's own wisdom, which almost all men think they have in a greater degree than the vulgar; that is, than all men but themselves, and a few others, whom by fame, or for concurring with themselves, they approve. For such is the nature of men that howsoever they may acknowledge many others to be more witty, or more eloquent, or more learned, yet they will hardly believe there be many so wise as themselves; for they see their own wit at hand, and other men's at a distance. But this proveth rather that men are in that point equal, than unequal. For there is not ordinarily a greater sign of the equal distribution of anything than that every man is contented with his share.

From this equality of ability ariseth equality of hope in the attaining of our ends. And therefore if any two men desire the same thing, which nevertheless they cannot both enjoy, they become enemies; and in the way to their end (which is principally their own conservation, and sometimes their delectation only) endeavour to destroy or subdue one another. And from hence it comes to pass that where an invader hath no more to fear than another man's single power, if one plant, sow, build, or possess a convenient seat, others may probably be expected to come prepared with forces united to dispossess and deprive him, not only of the fruit of his labour, but also of his life or liberty. And the invader again is in the like danger of another.

And from this diffidence of one another, there is no way for any man to secure himself so reasonable as anticipation; that is, by force, or wiles, to master the persons of all men he can so long till he see no other power great enough to endanger him: and this is no more than his own conservation requireth, and is generally allowed. Also because there be some that, taking pleasure in contemplating their own power in the acts of conquest, which they pursue farther than their security requires, if others, that otherwise would be glad to be at ease within modest bounds, should not by invasion increase their power, they would not be able, long time, by standing only on their defence, to subsist. And by consequence, such augmentation of dominion over men being necessary to a man's conservation, it ought to be allowed him.

Again, men have no pleasure (but on the contrary a great deal of grief) in keeping company where there is no power able to overawe them all. For every man looketh that his companion should value him at the same rate he sets upon himself, and upon all signs of contempt or undervaluing naturally endeavours, as far as he dares (which amongst them that have no common power to keep them in quiet is far enough to make them destroy each other), to extort a greater value from his contemners, by damage; and from others, by the example.

So that in the nature of man, we find three principal causes of quarrel. First, competition; secondly, diffidence; thirdly, glory.

The first maketh men invade for gain; the second, for safety; and the third, for reputation. The first use violence, to make themselves masters of other men's persons, wives, children, and cattle; the second, to defend them; the third, for trifles, as a word, a smile, a different opinion, and any other sign of undervalue, either direct in their persons or by reflection in their kindred, their friends, their nation, their profession, or their name.

Hereby it is manifest that during the time men live without a common power to keep them all in awe, they are in that condition which is called *war;* and such a war as is of every man against every man. For war consisteth not in battle only, or the act of fighting, but in a tract of time, wherein the will to contend by battle is sufficiently known: and therefore the notion of *time* is to be considered in the nature of war, as it is in the nature of weather. For as the nature of foul weather lieth not in a shower or two of rain, but in an inclination thereto of many days together: so the nature of war consisteth not in actual fighting, but in the known disposition thereto during all the time there is no assurance to the contrary. All other time is *peace*.

Whatsoever therefore is consequent to a time of war, where every man is enemy to every man, the same is consequent to the time wherein men live without other security than what their own strength and their own invention shall furnish them withal. In such condition there is no place for industry, because the fruit thereof is uncertain: and consequently no culture of the earth; no navigation, nor use of the commodities that may be imported by sea; no commodious buildings; no instruments of moving and removing such things as require much force; no knowledge of the face of the earth; no account of time; no arts; no letters; no society; and which is worst of all, continual fear, and danger of violent death; and the life of man, solitary, poor, nasty, brutish, and short.

It may seem strange to some man that has not well weighed these things that Nature should thus dissociate and render men apt to invade and destroy one another: and he may therefore, not trusting to this inference, made from the passions, desire perhaps to have the same confirmed by experience. Let him therefore consider with himself: when taking a journey, he arms himself and seeks to go well accompanied; when going to sleep, he locks his doors; when even in his house he locks his chests; and this when he knows there be laws and public officers, armed, to revenge all injuries shall be done him; what opinion he has of his fellow subjects, when he rides armed; of his fellow citizens, when he locks his doors; and of his children, and servants, when he locks his chests. Does he not there as much accuse mankind by his actions as I do by my words? But neither of us accuse man's nature in it. The desires, and other passions of man, are in themselves no sin. No more are the actions that proceed from those passions till they know a law that forbids them; which till laws be made they cannot know, nor can any law be made till they have agreed upon the person that shall make it.

It may peradventure be thought there was never such a time nor condition of war as this; and I believe it was never generally so, over all the world: but there are many places where they live so now. For the savage people in many places of America, except the government of small families, the concord whereof dependeth on natural lust, have no government at all, and live at this day in that brutish manner, as I said before. Howsoever, it may be perceived what manner of life there would be, where there were no common power to fear, by the manner of life which men that have formerly lived under a peaceful government use to degenerate into a civil war.

But though there had never been any time wherein particular men were in a condition of war one against another, yet in all times kings and persons of sovereign authority, because of their independency, are in continual jealousies, and in the state and posture of gladiators, having their weapons pointing, and their eyes fixed on one another; that is, their forts, garrisons, and guns upon the frontiers of their kingdoms, and continual spies upon their neighbours, which is a posture of war. But because they uphold thereby the industry of their subjects, there does not follow from it that misery which accompanies the liberty of particular men.

To this war of every man against every man, this also is consequent; that nothing can be unjust. The notions of right and wrong, justice and injustice, have there no place. Where there is no common power, there is no law; where no law, no injustice. Force and fraud are in war the two cardinal virtues. Justice and injustice are none of the faculties neither of the body nor mind. If they were, they might be in a man that were alone in the world, as well as his senses and passions. They are qualities that relate to men in society, not in solitude. It is consequent also to the same condition that there be no propriety, no dominion, no *mine* and *thine* distinct; but only that to be every man's that he can get, and for so long as he can keep it. And thus much for the ill condition which man by mere nature is actually placed in; though with a possibility to come out of it, consisting partly in the passions, partly in his reason.

The passions that incline men to peace are: fear of death; desire of such things as are necessary to commodious living; and a hope by their industry to obtain them. And reason suggesteth convenient articles of peace upon which men may be drawn to agreement. These articles are they which otherwise are called the *laws of nature,* whereof I shall speak more particularly in the two following chapters.

Chapter XIV
Of the First and Second Natural Laws, and of Contracts

The *right of nature,* which writers commonly call *jus naturale,* is the liberty each man hath to use his own power as he will himself for the preservation of his own nature; that is to say, of his own life; and consequently, of doing anything which, in his own judgement and reason, he shall conceive to be the aptest means thereunto.

By *liberty* is understood, according to the proper signification of the word, the absence of external impediments; which impediments may oft take away part of a man's power to do what he would, but cannot hinder him from using the power left him according as his judgement and reason shall dictate to him.

A *law of nature, lex naturalis,* is a precept, or general rule, found out by reason, by which a man is forbidden to do that which is destructive of his life, or taketh away the means of preserving the same, and to omit that by which he thinketh it may be best preserved. For though they that speak of this subject use to confound *jus* and *lex, right* and *law,* yet they ought to be distinguished, because *right* consisteth in liberty to do, or to forbear; whereas *law* determineth and bindeth to one of them: so that law and right differ as much as obligation and liberty, which in one and the same matter are inconsistent.

And because the condition of man (as hath been declared in the precedent chapter) is a condition of war of *every* one against *every* one, in which case every one is governed by his own reason, and there is nothing he can make use of that may not be a help unto him in preserving his life against his enemies; it followeth that in such a condition every man has a right to every thing, even to one another's body. And therefore, as long as this natural right of every man to every thing endureth, there can be no security to any man, how strong or wise soever he be, of living out the time which nature ordinarily alloweth men to live. And consequently it is a precept, or general rule of reason: *that every man ought to endeavour peace, as far as he has hope of obtaining it; and when he cannot obtain it, that he may seek and use all helps and advantages of war.* The first branch of which rule containeth the first and fundamental law of nature, which is: *to seek peace and follow it.* The second, the sum of the right of nature, which is: *by all means we can to defend ourselves.*

From this fundamental law of nature, by which men are commanded to endeavour peace, is derived this second law: *that a man be willing, when others are so too, as far forth as for peace and defence of himself he shall think it necessary, to lay down this right to all things; and be contented with so much liberty against other men as he would allow other men against himself.* For as long as every man holdeth this right, of doing anything he liketh; so long are all men in the condition of war. But if other men will not lay down their right, as well as he, then there is no reason for anyone to divest himself of his: for that were to expose himself to prey, which no man is bound to, rather than to dispose himself to peace. This is that law of the gospel: *Whatsoever you require that others should do to you, that do ye to them.* And that law of all men, *quod tibi fieri non vis, alteri ne feceris.*

To lay down a man's right to anything is to divest himself of the liberty of hindering another of the benefit of his own right to the same. For he that renounceth or passeth away his right giveth not to any other man a right which he had not before, because there is nothing to which every man had not right by nature, but only standeth out of his way that he may enjoy his own original right without hindrance from him, not without hindrance from another. So that the effect which redoundeth to one man by another man's defect of right is but so much diminution of impediments to the use of his own right original.

Right is laid aside, either by simply renouncing it, or by transferring it to another. By simply *renouncing,* when he cares not to whom the benefit thereof redoundeth. By *transferring,* when he intendeth the benefit thereof to some certain person or persons. And when a man hath in either manner abandoned or granted away his right, then is he said to be *obliged,* or *bound,* not to hinder those to whom such right is granted, or abandoned, from the benefit of it: and that he *ought,* and it is his *duty,* not to make void that voluntary act of his own: and that such hindrance is *injustice,* and *injury,* as being *sine jure;* the right being before renounced or transferred. So that *injury,* or *injustice,* in the controversies of the world, is somewhat like to that which in the disputations of scholars is called *absurdity.* For as it is there called an absurdity to contradict what one maintained in the beginning; so in the world it is called *injustice,* and *injury* voluntarily to undo that which from the beginning he had voluntarily done. The way by which a man either simply renounceth or transferreth his right is a declaration, or signification, by some voluntary and sufficient sign, or signs, that he doth so renounce or transfer, or hath so renounced or transferred the same, to him that accepteth it. And these signs are either words only, or actions only; or, as it happeneth most often, both words and actions. And the same are the *bonds,* by which men are bound and obliged: bonds that have their strength, not from their own nature (for nothing is more easily broken than a man's word), but from fear of some evil consequence upon the rupture.

Whensoever a man transferreth his right, or renounceth it, it is either in consideration of some right reciprocally transferred to himself, or for some other good he hopeth for thereby. For it is a voluntary act: and of the voluntary acts of every man, the object is some good to himself. And therefore there be some rights which no man can be understood by any words, or other signs, to have abandoned or transferred. As first a man cannot lay down the right of resisting them that assault him by force to take away his life, because he cannot be understood to aim thereby at any good to himself. The same may be said of wounds, and chains, and imprisonment, both because there is no benefit consequent to such patience, as there is to the patience of suffering another to be wounded or imprisoned, as also because a man cannot tell when he seeth men proceed against him by violence whether they intend his death or not. And lastly the motive and end for which this renouncing and transferring of right is introduced is nothing else but the security of a man's person, in his life, and in the means of so preserving life as not to be weary of it. And therefore if a man by words, or other signs, seem to despoil himself of the end for which those signs were intended, he is not to be understood as if he meant it, or that it was his will, but that he was ignorant of how such words and actions were to be interpreted.

The mutual transferring of right is that which men call *contract.*

There is difference between transferring of right to the thing, and transferring, or tradition, that is, delivery of the thing itself. For the thing may be delivered together with the translation of the right, as in buying and selling with ready money, or exchange of goods or lands, and it may be delivered some time after.

Again, one of the contractors may deliver the thing contracted for on his part, and leave the other to perform his part at some determinate time after, and in the meantime be trusted; and then the contract on his part is called *pact,* or *covenant:* or both parts may contract now to perform hereafter, in which cases he that is to perform in time to come, being trusted, his performance is called *keeping of promise,* or *faith,* and the failing of performance, if it be voluntary, *violation of faith.*

When the transferring of right is not mutual, but one of the parties transferreth in hope to gain thereby friendship or service from another, or from his friends; or in hope to gain the reputation of charity, or magnanimity; or to deliver his mind from the pain of compassion; or in hope of reward in heaven; this is not contract, but *gift, free gift, grace:* which words signify one and the same thing.

Signs of contract are either *express* or by *inference*. Express are words spoken with understanding of what they signify: and such words are either of the time present or past; as, *I give, I grant, I have given, I have granted, I will that this be yours:* or of the future; as, *I will give, I will grant,* which words of the future are called *promise.*

Signs by inference are sometimes the consequence of words; sometimes the consequence of silence; sometimes the consequence of actions; sometimes the consequence of forbearing an action: and generally a sign by inference, of any contract, is whatsoever sufficiently argues the will of the contractor.

Words alone, if they be of the time to come, and contain a bare promise, are an insufficient sign of a free gift and therefore not obligatory. For if they be of the time to come, as, *tomorrow I will give,* they are a sign I have not given yet, and consequently that my right is not transferred, but remaineth till I transfer it by some other act. But if the words be of the time present, or past, as, *I have given, or do give to be delivered tomorrow,* then is my tomorrow's right given away today; and that by the virtue of the words, though there were no other argument of my will. And there is a great difference in the signification of these words, *volo hoc tuum esse cras,* and *cras dabo;* that is, between *I will that this be thine tomorrow,* and, *I will give it thee tomorrow:* for the word *I will,* in the former manner of speech, signifies an act of the will present; but in the latter, it signifies a promise of an act of the will to come: and therefore the former words, being of the present, transfer a future right; the latter, that be of the future, transfer nothing. But if there be other signs of the will to transfer a right besides words; then, though the gift be free, yet may the right be understood to pass by words of the future: as if a man propounds a prize to him that comes first to the end of a race, the gift is free; and though the words be of the future, yet the right passeth: for if he would not have his words so be understood, he should not have let them run.

In contracts the right passeth, not only where the words are of the time present or past, but also where they are of the future, because all contract is mutual translation, or change of right; and therefore he that promiseth only, because he hath already received the benefit for which he promiseth, is to be understood as if he intended the right should pass: for unless he had been content to have his words so understood, the other would not have performed his part first. And for that cause, in buying, and selling, and other acts of contract, a promise is equivalent to a covenant, and therefore obligatory.

He that performeth first in the case of a contract is said to *merit* that which he is to receive by the performance of the other, and he hath it as *due.* Also when a prize is propounded to many, which is to be given to him only that winneth, or money is thrown amongst many to be enjoyed by them that catch it; though this be a free gift, yet so to win, or so to catch, is to merit, and to have it as due. For the right is transferred in the propounding of the prize, and in throwing down the money, though it be not determined to whom, but by the event of the contention. But there is between these two sorts of merit this difference, that in contract I merit by virtue of my own power and the contractor's need, but in this case of free gift I am enabled to merit only by the benignity of the givver: in contract I merit at the contractor's hand that he should depart with his right; in this case of gift, I merit not that the giver should part with his right, but that when he has parted with it, it should be mine rather than another's. And this I think to be the meaning of that distinction of the Schools between *meritum congrui,* and *meritum condigni.* For God Almighty, having promised paradise to those men, hoodwinked with carnal desires, that can walk through this world according to the precepts and limits prescribed by him, they say he that shall so walk shall merit paradise *ex congruo.* But because no man can demand a right to it by his own righteousness, or any other power in himself, but by the free grace of God only, they say no man can merit paradise *ex condigno.* This, I say, I think is the meaning of that distinction; but because disputers do not agree upon the signification of their own terms of art longer than it serves their turn, I will not affirm anything of their meaning: only this I say; when a gift is given indefinitely, as a prize to be contended for, he that winneth meriteth, and may claim the prize as due.

If a covenant be made wherein neither of the parties perform presently, but trust one another, in the condition of mere nature (which is a condition of war of every man against every man) upon any reasonable suspicion, it is void: but if there be a common power set over them both, with right and force sufficient to compel performance, it is not void. For he that performeth first has no assurance the other will perform after, because the bonds of words are too weak to bridle men's ambition, avarice, anger, and other passions, without the fear of some coercive power; which in the condition of mere nature, where all men are equal, and judges of the justness of their own fears, cannot possibly be supposed. And therefore he which performeth first does but betray himself to his enemy, contrary to the right he can never abandon of defending his life and means of living.

But in a civil estate, where there is a power set up to constrain those that would otherwise violate their faith, that fear is no more reasonable; and for that cause, he which by the covenant is to perform first is obliged so to do.

The cause of fear, which maketh such a covenant invalid, must be always something arising after the covenant made, as some new fact or other sign of the will not to perform, else it cannot make the covenant void. For that which could not hinder a man from promising ought not to be admitted as a hindrance of performing.

He that transferreth any right transferreth the means of enjoying it, as far as lieth in his power. As he that selleth land is understood to transfer the herbage and whatsoever grows upon it; nor can he that sells a mill turn away the stream that drives it. And they that give to a man the right of government in sovereignty are understood to give him the right of levying money to maintain soldiers, and of appointing magistrates for the administration of justice.

To make covenants with brute beasts is impossible, because not understanding our speech, they understand not, nor accept of any translation of right, nor can translate any right to another: and without mutual acceptation, there is no covenant.

To make covenant with God is impossible but by mediation of such as God speaketh to, either by revelation supernatural or by His lieutenants that govern under Him and in His name: for otherwise we know not whether our covenants be accepted or not. And therefore they that vow anything contrary to any law of nature, vow in vain, as being a thing unjust to pay such vow. And if it be a thing commanded by the law of nature, it is not the vow, but the law that binds them.

The matter or subject of a covenant is always something that falleth under deliberation, for to covenant is an act of the will; that is to say, an act, and the last act, of deliberation; and is therefore always understood to be something to come, and which is judged possible for him that covenanteth to perform.

And therefore, to promise that which is known to be impossible is no covenant. But if that prove impossible afterwards, which before was thought possible, the covenant is valid and bindeth, though not to the thing itself, yet to the value; or, if that also be impossible, to the unfeigned endeavour of performing as much as is possible, for to more no man can be obliged.

Men are freed of their covenants two ways; by performing, or by being forgiven. For performance is the natural end of obligation, and forgiveness the restitution of liberty, as being a retransferring of that right in which the obligation consisted.

Covenants entered into by fear, in the condition of mere nature, are obligatory. For example, if I covenant to pay a ransom, or service for my life, to an enemy, I am bound by it. For it is a contract, wherein one receiveth the benefit of life; the other is to receive money, or service for it, and consequently, where no other law (as in the condition of mere nature) forbiddeth the performance, the covenant is valid. Therefore prisoners of war, if trusted with the payment of their ransom, are obliged to pay it: and if a weaker prince make a disadvantageous peace with a stronger, for fear, he is bound to keep it; unless (as hath been said before) there ariseth some new and just cause of fear to renew the war. And even in Commonwealths, if I be forced to redeem myself from a thief by promising him money, I am bound to pay it, till the civil law discharge me. For whatsoever I may lawfully do without obligation, the same I may lawfully covenant to do through fear: and what I lawfuly covenant, I cannot lawfully break.

A former covenant makes void a later. For a man that hath passed away his right to one man today hath it not to pass tomorrow to another: and therefore the later promise passeth no right, but is null.

A covenant not to defend myself from force, by force, is always void. For (as I have shown before) no man can transfer or lay down his right to save himself from death, wounds, and imprisonment, the avoiding whereof is the only end of laying down any right; and therefore the promise of not resisting force, in no covenant transferreth any right, nor is obliging. For though a man may covenant thus, *unless I do so, or so, kill me;* he cannot covenant thus, *unless I do so, or so, I will not resist you when you come to kill me.* For man by nature chooseth the lesser evil, which is danger of death in resisting, rather than the greater, which is certain and present death in not resisting. And this is granted to be true by all men, in that they lead criminals to execution, and prison, with armed men, notwithstanding that such criminals have consented to the law by which they are condemned.

A covenant to accuse oneself, without assurance of pardon, is likewise invalid. For in the condition of nature, where every man is judge, there is no place for accusation: and in the civil state the accusation is followed with punishment, which, being force, a man is not obliged not to resist. The same is also true of the accusation of those by whose condemnation a man falls into misery; as of a father, wife, or benefactor. For the testimony of such an accuser, if it be not willingly given, is presumed to be corrupted by nature, and therefore not to be received: and where a man's testimony is not to be credited, he is not bound to give it. Also accusations upon torture are not to be reputed as testimonies. For torture is to be used but as means of conjecture, and light, in the further examination and search of truth; and what is in that case confessed tendeth to the ease of him that is tortured, not to the informing of the torturers, and therefore ought not to have the credit of a sufficient testimony: for whether he deliver himself by true or false accusation, he does it by the right of preserving his own life.

The force of words being (as I have formerly noted) too weak to hold men to the performance of their covenants, there are in man's nature but two imaginable helps to strengthen it. And those are either a fear of the consequence of breaking their word, or a glory or pride in appearing not to need to break it. This latter is a generosity too rarely found to be presumed on, especially in the pursuers of wealth, command, or sensual pleasure, which are the greatest part of mankind. The passion to be reckoned upon is fear; whereof there be two very general objects: one, the power of spirits invisible; the other, the power of those men they shall therein offend. Of these two, though the former be the greater power, yet the fear of the latter is commonly the greater fear. The fear of the former is in every man his own religion, which hath place in the nature of man before civil society. The latter hath not so; at least not place enough to keep men to their promises, because in the condition of mere nature, the inequality of power is not discerned, but by the event of battle. So that before the time of civil society, or in the interruption thereof by war, there is nothing can strengthen a covenant of peace agreed on against the temptations of avarice, ambition, lust, or other strong desire, but the fear of that invisible power which they every one worship as God, and fear as a revenger of their perfidy. All therefore that can be done between two men not subject to civil power is to put one another to swear by the God he feareth: which swearing, or *oath,* is a form of speech, added to a promise, by which he that promiseth signifieth that unless he perform he renounceth the mercy of his God, or calleth to him for vengeance on himself. Such was the heathen form, *Let Jupiter kill me else, as I kill this beast.* So is our form, *I shall do thus, and thus, so help me*

God. And this, with the rites and ceremonies which every one useth in his own religion, that the fear of breaking faith might be the greater.

By this it appears that an oath taken according to any other form, or rite, than his that sweareth is in vain and no oath, and that there is no swearing by anything which the swearer thinks not God. For though men have sometimes used to swear by their kings, for fear, or flattery; yet they would have it thereby understood they attributed to them divine honour. And that swearing unnecessarily by God is but profaning of his name: and swearing by other things, as men do in common discourse, is not swearing, but an impious custom, gotten by too much vehemence of talking.

It appears also that the oath adds nothing to the obligation. For a covenant, if lawful, binds in the sight of God, without the oath, as much as with it; if unlawful, bindeth not at all, though it be confirmed with an oath.

Chapter XV
Of Other Laws of Nature

From that law of nature by which we are obliged to transfer to another such rights as, being retained, hinder the peace of mankind, there followeth a third; which is this: *that men perform their covenants made;* without which covenants are in vain, and but empty words; and the right of all men to all things remaining, we are still in the condition of war.

And in this law of nature consisteth the fountain and original of *justice*. For where no covenant hath preceded, there hath no right been transferred, and every man has right to everything; and consequently, no action can be unjust. But when a covenant is made, then to break it is *unjust:* and the definition of *injustice* is no other than *the not performance of covenant*. And whatsoever is not unjust is just.

But because covenants of mutual trust, where there is a fear of not performance on either part (as hath been said in the former chapter), are invalid, though the original of justice be the making of covenants, yet injustice actually there can be none till the cause of such fear be taken away; which, while men are in the natural condition of war, cannot be done. Therefore before the names of *just* and *unjust* can have place, there must be some coercive power to compel men equally to the performance of their covenants, by the terror of some punishment greater than the benefit they expect by the breach of their covenant, and to make good that propriety which by mutual contract men acquire in recompense of the universal right they abandon: and such power there is none before the erection of a Commonwealth. And this is also to be gathered out of the ordinary definition of justice in the Schools, for they say that *justice is the constant will of giving to every man his own*. And therefore where there is no *own*, that is, no propriety, there is no injustice; and where there is no coercive power erected, that is, where there is no Commonwealth, there is no propriety, all men having right to all things: therefore where there is no Commonwealth, there nothing is unjust. So that the nature of justice consisteth in keeping of valid covenants, but the validity of covenants begins not but with

the constitution of a civil power sufficient to compel men to keep them: and
then it is also that propriety begins. . . .

Concerning Civil Government

by John Locke

Chapter VIII
Of the Beginning of Political Societies

MEN being, as has been said, by nature all free, equal, and independent, no one can be put out of this estate and subjected to the political power of another without his own consent, which is done by agreeing with other men, to join and unite into a community for their comfortable, safe, and peaceable living, one amongst another, in a secure enjoyment of their properties, and a greater security against any that are not of it. This any number of men may do, because it injures not the freedom of the rest; they are left, as it were, in the liberty of the state of Nature. When any number of men have so consented to make one community or government, they are thereby presently incorporated, and make one body politic, wherein the majority have a right to act and conclude the rest.

For, when any number of men have, by the consent of every individual, made a community, they have thereby made that community one body, with a power to act as one body, which is only by the will and determination of the majority. For that which acts any community, being only the consent of the individuals of it, and it being one body, must move one way, it is necessary the body should move that way whither the greater force carries it, which is the consent of the majority, or else it is impossible it should act or continue one body, one community, which the consent of every individual that united into it agreed that it should; and so every one is bound by that consent to be concluded by the majority. And therefore we see that in assemblies empowered to act by positive laws where no number is set by that positive law which empowers them, the act of the majority passes for the act of the whole, and of course determines as having, by the law of Nature and reason, the power of the whole.

And thus every man, by consenting with others to make one body politic under one government, puts himself under an obligation to every one of that society to submit to the determination of the majority, and to be concluded by it; or else this original compact, whereby he with others incorporates into one society, would signify nothing, and be no compact if he be left free and under no other ties than he was in before in the state of Nature. For what appearance would there be of any compact? What new engagement if he were no farther tied by any decrees of the society than he himself thought fit and did actually consent to? This would be still as great a liberty as he himself had before his compact, or any one else in the state of Nature, who may submit himself and consent to any acts of it if he thinks fit.

For if the consent of the majority shall not in reason be received as the act of the whole, and conclude every individual, nothing but the consent of every individual can make anything to be the act of the whole, which, considering the infirmities of health and avocations of business, which in a number though much less than that of a commonwealth, will necessarily keep many away from the public assembly; and the variety of opinions and contrariety of interests which unavoidably happen in all collections of men, it is next impossible ever to be had. And, therefore, if coming into society be upon such terms, it will be only like Cato's coming into the theatre, *tantum ut exiret.* Such a constitution as this would make the mighty leviathan of a shorter duration than the feeblest creatures, and not let it outlast the day it was born in, which cannot be supposed till we can think that rational creatures should desire and constitute societies only to be dissolved. For where the majority cannot conclude the rest, there they cannot act as one body, and consequently will be immediately dissolved again.

Whosoever, therefore, out of a state of Nature unite into a community, must be understood to give up all the power necessary to the ends for which they unite into society to the majority of the community, unless they expressly agreed in any number greater than the majority. And this is done by barely agreeing to unite into one political society, which is all the compact that is, or needs be, between the individuals that enter into or make up a commonwealth. And thus, that which begins and actually constitutes any political society is nothing but the consent of any number of freemen capable of majority, to unite and incorporate into such a society. And this is that, and that only, which did or could give beginning to any lawful government in the world.

To this I find two objections made: 1. That there are no instances to be found in story of a company of men, independent and equal one amongst another, that met together, and in this way began and set up a government. 2. It is impossible of right that men should do so, because all men, being born under government, they are to submit to that, and are not at liberty to begin a new one.

To the first there is this to answer: That it is not at all to be wondered that history gives us but a very little account of men that lived together in the state of Nature. The inconveniencies of that condition, and the love and want of society, no sooner brought any number of them together, but they presently united and incorporated if they designed to continue together. And if we may not suppose men ever to have been in the state of Nature, because we hear not much of them in such a state, we may as well suppose the armies of Salmanasser or Xerxes were never children, because we hear little of them till they were men and embodied in armies. Government is everywhere antecedent to records, and letters seldom come in amongst a people till a long continuation of civil society has, by other more necessary arts, provided for their safety, ease, and plenty. And then they began to look after the history of their founders, and search into their original when they have outlived the memory of it. For it is with commonwealths as with particular persons, they are commonly ignorant of their own births and infancies; and if they know anything of it, they are beholding for it to the accidental records that others have kept of it. And those that we have of the beginning of any polities in the world, excepting that of the Jews, where God Himself immediately interposed, and which favours not at all paternal dominion, are all either plain instances of such a beginning as I have mentioned, or at least have manifest footsteps of it.

He must show a strange inclination to deny evident matter of fact, when it agrees not with his hypothesis, who will not allow that the beginning of Rome and Venice were by the uniting together of several men, free and independent one of another, amongst whom there was no natural superiority or subjection. And if Josephus Acosta's word may be taken, he tells us that in many parts of America there was no government at all. "There are great and apparent conjectures," says he, "that these men [speaking of those of Peru] for a long time had neither kings nor commonwealths, but lived in troops, as they do this day in Florida—the Cheriquanas, those of Brazil, and many other nations, which have no certain kings, but, as occasion is offered in peace or war, they choose their captains as they please." If it be said, that every man there was born subject to his father, or the head of his family, that the subjection due from a child to a father took away not his freedom of uniting into what political society he thought fit, has been already proved; but be that as it will, these men, it is evident, were actually free; and whatever superiority some politicians now would place in any of them, they themselves claimed it not; but, by consent, were all equal, till, by the same consent, they set rulers over themselves. So that their politic societies all began from a voluntary union, and the mutual agreement of men freely acting in the choice of their governors and forms of government.

And I hope those who went away from Sparta, with Palantus, mentioned by Justin, will be allowed to have been freemen independent one of another, and to have set up a government over themselves by their own consent. Thus I have given several examples out of history of people, free and in the state of Nature, that, being met together, incorporated and began a commonwealth. And if the want of such instances be an argument to prove that government were not nor could not be so begun, I suppose the contenders for paternal empire were better let it alone than urge it against natural liberty; for if they can give so many instances out of history of governments begun upon paternal right, I think (though at least an argument from what has been to what should of right be of no great force) one might, without any great danger, yield them the cause. But if I might advise them in the case, they would do well not to search too much into the original of governments as they have begun *de facto*, lest they should find at the foundation of most of them something very little favourable to the design they promote, and such a power as they contend for.

But, to conclude: reason being plain on our side that men are naturally free; and the examples of history showing that the governments of the world, that were begun in peace, had their beginning laid on that foundation, and were made by the consent of the people; there can be little room for doubt, either where the right is, or what has been the opinion or practice of mankind about the first erecting of governments.

I will not deny that if we look back, as far as history will direct us, towards the original of commonwealths, we shall generally find them under the government and administration of one man. And I am also apt to believe that where a family was numerous enough to subsist by itself, and continued entire together, without mixing with others, as it often happens, where there is much land and few people, the government commonly began in the father. For the father having, by the law of Nature, the same power, with every man else, to punish, as he thought fit, any offences against that law, might thereby punish his transgressing children, even when they were men, and out of their pupilage; and they were very likely to submit to his punishment, and all join with him against the offender in their turns, giving him thereby power to execute his sentence against any transgression, and so, in effect, make him the law-maker and governor over all that remained in conjunction with his family. He was fittest to be trusted; paternal affection secured their property and interest under his care, and the custom of obeying him in their childhood made it easier to submit to him rather than any other. If, therefore, they must have one to rule them, as government is hardly to be avoided amongst men that live together, who so likely to be the man as he that was their common father, unless negligence, cruelty, or any other defect of mind or body, made him unfit for it? But when either the father died, and left his next heir—for want of age, wisdom, courage, or any other qualities—less fit for rule, or where several families met and consented to continue together, there, it is not to be doubted, but they used their natural freedom to set up him whom they judged the ablest and most likely to rule well over them. Conformable hereunto we find the people of America, who—living out of the reach of the conquering swords and spreading domination of the two great empires of Peru and Mexico—enjoyed their own natural freedom, though, *cœleris paribus*, they commonly prefer the heir of their deceased king; yet, if they find him any way weak or incapable, they pass him by, and set up the stoutest and bravest man for their ruler.

Thus, though looking back as far as records give us any account of peopling the world, and the history of nations, we commonly find the government to be in one hand, yet it destroys not that which I affirm—

viz., that the beginning of politic society depends upon the consent of the individuals to join into and make one society, who, when they are thus incorporated, might set up what form of government they thought fit. But this having given occasion to men to mistake and think that, by Nature, government was monarchical, and belonged to the father, it may not be amiss here to consider why people, in the beginning, generally pitched upon this form, which, though perhaps the father's pre-eminence might, in the first institution of some commonwealths, give a rise to and place in the beginning the power in one hand, yet it is plain that the reason that continued the form of government in a single person was not any regard or respect to paternal authority, since all petty monarchies—that is, almost all monarchies, near their original, have been commonly, at least upon occasion, elective.

First, then, in the beginning of things, the father's government of the childhood of those sprung from him having accustomed them to the rule of one man, and taught them that where it was exercised with care and skill, with affection and love to those under it, it was sufficient to procure and preserve men (all the political happiness they sought for in society), it was no wonder that they should pitch upon and naturally run into that form of government which, from their infancy, they had been all accustomed to, and which, by experience, they had found both easy and safe. To which if we add, that monarchy being simple and most obvious to men, whom neither experience had instructed in forms of government, nor the ambition or insolence of empire had taught to beware of the encroachments of prerogative or the inconveniencies of absolute power, which monarchy, in succession, was apt to lay claim to and bring upon them; it was not at all strange that they should not much trouble themselves to think of methods of restraining any exorbitances of those to whom they had given the authority over them, and of balancing the power of government by placing several parts of it in different hands. They had neither felt the oppression of tyrannical dominion, nor did the fashion of the age, nor their possessions or way of living, which afforded little matter for covetousness or ambition, give them any reason to apprehend or provide against it; and, therefore, it is no wonder they put themselves into such a frame of government as was not only, as I said, most obvious and simple, but also best suited to their present state and condition, which stood more in need of defence against foreign invasions and injuries than of multiplicity of laws where there was but very little property, and wanted not variety of rulers and abundance of officers to direct and look after their execution where there were but few trespassers and few offenders. Since, then, those who liked one another so well as to join into society cannot but be supposed to have some acquaintance and friendship together, they could not but have greater apprehensions of others than of one another; and, therefore, their first care and thought cannot but be supposed to be, how to secure themselves against foreign force. It was natural for them to put themselves under a frame of government which might best serve to that end, and choose the wisest and bravest man to conduct them in their wars and lead them out against their enemies, and in this chiefly be their ruler.

Thus we see that the kings of the Indians, in America, which is still a pattern of the first ages in Asia and Europe, whilst the inhabitants were too few for the country, and want of people and money gave men no temptation to enlarge their possessions of land or contest for wider extent of ground, are little more than generals of their armies; and though they command absolutely in war, yet at home, and in time of peace, they exercise very little dominion, and have but a very moderate sovereignty, the resolutions of peace and war being ordinarily either in the people or in a council, though the war itself, which admits not of pluralities of governors, naturally evolves the command into the king's sole authority.

And thus, in Israel itself, the chief business of their judges and first kings seems to have been to be captains in war and leaders of their armies, which (besides what is signified by "going out and in before the people," which was, to march forth to wars and home again at the heads of their forces) appears plainly in the story of Jephtha. The Ammonites making war upon Israel, the Gileadites, in fear, send to Jephtha, a bastard of their family, whom they had cast off, and article with him, if he will assist them against the Ammonites, to make him their ruler, which they do in these words: "And the people made him head and captain over them" (Judges 11. 11), which was, as it seems, all one as to be judge. "And he judged Israel" (Judges 12. 7)—that is, was their captain-general—"six years." So when Jotham upbraids the Shechemites with the obligation they had to Gideon, who had been their judge and ruler, he tells them: "He fought for you, and adventured his life for, and delivered you out of the hands of Midian" (Judges 9. 17). Nothing mentioned of him but what he did as a general, and, indeed, that is all is found in his history, or in any of the rest of the Judges. And Abimelech particularly is called king, though at most he was but their general. And when, being weary of the ill-conduct of Samuel's sons, the children of Israel desired a king, "like all the nations, to judge them, and to go out before them, and to fight their battles" (1 Sam. 8. 20), God, granting their desire, says to Samuel, "I will send thee a man, and thou shalt anoint him to be captain over my people Israel, that he may save my people out of the hands of the Philistines" (ch. 9. 16). As if the only business of a king had been to lead out their armies and fight in their defence; and, accordingly, at his inauguration, pouring a vial of oil upon him, declares to Saul that "the Lord had anointed him to be captain over his inheritance" (ch. 10. 1). And therefore those who, after Saul being solemnly chosen and saluted king by the tribes at Mispah, were unwilling to have him their king, make no other objection but this, "How shall this man save us?" (ch. 10. 27), as if they should have said: "This man is unfit to be our king, not having skill and conduct enough in war to be able to defend us." And when God resolved to transfer the government to David, it is in these words: "But now thy kingdom shall not continue: the Lord hath sought Him a man after His own heart, and the Lord hath commanded him to be captain over His people" (ch. 13. 14). As if the whole kingly authority were nothing else but to be their general; and therefore the tribes who had stuck to Saul's family, and opposed David's reign, when they came to Hebron with terms of submission to him, they tell him, amongst other arguments, they had to submit to him as to their king, that he was, in effect, their king in Saul's time, and therefore they had no reason but to receive him as their king now. "Also," they say, "in time past, when Saul was king over us, thou wast he that leddest out and broughtest in Israel, and the Lord said unto thee, Thou shalt feed my people Israel, and thou shalt be a captain over Israel."

Thus, whether a family, by degrees, grew up into a commonwealth, and the fatherly authority being continued on to the elder son, every one in his turn growing up under it tacitly submitted to it, and the easiness and equality of it not offending any one, every one acquiesced till time seemed to have confirmed it and settled a right of succession by prescription; or whether several families, or the descendants of several families, whom chance, neighbourhood, or business brought together, united into society; the need of a general whose conduct might defend them against their enemies in war, and the great confidence the innocence and sincerity of that poor but virtuous age, such as are almost all those which begin governments that ever come to last in the world, gave men one of another, made the first beginners of commonwealths generally put the rule into one man's hand, without any other express limitation or restraint but what the nature of the thing and the end of government required. It was given them for the public good and safety, and to those ends, in the infancies of commonwealths, they commonly used it; and unless they had done so, young societies could not have subsisted. Without such nursing fathers, without this care of the governors, all governments would have sunk under the weakness and infirmities of their infancy, the prince and the people had soon perished together.

But the golden age (though before vain ambition, and *amor sceleratus habendi*, evil concupiscence had corrupted men's minds into a mistake of true power and honour) had more virtue, and consequently better governors, as well as less vicious subjects; and there was then no stretching prerogative on the one side to oppress the people, nor, consequently, on the other, any dispute about privilege, to lessen or restrain the power of the magistrate; and so no contest betwixt rulers and people about governors or government.[1] Yet, when ambition and luxury, in future ages, would retain and increase the power, without doing the business for which it was given, and aided by flattery, taught princes to have distinct and separate interests from their people, men found it necessary to examine more carefully the original and rights of government, and to find out ways to restrain the exorbitances and prevent the abuses of that power, which they having entrusted in another's hands, only for their own good, they found was made use of to hurt them.

Thus we may see how probable it is that people that were naturally free, and, by their own consent, either submitted to the government of their father, or united together, out of different families, to make a government, should generally put the rule into one man's hands, and choose to be under the conduct of a single person, without so much, as by express conditions, limiting or regulating his power, which they thought safe enough in his honesty and prudence; though they never dreamed of monarchy being *jure Divino,* which we never heard of among mankind till it was revealed to us by the divinity of this last age, nor ever allowed paternal power to have a right to dominion or to be the foundation of all government. And thus much may suffice to show that, as far as we have any light from history, we have reason to conclude that all peaceful beginnings of government have been laid in the consent of the people. I say "peaceful," because I shall have occasion, in another place, to speak of conquest, which some esteem a way of beginning of governments.

The other objection, I find, urged against the beginning of polities, in the way I have mentioned, is this, viz.:

"That all men being born under government, some or other, it is impossible any of them should ever be free and at liberty to unite together and begin a new one, or ever be able to erect a lawful government." If this argument be good, I ask, How came so many lawful monarchies into the world? For if anybody, upon this supposition, can show me any one man, in any age of the world, free to begin a lawful monarchy, I will be bound to show him ten other free men at liberty, at the same time, to unite and begin a new government under a regal or any other form. It being demonstration that if any one born under the dominion of another may be so free as to have a right to command others in a new and distinct empire, every one that is born under the dominion of another may be so free too, and may become a ruler or subject of a distinct separate government. And so, by this their own principle, either all men, however born, are free, or else there is but one lawful prince, one lawful government in the world; and then they have nothing to do but barely to show us which that is, which, when they have done, I doubt not but all mankind will easily agree to pay obedience to him.

Though it be a sufficient answer to their objection to show that it involves them in the same difficulties that it doth those they use it against, yet I shall endeavour to discover the weakness of this argument a little further.

"All men," say they, "are born under government, and therefore they cannot be at liberty to begin a new one. Every one is born a subject to his father or his prince, and is therefore under the perpetual tie of subjection and allegiance." It is plain mankind never owned nor considered any such natural subjection that they were born in, to one or to the other, that tied them, without their own consents, to a subjection to them and their heirs.

For there are no examples so frequent in history, both sacred and profane, as those of men withdrawing themselves and their obedience from the jurisdiction they were born under, and the family or community they were bred up in, and setting up new governments in other places, from whence sprang all that number of petty commonwealths in the beginning of ages, and which always multiplied as long as there was room enough, till the stronger or more fortunate swallowed the weaker; and those great ones, again breaking to pieces, dissolved into lesser dominions; all which are so many testimonies against paternal sovereignty, and plainly prove that it was not the natural right of the father descending to his heirs that made governments in the beginning; since it was impossible, upon that ground, there should have been so many little kingdoms but only one universal monarchy if men had not been at liberty to separate themselves from their families and their government, be it what it will that was set up in it, and go and make distinct commonwealths and other governments as they thought fit.

This has been the practice of the world from its first beginning to this day; nor is it now any more hindrance to the freedom of mankind, that they are born under constituted and ancient polities that have established laws and set forms of government, than if they were born in the woods amongst the unconfined inhabitants that run loose in them. For those who would persuade us that by being born under any government we are naturally subjects to it, and have no more any title or pretence to the freedom of the state of Nature, have no other reason (bating that of paternal power, which we have already answered) to produce for it, but only because our fathers or progenitors passed away their natural liberty, and thereby bound up themselves and their posterity to a perpetual subjection to the government which they themselves submitted to. It is true that whatever engagements or promises any one made for himself, he is under the obligation of them, but cannot by any compact whatsoever bind his children or posterity. For his son, when a man, being altogether as free as the father, any act of the father can no more give away the liberty of the son than it can of anybody else. He may, indeed, annex such conditions to the land he enjoyed, as a subject of any commonwealth, as may oblige his son to be of that community, if he will enjoy those possessions which were his father's, because that estate being his father's property, he may dispose or settle it as he pleases.

And this has generally given the occasion to the mistake in this matter; because commonwealths not permitting any part of their dominions to be dismembered, nor to be enjoyed by any but those of their community, the son cannot ordinarily enjoy the possessions of his father but under the same terms his father did, by becoming a member of the society, whereby he puts himself presently under the government he finds there established, as much as any other subject of that commonweal. And thus the consent of free men, born under government, which only makes them members of it, being given separately in their turns, as each comes to be of age, and not in a multitude together, people take no notice of it, and thinking it not done at all, or not necessary, conclude they are naturally subjects as they are men.

But it is plain governments themselves understand it otherwise; they claim no power over the son because of that they had over the father; nor look on children as being their subjects, by their fathers being so. If a subject of England has a child by an Englishwoman in France, whose subject is he? Not the King of England's; for he must have leave to be admitted to the privileges of it. Nor the King of France's, for how then has his father a liberty to bring him away, and breed him as he pleases; and whoever was judged as a traitor or deserter, if he left, or warred against a country, for being barely born in it of parents that were aliens there? It is plain, then, by the practice of governments themselves, as well as by the law of right reason, that a child is born a subject of no country nor government. He is born under his father's tuition and authority till he come to age of discretion, and then he is a free man, at liberty what government he will put himself under, what body politic he will unite himself to. For if an Englishman's son born in France be at liberty, and may do so, it is evident there is no tie upon him by his father being a subject of that kingdom, nor is he bound up by any compact of his ancestors; and why then hath not his son, by the same reason, the same liberty, though he be born anywhere else? Since the power that a father hath naturally over his children is the same wherever they be born, and the ties of natural obligations are not bounded by the positive limits of kingdoms and commonwealths.

Every man being, as has been showed, naturally free, and nothing being able to put him into subjection to any earthly power, but only his own consent, it is to be considered what shall be understood to be a sufficient declaration of a man's consent to make him subject to the laws of any government. There is a common distinction of an express and a tacit consent, which will concern our present case. Nobody doubts but an express consent of any man, entering into any society, makes him a perfect member of that society, a subject of that government. The difficulty is, what ought to be looked upon as a tacit consent, and how far it binds— *i.e.*, how far any one shall be looked on to have consented, and thereby submitted to any government, where he has made no expressions of it at all. And to this I say, that every man that hath any possession or enjoyment of any part of the dominions of any government doth hereby give his tacit consent, and is as far forth obliged to obedience to the laws of that government, during such enjoyment, as any one under it, whether this his possession be of land to him and his heirs for ever, or a lodging only for a week; or whether it be barely travelling freely on the highway; and, in effect, it reaches as far as the very being of any one within the territories of that government.

To understand this the better, it is fit to consider that every man when he at first incorporates himself into any commonwealth, he, by his uniting himself thereunto, annexes also, and submits to the community those possessions which he has, or shall acquire, that do not already belong to any other government. For it would be a direct contradiction for any one to enter into society with others for the securing and regulating of property, and yet to suppose his land, whose property is to be regulated by the laws of the society, should be exempt from the jurisdiction of that government to which he himself, and the property of the land, is a subject. By the same act, therefore, whereby any one unites his person, which was before free, to any commonwealth, by the same he unites his possessions, which were before free, to it also; and they become, both of them, person and possession, subject to the government and dominion of that commonwealth as long as it hath a being. Whoever therefore, from thenceforth, by inheritance, purchases permission, or otherwise enjoys any part of the land so annexed to, and under the government of that commonweal, must take it with the condition it is under—that is, of submitting to the government of the commonwealth, under whose jurisdiction it is, as far forth as any subject of it.

But since the government has a direct jurisdiction only over the land and reaches the possessor of it (before he has actually incorporated himself in the society) only as he dwells upon and enjoys that, the obligation any one is under by virtue of such enjoyment to submit to the government begins and ends with the enjoyment; so that whenever the owner, who has given nothing but such a tacit consent to the government will, by donation, sale or otherwise, quit the said possession, he is at liberty to go and incorporate himself into any other commonwealth, or agree with others to begin a new one *in vacuis locis*, in any part of the world they can find free and unpossessed; whereas he that has once, by actual agreement and any express declaration, given his consent to be of any commonweal, is perpetually and indispensably obliged to be, and remain unalterably a subject to it, and can never be again in the liberty of the state of Nature, unless by any calamity the government he was under comes to be dissolved.

But submitting to the laws of any country, living quietly and enjoying privileges and protection under them, makes not a man a member of that society; it is only a local protection and homage due to and from all those who, not being in a state of war, come within the territories belonging to any government, to all parts whereof the force of its law extends. But this no more makes a man a member of that society, a perpetual subject of that commonwealth, than it would make a man a subject to another in whose family he found it convenient to abide for some time, though, whilst he continued in it, he were obliged to comply with the laws and submit to the government he found there. And thus we see that foreigners, by living all their lives under another government, and enjoying the privileges and protection of it, though they are bound, even in conscience, to submit to its administration as far forth as any denizen, yet do not thereby come to be subjects or members of that commonwealth. Nothing can make any man so but his actually entering into it by positive engagement and express promise and compact. This is that which, I think, concerning the beginning of political societies, and that consent which makes any one a member of any commonwealth.

---

[1] "At the first, when some certain kind of regimen was once approved, it may be that nothing was then further thought upon for the manner of governing, but all permitted unto their wisdom and discretion, which were to rule till, by experience, they found this for all parts very inconvenient, so as the thing which they had devised for a remedy did indeed but increase the sore which it should have cured. They saw that to live by one man's will became the cause of all men's misery. This constrained them to come unto laws wherein all men might see their duty beforehand, and know the penalties of transgressing them." Hooker, *Eccl. Pol.* i. 10.

First Week — Fifth Day

Aristotle, *Politics*, Book I, Chapters 1-7

Jean Jacques Rousseau,
The Social Contract, Book I, Chapters 1-8

Alexis de Tocqueville,
Democracy in America, Fourth Book, Chapter 6

Virginia Woolf, *A Room of One's Own*
(selection)

Politics

by Aristotle

BOOK I

I

EVERY state is a community of some kind, and every community is established with a view to some good; for mankind always act in order to obtain that which they think good. But, if all communities aim at some good, the state or political community, which is the highest of all, and which embraces all the rest, aims at good in a greater degree than any other, and at the highest good.

Some people think that the qualifications of a statesman, king, householder, and master are the same, and that they differ, not in kind, but only in the number of their subjects. For example, the ruler over a few is called a master; over more, the manager of a household; over a still larger number, a statesman or king, as if there were no difference between a great household and a small state. The distinction which is made between the king and the statesman is as follows: When the government is personal, the ruler is a king; when, according to the rules of the political science, the citizens rule and are ruled in turn, then he is called a statesman.

But all this is a mistake; for governments differ in kind, as will be evident to any one who considers the matter according to the method which has hitherto guided us. As in other departments of science, so in politics, the compound should always be resolved into the simple elements or least parts of the whole. We must therefore look at the elements of which the state is composed, in order that we may see in what the different kinds of rule differ from one another, and whether any scientific result can be attained about each one of them.

2

He who thus considers things in their first growth and origin, whether a state or anything else, will obtain the clearest view of them. In the first place there must be a union of those who cannot exist without each other; namely, of male and female, that the race may continue (and this is a union which is formed, not of deliberate purpose, but because, in common with other animals and with plants, mankind have a natural desire to leave behind them an image of themselves), and of natural ruler and subject, that both may be preserved. For that which can foresee by the exercise of mind is by nature intended to be lord and master, and that which can with its body give effect to such foresight is a subject, and by nature a slave; hence master and slave have the same interest. Now nature has distinguished between the female and the slave. For she is not niggardly, like the smith who fashions the Delphian knife for many uses; she makes each thing for a single use, and every instrument is best made when intended for one and not for many uses. But among barbarians no distinction is made between women and slaves, because there is no natural ruler among them: they are a community of slaves, male and female. Wherefore the poets say, —

It is meet that Hellenes should rule over barbarians; —

as if they thought that the barbarian and the slave were by nature one.

Out of these two relationships between man and woman, master and slave, the first thing to arise is the family, and Hesiod is right when he says, —

First house and wife and an ox for the plough,

for the ox is the poor man's slave. The family is the association established by nature for the supply of men's everyday wants, and the members of it are called by Charondas 'companions of the cupboard', and by Epimenides the Cretan, 'companions of the manger'. But when several families are united, and the association aims at something more than the supply of daily needs, the first society to be formed is the village. And the most natural form of the village appears to be that of a colony from the family, composed of the children and grandchildren, who are said to be 'suckled with the same milk'. And this is the reason why Hellenic states were originally governed by kings; because the Hellenes were under royal rule before they came together, as the barbarians still are. Every family is ruled by the eldest, and therefore in the colonies of the family the kingly form of government prevailed because they were of the same blood. As Homer says:

Each one gives law to his children and to his wives.

For they lived dispersedly, as was the manner in ancient times. Wherefore men say that the Gods have a king, because they themselves either are or were in ancient times under the rule of a king. For they imagine, not only the forms of the Gods, but their ways of life to be like their own.

When several villages are united in a single complete community, large enough to be nearly or quite self-sufficing, the state comes into existence, originating in the bare needs of life, and continuing in existence for the sake of a good life. And therefore, if the earlier forms of society are natural, so is the state, for it is the end of them, and the nature of a thing is its end. For what each thing is when fully developed, we call its nature, whether we are speaking of a man, a horse, or a family. Besides, the final cause and end of a thing is the best, and to be self-sufficing is the end and the best.

Hence it is evident that the state is a creation of nature, and that man is by nature a political animal. And he who by nature and not by mere accident is without a state, is either a bad man or above humanity; he is like the

> Tribeless, lawless, hearthless one,

whom Homer denounces—the natural outcast is forthwith a lover of war; he may be compared to an isolated piece at draughts.

Now, that man is more of a political animal than bees or any other gregarious animals is evident. Nature, as we often say, makes nothing in vain, and man is the only animal whom she has endowed with the gift of speech. And whereas mere voice is but an indication of pleasure or pain, and is therefore found in other animals (for their nature attains to the perception of pleasure and pain and the intimation of them to one another, and no further), the power of speech is intended to set forth the expedient and inexpedient, and therefore likewise the just and the unjust. And it is a characteristic of man that he alone has any sense of good and evil, of just and unjust, and the like, and the association of living beings who have this sense makes a family and a state.

Further, the state is by nature clearly prior to the family and to the individual, since the whole is of necessity prior to the part; for example, if the whole body be destroyed, there will be no foot or hand, except in an equivocal sense, as we might speak of a stone hand; for when destroyed the hand will be no better than that. But things are defined by their working and power; and we ought not to say that they are the same when they no longer have their proper quality, but only that they have the same name. The proof that the state is a creation of nature and prior to the individual is that the individual, when isolated, is not self-sufficing; and therefore he is like a part in relation to the whole. But he who is unable to live in society, or who has no need because he is sufficient for himself, must be either a beast or a god: he is no part of a state. A social instinct is implanted in all men by nature, and yet he who first founded the state was the greatest of benefactors. For man, when perfected, is the best of animals, but, when separated from law and justice, he is the worst of all; since armed injustice is the more dangerous, and he is equipped at birth with arms, meant to be used by intelligence and virtue, which he may use for the worst ends.

Wherefore, if he have not virtue, he is the most unholy and the most savage of animals, and the most full of lust and gluttony. But justice is the bond of men in states, for the administration of justice, which is the determination of what is just, is the principle of order in political society.

3

Seeing then that the state is made up of households, before speaking of the state we must speak of the management of the household. The parts of household management correspond to the persons who compose the household, and a complete household consists of slaves and freemen. Now we should begin by examining everything in its fewest possible elements; and the first and fewest possible parts of a family are master and slave, husband and wife, father and children. We have therefore to consider what each of these three relations is and ought to be: I mean the relation of master and servant, the marriage relation (the conjunction of man and wife has no name of its own), and thirdly, the procreative relation (this also has no proper name). And there is another element of a household, the so-called art of getting wealth, which, according to some, is identical with household management, according to others, a principal part of it; the nature of this art will also have to be considered by us.

Let us first speak of master and slave, looking to the needs of practical life and also seeking to attain some better theory of their relation than exists at present. For some are of opinion that the rule of a master is a science, and that the management of a household, and the mastership of slaves, and the political and royal rule, as I was saying at the outset, are all the same. Others affirm that the rule of a master over slaves is contrary to nature and that the distinction between slave and freeman exists by law only, and not by nature; and being an interference with nature is therefore unjust.

4

Property is a part of the household, and the art of acquiring property is a part of the art of managing the household; for no man can live well, or indeed live at all, unless he be provided with necessaries. And as in the arts which have a definite sphere the workers must have their own proper instruments for the accomplishment of their work, so it is in the management of a household. Now instruments are of various sorts; some are living, others lifeless; in the rudder, the pilot of a ship has a lifeless, in the look-out man, a living instrument; for in the arts the servant is a kind of instrument. Thus, too, a possession is an instrument for maintaining life. And so, in the arrangement of the family, a slave is a living possession, and property a number of such instruments; and the servant is himself an instrument which takes precedence of all other instruments. For if every instrument could accomplish its own work, obeying or anticipating the will of others, like the statues of Daedalus, or the tripods of Hephaestus, which, says the poet, *of their own accord entered the assembly of the Gods;*

if, in like manner, the shuttle would weave and the plectrum touch the lyre without a hand to guide them, chief workmen would not want servants, nor masters slaves. Here, however, another distinction must be drawn: the instruments commonly so called are instruments of production, whilst a possession is an instrument of action. The shuttle, for example, is not only of use; but something else is made by it, whereas of a garment or of a bed there is only the use. Further, as production and action are different in kind, and both require instruments, the instruments which they employ must likewise differ in kind. But life is action and not production, and therefore the slave is the minister of action. Again, a possession is spoken of as a part is spoken of; for the part is not only a part of something else, but wholly belongs to it; and this is also true of a possession. The master is only the master of the slave; he does not belong to him, whereas the slave is not only the slave of his master, but wholly belongs to him. Hence we see what is the nature and office of a slave; he who is by nature not his own but another's man, is by nature a slave; and he may be said to be another's man who, being a human being, is also a possession. And a possesion may be defined as an instrument of action, separable from the possessor.

5

But is there any one thus intended by nature to be a slave, and for whom such a condition is expedient and right, or rather is not all slavery a violation of nature?

There is no difficulty in answering this question, on grounds both of reason and of fact. For that some should rule and others be ruled is a thing not only necessary, but expedient; from the hour of their birth, some are marked out for subjection, others for rule.

And there are many kinds both of rulers and subjects (and that rule is the better which is exercised over better subjects—for example, to rule over men is better than to rule over wild beasts; for the work is better which is executed by better workmen, and where one man rules and another is ruled, they may be said to have a work); for in all things which form a composite whole and which are made up of parts, whether continuous or discrete, a distinction between the ruling and the subject element comes to light. Such a duality exists in living creatures, but not in them only; it originates in the constitution of the universe; even in things which have no life there is a ruling principle, as in a musical mode. But we are wandering from the subject. We will therefore restrict ourselves to the living creature, which, in the first place, consists of soul and body: and of these two, the one is by nature the ruler, and the other the subject. But then we must look for the intentions of nature in things which retain their nature, and not in things which are corrupted. And therefore we must study the man who is in the most perfect state both of body and soul, for in him we shall see the true relation of the two; although in bad or corrupted natures the body will often appear to rule over the soul, because they are in an evil and unnatural condition. At all events we may firstly observe in living creatures both a despotical and a constitutional rule; for the soul rules the body with a despotical rule, whereas the intellect rules the appetites with a constitutional and royal rule. And it is clear that the rule of the soul over the body, and of the mind and the rational element over the passionate, is natural and expedient; whereas the equality of the two or the rule of the inferior is always hurtful. The same holds good of animals in relation to men; for tame animals have a better nature than wild, and all tame animals are better off when they are ruled by man; for then they are preserved. Again, the male is by nature superior, and the female inferior; and the one rules, and the other is ruled; this principle, of necessity, extends to all mankind. Where then there is such a difference as that between soul and body, or between men and animals (as in the case of those whose business is to use their body, and who can do nothing better), the lower sort are by nature slaves, and it is better for them as for all inferiors that they should be under the rule of a master. For he who can be, and therefore is, another's, and he who participates in rational principle enough to apprehend, but not to have, such a principle, is a slave by nature. Whereas the lower animals cannot even apprehend a principle; they obey their instincts. And indeed the use made of slaves and of tame animals is not very different; for both with their bodies minister to the needs of life. Nature would like to distinguish between the bodies of freemen and slaves, making the one strong for servile labour, the other upright, and although useless for such services, useful for political life in the arts both of war and peace. But the opposite often happens— that some have the souls and others have the bodies of freemen. And doubtless if men differed from one another in the mere forms of their bodies as much as the statues of the Gods do from men, all would acknowledge that the inferior class should be slaves of the superior. And if this is true of the body, how much more just that a similar distinction should exist in the soul? but the beauty of the body is seen, whereas the beauty of the soul is not seen. It is clear, then, that some men are by nature free, and others slaves, and that for these latter slavery is both expedient and right.

6

But that those who take the opposite view have in a certain way right on their side, may be easily seen. For the words slavery and slave are used in two senses. There is a slave or slavery by law as well as by nature. The law of which I speak is a sort of convention—the law by which whatever is taken in war is supposed to belong to the victors. But this right many jurists impeach, as they would an orator who brought forward an unconstitutional measure: they detest the notion that, because one man has the power of doing violence and is superior in brute strength, another shall be his slave and subject. Even among philosophers there is a difference of opinion. The origin of the dispute, and what makes the views invade each other's territory, is as follows: in some sense virtue, when furnished with means, has actually the greatest power of exercising force: and as superior power is only found where there is superior excellence of some kind, power seems to imply virtue, and the dispute to be simply one about justice (for it is due to one party identifying justice with goodwill, while the other identifies it with the mere rule of the stronger). If these views are thus set out separately, the other views have no force or plausibility against the view that the superior in virtue ought to rule, or be master. Others clinging, as they think, simply to a principle of justice (for law and custom are a sort of justice), assume that slavery in accordance with the custom of war is justified by law, but at the same moment they deny this. For what if the cause of the war be unjust? And again, no one would ever say that he is a slave who is unworthy to be a slave. Were this the case, men of the highest rank would be slaves and the children of slaves if they or their parents chance to have been taken captive and sold. Wherefore Hellenes do not like to call Hellenes slaves, but confine the term to barbarians. Yet, in using this language, they really mean the natural slave of whom we spoke at first, for it must be admitted that some are slaves everywhere, others nowhere. The same principle applies to nobility. Hellenes regard themselves as noble everywhere, and not only in their own country, but they deem the barbarians noble only when at home, thereby implying that there are two sorts of nobility and freedom, the one absolute, the other relative. The Helen of Theodectes says:[2]

> Who would presume to call me servant who am on both sides
> sprung from the stem of the Gods?

What does this mean but that they distinguish freedom and slavery, noble and humble birth, by the two principles of good and evil? They think that as men and animals beget men and animals, so from good men a good man springs. But this is what nature, though she may intend it, cannot always accomplish.

We see then that there is some foundation for this difference of opinion, and that all are not either slaves by nature or freemen by nature, and also that there is in some cases a marked distinction between the two classes, rendering it expedient and right for the one to be slaves and the others to be masters: the one practising obedience, the others exercising the authority and lordship which nature intended them to have. The abuse of this authority is injurious to both; for the interests of part and whole, of body and soul, are the same, and the slave is a part of the master, a living but separated part of his bodily frame. Hence. where the relation of master and slave between them is natural they are friends and have a common interest, but where it rests merely on law and force the reverse is true.

7

The previous remarks are quite enough to show that the rule of a master is not a constitutional rule, and that all the different kinds of rule are not as some affirm, the same with each other. For there is one rule exercised over subjects who are by nature slaves. The rule of a household is a monarchy, for every house is under one head: whereas constitutional rule is a government of freemen and equals. The master is not called a master because he has science, but because he is of a certain character, and the same remark applies to the slave and the freeman. Still there may be a science for the master and a science for the slave. The science of the slave would be such as the man of Syracuse taught, who made money by instructing slaves in their ordinary duties. And such a knowledge may be carried further, so as to include cookery and similar menial arts. For some duties are of the more necessary, others of the more honourable sort; as the proverb says, 'slave before slave, master before master'.[3] But all such branches of knowledge are servile. There is likewise a science of the master, which teaches the use of slaves; for the master as such is concerned, not with the acquisition, but with the use of them. Yet this so-called science is not anything great or wonderful; for the master need only know how to order that which the slave must know how to execute. Hence those who are in a position which places them above toil have stewards who attend to their households while they occupy themselves with philosophy or with politics. But the art of acquiring slaves, I mean of justly acquiring them, differs both from the art of the master and the art of the slave, being a species of hunting or war. Enough of the distinction between master and slave.

The Social Contract

or

Principles of Political Right

by Jean Jacques Rousseau

FOREWORD

This little treatise is part of a longer work which I began years ago without realising my limitations, and long since abandoned. Of the various fragments that might have been extracted from what I wrote, this is the most considerable, and, I think, the least unworthy of being offered to the public. The rest no longer exists.

BOOK I

I MEAN to inquire if, in the civil order, there can be any sure and legitimate rule of administration, men being taken as they are and laws as they might be. In this inquiry I shall endeavour always to unite what right sanctions with what is prescribed by interest, in order that justice and utility may in no case be divided.

I enter upon my task without proving the importance of the subject. I shall be asked if I am a prince or a legislator, to write on politics. I answer that I am neither, and that is why I do so. If I were a prince or a legislator, I should not waste time in saying what wants doing; I should do it, or hold my peace.

As I was born a citizen of a free State, and a member of the Sovereign, I feel that, however feeble the influence my voice can have on public affairs, the right of voting on them makes it my duty to study them: and I am happy, when I reflect upon governments, to find my inquiries always furnish me with new reasons for loving that of my own country.

1. Subject of the First Book

Man is born free; and everywhere he is in chains. One thinks himself the master of others, and still remains a greater slave than they. How did this change come about? I do not know. What can make it legitimate? That question I think I can answer.

If I took into account only force, and the effects derived from it, I should say: "As long as a people is compelled to obey, and obeys, it does well; as soon as it can shake off the yoke, and shakes it off, it does still better; for, regaining its liberty by the same right as took it away, either it is justified in resuming it, or there was no justification for those who took it away." But the social order is a sacred right which is the basis of all other rights. Nevertheless, this right does not come from nature, and must therefore be founded on conventions. Before coming to that, I have to prove what I have just asserted.

2. The First Societies

The most ancient of all societies, and the only one that is natural, is the family: and even so the children remain attached to the father only so long as they need him for their preservation. As soon as this need ceases, the natural bond is dissolved. The children, released from the obedience they owed to the father, and the father, released from the care he owed his children, return equally to independence. If they remain united, they continue so no longer naturally, but voluntarily; and the family itself is then maintained only by convention.

This common liberty results from the nature of man. His first law is to provide for his own preservation, his first cares are those which he owes to himself; and, as soon as he reaches years of discretion, he is the sole judge of the proper means of preserving himself, and consequently becomes his own master.

The family then may be called the first model of political societies: the ruler corresponds to the father, and the people to the children; and all, being born free and equal, alienate their liberty only for their own advantage. The whole difference is that, in the family, the love of the father for his children repays him for the care he takes of them, while, in the State, the pleasure of commanding takes the place of the love which the chief cannot have for the peoples under him.

Grotius denies that all human power is established in favour of the governed, and quotes slavery as an example. His usual method of reasoning is constantly to establish right by fact.[1] It would be possible to employ a more logical method, but none could be more favourable to tyrants.

It is then, according to Grotius, doubtful whether the human race belongs to a hundred men, or that hundred men to the human race: and, throughout his book, he seems to incline to the former alternative, which is also the view of Hobbes. On this showing, the human species is divided into so many herds of cattle, each with its ruler, who keeps guard over them for the purpose of devouring them.

As a shepherd is of a nature superior to that of his flock, the shepherds of men, i.e., their rulers, are of a nature superior to that of the peoples under them. Thus, Philo tells us, the Emperor Caligula reasoned, concluding equally well either that kings were gods, or that men were beasts.

The reasoning of Caligula agrees with that of Hobbes and Grotius. Aristotle, before any of them, had said that men are by no means equal naturally, but that some are born for slavery, and others for dominion.

Aristotle was right; but he took the effect for the cause. Nothing can be more certain than that every man born in slavery is born for slavery. Slaves lose everything in their chains, even the desire of escaping from them: they love their servitude, as the comrades of Ulysses loved their brutish condition.[2] If then there are slaves by nature, it is because there have been slaves against nature. Force made the first slaves, and their cowardice perpetuated the condition.

I have said nothing of King Adam, or Emperor Noah, father of the three great monarchs who shared out the universe, like the children of Saturn, whom some scholars have recognised in them. I trust to getting due thanks for my moderation; for, being a direct descendant of one of these princes, perhaps of the eldest branch, how do I know that a verification of titles might not leave me the legitimate king of the human race? In any case, there can be no doubt that Adam was sovereign of the world, as Robinson Crusoe was of his island, as long as he was its only inhabitant; and this empire had the advantage that the monarch, safe on his throne, had no rebellions, wars, or conspirators to fear.

3. The Right of the Strongest

The strongest is never strong enough to be always the master, unless he transforms strength into right, and obedience into duty. Hence the right of the strongest, which, though to all seeming meant ironically, is really laid down as a fundamental principle. But are we never to have an explanation of this phrase? Force is a physical power, and I fail to see what moral effect it can have. To yield to force is an act of necessity, not of will—at the most, an act of prudence. In what sense can it be a duty?

Suppose for a moment that this so-called "right" exists. I maintain that the sole result is a mass of nonsense. For, if force creates right, the effect changes with the cause: every force that is greater than the first succeeds to its right. As soon as it is possible to disobey with impunity, disobedience is legitimate; and, the strongest being always in the right, the only thing that matters is to act so as to become the strongest. But what kind of right is that which perishes when force fails? If we must obey perforce, there is no need to obey because we ought; and if we are not forced to obey, we are under no obligation to do so. Clearly, the word "right" adds nothing to force: in this connection, it means absolutely nothing.

Obey the powers that be. If this means yield to force, it is a good precept, but superfluous: I can answer for its never being violated. All power comes from God, I admit; but so does all sickness: does that mean that we are forbidden to call in the doctor? A brigand surprises me at the edge of a wood: must I not merely surrender my purse on compulsion; but, even if I could withhold it, am I in conscience bound to give it up? For certainly the pistol he holds is also a power.

Let us then admit that force does not create right, and that we are obliged to obey only legitimate powers. In that case, my original question recurs.

4. Slavery

Since no man has a natural authority over his fellow, and force creates no right, we must conclude that conventions form the basis of all legitimate authority among men.

If an individual, says Grotius, can alienate his liberty and make himself the slave of a master, why could not a whole people do the same and make itself subject to a king? There are in this passage plenty of ambiguous words which would need explaining; but let us confine ourselves to the word *alienate*. To alienate is to give or to sell. Now, a man who becomes the slave of another does not give himself; he sells himself, at the least for his subsistence: but for what does a people sell itself? A king is so far from furnishing his subjects with their subsistence that he gets his own only from them; and, according to Rabelais, kings do not live on nothing. Do subjects then give their persons on condition that the king takes their goods also? I fail to see what they have left to preserve.

It will be said that the despot assures his subjects civil tranquillity. Granted; but what do they gain, if the wars his ambition brings down upon them, his insatiable avidity, and the vexatious conduct of his ministers press harder on them than their own dissensions would have done? What do they gain, if the very tranquillity they enjoy is one of their miseries? Tranquillity is found also in dungeons; but is that enough to make them desirable places to live in? The Greeks imprisoned in the cave of the Cyclops lived there very tranquilly, while they were awaiting their turn to be devoured.

To say that a man gives himself gratuitously, is to say what is absurd and inconceivable; such an act is null and illegitimate, from the mere fact that he who does it is out of his mind. To say the same of a whole people is to suppose a people of madmen; and madness creates no right.

Even if each man could alienate himself, he could not alienate his children: they are born men and free; their liberty belongs to them, and no one but they has the right to dispose of it. Before they came to years of discretion, the father can, in their name, lay down conditions for their preservation and well-being, but he cannot give them irrevocably and without conditions: such a gift is contrary to the ends of nature, and exceeds the rights of paternity. It would therefore be necessary, in order to legitimise an arbitrary government, that in every generation the people should be in a position to accept or reject it; but, were this so, the government would be no longer arbitrary.

To renounce liberty is to renounce being a man, to surrender the rights of humanity and even its duties. For him who renounces everything no indemnity is possible. Such a renunciation is incompatible with man's nature; to remove all liberty from his will is to remove all morality from his acts. Finally, it is an empty and contradictory convention that sets up, on the one side, absolute authority, and, on the other, unlimited obedience. Is it not clear that we can be under no obligation to a person from whom we have the right to exact everything? Does not this condition alone, in the absence of equivalence or exchange, in itself involve the nullity of the act? For what right can my slave have against me, when all that he has belongs to me, and, his right being mine, this right of mine against myself is a phrase devoid of meaning?

Grotius and the rest find in war another origin for the so-called right of slavery. The victor having, as they hold, the right of killing the vanquished, the latter can buy back his life at the price of his liberty; and this convention is the more legitimate because it is to the advantage of both parties.

But it is clear that this supposed right to kill the conquered is by no means deducible from the state of war. Men, from the mere fact that, while they are living in their primitive independence, they have no mutual relations stable enough to constitute either the state of peace or the state of war, cannot be naturally enemies. War is constituted by a relation between things, and not between persons; and, as the state of war cannot arise out of simple personal relations, but only out of real relations, private war, or war of man with man, can exist neither in the state of nature, where there is no constant property, nor in the social state, where everything is under the authority of the laws.

Individual combats, duels and encounters, are acts which cannot constitute a state; while the private wars, authorised by the Establishments of Louis IX, King of France, and suspended by the Peace of God, are abuses of feudalism, in itself an absurd system if ever there was one, and contrary to the principles of natural right and to all good polity.

War then is a relation, not between man and man, but between State and State, and individuals are enemies only accidentally, not as men, nor even as citizens,[3] but as soldiers; not as members of their country, but as its defenders. Finally, each State can have for enemies only other States, and not men; for between things disparate in nature there can be no real relation.

Furthermore, this principle is in conformity with the established rules of all times and the constant practice of all civilised peoples. Declarations of war are intimations less to powers than to their subjects. The foreigner, whether king, individual, or people, who robs, kills or detains the subjects, without declaring war on the prince, is not an enemy, but a brigand. Even in real war, a just prince, while laying hands, in the enemy's country, on all that belongs to the public, respects the lives and goods of individuals: he respects rights on which his own are founded. The object of the war being the destruction of the hostile State, the other side has a right to kill its defenders, while they are bearing arms; but as soon as they lay them down and surrender, they cease to be enemies or instruments of the enemy, and become once more merely men, whose life no one has any right to take. Sometimes it is possible to kill the State without killing a single one of its members; and war gives no right which is not necessary to the gaining of its object. These principles are not those of Grotius: they are not based on the authority of poets, but derived from the nature of reality and based on reason.

The right of conquest has no foundation other than the right of the strongest. If war does not give the conqueror the right to massacre the conquered peoples, the right to enslave them cannot be based upon a right which does not exist. No one has a right to kill an enemy except when he cannot make him a slave, and the right to enslave him cannot therefore be derived from the right to kill him. It is accordingly an unfair exchange to make him buy at the price of his liberty his life, over which the victor holds no right. Is it not clear that there is a vicious circle in founding the right of life and death on the right of slavery, and the right of slavery on the right of life and death?

Even if we assume this terrible right to kill everybody, I maintain that a slave made in war, or a conquered people, is under no obligation to a master, except to obey him as far as he is compelled to do so. By taking an equivalent for his life, the victor has not done him a favour; instead of killing him without profit, he has killed him usefully. So far then is he from acquiring over him any authority in addition to that of force, that the state of war continues to subsist between them: their mutual relation is the effect of it, and the usage of the right of war does not imply a treaty of peace. A convention has indeed been made; but this convention, so far from destroying the state of war, presupposes its continuance.

So, from whatever aspect we regard the question, the right of slavery is null and void, not only as being illegitimate, but also because it is absurd and meaningless. The words *slave* and *right* contradict each other, and are mutually exclusive. It will always be equally foolish for a man to say to a man or to a people: "I make with you a convention wholly at your expense and wholly to my advantage; I shall keep it as long as I like, and you will keep it as long as I like."

5. That We Must Always Go Back to a First Convention

Even if I granted all that I have been refuting, the friends of despotism would be no better off. There will always be a great difference between subduing a multitude and ruling a society. Even if scattered individuals were successively enslaved by one man, however numerous they might be, I still see no more than a master and his slaves, and certainly not a people and its ruler; I see what may be termed an aggregation, but not an association; there is as yet neither public good nor body politic. The man in question, even if he has enslaved half the world, is still only an individual; his interest, apart from that of others, is still a purely private interest. If this same man comes to die, his empire, after him, remains scattered and without unity, as an oak falls and dissolves into a heap of ashes when the fire has consumed it.

A people, says Grotius, can give itself to a king. Then, according to Grotius, a people is a people before it gives itself. The gift is itself a civil act, and implies public deliberation. It would be better, before examining the act by which a people gives itself to a king, to examine that by which it has become a people; for this act, being necessarily prior to the other, is the true foundation of society.

Indeed, if there were no prior convention, where, unless the election were unanimous, would be the obligation on the minority to submit to the choice of the majority? How have a hundred men who wish for a master the right to vote on behalf of ten who do not? The law of majority voting is itself something established by convention, and presupposes unanimity, on one occasion at least.

6. The Social Compact

I suppose men to have reached the point at which the osbstacles in the way of their preservation in the state of nature show their power of resistance to be greater than the resources at the disposal of each individual for his maintenance in that state. That primitive condition can then subsist no longer; and the human race would perish unless it changed its manner of existence.

But, as men cannot engender new forces, but only unite and direct existing ones, they have no other means of preserving themselves than the formation, by aggregation, of a sum of forces great enough to overcome the resistance. These they have to bring into play by means of a single motive power, and cause to act in concert.

This sum of forces can arise only where several persons come together; but, as the force and liberty of each man are the chief instruments of his self-preservation, how can he pledge them without harming his own interests, and neglecting the care he owes to himself? This difficulty, in its bearing on my present subject, may be stated in the following terms:

"The problem is to find a form of association which will defend and protect with the whole common force the person and goods of each associate, and in which each, while uniting himself with all, may still obey himself alone, and remain as free as before." This is the fundamental problem of which the *Social Contract* provides the solution.

The clauses of this contract are so determined by the nature of the act that the slightest modification would make them vain and ineffective; so that, although they have perhaps never been formally set forth, they are everywhere the same and everywhere tacitly admitted and recognised, until, on the violation of the social compact, each regains his original rights and resumes his natural liberty, while losing the conventional liberty in favour of which he renounced it.

These clauses, properly understood, may be reduced to one—the total alienation of each associate, together with all his rights, to the whole community; for, in the first place, as each gives himself absolutely, the conditions are the same for all; and, this being so, no one has any interest in making them burdensome to others.

Moreover, the alienation being with reserve, the union is as perfect as it can be, and no associate has anything more to demand: for, if the individuals retained certain rights, as there would be no common superior to decide between them and the public, each, being on one point his own judge, would ask to be so on all; the state of nature would thus continue, and the association would necessarily become inoperative or tyrannical.

Finally, each man, in giving himself to all, gives himself to nobody; and as there is no associate over whom he does not acquire the same right as he yields others over himself, he gains an equivalent for everything he loses, and an increase of force for the preservation of what he has.

If then we discard from the social compact what is not of its essence, we shall find that it reduces itself to the following terms:

"Each of us puts his person and all his power in common under the supreme direction of the general will, and, in our corporate capacity, we receive each member as an indivisible part of the whole."

At once, in place of the individual personality of each contracting party, this act of association creates a moral and collective body, composed of as many members as the assembly contains votes, and receiving from this act its unity, its common identity, its life and its will. This public person, so formed by the union of all other persons, formerly took the name of *city*,[4] and now takes that of *Republic* or *body politic*; it is called by its members *State* when passive, *Sovereign* when active, and *Power* when compared with others like itself. Those who are associated in it take collectively the name of *people,* and severally are called *citizens,* as sharing in the sovereign power, and *subjects,* as being under the laws of the State. But these terms are often confused and taken one for another: it is enough to know how to distinguish them when they are being used with precision.

7. The Sovereign

This formula shows us that the act of association comprises a mutual undertaking between the public and the individuals, and that each individual, in making a contract, as we may say, with himself, is bound in a double capacity; as a member of the Sovereign he is bound to the individuals, and as a member of the State to the Sovereign. But the maxim of civil right, that no one is bound by undertakings made to himself, does not apply in this case; for there is a great difference between incurring an obligation to yourself and incurring one to a whole of which you form a part.

Attention must further be called to the fact that public deliberation, while competent to bind all the subjects to the Sovereign, because of the two different capacities in which each of them may be regarded, cannot, for the opposite reason, bind the Sovereign to itself; and that it is consequently against the nature of the body politic for the Sovereign to impose on itself a law which it cannot infringe. Being able to regard itself in only one capacity, it is in the position of an individual who makes a contract with himself; and this makes it clear that there neither is nor can be any kind of fundamental law binding on the body of the people—not even the social contract itself. This does not mean that the body politic cannot enter into undertakings with others, provided the contract is not infringed by them; for in relation to what is external to it, it becomes a simple being, an individual.

But the body politic or the Sovereign, drawing its being wholly from the sanctity of the contract, can never bind itself, even to an outsider, to do anything derogatory to the original act, for instance, to alienate any part of itself, or to submit to another Sovereign. Violation of the act by which it exists would be self-annihilation; and that which is itself nothing can create nothing.

As soon as this multitude is so united in one body, it is impossible to offend against one of the members without attacking the body, and still more to offend against the body without the members resenting it. Duty and interest therefore equally oblige the two contracting parties to give each other help; and the same men should seek to combine, in their double capacity, all the advantages dependent upon that capacity.

Again, the Sovereign, being formed wholly of the individuals who compose it, neither has nor can have any interest contrary to theirs; and consequently the sovereign power need give no guarantee to its subjects, because it is impossible for the body to wish to hurt all its members. We shall also see later on that it cannot hurt any in particular. The Sovereign, merely by virtue of what it is, is always what it should be.

This, however, is not the case with the relation of the subjects to the Sovereign, which, despite the common interest, would have no security that they would fulfil their undertakings, unless it found means to assure itself of their fidelity.

In fact, each individual, as a man, may have a particular will contrary or dissimilar to the general will which he has as a citizen. His particular interest may speak to him quite differently from the common interest: his absolute and naturally independent existence may make him look upon what he owes to the common cause as a gratuitous contribution, the loss of which will do less harm to others than the payment of it is burdensome to himself; and, regarding the moral person which constitutes the State as a *persona ficta*, because not a man, he may wish to enjoy the rights of citizenship without being ready to fulfil the duties of a subject. The continuance of such an injustice could not but prove the undoing of the body politic.

In order then that the social compact may not be an empty formula, it tacitly includes the undertaking, which alone can give force to the rest, that whoever refuses to obey the general will shall be compelled to do so by the whole body. This means nothing less than that he will be forced to be free; for this is the condition which, by giving each citizen to his country, secures him against all personal dependence. In this lies the key to the working of the political machine; this alone legitimises civil undertakings, which, without it, would be absurd, tyrannical, and liable to the most frightful abuses.

8. The Civil State

The passage from the state of nature to the civil state produces a very remarkable change in man, by substituting justice for instinct in his conduct, and giving his actions the morality they had formerly lacked. Then only, when the voice of duty takes the place of physical impulses and right of appetite, does man, who so far had considered only himself, find that he is forced to act on different principles, and to consult his reason before listening to his inclinations. Although, in this state, he deprives himself of some advantages which he got from nature, he gains in return others so great, his faculties are so stimulated and developed, his ideas so extended, his feelings so ennobled, and his whole soul so uplifted, that, did not the abuses of this new condition often degrade him below that which he left, he would be bound to bless continually the happy moment which took him from it for ever, and, instead of a stupid and unimaginative animal, made him an intelligent being and a man.

Let us draw up the whole account in terms easily commensurable. What man loses by the social contract is his natural liberty and an unlimited right to everything he tries to get and succeeds in getting; what he gains is civil liberty and the proprietorship of all he possesses. If we are to avoid mistake in weighing one against the other, we must clearly distinguish natural liberty, which is bounded only by the strength of the individual, from civil liberty, which is limited by the general will; and possession, which is merely the effect of force or the right of the first occupier, from property, which can be founded only on a positive title.

We might, over and above all this, add, to what man acquires in the civil state, moral liberty, which alone makes him truly master of himself; for the mere impulse of appetite is slavery, while obedience to a law which we prescribe to ourselves is liberty. But I have already said too much on this head, and the philosophical meaning of the word liberty does not now concern us.

---

[1] "Learned inquiries into public right are often only the history of past abuses; and troubling to study them too deeply is a profitless infatuation" (*Essay on the Interests of France in Relation to its Neighbours*, by the Marquis d'Argenson). This is exactly what Grotius has done.

[2] See a short treatise of Plutarch's entitled *That Animals Reason*.

[3] The Romans, who understood and respected the right of war more than any other nation on earth, carried their scruples on this head so far that a citizen was not allowed to serve as a volunteer without engaging himself expressly against the enemy, and against such and such an enemy by name. A legion in which the younger Cato was seeing his first service under Popilius having been reconstructed, the elder Cato wrote to Popilius that, if he wished his son to continue serving under him, he must administer to him a new military oath, because, the first having been annulled, he was no longer able to bear arms against the enemy. The same Cato wrote to his son telling him to take great care not to go into battle before taking this new oath. I know that the siege of Clusium and other isolated events can be quoted against me; but I am citing laws and customs. The Romans are the people that least often transgressed its laws; and no other people has had such good ones.

[4] The real meaning of this word has been almost wholly lost in modern times; most people mistake a town for a city, and a townsman for a citizen. They do not know that houses make a town, but citizens a city. The same mistake long ago cost the Carthaginians dear. I have never read of the title of citizens being given to the subjects of any prince, not even the

ancient Macedonians or the English of to-day, though they are nearer liberty than any one else. The French alone everywhere familiarly adopt the name of citizens, because, as can be seen from their dictionaries, they have no idea of its meaning; otherwise they would be guilty in usurping it, of the crime of *lèse-majesté:* among them, the name expresses a virtue, and not a right. When Bodin spoke of our citizens and townsmen, he fell into a bad blunder in taking the one class for the other. M. d'Alembert has avoided the error, and, in his article on Geneva, has clearly distinguished the four orders of men (or even five, counting mere foreigners) who dwell in our town, of which two only compose the Republic. No other French writer, to my knowledge, has understood the real meaning of the word citizen.

Democracy in America

by Alexis de Tocqueville

Fourth Book – Chapter VI
What Sort of Despotism Democratic Nations Have to Fear

...DEMOCRATIC governments may become violent, and even cruel, at certain periods of extreme effervescence or of great danger; but these crises will be rare and brief. When I consider the petty passions of our contemporaries, the mildness of their manners, the extent of their education, the purity of their religion, the gentleness of their morality, their regular and industrious habits, and the restraint which they almost all observe in their vices no less than in their virtues, I have no fear that they will meet with tyrants in their rulers but rather with guardians.

I think, then, that the species of oppression by which democratic nations are menaced is unlike anything which ever before existed in the world; our contemporaries will find no prototype of it in their memories. I seek in vain for an expression which will accurately convey the whole of the idea I have formed of it; the old words "despotism" and "tyranny" are inappropriate. The thing itself is new, and, since I cannot name it, I must attempt to define it.

I seek to trace the novel features under which despotism may appear in the world. The first thing that strikes the observation is an innumerable multitude of men, all equal and alike, incessantly endeavoring to procure the petty and paltry pleasures with which they glut their lives. Each of them, living apart, is as a stranger to the fate of all the rest—his children and his private friends constitute to him the whole of mankind; as to the rest of his fellow-citizens, he is close to them, but he sees them not—he touches them, but he feels them not; he exists but in himself and for himself alone; and if his kindred still remain to him, he may be said, at any rate, to have lost his country.

Above this race of men stands an immense and tutelary power which takes upon itself alone to secure their gratifications and to watch over their fate. That power is absolute, minute, regular, provident, and mild. It would be like the authority of a parent, if, like that authority, its object was to prepare men for manhood; but it seeks, on the contrary, to keep them in perpetual childhood; it is well content that the people should rejoice, provided they think of nothing but rejoicing. For their happiness such a government willingly labors, but it chooses to be the sole agent and the only arbiter of that happiness; it provides for their security, foresees and supplies their necessities, facilitates their pleasures, manages their principal concerns, directs their industry, regulates the descent of property, and subdivides their inheritances: what remains but to spare them all the care of thinking and all the trouble of living?

Thus, it every day renders the exercise of the free agency of man less useful and less frequent; it circumscribes the will within a narrower range and gradually robs a man of all the uses of himself. The principle of equality has prepared men for these things; it has predisposed men to endure them, and oftentimes to look on them as benefits.

After having thus successively taken each member of the community in its powerful grasp, and fashioned him at will, the supreme power then extends its arm over the whole community. It covers the surface of society with a network of small complicated rules, minute and uniform, through which the most original minds and the most energetic characters cannot penetrate to rise above the crowd. The will of man is not shattered but softened, bent, and guided; men are seldom forced by it to act, but they are constantly restrained from acting. Such a power does not destroy, but it prevents existence; it does not tyrannize, but it compresses, enervates, extinguishes, and stupefies a people, till each nation is reduced to be nothing better than a flock of timid and industrious animals, of which the government is the shepherd.

I have always thought that servitude of the regular, quiet, and gentle kind which I have just described might be combined more easily than is commonly believed with some of the outward forms of freedom and that it might even establish itself under the wing of the sovereignty of the people. . . .

A Room of One's Own

by Virginia Woolf

IT would be ambitious beyond my daring, I thought, looking about the shelves for books that were not there, to suggest to the students of those famous colleges that they should re-write history, though I own that it often seems a little queer as it is, unreal, lop-sided; but why should they not add a supplement to history? Calling it, of course, by some inconspicuous name so that women might figure there without impropriety? For one often catches a glimpse of them in the lives of the great, whisking away into the background, concealing, I sometimes think, a wink, a laugh, perhaps a tear. And, after all, we have lives enough of Jane Austen; it scarcely seems necessary to consider again the influence of the tragedies of Joanna Baillie upon the poetry of Edgar Allan Poe; as for myself, I should not mind if the homes and haunts of Mary Russell Mitford were closed to the public for a century at least. But what I find deplorable, I continued, looking about the bookshelves again, is that nothing is known about women before the eighteenth century. I have no model in my mind to turn about this way and that. Here am I asking why women did not write poetry in the Elizabethan age, and I am not sure how they were educated; whether they were taught to write; whether they had sitting-rooms to themselves; how many women had children before they were twenty-one; what, in short, they did from eight in the morning till eight at night. They had no money, evidently; according to Professor Trevelyan they were married whether they liked it or not before they were out of the nursery, at fifteen or sixteen very likely. It would have been extremely odd, even upon this showing, had one of them suddenly written the plays of Shakespeare, I concluded, and I thought of that old gentleman, who is dead now, but was a bishop, I think, who declared that it was impossible for any woman, past, present, or to come, to have the genius of Shakespeare. He wrote to the papers about it. He also told a lady who applied to him for information that cats do not as a matter of fact go to heaven, though they have, he added, souls of a sort. How much thinking those old gentlemen used to save one! How the borders of ignorance shrank back at their approach! Cats do not go to heaven. Women cannot write the plays of Shakespeare.

Be that as it may, I could not help thinking, as I looked at the works of Shakespeare on the shelf, that the bishop was right at least in this; it would have been impossible, completely and entirely, for any woman to have written the plays of Shakespeare in the age of Shakespeare. Let me imagine, since facts are so hard to come by, what would have happened had Shakespeare had a wonderfully gifted sister, called Judith, let us say. Shakespeare himself went, very probably—his mother was an heiress—to the grammar school, where he may have learnt Latin—Ovid, Virgil and Horace—and the elements of grammar and logic. He was, it is well known, a wild boy who poached rabbits, perhaps shot a deer, and had, rather sooner than he should have done, to marry a woman in the neighbourhood, who bore him a child rather quicker than was right. That escapade sent him to seek his fortune in London. He had, it seemed, a taste for the theatre; he began by holding horses at the stage door. Very soon he got work in the theatre, became a successful actor, and lived at the hub of the universe, meeting everybody, knowing everybody, practising his art on the boards, exercising his wits in the streets, and even getting access to the palace of the queen. Meanwhile his extraordinarily gifted sister, let us suppose, remained at home. She was as adventurous, as imaginative, as agog to see the world as he was. But she was not sent to school. She had no chance of learning grammar and logic, let alone of reading Horace and Virgil. She picked up a book now and then, one of her brother's perhaps, and read a few pages. But then her parents came in and told her to mend the stockings or mind the stew and not moon about with books and papers. They would have spoken sharply but kindly, for they were substantial people who knew the conditions of life for a woman and loved their daughter—indeed, more likely than not she was the apple of her father's eye. Perhaps she scribbled some pages up in an apple loft on the sly, but was careful to hide them or set fire to them. Soon, however, before she was out of her teens, she was to be betrothed to the son of a neighbouring woolstapler. She cried out that marriage was hateful to her, and for that she was severely beaten by her father. Then he ceased to scold her. He begged her instead not to hurt him, not to shame him in this matter of her marriage. He would give her a chain of beads or a fine petticoat, he said; and there were tears in his eyes. How could she disobey him? How could she break his heart? The force of her own gift alone drove her to it. She made up a small parcel of her belongings, let herself down by a rope one summer's night and took the road to London. She was not seventeen. The birds that sang in the hedge were not more musical than she was. She had the quickest fancy, a gift like her brother's, for the tune of words. Like him, she had a taste for the theatre. She stood at the stage door; she wanted to act, she said. Men laughed in her face. The manager—a fat, loose-lipped man—guffawed. He bellowed something about poodles dancing and women acting—no woman, he said, could possibly be an actress. He hinted—you can imagine what. She could get no training in her craft. Could she even seek her dinner in a tavern or roam the streets at midnight? Yet her genius was for fiction and lusted to feed abundantly upon the lives of men and women and the study of their ways. At last—for she was very young, oddly like Shakespeare the poet in her face, with the same grey eyes and rounded brows—at last Nick Greene the actor-manager took pity on her; she found herself with child by that gentleman and so—who shall measure the heat and violence of the poet's heart when caught and tangled in a woman's body?—killed herself one winter's night and lies buried at some cross-roads where the omnibuses now stop outside the Elephant and Castle.

That, more or less, is how the story would run, I think, if a woman in Shakespeare's day had had Shakespeare's genius. But for my part, I agree with the deceased bishop, if such he was—it is unthinkable that any woman in Shakespeare's day should have had Shakespeare's genius. For genius like Shakespeare's is not born among labouring, uneducated, servile people. It was not born in England among the Saxons and the Britons. It is not born today among the working classes. How, then, could it have been born among women whose work began, according to Professor Trevelyan, almost before they were out of the nursery, who were forced to it by their parents and held to it by all the power of law and custom? Yet genius of a sort must have existed among women as it must have existed among the working classes. Now and again an Emily Brontë or a Robert Burns blazes out and proves its presence. But certainly it never got itself on to paper. When, however, one reads of a witch being ducked, of a woman possessed by devils, of a wise woman selling herbs, or even of a very remarkable man who had a mother, then I think we are on the track of a lost novelist, a suppressed poet, of some mute and inglorious Jane Austen, some Emily Brontë who dashed her brains out on the moor or mopped and mowed about the highways crazed with the torture that her gift had put her to. Indeed, I would venture to guess that Anon, who wrote so many poems without signing them, was often a woman. It was a woman Edward Fitzgerald, I think, suggested who made the ballads and the folk-songs, crooning them to her children, beguiling her spinning with them, or the length of the winter's night.

This may be true or it may be false—who can say?—but what is true in it, so it seemed to me, reviewing the story of Shakespeare's sister as I had made it, is that any woman born with a great gift in the sixteenth century would certainly have gone crazed, shot herself, or ended her days in some lonely cottage outside the village, half witch, half wizard, feared and mocked at. For it needs little skill in psychology to be sure that a highly gifted girl who had tried to use her gift for poetry would have been so thwarted and hindered by other people, so tortured and pulled asunder by her own contrary instincts, that she must have lost her health and sanity to a degree. No girl could have walked to London and stood at a stage door and forced her way into the presence of actor-managers without doing herself a violence and suffering an anguish which may have been irrational—for chastity may be a fetish invented by certain societies for unknown reasons—but were none the less inevitable. Chastity had then, as it has even now, a religious importance in a woman's life, and has so wrapped itself round with nerves and instincts that to cut it free and bring it to the light of day demands courage of the rarest. To have lived a free life in London in the sixteenth century would have meant for a woman who was poet and playwright a nervous stress and dilemma which might well have killed her. Had she survived, whatever she had written would have been twisted and deformed, issuing from a strained and morbid imagination. And undoubtedly, I thought, looking at the shelf where there are no plays by women, her work would have gone unsigned. That refuge she would have sought certainly. It was the relic of the sense of chastity that dictated anonymity to women even so late as the nineteenth century. Currer Bell, George Eliot, George Sand, all the victims of inner strife as their writings prove, sought ineffectively to veil themselves by using the name of a man. Thus they did homage to the convention, which if not implanted by the other sex was liberally encouraged by them (the chief glory of a woman is not to be talked of, said Pericles, himself a much-talked-of man), that publicity in women is detestable. Anonymity runs in their blood. The desire to be veiled still possesses them. They are not even now as concerned about the health of their fame as men are, and, speaking generally, will pass a tombstone or a signpost without feeling an irresistible desire to cut their names on it, as Alf, Bert or Chas. must do in obedience to their instinct, which murmurs if it sees a fine woman go by, or even a dog, Ce chien est A moi. And, of course, it may not be a dog, I thought, remembering Parliament Square, the Sieges Allee and other avenues; it may be a piece of land or a man with curly black hair. It is one of the great advantages of being a woman that one can pass even a very fine negress without wishing to make an Englishwoman of her.

That woman, then, who was born with a gift of poetry in the sixteenth century, was an unhappy woman, a woman at strife against herself. All the conditions of her life, all her own instincts, were hostile to the state of mind which is needed to set free whatever is in the brain. But what is the state of mind that is most propitious to the act of creation, I asked. Can one come by any notion of the state that furthers and makes possible that strange activity? Here I opened the volume containing the Tragedies of Shakespeare. What was Shakespeare's state of mind, for instance, when he wrote *Lear* and *Antony and Cleopatra*? It was certainly the state of mind most favourable to poetry that there has ever existed. But Shakespeare himself said nothing about it. We only know casually and by chance that he "never blotted a line." Nothing indeed was ever said by the artist himself about his state of mind until the eighteenth century perhaps. Rousseau perhaps began it. At any rate, by the nineteenth century self-consciousness had developed so far that it was the custom for men of letters to describe their minds in confessions and autobiographies. Their lives also were written, and their letters were printed after their deaths. Thus, though we do not know what Shakespeare went through when he wrote *Lear*, we do know what Carlyle went through when he wrote the *French Revolution;* what Flaubert went through when he wrote *Madame Bovary;* what Keats was going through when he tried to write poetry against the coming of death and the indifference of the world.

And one gathers from this enormous modern literature of confession and self-analysis that to write a work of genius is almost always a feat of prodigious difficulty. Everything is against the likelihood that it will come from the writer's mind whole and entire. Generally material circumstances are against it. Dogs will bark; people will interrupt; money must be made; health will break down. Further, accentuating all these difficulties and making them harder to bear is the world's notorious indifference. It does not ask people to write poems and novels and histories; it does not need them. It does not care whether Flaubert finds the right word or whether Carlyle scrupulously verifies this or that fact. Naturally, it will not pay for what it does not want. And so the writer, Keats, Flaubert, Carlyle, suffers, especially in the creative years of youth, every form of distraction and discouragement. A curse, a cry of agony, rises from those books of analysis and confession. "Mighty poets in their misery dead"—that is the burden of their song. If anything comes through in spite of all this, it is a miracle, and probably no book is born entire and uncrippled as it was conceived.

But for women, I thought, looking at the empty shelves, these difficulties were infinitely more formidable. In the first place, to have a room of her own, let alone a quiet room or a sound-proof room, was out of the question, unless her parents were exceptionally rich or very noble, even up to the beginning of the nineteenth century. Since her pin money, which depended on the good will of her father, was only enough to keep her clothed, she was debarred from such alleviations as came even to Keats or Tennyson or Carlyle, all poor men, from a walking tour, a little journey to France, from the separate lodging which, even if it were miserable enough, sheltered them from the claims and tyrannies of their families. Such material difficulties were formidable; but much worse were the immaterial. The indifference of the world which Keats and Flaubert and other men of genius have found so hard to bear was in her case not indifference but hostility. The world did not say to her as it said to them, Write if you choose; it makes no difference to me. The world said with a guffaw, Write? What's the good of your writing; Here the psychologists of Newnham and Girton might come to our help, I thought, looking again at the blank spaces on the shelves. For surely it is time that the effect of discouragement upon the mind of the artist should be measured, as I have seen a dairy company measure the effect of ordinary milk and Grade A milk upon the body of the rat. They set two rats in cages side by side, and of the two one was furtive, timid and small, and the other was glossy, bold and big. Now what food do we feed women as artists upon? I asked, remembering, I suppose, that dinner of prunes and custard. To answer that question I had only to open the evening paper and to read that Lord Birkenhead is of opinion—but really I am not going to trouble to copy out Lord Birkenhead's opinion upon the writing of women. What Dean Inge says I will leave in peace. The Harley Street specialist may be allowed to rouse the echoes of Harley Street with his vociferations without raising a hair on my head. I will quote, however, Mr. Oscar Browning, because Mr. Oscar Browning was a great figure in Cambridge at one time, and used to examine the students at Girton and Newnham. Mr. Oscar Browning was wont to declare "that the impression left on his mind, after looking over any set of examination papers, was that, irrespective of the marks he might give, the best woman was intellectually the inferior of the worst man." After saying that Mr. Browning went back to his rooms—and it is this sequel that endears him and makes him a human figure of some bulk and majesty—he went back to his rooms and found a stable-boy lying on the sofa—"a mere skeleton, his cheeks were cavernous and sallow, his teeth were black, and he did not appear to have the full use of his limbs. . . . 'That's Arthur' [said Mr. Browning]. 'He's a dear boy really and most high-minded.' " The two pictures always seem to me to complete each other. And happily in this age of biography the two pictures often do complete each other, so that we are able to interpret the opinions of great men not only by what they say, but by what they do.

But though this is possible now, such opinions coming from the lips of important people must have been formidable enough even fifty years ago. Let us suppose that a father from the highest motives did not wish his daughter to leave home and become writer, painter or scholar. "See what Mr. Oscar Browning says," he would say; and there was not only Mr. Oscar Browning; there was the *Saturday Review*; there was Mr. Greg—the "essentials of a woman's being," said Mr. Greg emphatically, "are that *they are supported by, and they minister to, men*"—there was an enormous body of masculine opinion to the effect that nothing could be expected of women intellectually. Even if her father did not read out loud these opinions, any girl could read them for herself; and the reading, even in the nineteenth century, must have lowered her vitality, and told profoundly upon her work. There would always have been that assertion—you cannot do this, you are incapable of doing that—to protest against, to overcome. Probably for a novelist this germ is no longer of much effect; for there have been women novelists of merit. But for painters it must still have some sting in it; and for musicians, I imagine, is even now active and poisonous in the extreme. The woman composer stands where the actress stood in the time of Shakespeare. Nick Greene, I thought, remembering the story I had made about Shakespeare's sister, said that a woman acting put him in mind of a dog dancing. Johnson repeated the phrase two hundred years later of women preaching. And here, I said, opening a book about music, we have the very words used again in this year of grace, 1928, of women who try to write music. "Of Mlle. Germaine Tailleferre one can only repeat Dr. Johnson's dictum concerning a woman preacher, transposed into terms of music. 'Sir, a woman's composing is like a dog's walking on his hind legs. It is not done well, but you are surprised to find it done at all.' " So accurately does history repeat itself.

Thus, I concluded, shutting Mr. Oscar Browning's life and pushing away the rest, it is fairly evident that even in the nineteenth century a woman was not encouraged to be an artist. On the contrary, she was snubbed, slapped, lectured and exhorted. Her mind must have been strained and her vitality lowered by the need of opposing this, of disproving that. For here again we come within range of that very interesting and masculine complex which has had so much influence upon the woman's movement; that deep-seated desire, not so much that *she* shall be inferior as that *he* shall be superior, which plants him wherever one looks, not only in front of the arts, but barring the way to politics too, even when the risk to himself seems infinitesimal and the suppliant humble and devoted. Even Lady Bessborough, I remembered, with all her passion for politics, must humbly bow herself and write to Lord Granville Leveson-Gower: ". . . notwithstanding all my violence in politics and talking so much on that subject, I perfectly agree with you that no woman has any business to meddle with that or any other serious business, farther than giving her opinion (if she is ask'd)." And so she goes on to spend her enthusiasm where it meets with no obstacle whatsoever upon that immensely important subject, Lord Granville's maiden speech in the House of Commons. The spectacle is certainly a strange one, I thought. The history of men's opposition to women's emancipation is more interesting perhaps than the story of that emancipation itself. An amusing book might be made of it if some young student at Girton or Newnham would collect examples and deduce a theory—but she would need thick gloves on her hands, and bars to protect her of solid gold. . . .

Property

First Week — Sixth Day

John Locke,
Concerning Civil Government, Chapter V

Karl Marx and Friedrich Engels,
The Communist Manifesto

Mao Tse-tung,
"To Reveal One's True Feelings"

E. F. Schumacher,
Small is Beautiful,
"Buddhist Economics"

Concerning Civil Government

by John Locke

Chapter V
Of Property

WHETHER we consider natural reason, which tells us that men, being once born, have a right to their preservation, and consequently to meat and drink and such other things as Nature affords for their subsistence, or "revelation," which gives us an account of those grants God made of the world to Adam, and to Noah and his sons, it is very clear that God, as King David says (Psalm 115. 16), "has given the earth to the children of men," given it to mankind in common. But, this being supposed, it seems to some a very great difficulty how any one should ever come to have a property in anything, I will not content myself to answer, that, if it be difficult to make out "property" upon a supposition that God gave the world to Adam and his posterity in common, it is impossible that any man but one universal monarch should have any "property" upon a supposition that God gave the world to Adam and his heirs in succession, exclusive of all the rest of his posterity; but I shall endeavor to show how men might come to have a property in several parts of that which God gave to mankind in common, and that without any express compact of all the commoners.

God, who hath given the world to men in common, hath also given them reason to make use of it to the best advantage of life and convenience. The earth and all that is therein is given to men for the support and comfort of their being. And though all the fruits it naturally produces, and beasts it feeds, belong to mankind in common, as they are produced by the spontaneous hand of Nature, and nobody has originally a private dominion exclusive of the rest of mankind in any of them, as they are thus in their natural state, yet being given for the use of men, there must of necessity be a means to appropriate them some way or other before they can be of any use, or at all beneficial, to any particular men. The fruit or venison which nourishes the wild Indian, who knows no enclosure, and is still a tenant in common, must be his, and so his—*i.e.*, a part of him, that another can no longer have any right to it before it can do him any good for the support of his life.

Though the earth and all inferior creatures be common to all men, yet every man has a "property" in his own "person." This nobody has any right to but himself. The "labour" of his body and the "work" of his hands, we may say, are properly his. Whatsoever, then, he removes out of the state that Nature hath provided and left it in, he hath mixed his labour with it, and joined to it something that is his own, and thereby makes it his property. It being by him removed from the common state Nature placed it in, it hath by this labour something annexed to it that excludes the common right of other men. For this "labour" being the unquestionable property of the labourer, no man but he can have a right to what that is once joined to, at least where there is enough, and as good left in common for others.

He that is nourished by the acorns he picked up under an oak, or the apples he gathered from the trees in the wood, has certainly appropriated them to himself. Nobody can deny but the nourishment is his. I ask, then, when did they begin to be his? when he digested? or when he ate? or when he boiled? or when he brought them home? or when he picked them up? And it is plain, if the first gathering made them not his, nothing else could. That labour put a distinction between them and common. That added something to them more than Nature, the common mother of all, had done, and so they became his private right. And will any one say he had no right to those acorns or apples he thus appropriated because he had not the consent of all mankind to make them his? Was it a robbery thus to assume to himself what belonged to all in common? If such a consent as that was necessary, man had starved, notwithstanding the plenty God had given him. We see in commons, which remain so by compact, that it is the taking any part of what is common, and removing it out of the state Nature leaves it in, which begins the property, without which the common is of no use. And the taking of this or that part does not depend on the express consent of all the commoners. Thus, the grass my horse has bit, the turfs my servant has cut, and the ore I have digged in any place, where I have a right to them in common with others, become my property without the assignation or consent of anybody. The labour that was mine, removing them out of that common state they were in, hath fixed my property in them.

By making an explicit consent of every commoner necessary to any one's appropriating to himself any part of what is given in common, children or servants could not cut the meat which their father or master had provided for them in common without assigning to every one his peculiar part. Though the water running in the fountain be every one's, yet who can doubt but that in the pitcher is his only who drew it out? His labour hath taken it out of the hands of Nature where it was common, and belonged equally to all her children, and hath thereby appropriated it to himself.

Thus this law of reason makes the deer that Indian's who hath killed it;

it is allowed to be his goods who hath bestowed his labour upon it, though, before, it was the common right of every one. And amongst those who are counted the civilised part of mankind, who have made and multiplied positive laws to determine property, this original law of Nature for the beginning of property, in what was before common, still takes place, and by virtue thereof, what fish any one catches in the ocean, that great and still remaining common of mankind; or what ambergris any one takes up here is by the labour that removes it out of that common state Nature left it in, made his property who takes that pains about it. And even amongst us, the hare that any one is hunting is thought his who pursues her during the chase. For being a beast that is still looked upon as common, and no man's private possession, whoever has employed so much labour about any of that kind as to find and pursue her has thereby removed her from the state of Nature wherein she was common, and hath begun a property.

It will, perhaps, be objected to this, that if gathering the acorns or other fruits of the earth, etc., makes a right to them, then any one may engross as much as he will. To which I answer, Not so. The same law of Nature that does by this means give us property, does also bound that property too. "God has given us all things richly." Is the voice of reason confirmed by inspiration? But how far has He given it us—"to enjoy"? As much as any one can make use of to any advantage of life before it spoils, so much he may by his labour fix a property in. Whatever is beyond this is more than his share, and belongs to others. Nothing was made by God for man to spoil or destroy. And thus considering the plenty of natural provisions there was a long time in the world, and the few spenders, and to how small a part of that provision the industry of one man could extend itself and engross it to the prejudice of others, especially keeping within the bounds set by reason of what might serve for his use, there could be then little room for quarrels or contentions about property so established.

But the chief matter of property being now not the fruits of the earth and the beasts that subsist on it, but the earth itself, as that which takes in and carries with it all the rest, I think it is plain that property in that too is acquired as the former. As much land as a man tills, plants, improves, cultivates, and can use the product of, so much is his property. He by his labour does, as it were, enclose it from the common. Nor will it invalidate his right to say everybody else has an equal title to it, and therefore he cannot appropriate, he cannot enclose, without the consent of all his fellow-commoners, all mankind. God, when He gave the world in common to all mankind, commanded man also to labour, and the penury of his condition required it of him. God and his reason commanded him to subdue the earth—*i.e.*, improve it for the benefit of life and therein lay out something upon it that was his own, his labour. He that, in obedience to this command of God, subdued, tilled, and sowed any part of it, thereby annexed to it something that was his property, which another had no title to, nor could without injury take from him.

Nor was this appropriation of any parcel of land, by improving it, any prejudice to any other man, since there was still enough and as good left, and more than the yet unprovided could use. So that, in effect, there was never the less left for others because of his enclosure for himself. For he that leaves as much as another can make use of does as good as take nothing at all. Nobody could think himself injured by the drinking of another man, though he took a good draught, who had a whole river of the same water left him to quench his thirst. And the case of land and water, where there is enough of both, is perfectly the same.

God gave the world to men in common, but since He gave it them for their benefit and the greatest conveniencies of life they were capable to draw from it, it cannot be supposed He meant it should always remain common and uncultivated. He gave it to the use of the industrious and rational (and labour was to be his title to it); not to the fancy or covetousness of the quarrelsome and contentious. He that had as good left for his improvement as was already taken up needed not complain, ought not to meddle with what was already improved by another's labour; if he did it is plain he desired the benefit of another's pains, which he had no right to, and not the ground which God had given him, in common with others, to labour on, and whereof there was as good left as that already possessed, and more than he knew what to do with, or his industry could reach to.

It is true, in land that is common in England or any other country, where there are plenty of people under government who have money and commerce, no one can enclose or appropriate any part without the consent of all his fellow-commoners; because this is left common by compact—*i.e.*, by the law of the land, which is not to be violated. And, though it be common in respect of some men, it is not so to all mankind, but is the joint propriety of this country, or this parish. Besides, the remainder, after such enclosure, would not be as good to the rest of the commoners as the whole was, when they could all make use of the whole; whereas in the beginning and first peopling of the great common of the world it was quite otherwise. The law man was under was rather for appropriating. God commanded, and his wants forced him to labour. That was his property, which could not be taken from him wherever he had fixed it. And hence subduing or cultivating the earth and having dominion, we see, are joined together. The one gave title to the other. So that God, by commanding to subdue, gave authority so far to appropriate. And the condition of human life, which requires labour and materials to work on, necessarily introduces private possessions.

The measure of property Nature well set, by the extent of men's labour and the conveniency of life. No man's labour could subdue or appropriate all, nor could his enjoyment consume more than a small part; so that it was impossible for any man, this way, to entrench upon the right of another or acquire to himself a property to the prejudice of his neighbour, who would still have room for as good and as large a possession (after the other had taken out his) as before it was appropriated. Which measure did confine every man's possession to a very moderate proportion, and such as he might appropriate to himself without injury to anybody in the first ages of the world, when men were more in danger to be lost, by wandering from their company, in the then vast wilderness of the earth than to be straitened for want of room to plant in.

The same measure may be allowed still, without prejudice to anybody, full as the world seems. For, supposing a man or family, in the state they were at first, peopling of the world by the children of Adam or Noah, let him plant in some inland vacant places of America. We shall find that the possessions he could make himself, upon the measures we have given, would not be very large, nor, even to this day, prejudice the rest of mankind or give them reason to complain or think themselves injured by this man's encroachment, though the race of men have now spread themselves to all the corners of the world, and do infinitely exceed the small number was at the beginning. Nay, the extent of ground is of so little value without labour that I have heard it affirmed that in Spain itself a man may be permitted to plough, sow, and reap, without being disturbed, upon land he has no other title to, but only his making use of it. But, on the contrary, the inhabitants think themselves beholden to him who, by his industry on neglected, and consequently waste land, has increased the stock of corn, which they wanted. But be this as it will, which I lay no stress on, this I dare boldly affirm, that the same rule of propriety—viz., that every man should have as much as he could make use of, would hold still in the world, without straitening anybody, since there is land enough in the world to suffice double the inhabitants, had not the invention of money, and the tacit agreement of men to put a value on it, introduced (by consent) larger possessions and a right to them; which, how it has done, I shall by and by show more at large.

This is certain, that in the beginning, before the desire of having more than men needed had altered the intrinsic value of things, which depends only on their usefulness to the life of man, or had agreed that a little piece of yellow metal, which would keep without wasting or decay, should be worth a great piece of flesh or a whole heap of corn, though men had a right to appropriate by their labour, each one to himself, as much of the things of Nature as he could use, yet this could not be much, nor to the prejudice of others, where the same plenty was still left, to those who would use the same industry.

Before the appropriation of land, he who gathered as much of the wild fruit, killed, caught, or tamed as many of the beasts as he could—he that so employed his pains about any of the spontaneous products of Nature as any way to alter them from the state Nature put them in, by placing any of his labour on them, did thereby acquire a propriety in them; but if they perished in his possession without their due use—if the fruits rotted or the venison putrefied before he could spend it, he offended against the common law of Nature, and was liable to be punished: he invaded his neighbour's share, for he had no right farther than his use called for any of them, and they might serve to afford him conveniencies of life.

The same measures governed the possession of land, too. Whatsoever he tilled and reaped, laid up and made use of before it spoiled, that was his peculiar right; whatsoever he enclosed, and could feed and make use of, the cattle and product was also his. But if either the grass of his enclosure rotted on the ground, or the fruit of his planting perished without gathering and laying up, this part of the earth, notwithstanding his enclosure, was still to be looked on as waste, and might be the possession of any other. Thus, at the beginning, Cain might take as much ground as he could till and make it his own land, and yet leave enough to Abel's sheep to feed on: a few acres would serve for both their possessions. But as families increased and industry enlarged their stocks, their possessions enlarged with the need of them; but yet it was commonly without any fixed property in the ground they made use of till they incorporated, settled themselves together, and built cities, and then, by consent, they came in time to set out the bounds of their distinct territories and agree on limits between them and their neighbours, and by laws within themselves settled the properties of those of the same society. For we see that in that part of the world which was first inhabited, and therefore like to be best peopled, even as low down as Abraham's time, they wandered with their flocks and their herds, which was their substance, freely up and down—and this Abraham did in a country where he was a stranger; whence it is plain that, at least, a great part of the land lay in common, that the inhabitants valued it not, nor claimed property in any more than they made use of; but when there was not room enough in the same place for their herds to feed together, they, by consent, as Abraham and Lot did (Gen. 13.5), separated and enlarged their pasture where it best liked them. And for the same reason, Esau went from his father and his brother, and planted in Mount Seir (Gen. 36. 6).

And thus, without supposing any private dominion and property in Adam over all the world, exclusive of all other men, which can no way be proved, nor any one's property be made out from it, but supposing the world, given as it was to the children of men in common, we see how labour could make men distinct titles to several parcels of it for their private uses, wherein there could be no doubt of right, no room for quarrel.

Nor is it so strange as, perhaps, before consideration, it may appear, that the property of labour should be able to overbalance the community of land, for it is labour indeed that puts the difference of value on everything; and let any one consider what the difference is between an acre of land planted with tobacco or sugar, sown with wheat or barley, and an acre of the same land lying in common without any husbandry upon it, and he will find that the improvement of labour makes the far greater part of the value. I think it will be but a very modest computation to say, that of the products of the earth useful to the life of man, nine-tenths are the effects of labour. Nay, if we will rightly estimate things as they come to our use, and cast up the several expenses about them—what in them is purely owing to Nature and what to labour—we shall find that in most of them ninety-nine hundredths are wholly to be put on the account of labour.

There cannot be a clearer demonstration of anything than several nations of the Americans are of this, who are rich in land and poor in all the comforts of life; whom Nature, having furnished as liberally as any other people with the materials of plenty—*i.e.*, a fruitful soil, apt to produce in abundance what might serve for food, raiment, and delight; yet, for want of improving it by labour, have not one hundredth part of the conveniencies we enjoy, and a king of a large and fruitful territory there feeds, lodges, and is clad worse than a day labourer in England.

To make this a little clearer, let us but trace some of the ordinary provisions of life, through their several progresses, before they come to our use, and see how much they receive of their value from human industry. Bread, wine, and cloth are things of daily use and great plenty; yet notwithstanding acorns, water, and leaves, or skins must be our bread, drink and clothing, did not labour furnish us with these more useful commodities. For whatever bread is more worth than acorns, wine than water, and cloth or silk than leaves, skins or moss, that is wholly owing to labour and industry. The one of these being the food and raiment which unassisted Nature furnishes us with; the other provisions which our industry and pains prepare for us, which how much they exceed the other in value, when any one hath computed, he will then see how much labour makes the far greatest part of the value of things we enjoy in this world; and the ground which produces the materials is scarce to be reckoned in as any, or at most, but a very small part of it; so little, that even amongst us, land that is left wholly to nature, that hath no improvement of pasturage, tillage, or planting, is called, as indeed it is, waste; and we shall find the benefit of it amount to little more than nothing.

An acre of land that bears here twenty bushels of wheat, and another in America, which, with the same husbandry, would do the like, are, without doubt, of the same natural, intrinsic value. But yet the benefit mankind receives from one in a year is worth five pounds, and the other possibly not worth a penny; if all the profit an Indian received from it were to be valued and sold here, at least I may truly say, not one thousandth. It is labour, then, which puts the greatest part of value upon land, without which it would scarcely be worth anything; it is to that we owe the greatest part of all its useful products; for all that the straw, bran, bread, of that acre of wheat, is more worth than the product of an acre of as good land which lies waste is all the effect of labour. For it is not barely the ploughman's pains, the reaper's and thresher's toil, and the baker's sweat, is to be counted into the bread we eat; the labour of those who broke the oxen, who digged and wrought the iron and stones, who felled and framed the timber employed about the plough, mill, oven, or any other utensils, which are a vast number, requisite to this corn, from its sowing to its being made bread, must all be charged on the account of labour, and received as an effect of that; Nature and the earth furnished only the almost worthless materials as in themselves. It would be a strange catalogue of things that industry provided and made use of about every loaf of bread before it came to our use if we could trace them; iron, wood, leather, bark, timber, stone, bricks, coals, lime, cloth, dyeing-drugs, pitch, tar, masts, ropes, and all the materials made use of in the ship that brought any of the commodities made use of by any of the workmen, to any part of the work, all which it would be almost impossible, at least too long, to reckon up.

From all which it is evident, that though the things of Nature are given in common, man (by being master of himself, and proprietor of his own person, and the actions or labour of it) had still in himself the great foundation of property; and that which made up the great part of what he applied to the support or comfort of his being, when invention and arts had improved the conveniencies of life, was perfectly his own, and did not belong in common to others.

Thus labour, in the beginning, gave a right of property, wherever any one was pleased to employ it, upon what was common, which remained a long while, the far greater part, and is yet more than mankind makes use of. Men at first, for the most part, contented themselves with what unassisted Nature offered to their necessities; and though afterwards, in some parts of the world, where the increase of people and stock, with the use of money, had made land scarce, and so of some value, the several communities settled the bounds of their distinct territories, and, by laws, within themselves, regulated the properties of the private men of their society, and so, by compact and agreement, settled the property which labour and industry began. And the leagues that have been made between several states and kingdoms, either expressly or tacitly disowning all claim and right to the land in the other's possession, have, by common consent, given up their pretences to their natural common right, which originally they had to those countries; and so have, by positive agreement, settled a property amongst themselves, in distinct parts of the world; yet there are still great tracts of ground to be found, which the inhabitants thereof, not having joined with the rest of mankind in the consent of the use of their common money, lie waste, and are more than the people who dwell on it, do, or can make use of, and so still lie in common; though this can scarce happen amongst that part of mankind that have consented to the use of money. The greatest part of things really useful to the life of man, and such as the necessity of subsisting made the first commoners of the world look after— as it doth the Americans now—are generally things of short duration, such as—if they are not consumed by use—will decay and perish of themselves. Gold, silver, and diamonds are things that fancy or agreement hath put the value on, more than real use and the necessary support of life. Now of those good things which Nature hath provided in common, every one hath a right (as hath been said) to as much as he could use; and had a property in all he could effect with his labour; all that his industry could extend to, or alter from the state Nature had put it in, was his. He that gathered a hundred bushels of acorns or apples had thereby a property in them; they were his goods as soon as gathered. He was only to look that he used them before they spoiled, else he took more than his share, and robbed others. And, indeed, it was a foolish thing, as well as dishonest, to hoard up more than he could make use of. If he gave away a part to anybody else, so that it perished not uselessly in his possession, these he also made use of. And if he also bartered away plums that would have rotted in a week, for nuts that would last good for his eating a whole year, he did no injury; he wasted not the common stock; destroyed no part of the portion of goods that belonged to others, so long as nothing perished uselessly in his hands. Again, if he would give his nuts for a piece of metal, pleased with its colour, or exchange his sheep for shells, or wool for a sparkling pebble or a diamond, and keep those by him all his life, he invaded not the rights of others; he might heap up as much of these durable things as he pleased; the exceeding of the bounds of his just property not lying in the largeness of his possession, but the perishing of anything uselessly in it.

And thus came in the use of money; some lasting thing that men might keep without spoiling, and that, by mutual consent, men would take in exchange for the truly useful but perishable supports of life.

And as different degrees of industry were apt to give men possessions in different proportions, so this invention of money gave them the opportunity to continue and enlarge them. For supposing an island, separate from all possible commerce with the rest of the world, wherein there were but a hundred families, but there were sheep, horses, and cows, with other useful animals, wholesome fruits, and land enough for corn for a hundred thousand times as many, but nothing in the island, either because of its commonness or perishableness, fit to supply the place of money. What reason could any one have there to enlarge his possessions beyond the use of his family, and a plentiful supply to its consumption, either in what their own industry produced, or they could barter for like perishable, useful commodities with others? Where there is not something both lasting and scarce, and so valuable to be hoarded up, there men will not be apt to enlarge their possessions of land, were it never so rich, never so free for them to take. For I ask, what would a man value ten thousand or an hundred thousand acres of excellent land, ready cultivated and well stocked, too, with cattle, in the middle of the inland parts of America, where he had no hopes of commerce with other parts of the world, to draw money to him by the sale of the product? It would not be worth the enclosing, and we should see him give up again to the wild common of Nature whatever was more than would supply the conveniencies of life, to be had there for him and his family.

Thus, in the beginning, all the world was America, and more so than that is now; for no such thing as money was anywhere known. Find out something that hath the use and value of money amongst his neighbours, you shall see the same man will begin presently to enlarge his possessions.

But, since gold and silver, being little useful to the life of man, in proportion to food, raiment, and carriage, has its value only from the consent of men—whereof labour yet makes in great part the measure—it is plain that the consent of men have agreed to a disproportionate and unequal possession of the earth—I mean out of the bounds of society and compact; for in governments the laws regulate it; they having, by consent, found out and agreed in a way how a man may, rightfully and without injury, possess more than he himself can make use of by receiving gold and silver, which may continue long in a man's possession without decaying for the overplus, and agreeing those metals should have a value.

And thus, I think, it is very easy to conceive, without any difficulty, how labour could at first begin a title of property in the common things of

Nature, and how the spending it upon our uses bounded it; so that there could then be no reason of quarrelling about title, nor any doubt about the largeness of possession it gave. Right and conveniency went together. For as a man had a right to all he could employ his labour upon, so he had no temptation to labour for more than he could make use of. This left no room for controversy about the title, nor for encroachment on the right of others. What portion a man carved to himself was easily seen; and it was useless, as well as dishonest, to carve himself too much, or take more than he needed.

The Communist Manifesto

by Karl Marx and Friedrich Engels

Preface by Friedrich Engels

THE *Manifesto* was published as the platform of the Communist League, a workingmen's association, first exclusively German, later on international, and, under the political conditions of the Continent before 1848, unavoidably a secret society. At a Congress of the League, held in London in November, 1847, Marx and Engels were commissioned to prepare for publication a complete theoretical and practical party program. Drawn up in German in January, 1848, the manuscript was sent to the printer in London a few weeks before the French revolution of February 24th. A French translation was brought out in Paris shortly before the insurrection of June, 1848. The first English translation, by Miss Helen Macfarlane, appeared in George Julian Harney's *Red Republican*, London, 1850. A Danish and a Polish edition had also been published.

The defeat of the Parisian insurrection of June, 1848—the first great battle between proletariat and bourgeoisie—drove again into the background, for a time, the social and political aspirations of the European working class. Thenceforth, the struggle for supremacy was again, as it had been before the revolution of February, solely between different sections of the propertied class; the working class was reduced to a fight for political elbow-room, and to the position of extreme wing of the middle class radicals. Wherever independent proletarian movements continued to show signs of life, they were ruthlessly hunted down. Thus the Prussian police hunted out the central board of the Communist League, then located in Cologne. The members were arrested, and, after eighteen months' imprisonment, they were tried in October, 1852. This celebrated "Cologne Communist Trial" lasted from October 4th till November 12th; seven of the prisoners were sentenced to terms of imprisonment in a fortress, varying from three to six years. Immediately after the sentence, the League was formally dissolved by the remaining members. As to the *Manifesto*, it seemed thenceforth to be doomed to oblivion.

When the European working class had recovered sufficient strength for another attack on the ruling classes, the International Workingmen's Association sprang up. But this association, formed with the express aim of welding into one body the whole militant proletariat of Europe and America, could not at once proclaim the principles laid down in the *Manifesto*. The International was bound to have a program broad enough to be acceptable to the English trades unions, to the followers of Proudhon in France, Belgium, Italy, and Spain, and to the Lassalleans[1] in Germany. Marx, who drew up this program to the satisfaction of all parties, entirely trusted to the intellectual development of the working class which was sure to result from combined action and mutual discussion. The very events and vicissitudes of the struggle against capital, the defeats even more than the victories, could not help bringing home to men's minds the insufficiency of their various favourite nostrums, and preparing the way for a more complete insight into the true conditions of working class emancipation. And Marx was right. The International, on its breaking up in 1874, left the workers quite different men from what it had found them in 1864. Proudhonism in France, Lassalleanism in Germany were dying out, and even the conservative English trades unions, though most of them had long since severed their connection with the International, were gradually advancing towards that point at which, last year at Swansea, their president could say in their name "continental Socialism has lost its terrors for us." In fact, the principles of the *Manifesto* had made considerable headway among the workingmen of all countries.

The *Manifesto* itself thus came to the front again. Since 1850 the German text had been reprinted several times in Switzerland, England, and America. In 1872 it was translated into English in New York, where the translation was published in *Woodhull and Claflin's Weekly*. From this English version, a French one was made in *Le Socialiste* of New York. Since then at least two more English translations, more or less mutilated, have been brought out in America, and one of them has been reprinted in England. The first Russian translation, made by Bakunin, was published at Herzen's *Kolokol* office in Geneva, about 1863; a second one, by the heroic Vera Zasulich, also in Geneva, in 1882.[2] A new Danish edition is to be found in *Socialdemokratisk Bibliothek*, Copenhagen, 1885; a fresh French translation in *Le Socialiste*, Paris, 1886. From this latter, a Spanish version was prepared and published in Madrid in 1886. Not counting the German reprints there had been at least twelve editions. An Armenian translation, which was to be published in Constantinople some months ago, did not see the light, I am told, because the publisher was afraid of bringing out a book with the name of Marx on it, while the translator declined to call it his own production. Of further translations into other languages I have heard, but have not seen. Thus the history of the *Manifesto* reflects to a great extent the history of the modern working class movement; at present it is undoubtedly the most widespread, the most international production of all Socialist literature, the common platform acknowledged by millions of workingmen from Siberia to California.

Yet, when it was written, we could not have called it a *Socialist* manifesto. By Socialists, in 1847, were understood, on the one hand, the adherents of the various Utopian systems: Owenites in England, Fourierists in France, both of them already reduced to the position of mere sects, and gradually dying out; on the other hand, the most multifarious social quacks, who, by all manners of tinkering, professed to redress, without any danger to capital and profit, all sorts of social grievances; in both cases men outside the working class movement, and looking rather to the "educated" classes for support. Whatever portion of the working class had become convinced of the insufficiency of mere political revolutions and had proclaimed the necessity of a total social change, called itself *Communist*. It was a crude, rough-hewn, purely instinctive sort of Communism; still, it touched the cardinal point and was powerful enough amongst the working class to produce the Utopian Communism of Cabet in France, and of Weitling in Germany. Thus, in 1847, Socialism was a middle class movement; Communism, a working class movement. Socialism was, on the continent at least, "respectable"; Communism was the very opposite. And as our notion from the very beginning was that "the emancipation of the working class must be the act of the working class itself," there could be no doubt as to which of the two names we must take. Moreover, we have ever since been far from repudiating it.

The *Manifesto* being our joint production, I consider myself bound to state that the fundamental proposition which forms its nucleus belongs to Marx. That proposition is: That in every historical epoch the prevailing mode of economic production and exchange, and the social organization necessarily following from it, form the basis upon which is built up, and from which alone can be explained, the political and intellectual history of that epoch; that, consequently, the whole history of mankind (since the dissolution of primitive tribal society, holding land in common ownership) has been a history of class struggles, contests between exploiting and exploited, ruling and oppressed classes; that the history of these class struggles forms a series of evolutions in which, nowadays, a stage has been reached where the exploited and oppressed class—the proletariat—cannot attain its emancipation from the sway of the exploiting and ruling class—the bourgeoisie—without at the same time, and once and for all, emancipating society at large from all exploitation, oppression, class distinctions and class struggles.

This proposition, which in my opinion is destined to do for history what Darwin's theory has done for biology, we, both of us, had been gradually approaching for some years before 1845. How far I had independently progressed towards it is best shown by my *Condition of the Working Class in England*. But when I again met Marx at Brussels in the spring of 1845, he had it already worked out, and put it before me in terms almost as clear as those in which I have stated it here.

From our joint preface to the German edition of 1872 I quote:

"However much the state of things may have altered during the last 25 years, the general principles laid down in this *Manifesto* are, on the whole, as correct today as ever. Here and there some detail might be improved. The practical application of the principles will depend, as the *Manifesto* itself states, everywhere and at all times, on the historical conditions for the time being existing, and, for that reason, no special stress is laid on the revolutionary measures proposed at the end of Section II. That passage would in many respects be very differently worded today. In view of the gigantic strides of modern industry since 1848, and of the accompanying improved and extended organization of the working class; in view of the practical experience gained, first in the February revolution, and then, still more, in the Paris Commune, where the proletariat for the first time held political power for two whole months, this program has in some details become antiquated. One thing especially was proved by the Commune, viz., that 'the working class cannot simply lay hold of the ready made state machinery, and wield it for its own purposes.' (See, *The Civil War in France; Address by the General Council of the International Workingmen's Association,* 1871, where this point is further developed.) Further, it is self-evident that the criticism of Socialist literature is deficient in relation to the present time, because it comes down only to 1847; also, that the remarks on the relation of the Communists to the various opposition parties (Section IV), although in principle still correct, yet in practice are antiquated, because the political situation has been entirely changed, and the progress of history has swept from off the earth the greater portion of the political parties there enumerated.

"But then, the *Manifesto* has become a historical document which we have no longer any right to alter."

The present translation is by Mr. Samuel Moore, the translator of the greater portion of Marx's *Capital.* We have revised it in common, and I have added a few notes explanatory of historical allusions.

—*London, January 30th, 1888.*

Manifesto of the Communist Party

A SPECTRE is haunting Europe—the spectre of Communism. All the powers of old Europe have entered into a holy alliance to exorcise this spectre: Pope and Czar, Metternich and Guizot, French Radicals and German police spies.

Where is the party in opposition that has not been decried as communistic by its opponents in power? Where the opposition that has not hurled back the branding reproach of Communism against the more advanced opposition parties, as well as against its reactionary adversaries?

Two things result from this fact:

I. Communism is already acknowledged by all European powers to be itself a power.

II. It is high time that Communists should openly, in the face of the whole world, publish their views, their aims, their tendencies, and meet this nursery tale of the spectre of Communism with a manifesto of the party itself.

To this end, Communists of various nationalities have assembled in London and sketched the following manifesto, to be published in the English, French, German, Italian, Flemish, and Danish languages.

Chapter I
Bourgeois and Proletarians[3]

The history of all hitherto existing society[4] is the history of class struggles.

Freeman and slave, patrician and plebeian, lord and serf, guild-master[5] and journeyman, in a word, oppressor and oppressed stood in constant opposition to one another, carried on an uninterrupted, now hidden, now open fight, a fight that each time ended either in a revolutionary reconstitution of society at large, or in the common ruin of the contending classes.

In the earlier epochs of history we find almost everywhere a complicated arrangement of society into various orders, a manifold gradation of social rank. In ancient Rome we have patricians, knights, plebeians, slaves; in the Middle Ages, feudal lords, vassals, guild-masters, journeymen, apprentices, serfs; in almost all of these classes, again, subordinate gradations.

The modern bourgeois society that has sprouted from the ruins of feudal society has not done away with class antagonisms. It has but established new classes, new conditions of oppression, new forms of struggle in place of the old ones.

Our epoch, the epoch of the bourgeoisie, possesses, however, this distinctive feature: it has simplified the class antagonisms. Society as a whole is more and more splitting up into two great hostile camps, into two great classes directly facing each other—bourgeoisie and proletariat.

From the serfs of the Middle Ages sprang the chartered burghers of the earliest towns. From these burgesses the first elements of the bourgeoisie were developed.

The discovery of America, the rounding of the Cape, opened up fresh ground for the rising bourgeoisie. The East Indian and Chinese markets, the colonization of America, trade with the colonies, the increase in the means of exchange and in commodities generally, gave to commerce, to navigation, to industry, an impulse never before known, and thereby, to the revolutionary element in the tottering feudal society, a rapid development.

The feudal system of industry, in which industrial production was monopolized by closed guilds, now no longer sufficed for the growing wants of the new markets. The manufacturing system took its place. The guild-masters were pushed aside by the manufacturing middle class; division of labour between the different corporate guilds vanished in the face of division of labour in each single workshop.

Meantime the markets kept ever growing, the demand ever rising. Even manufacture no longer sufficed. Thereupon, steam and machinery revolutionized industrial production. The place of manufacture was taken by the giant, modern industry, the place of the industrial middle class, by industrial millionaires—the leaders of whole industrial armies, the modern bourgeois.

Modern industry has established the world market, for which the discovery of America paved the way. This market has given an immense development to commerce, to navigation, to communication by land. This development has, in its turn, reacted on the extension of industry; and in proportion as industry, commerce, navigation, railways extended, in the same proportion the bourgeoisie developed, increased its capital, and pushed into the background every class handed down from the Middle Ages.

We see, therefore, how the modern bourgeoisie is itself the product of a long course of development, of a series of revolutions in the modes of production and of exchange.

Each step in the development of the bourgeoisie was accompanied by a corresponding political advance of that class. An oppressed class under the sway of the feudal nobility, it became an armed and self-governing association in the mediæval commune:[6] here, independent urban republic (as in Italy and Germany); there, taxable "third estate" of the monarchy (as in France); afterwards, in the period of manufacture proper, serving either the semi-feudal or the absolute monarchy as a counterpoise against the nobility, and, in fact, corner stone of the great monarchies in general. The bourgeoisie has at last, since the establishment of modern industry and of the world market, conquered for itself, in the modern representative state, exclusive political sway. The executive of the modern state is but a committee for managing the common affairs of the whole bourgeoisie.

The bourgeoisie has played a most revolutionary role in history.

The bourgeoisie, wherever it has got the upper hand, has put an end to all feudal, patriarchal, idyllic relations. It has pitilessly torn asunder the motley feudal ties that bound man to his "natural superiors," and has left no other bond between man and man than naked self-interest, than callous "cash payment." It has drowned the most heavenly ecstasies of religious fervour, of chivalrous enthusiasm, of philistine sentimentalism, in the icy water of egotistical calculation. It has resolved personal worth into exchange value, and in place of the numberless indefeasible chartered freedoms has set up that single, unconscionable freedom—Free Trade. In one word, for exploitation, veiled by religious and political illusions, it has substituted naked, shameless, direct, brutal exploitation.

The bourgeoisie has stripped of its halo every occupation hitherto honoured and looked up to with reverent awe. It has converted the physician, the lawyer, the priest, the poet, the man of science, into its paid wage labourers.

The bourgeoisie has torn away from the family its sentimental veil, and has reduced the family relation to a mere money relation.

The bourgeoisie has disclosed how it came to pass that the brutal display of vigour in the Middle Ages which reactionaries so much admire found its fitting complement in the most slothful indolence. It has been the first to show what man's activity can bring about. It has accomplished wonders far surpassing Egyptian pyramids, Roman aqueducts, and Gothic cathedrals; it has conducted expeditions that put in the shade all former migrations of nations and crusades.

The bourgeoisie cannot exist without constantly revolutionizing the instruments of production, and thereby the relations of production, and with them the whole relations of society. Conservation of the old modes of production in unaltered form was, on the contrary, the first condition of existence for all earlier industrial classes. Constant revolutionizing of production, uninterrupted disturbance of all social conditions, everlasting uncertainty and agitation distiguish the bourgeois epoch from all earlier ones. All fixed, fast-frozen relations with their train of ancient and venerable prejudices and opinions are swept away; all new-formed ones become antiquated before they can ossify. All that is solid melts in air, all that is holy is profaned, and man is at last compelled to face with sober senses his real conditions of life and his relations with his kind.

The need of a constantly expanding market for its products chases the bourgeoisie over the whole surface of the globe. It must nestle everywhere, settle everywhere, establish connections everywhere.

The bourgeoisie has through its exploitation of the world market given a cosmopolitan character to production and consumption in every country. To the great chagrin of reactionaries it has drawn from under the feet of industry the national ground on which it stood. All old-established national industries have been destroyed or are daily being destroyed. They are dislodged by new industries whose introduction becomes a life and death question for all civilized nations; by industries that no longer work up indigenous raw material, but raw material drawn from the remotest zones; industries whose products are consumed, not only at home, but in every quarter of the globe. In place of the old wants, satisfied by the production of the country, we find new wants, requiring for their satisfaction the products of distant lands and climes. In place of the old local and national seclusion and self-sufficiency we have intercourse in every direction, universal inter-dependence of nations. And as in material, so also in intellectual production. The intellectual creations of individual nations become common property. National one-sidedness and narrow-mindedness become more and more impossible, and from the numerous national and local literatures there arises a world literature.

The bourgeoisie, by the rapid improvement of all instruments of production, by the immensely facilitated means of communication, draws all nations, even the most barbarian, into civilization. The cheap prices of its commodities are the heavy artillery with which it batters down all Chinese walls, with which it forces the barbarians' intensely obstinate hatred of foreigners to capitulate. It compels all nations, on pain of extinction, to adopt the bourgeois mode of production; it compels them to introduce what it calls civilization into their midst, *i.e.*, to become bourgeois themselves. In a word, it creates a world after its own image.

The bourgeoisie has subjected the country to the rule of the towns. It has created enormous cities, has greatly increased the urban population as compared with the rural, and has thus rescued a considerable part of the population from the idiocy of rural life. Just as it has made the country dependent on the towns, so it has made barbarian and semi-barbarian countries dependent on the civilized ones, nations of peasants on nations of bourgeois, the East on the West.

More and more the bourgeoisie keeps doing away with the scattered state of the population, of the means of production, and of property. It has agglomerated population, centralized means of production, and has concentrated property in a few hands. The necessary consequence of this was political centralization. Independent, or but loosely connected provinces, with separate interests, laws, governments and systems of taxation, become lumped together into one nation, with one government, one code of laws, one national class interest, one frontier and one customs tariff.

The bourgeoisie during its rule of scarce one hundred years has created more massive and more colossal productive forces than have all preceding generations together. Subjection of nature's forces to man, machinery, application of chemistry to industry and agriculture, steam-navigation, railways, electric telegraphs, clearing of whole continents for cultivation, canalization of rivers, whole populations conjured out of the ground—what earlier century had even a presentiment that such productive forces slumbered in the lap of social labour?

We see, then, that the means of production and of exchange which served as the foundation for the growth of the bourgeoisie were generated in feudal society. At a certain stage in the development of these means of production and of exchange, the conditions under which feudal society produced and exchanged, the feudal organization of agriculture and manufacturing industry, in a word, the feudal relations of property became no longer compatible with the already developed productive forces; they became so many fetters. They had to be burst asunder; they were burst asunder.

Into their place stepped free competition, accompanied by a social and political constitution adapted to it, and by the economic and political sway of the bourgeois class.

A similar movement is going on before our own eyes. Modern bourgeois society with its relations of production, of exchange and of property, a society that has conjured up such gigantic means of production and of exchange, is like the sorcerer who is no longer able to control the powers of the nether world whom he has called up by his spells. For many a decade past the history of industry and commerce is but the history of the revolt of modern productive forces against modern conditions of production, against the property relations that are the conditions for the existence of the bourgeoisie and of its rule. It is enough to mention the commercial crises that by their periodical return put the existence of the entire bourgeois society on trial, each time more threateningly. In these crises a great part not only of the existing products, but also of the previously created productive forces, are periodically destroyed. In these crises there breaks out an epidemic that, in all earlier epochs, would have seemed an absurdity—the epidemic of over-production. Society suddenly finds itself put back into a state of momentary barbarism; it appears as if a famine, a universal war of devastation had cut off the supply of every means of subsistence; industry and commerce seem to be destroyed. And why? Because there is too much civilization, too much means of subsistence, too much industry, too much commerce. The productive forces at the disposal of society no longer tend to further the development of the conditions of bourgeois property; on the contrary, they have become too powerful for these conditions, by which they are fettered, and no sooner do they overcome these fetters than they bring disorder into the whole of bourgeois society, endanger the existence of bourgeois property. The conditions of bourgeois society are too narrow to comprise the wealth created by them. And how does the bourgeoisie get over these crises? On the one hand by enforced destruction of a mass of productive forces; on the other, by the conquest of new markets and by the more thorough exploitation of the old ones. That is to say, by paving the way for more extensive and more destructive crises, and by diminishing the means whereby crises are prevented.

The weapons with which the bourgeoisie felled feudalism to the ground are now turned against the bourgeoisie itself.

But not only has the bourgeoisie forged the weapons that bring death to itself; it has also called into existence the men who are to wield those weapons—the modern working class, the proletarians.

In proportion as the bourgeoisie, i.e., capital, is developed, in the same proportion is the proletariat, the modern working class, developed—a class of labourers, who live only so long as they find work, and who find work only so long as their labour increases capital. These labourers, who must sell themselves piecemeal, are a commodity like every other article of commerce, and are consequently exposed to all the vicissitudes of competition, to all the fluctuations of the market.

Owing to the extensive use of machinery and to division of labour, the work of the proletarians has lost all individual character, and, consequently, all charm for the workman. He becomes an appendage of the machine, and it is only the most simple, most monotonous, and most easily acquired knack that is required of him. Hence, the cost of production of a workman is restricted almost entirely to the means of subsistence that he requires for his maintenance and for the propagation of his race. But the price of a commodity, and therefore also of labour, is equal to its cost of production. In proportion, therefore, as the repulsiveness of the work increases, the wage decreases. Nay more, in proportion as the use of machinery and division of labour increases, in the same proportion the burden of toil also increases, whether by prolongation of the working hours, by increase of the work exacted in a given time, or by increased speed of the machinery, etc.

Modern industry has converted the little workshop of the patriarchal master into the great factory of the industrial capitalist. Masses of labourers, crowded into the factory, are organized like soldiers. As privates of the industrial army they are placed under the command of a perfect hierarchy of officers and sergeants. Not only are they slaves of the bourgeois class and of the bourgeois state; they are daily and hourly enslaved by the machine, by the overseer, and, above all, by the individual bourgeois manufacturer himself. The more openly this despotism proclaims gains to be its end and aim, the more petty, the more hateful, and the more embittering it is.

The less the skill and exertion of strength implied in manual labour—in other words, the more modern industry develops—the more is the labour of men superseded by that of women. Differences of age and sex have no longer any distinctive social validity for the working class. All are instruments of labour, more or less expensive to use, according to their age and sex.

No sooner has the labourer received his wages in cash, for the moment escaping exploitation by the manufacturer, than he is set upon by the other portions of the bourgeoisie—the landlord, the shopkeeper, the pawnbroker, etc.

The lower strata of the middle class—the small tradespeople, shopkeepers, and retired tradesmen generally, the handicraftsmen and peasants—all these sink gradually into the proletariat, partly because their diminutive capital does not suffice for the scale on which modern industry is carried on and is swamped in the competition with the large capitalists, partly because their specialized skill is rendered worthless by new methods of production. Thus the proletariat is recruited from all classes of the population.

The proletariat goes through various stages of development. With its birth begins its struggle with the bourgeoisie. At first the contest is carried on by individual labourers, then by the workpeople of a factory, then by the operatives of one trade, in one locality, against the individual bourgeois who directly exploits them. They direct their attacks not against the bourgeois conditions of production, but against the instruments of production themselves; they destroy imported wares that compete with their labour, they smash machinery to pieces, they set factories ablaze, they seek to restore by force the vanished status of the workman of the Middle Ages.

At this stage the labourers still form an incoherent mass scattered over the whole country, and broken up by their mutual competition. If anywhere they unite to form more compact bodies, this is not yet the consequence of their own active union, but of the union of the bourgeoisie, which class, in order to attain its own political ends, is compelled to set the whole proletariat in motion, and is, moreover, still able to do so for a time. At this stage, therefore, the proletarians do not fight their enemies, but the enemies of their enemies, the remnants of absolute monarchy, the landowners, the non-industrial bourgeois, the petty bourgeoisie. Thus the whole historical movement is concentrated in the hands of the bourgeoisie; every victory so obtained is a victory for the bourgeoisie.

But with the development of industry the proletariat not only increases in number; it becomes concentrated in greater masses, its strength grows, and it feels that strength more. The various interests and conditions of life within the ranks of the proletariat are more and more equalized, in proportion as machinery obliterates all distinctions of labour and nearly everywhere reduces wages to the same low level. The growing competition among the bourgeois and the resulting commercial crises make the wages of the workers ever more fluctuating. The unceasing improvement of machinery, ever more rapidly developing, makes their livelihood more and more precarious; the collisions between individual workmen and individual bourgeois take more and more the character of collisions between two classes. Thereupon the workers begin to form combinations (trade unions) against the bourgeoisie; they club together in order to keep up the rate of wages; they found permanent associations in order to make provisions beforehand for these occasional revolts. Here and there the contest breaks out into riots.

Now and then the workers are victorious, but only for a time. The real fruit of their battles lies not in the immediate result but in the ever expanding union of the workers. This union is furthered by the improved means of communication which are created by modern industry, and which place the workers of different localities in contact with one another. It was just this contact that was needed to centralize the numerous local struggles, all of the same character, into one national struggle between classes. But every class struggle is a political struggle. And that union, which the burghers of the Middle Ages, with their miserable highways, required centuries to attain, the modern proletarians, thanks to railways, achieve in a few years.

This organization of the proletarians into a class, and consequently into a political party, is continually being upset again by the competition between the workers themselves. But it ever rises up again, stronger, firmer, mightier. It compels legislative recognition of particular interests of the workers by taking advantage of the divisions among the bourgeoisie itself. Thus the Ten Hour bill in England was carried.

Altogether, collisions between the classes of the old society further the course of development of the proletariat in many ways. The bourgeoisie finds itself involved in a constant battle—at first with the aristocracy; later on, with those portions of the bourgeoisie itself whose interests have become antagonistic to the progress of industry; at all times with the bourgeoisie of foreign countries. In all these battles it sees itself compelled to appeal to the proletariat, to ask for its help, and thus to drag it into the political arena. The bourgeoisie itself, therefore, supplies the proletariat with its own elements of political and general education; in other words, it furnishes the proletariat with weapons for fighting the bourgeoisie.

Further, as we have already seen, entire sections of the ruling classes are, by the advance of industry, precipitated into the proletariat, or are at least threatened in their conditions of existence. These also supply the proletariat with fresh elements of enlightenment and progress.

Finally, in times when the class struggle nears the decisive hour, the process of dissolution going on within the ruling class, in fact within the whole range of old society, assumes such a violent, glaring character that a small section of the ruling class cuts itself adrift and joins the revolutionary class, the class that holds the future in its hands. Just as, therefore, at an earlier period a section of the nobility went over to the bourgeoisie, so now a portion of the bourgeoisie goes over to the proletariat, and in particular, a portion of the bourgeois ideologists who have raised themselves to the level of comprehending theoretically the historical movement as a whole.

Of all the classes that stand face to face with the bourgeoisie today, the proletariat alone is a really revolutionary class. The other classes decay and finally disappear in the face of modern industry; the proletariat is its special and essential product.

The lower middle class, the small manufacturer, the shopkeeper, the artisan, the peasant—all these fight against the bourgeoisie, to save from extinction their existence as fractions of the middle class. They are, therefore, not revolutionary but conservative. Nay more, they are reactionary, for they try to roll back the wheel of history. If by chance they are revolutionary they are so only in view of their impending transfer into the proletariat; they thus defend not their present but their future interests; they desert their own standpoint to adopt that of the proletariat.

The "dangerous class," the social scum (Lumpenproletariat), that passively rotting mass thrown off by the lowest layers of old society, may here and there be swept into the movement by a proletarian revolution; its conditions of life, however, prepare it far more for the part of a bribed tool of reactionary intrigue.

The social conditions of the old society no longer exist for the proletariat. The proletarian is without property; his relation to his wife and children has no longer anything in common with bourgeois family relations; modern industrial labour, modern subjection to capital, the same in England as in France, in America as in Germany, has stripped him of every trace of national character. Law, morality, religion are to him so many bourgeois prejudices, behind which lurk in ambush just as many bourgeois interests.

All the preceding classes that got the upper hand sought to fortify their already acquired status by subjecting society at large to their conditions of appropriation. The proletarians cannot become masters of the productive forces of society except by abolishing their own previous mode of appropriation, and thereby also every other previous mode of appropriation. They have nothing of their own to secure and to fortify; their mission is to destroy all previous securities for, and insurances of, individual property.

All previous historical movements were movements of minorities, or in the interest of minorities. The proletarian movement is the self-conscious, independent movement of the immense majority, in the interest of the immense majority. The proletariat, the lowest stratum of our present society, cannot stir, cannot raise itself up, without the whole superincumbent strata of official society being sprung into the air.

Though not in substance, yet in form, the struggle of the proletariat with the bourgeoisie is at first a national struggle. The proletariat of each country must, of course, first of all settle matters with its own bourgeoisie.

In depicting the most general phases of the development of the proletariat we traced the more or less veiled civil war raging within existing society, up to the point where that war breaks out into open revolution, and where the violent overthrow of the bourgeoisie lays the foundation for the sway of the proletariat.

Hitherto, every form of society has been based, as we have already seen, on the antagonism of oppressing and oppressed classes. But in order to oppress a class certain conditions must be assured to it under which it can, at least, continue its slavish existence. The serf, in the period of serfdom, raised himself to membership in the commune, just as the petty bourgeois, under the yoke of feudal absolutism, managed to develop into a bourgeois. The modern labourer, on the contrary, instead of rising with the progress of industry, sinks deeper and deeper below the conditions of existence of his own class. He becomes a pauper, and pauperism develops more rapidly than population and wealth. And here it becomes evident that the bourgeoisie is unfit any longer to be the ruling class in society and to impose its conditions of existence upon society as an overriding law. It is unfit to rule because it is incompetent to assure an existence to its slave within his slavery, because it cannot help letting him sink into such a state that it has to feed him, instead of being fed by him. Society can no longer live under this bourgeoisie, in other words, its existence is no longer compatible with society.

The essential condition for the existence and sway of the bourgeois class is the formation and augmentation of capital; the condition for capital is wage labour. Wage labour rests exclusively on competition between the labourers. The advance of industry, whose involuntary promoter is the bourgeoisie, replaces the isolation of the labourers, due to competition, by their revolutionary combination, due to association. The development of modern industry, therefore, cuts from under its feet the very foundation on which the bourgeoisie produces and appropriates products. What the bourgeoisie, therefore, produces above all are its own grave-diggers. Its fall and the victory of the proletariat are equally inevitable.

Chapter II
Proletarians and Communists

In what relation do the Communists stand to the proletarians as a whole?

The Communists do not form a separate party opposed to other working class parties.

They have no interests separate and apart from those of the proletariat as a whole.

They do not set up any sectarian principles of their own by which to shape and mould the proletarian movement.

The Communists are distinguished from the other working class parties by this only: 1. In the national struggles of the proletarians of the different countries they point out and bring to the front the common interests of the entire proletariat, independently of all nationality; 2. In the various stages of development which the struggle of the working class against the bourgeoisie has to pass through they always and everywhere represent the interests of the movement as a whole.

The Communists, therefore, are on the one hand, practically, the most advanced and resolute section of the working class parties of every country, that section which pushes forward all others; on the other hand, theoretically, they have over the great mass of the proletariat the advantage of clearly understanding the line of march, the conditions, and the ultimate general results of the proletarian movement.

The immediate aim of the Communists is the same as that of all the other proletarian parties: formation of the proletariat into a class, overthrow of bourgeois supremacy, conquest of political power by the proletariat.

The theoretical conclusions of the Communists are in no way based on ideas or principles that have been invented or discovered by this or that would-be universal reformer.

They merely express in general terms actual relations springing from an existing class struggle, from a historical movement going on under our very eyes. The abolition of existing property relations is not at all a distinctive feature of Communism.

All property relations in the past have continually been subject to historical change consequent upon the change in historical conditions.

The French Revolution, for example, abolished feudal property in favour of bourgeois property.

The distinguishing feature of Communism is not the abolition of property generally, but the abolition of bourgeois property. But modern bourgeois private property is the final and most complete expression of the system of producing and appropriating products that is based on class antagonisms, on the exploitation of the many by the few.

In this sense the theory of the Communists may be summed up in the single sentence: abolition of private property.

We Communists have been reproached with the desire of abolishing the right of personally acquiring property as the fruit of a man's own labour, which property is alleged to be the groundwork of all personal freedom, activity and independence.

Hard-won, self-acquired, self-earned property! Do you mean the property of the petty artisan and of the small peasant, a form of property that preceded the bourgeois form? There is no need to abolish that; the development of industry has to a great extent already destroyed it and is still destroying it daily.

Or do you mean modern bourgeois private property?

But does wage labour create any property for the labourer? Not a bit. It creates capital, i.e., that kind of property which exploits wage labour and which cannot increase except upon condition of begetting a new supply of wage labour for fresh exploitation. Property in its present form is based on the antagonism of capital and wage labour. Let us examine both sides of this antagonism.

To be a capitalist is to have not only a purely personal, but a social, *status* in production. Capital is a collective product, and only by the united action of many members—nay, in the last resort, only by the united action of all members of society—can it be set in motion.

Capital is, therefore, not a personal, it is a social, power.

When, therefore, capital is converted into common property, into the property of all members of society, personal property is not thereby transformed into social property. It is only the social character of the property that is changed. It loses its class character.

Let us now take wage labour.

The average price of wage labour is the minimum wage, i.e., that quantum of the means of subsistence which is absolutely requisite to keep the labourer in bare existence as a labourer. What, therefore, the wage labourer appropriates by means of his labour merely suffices to prolong and reproduce a bare existence. We by no means intend to abolish this personal appropriation of the products of labour, an appropriation that is made for the maintenance and reproduction of human life and that leaves no surplus wherewith to command the labour of others. All that we want to do away with is the miserable character of this appropriation, under which the labourer lives merely to increase capital, and is allowed to live only insofar as the interest of the ruling class requires it.

In bourgeois society living labour is but a means to increase accumulated labour. In Communist society accumulated labour is but a means to widen, to enrich, to promote the existence of the labourer.

In bourgeois society, therefore, the past dominates the present; in Communist society, the present dominates the past. In bourgeois society capital is independent and has individuality, while the living person is dependent and has no individuality.

And the abolition of this state of things is called by the bourgeois, abolition of individuality and freedom! And rightly so. The abolition of bourgeois individuality, bourgeois independence, and bourgeois freedom is undoubtedly aimed at.

By freedom is meant, under the present bourgeois conditions of production, free trade, free selling and buying.

But if selling and buying disappears, free selling and buying disappears also. This talk about free selling and buying, and all the other "brave words" of our bourgeoisie about freedom in general, have a meaning, if any, only in contrast with restricted selling and buying, with the fettered traders of the Middle Ages, but have no meaning when opposed to the Communist abolition of buying and selling, of the bourgeois conditions of production, and of the bourgeoisie itself.

You are horrified at our intending to do away with private property. But in your existing society private property is already done away with for nine-tenths of the population; its existence for the few is solely due to its non-existence in the hands of those nine-tenths. You reproach us, therefore, with intending to do away with a form of property, the necessary condition for whose existence is the non-existence of any property for the immense majority of a society.

In a word, you reproach us with intending to do away with your property. Precisely so; that is just what we intend.

From the moment when labour can no longer be converted into

capital, money, or rent—into a social power capable of being monopolised —i.e., from the moment when individual property can no longer be transformed into bourgeois property, into capital; from that moment, you say, individuality vanishes.

You must, therefore, confess that by "individual" you mean no other person than the bourgeois, than the middle class owner of property. This person must, indeed, be swept out of the way and made impossible.

Communism deprives no man of the power to appropriate the products of society; all that it does is to deprive him of the power to subjugate the labour of others by means of such appropriation.

It has been objected that upon the abolition of private property all work will cease and universal laziness will overtake us.

According to this, bourgeois society ought long ago to have gone to the dogs through sheer idleness; for those of its members who work acquire nothing, and those who acquire anything do not work. The whole of this objection is but another expression of the tautology: there can no longer be any wage labour when there is no longer any capital.

All objections urged against the Communist mode of producing and appropriating material products have in the same way been urged against the Communist modes of producing and appropriating intellectual products. Just as to the bourgeois the disappearance of class property is the disappearance of production itself, so the disappearance of class culture is to him identical with the disappearance of all culture.

That culture, the loss of which he laments, is for the enormous majority a mere training to act as a machine.

But don't wrangle with us so long as you apply to our intended abolition of bourgeois property the standard of your bourgeois notions of freedom, culture, law, etc. Your very ideas are but the outgrowth of the conditions of your bourgeois production and bourgeois property, just as your jurisprudence is but the will of your class made into a law for all, a will whose essential character and direction are determined by the economic conditions of existence of your class.

The selfish misconception that induces you to transform into eternal laws of nature and of reason the social forms springing from your present mode of production and form of property—historical relations that rise and disappear in the progress of production—this misconception you share with every ruling class that has preceded you. What you see clearly in the case of ancient property, what you admit in the case of feudal property, you are, of course, forbidden to admit in the case of your own bourgeois form of property.

Abolition of the family! Even the most radical flare up at this infamous proposal of the Communists.

On what foundation is the present family, the bourgeois family, based? On capital, on private gain. In its completely developed form this family exists only among the bourgeoisie. But this state of things finds its complement in the practical absence of the family among the proletarians, and in public prostitution.

The bourgeois family will vanish as a matter of course when its complement vanishes, and both will vanish with the vanishing of capital.

Do you charge us with wanting to stop the exploitation of children by their parents? To this crime we plead guilty.

But, you will say, we destroy the most hallowed of relations when we replace home education by social.

And your education! Is not that also social, and determined by the social conditions under which you educate, by the intervention of society, direct or indirect, by means of schools, etc.? The Communists have not invented the intervention of society in education; they do but seek to alter the character of that intervention and to rescue education from the influence of the ruling class.

The bourgeois claptrap about the family and education, about the hallowed co-relation of parent and child, becomes all the more disgusting, the more, by the action of modern industry, all family ties among the proletarians are torn asunder and their children transformed into simple articles of commerce and instruments of labour.

But you Communists would introduce community of women, screams the whole bourgeoisie in chorus.

The bourgeois sees in his wife a mere instrument of production. He hears that the instruments of production are to be exploited in common, and, naturally, can come to no other conclusion than that the lot of being common to all will likewise fall to the women.

He has not even a suspicion that the real point aimed at is to do away with the status of women as mere instruments of production.

For the rest, nothing is more ridiculous than the virtuous indignation of our bourgeois at the community of women which, they pretend, is to be openly and officially established by the Communists. The Communists have no need to introduce community of women; it has existed almost from time immemorial.

Our bourgeois, not content with having the wives and daughters of their proletarians at their disposal, not to speak of common prostitutes, take the greatest pleasure in seducing each other's wives.

Bourgeois marriage is in reality a system of wives in common and thus at the most what the Communists might possibly be reproached with is that they desire to introduce, in substitution for a hypocritically concealed, an openly legalized, community of women. For the rest, it is self-evident that the abolition of the present system of production must bring with it the abolition of the community of women springing from that system, i.e., of prostitution both public and private.

The Communists are further reproached with desiring to abolish countries and nationality.

The workingmen have no country. We cannot take from them what they have not got. Since the proletariat must first of all acquire political supremacy, must rise to be the leading class of the nation, must constitute itself *the* nation, it is, so far, itself national, though not in the bourgeois sense of the word.

National differences and antagonisms between peoples are vanishing gradually from day to day, owing to the development of the bourgeoisie, to freedom of commerce, to the world market, to uniformity in the mode of production and in the conditions of life corresponding thereto.

The supremacy of the proletariat will cause them to vanish still faster. United action, of the leading civilized countries at least, is one of the first conditions for the emancipation of the proletariat.

In proportion as the exploitation of one individual by another is put an end to, the exploitation of one nation by another will also be put an end to. In proportion as the antagonism between classes within the nation vanishes, the hostility of one nation to another will come to an end.

The charges against Communism made from a religious, a philosophical, and, generally, from an ideological standpoint are not deserving of serious examination.

Does it require deep intuition to comprehend that man's ideas, views, and conceptions—in one word, man's consciousness—changes with every change in the conditions of his material existence, in his social relations and in his social life?

What else does the history of ideas prove than that intellectual production changes its character in proportion as material production is changed? The ruling ideas of each age have ever been the ideas of its ruling class.

When people speak of ideas that revolutionize society, they do but express the fact that within the old society the elements of a new one have been created and that the dissolution of the old ideas keeps even pace with the dissolution of the old conditions of existence.

When the ancient world was in its last throes the ancient religions were overcome by Christianity. When Christian ideas succumbed in the 18th century to rationalist ideas, feudal society fought its death-battle with the then revolutionary bourgeoisie. The ideas of religious liberty and freedom of conscience merely gave expression to the sway of free competition within the domain of knowledge.

"Undoubtedly," it will be said, "religion, moral, philosophical and juridical ideas have been modified in the course of historical development. But religion, morality, philosophy, political science, and law, constantly survived this change."

"There are, besides, eternal truths such as freedom, justice, etc., that are common to all states of society. But Communism abolishes eternal truths, it abolishes all religion and all morality, instead of constituting them on a new basis; it, therefore, acts in contradiction to all past historical experience."

What does this accusation reduce itself to? The history of all past society has consisted in the development of class antagonisms, antagonisms that assumed different forms at different epochs.

But whatever form they may have taken, one fact is common to all past ages, viz., the exploitation of one part of society by the other. No wonder, then, that the social consciousness of past ages, despite all the multiplicity and variety it displays, moves within certain common forms, or general ideas, which cannot completely vanish except with the total disappearance of class antagonisms.

The Communist revolution is the most radical rupture with traditional property relations; no wonder that its development involves the most radical rupture with traditional ideas.

But let us have done with the bourgeois objections to Communism.

We have seen above that the first step in the revolution by the working class is to raise the proletariat to the position of ruling class, to establish democracy.

The proletariat will use its political supremacy to wrest by degrees all capital from the bourgeoisie, to centralize all instruments of production in the hands of the state, i.e., of the proletariat organized as the ruling class, and to increase the total of productive forces as rapidly as possible.

Of course, in the beginning this cannot be effected except by means of despotic inroads on the rights of property and on the conditions of bourgeois production; by means of measures, therefore, which appear economically insufficient and untenable, but which, in the course of the movement outstrip themselves, necessitate further inroads upon the old social order, and are unavoidable as a means of entirely revolutionizing the mode of production.

These measures will, of course, be different in different countries.

Nevertheless, in the most advanced countries the following will be pretty generally applicable:

1. Abolition of property in land and application of all rents of land to public purposes.

2. A heavy progressive or graduated income tax.

3. Abolition of all right of inheritance.

4. Confiscation of the property of all emigrants and rebels.

5. Centralization of credit in the hands of the state by means of a national bank with state capital and an exclusive monopoly.

6. Centralization of the means of communication and transport in the hands of the state.

7. Extension of factories and instruments of production owned by the state; the bringing into cultivation of waste lands, and the improvement of the soil generally in accordance with a common plan.

8. Equal obligation of all to work. Establishment of industrial armies, especially for agriculture.

9. Combination of agriculture with manufacturing industries; gradual abolition of the distinction between town and country by a more equable distribution of the population over the country.

10. Free education for all children in public schools. Abolition of child factory labour in its present form. Combination of education with industrial production, etc.

When in the course of development class distinctions have disappeared and all production has been concentrated in the hands of a vast association of the whole nation, the public power will lose its political character. Political power, properly so called, is merely the organized power of one class for oppressing another. If the proletariat during its contest with the bourgeoisie is compelled by the force of circumstances to organize itself as a class; if by means of a revolution it makes itself the ruling class and, as such, sweeps away by force the old conditions of production, then it will, along with these conditions, have swept away the conditions for the existence of class antagonisms and of classes generally, and will thereby have abolished its own supremacy as a class.

In place of the old bourgeois society, with its classes and class antagonisms, we shall have an association in which the free development of each is the condition for the free development of all.

[1] Lassalle always acknowledged himself to us personally to be a disciple of Marx and, as such, stood on the ground of the *Manifesto*. But, in his public agitation, 1862-64, he did not go beyond demanding cooperative workshops supported by state credit.

[2] This version was actually made by Plekhanov. Bakunin's translation appeared in 1870. —EDITOR.

[3] By *bourgeoisie* is meant the class of modern capitalists, owners of the means of social production, and employers of wage labour; by *proletariat*, the class of modern wage labourers who, having no means of production of their own, are reduced to selling their labour power in order to live.

[4] That is, all *written* history. In 1837, the pre-history of society, the social organization existing previous to recorded history, was all but unknown. Since then Haxthausen discovered common ownership of land in Russia; Maurer proved it to be the social foundation from which all Teutonic races started in history, and, by and by, village communities were found to be, or to have been, the primitive form of society everywhere from India to Ireland. The inner organization of this primitive communistic society was laid bare, in its typical form, by Morgan's crowning discovery of the true nature of the *gens* and its relation to the *tribe*. With the dissolution of these primæval communities society begins to be differentiated into separate and finally antagonistic classes. I have attempted to retrace this process of dissolution in *The Origin of the Family, Private Property and the State*.

[5] Guild-master, that is, a full member of a guild, a master within, not a head of a guild.

[6] "Commune" was the name taken in France by the nascent towns even before they had conquered from their feudal lords and masters local self-government and political rights as the "Third Estate." Generally speaking, for the economic development of the bourgeoisie, England is here taken as the typical country; for its political development, France.

To Reveal
One's True Feelings

by Mao Tse-tung
(with surrounding commentary by Lucian Pye)

THE CLIMAX of Mao as Public Man and as Private Man is perfectly captured by his words in a poem written to Chou En-lai early in 1975 shortly before the meeting of the Second Plenum of the Tenth Party Congress. As we have so frequently found, starting with his poem of mourning for his mother, Mao's use of words reveals both his conscious concerns and his deeper inner anxieties. The title of the poem is, appropriately, "To Reveal One's True Feelings" and reads as follows:

> *Loyal parents who sacrificed so much for the nation*
> *Never feared the ultimate fate.*
> *Now that the country has become red, who will be its guardian?*
>
> *Our mission unfinished may take a thousand years.*
> *The struggle tires us, and our hair is grey.*
> *You and I, old friends, can we just watch our efforts*
>   *be washed away?*

The first two lines sound a note of solid confidence as they uphold the idea that parents who make sacrifices can be absolutely sure of what will follow for their children. In the next line doubt emerges and Mao reveals his uncertainty and anxiety about what might happen when there is no strong "guardian" or real "father." Then in the last lines despair takes over as Mao acknowledges the limits of his own capacity as "parent." The contrast between the first and the last lines gives emphasis to Mao's view that while others can be firm and confident parents, he knows that he himself, who was so successful as a rebellious son, lacks the capacity to be an influencing "father." Behind the surface appearances of self-assurance, there lie the insecurities and self-doubts which have produced his remarkable spirit of the "monkey" and the "tiger."

This poem, written late in Mao's life when he must have been contemplating all the varied roles he had played as Public Man, provides confirmation for the psychological interpretation which has run through this entire book. . . .

Small Is Beautiful

by E. F. Schumacher

4
Buddhist Economics

"**R**IGHT Livelihood" is one of the requirements of the Buddha's Noble Eightfold Path. It is clear, therefore, that there must be such a thing as Buddhist economics.

Buddhist countries have often stated that they wish to remain faithful to their heritage. So Burma: "The New Burma sees no conflict between religious values and economic progress. Spiritual health and material well-being are not enemies: they are natural allies." Or: "We can blend successfully the religious and spiritual values of our heritage with the benefits of modern technology." Or: "We Burmans have a sacred duty to conform both our dreams and our acts to our faith. This we shall ever do."

All the same, such countries invariably assume that they can model their economic development plans in accordance with modern economics, and they call upon modern economists from so-called advanced countries to advise them, to formulate the policies to be pursued, and to construct the grand design for development, the Five-Year Plan or whatever it may be called. No one seems to think that a Buddhist way of life would call for Buddhist economics, just as the modern materialist way of life has brought forth modern economics.

Economists themselves, like most specialists, normally suffer from a kind of metaphysical blindness, assuming that theirs is a science of absolute and invariable truths, without any presuppositions. Some go as far as to claim that economic laws are as free from "metaphysics" or "values" as the law of gravitation. We need not, however, get involved in arguments of methodology. Instead, let us take some fundamentals and see what they look like when viewed by a modern economist and a Buddhist economist.

257

There is universal agreement that a fundamental source of wealth is human labour. Now, the modern economist has been brought up to consider "labour" or work as little more than a necessary evil. From the point of view of the employer, it is in any case simply an item of cost, to be reduced to a minimum if it cannot be eliminated altogether, say, by automation. From the point of view of the workman, it is a "disutility"; to work is to make a sacrifice of one's leisure and comfort, and wages are a kind of compensation for the sacrifice. Hence the ideal from the point of view of the employer is to have output without employees, and the ideal from the point of view of the employee is to have income without employment.

The consequences of these attitudes both in theory and in practise are, of course, extremely far-reaching. If the ideal with regard to work is to get rid of it, every method that "reduces the work load" is a good thing. The most potent method, short of automation, is the so-called "division of labour" and the classical example is the pin factory eulogised in Adam Smith's *Wealth of Nations*. Here it is not a matter of ordinary specialisation, which mankind has practised from time immemorial, but of dividing up every complete process of production into minute parts, so that the final product can be produced at great speed without anyone having had to contribute more than a totally insignificant and, in most cases, unskilled movement of his limbs.

The Buddhist point of view takes the function of work to be at least threefold: to give a man a chance to utilise and develop his faculties; to enable him to overcome his ego-centredness by joining with other people in a common task; and to bring forth the goods and services needed for a becoming existence. Again, the consequences that flow from this view are endless. To organise work in such a manner that it becomes meaningless, boring, stultifying, or nerve-racking for the worker would be little short of criminal; it would indicate a greater concern with goods than with people, an evil lack of compassion and a soul-destroying degree of attachment to the most primitive side of this worldly existence. Equally, to strive for leisure as an alternative to work would be considered a complete misunderstanding of one of the basic truths of human existence, namely that work and leisure are complementary parts of the same living process and cannot be separated without destroying the joy of work and the bliss of leisure.

From the Buddhist point of view, there are therefore two types of mechanisation which must be clearly distinguished: one that enhances a man's skill and power and one that turns the work of man over to a mechanical slave, leaving man in a position of having to serve the slave. How to tell the one from the other? "The craftsman himself," says Ananda Coomaraswamy, a man equally competent to talk about the modern West as the ancient East, "can always, if allowed to, draw the delicate distinction between the machine and the tool. The carpet loom is a tool, a contrivance for holding warp threads at a stretch for the pile to be woven around them by the craftsmen's fingers; but the power loom is a machine, and its significance as a destroyer of culture lies in the fact that it does the essentially human part of the work." It is clear, therefore, that Buddhist economics must be very different from the economics of modern materialism, since the Buddhist sees the essence of civilisation not in a multiplication of wants but in the purification of human character. Character, at the same time, is formed primarily by a man's work. And work, properly conducted in conditions of human dignity and freedom, blesses those who do it and equally their products. The Indian philosopher and economist J. C. Kumarappa sums the matter up as follows:

> If the nature of the work is properly appreciated and applied, it will stand in the same relation to the higher faculties as food is to the physical body. It nourishes and enlivens the higher man and urges him to produce the best he is capable of. It directs his free will along the proper course and disciplines the animal in him into progressive channels. It furnishes an excellent background for man to display his scale of values and develop his personality.

If a man has no chance of obtaining work he is in a desperate position, not simply because he lacks an income but because he lacks this nourishing and enlivening factor of disciplined work which nothing can replace. A modern economist may engage in highly sophisticated calculations on whether full employment "pays" or whether it might be more "economic" to run an economy at less than full employment so as to ensure a greater mobility of labour, a better stabiity of wages, and so forth. His fundamental criterion of success is simply the total quantity of goods produced during a given period of time. "If the marginal urgency of goods is low," says Professor Galbraith in *The Affluent Society*, "then so is the urgency of employing the last man or the last million men in the labour force." And again: "If. . . we can afford some unemployment in the interest of stability— a proposition, incidentally, of impeccably conservative antecedents—then we can afford to give those who are unemployed the goods that enable them to sustain their accustomed standard of living."

From a Buddhist point of view, this is standing the truth on its head by considering goods as more important than people and consumption as more important than creative activity. It means shifting the emphasis from the worker to the product of work, that is, from the human to the sub-human, a surrender to the forces of evil. The very start of Buddhist economic planning would be a planning for full employment, and the primary purpose of this would in fact be employment for everyone who needs an "outside" job: it would not be the maximisation of employment nor the maximisation of production. Women, on the whole, do not need an "outside" job, and the large-scale employment of women in offices or factories would be considered a sign of serious economic failure. In particular, to let mothers of young children work in factories while the children run wild would be as uneconomic in the eyes of a Buddhist economist as the employment of a skilled worker as a soldier in the eyes of a modern economist.

While the materialist is mainly interested in goods, the Buddhist is mainly interested in liberation. But Buddhism is "The Middle Way" and therefore in no way antagonistic to physical well-being. It is not wealth that stands in the way of liberation but the attachment to wealth; not the enjoyment of pleasurable things but the craving for them. The keynote of Buddhist economics, therefore, is simplicity and non-violence. From an economist's point of view, the marvel of the Buddhist way of life is the utter rationality of its pattern—amazingly small means leading to extraordinarily satisfactory results.

For the modern economist this is very difficult to understand. He is used to measuring the "standard of living" by the amount of annual consumption, assuming all the time that a man who consumes more is "better off" than a man who consumes less. A Buddhist economist would consider this approach excessively irrational: since consumption is merely a means to human well-being, the aim should be to obtain the maximum of well-being with the minimum of consumption. Thus, if the purpose of clothing is a certain amount of temperature comfort and an attractive appearance, the task is to attain this purpose with the smallest possible effort, that is, with the smallest annual destruction of cloth and with the help of designs that involve the smallest possible input of toil. The less toil there is, the more time and strength is left for artistic creativity. It would be highly uneconomic, for instance, to go in for complicated tailoring, like the modern West, when a much more beautiful effect can be achieved by the skilful draping of uncut material. It would be the height of folly to make material so that it should wear out quickly and the height of barbarity to make anything ugly, shabby or mean. What has just been said about clothing applies equally to all other human requirements. The ownership and the consumption of goods is a means to an end, and Buddhist economics is the systematic study of how to attain given ends with the minimum means.

Modern economics, on the other hand, considers consumption to be the sole end and purpose of all economic activity, taking the factors of production—land, labour, and capital—as the means. The former, in short, tries to maximise human satisfactions by the optimal pattern of consumption, while the latter tries to maximise consumption by the optimal pattern of productive effort. It is easy to see that the effort needed to sustain a way of life which seeks to attain the optimal pattern of consumption is likely to be much smaller than the effort needed to sustain a drive for maximum consumption. We need not be surprised, therefore, that the pressure and strain of living is very much less in, say, Burma than it is in the United States, in spite of the fact that the amount of labour-saving machinery used in the former country is only a minute fraction of the amount used in the latter.

Simplicity and non-violence are obviously closely related. The optimal pattern of consumption, producing a high degree of human satisfaction by means of a relatively low rate of consumption, allows people to live without great pressure and strain and to fulfil the primary injunction of Buddhist teaching: "Cease to do evil; try to do good." As physical resources are everywhere limited, people satisfying their needs by means of a modest use of resources are obviously less likely to be at each other's throats than people depending upon a high rate of use. Equally, people who live in highly self-sufficient local communities are less likely to get involved in large-scale violence than people whose existence depends upon worldwide systems of trade.

From the point of view of Buddhist economics, therefore, production from local resources for local needs is the most rational way of economic life, while dependence on imports from afar and the consequent need to produce for export to unknown and distant peoples is highly uneconomic and justifiable only in exceptional cases and on a small scale. Just as the modern economist would admit that a high rate of consumption of transport services between a man's home and his place of work signifies a misfortune and not a high standard of life, so the Buddhist economist would hold that to satisfy human wants from faraway sources rather than from sources nearby signifies failure rather than success. The former tends to take statistics showing an increase in the number of ton/miles per head of the population carried by a country's transport system as proof of economic progress, while to the latter—the Buddhist economist—the same statistics would indicate a highly undesirable deterioration in the *pattern* of consumption.

Another striking difference between modern economics and Buddhist economics arises over the use of natural resources. Bertrand de Jouvenel, the eminent French political philosopher, has characterised "Western man" in words which may be taken as a fair description of the modern economist:

> He tends to count nothing as an expenditure, other than human effort; he does not seem to mind how much mineral matter he wastes and, far worse, how much living matter he destroys. He does not seem to realise at all that human life is a dependent part of an ecosystem of many different forms of life. As the world is ruled from towns where men are cut off from any form of life other than human, the feeling of belonging to an ecosystem is not revived. This results in a harsh and improvident treatment of things upon which we ultimately depend, such as water and trees.

The teaching of the Buddha, on the other hand, enjoins a reverent and non-violent attitude not only to all sentient beings but also, with great emphasis, to trees. Every follower of the Buddha ought to plant a tree every few years and look after it until it is safely established, and the Buddhist economist can demonstrate without difficulty that the universal observation of this rule would result in a high rate of genuine economic development independent of any foreign aid. Much of the economic decay of southeast Asia (as of many other parts of the world) is undoubtedly due to a heedless and shameful neglect of trees.

Modern economics does not distinguish between renewable and non-renewable materials, as its very method is to equalise and quantify everything by means of a money price. Thus, taking various alternative fuels, like coal, oil, wood, or water-power: the only difference between them recognised by modern economics is relative cost per equivalent unit. The cheapest is automatically the one to be preferred, as to do otherwise would be irrational and "uneconomic." From a Buddhist point of view, of course, this will not do; the essential difference between non-renewable fuels like coal and oil on the one hand and renewable fuels like wood and water-power on the other cannot be simply overlooked. Non-renewable goods must be used only if they are indispensable, and then only with the greatest care and the most meticulous concern for conservation. To use them heedlessly or extravagantly is an act of violence, and while complete non-violence may not be attainable on this earth, there is nonetheless an ineluctable duty on man to aim at the ideal of non-violence in all he does.

Just as a modern European economist would not consider it a great economic achievement if all European art treasures were sold to America at attractive prices, so the Buddhist economist would insist that a population basing its economic life on non-renewable fuels is living parasitically, on capital instead of income. Such a way of life could have no permanence and could therefore be justified only as a purely temporary expedient. As the world's resources of non-renewable fuels—coal, oil and natural gas— are exceedingly unevenly distributed over the globe and undoubtedly limited in quantity, it is clear that their exploitation at an ever-increasing rate is an act of violence against nature which must almost inevitably lead to violence between men.

This fact alone might give food for thought even to those people in Buddhist countries who care nothing for the religious and spiritual values of their heritage and ardently desire to embrace the materialism of modern economics at the fastest possible speed. Before they dismiss Buddhist economics as nothing better than a nostalgic dream, they might wish to consider whether the path of economic development outlined by modern economics is likely to lead them to places where they really want to be. Towards the end of his courageous book *The Challenge of Man's Future*, Professor Harrison Brown of the California Institute of Technology gives the following appraisal:

> Thus we see that, just as industrial society is fundamentally unstable and subject to reversion to agrarian existence, so within it the conditions which offer individual freedom are unstable in their ability to avoid the conditions which impose rigid organisation and totalitarian control. Indeed, when we examine all of the foreseeable difficulties which threaten the survival of industrial civilisation, it is difficult to see how the achievement of stability and the maintenance of individual liberty can be made compatible.

Even if this were dismissed as a long-term view there is the immediate question of whether "modernisation," as currently practised without regard to religious and spiritual values, is actually producing agreeable results. As far as the masses are concerned, the results appear to be disastrous—a collapse of the rural economy, a rising tide of unemployment in town and country, and the growth of a city proletariat without nourishment for either body or soul.

It is in the light of both immediate experience and long-term prospects that the study of Buddhist economics could be recommended even to those who believe that economic growth is more important than any spiritual or religious values. For it is not a question of choosing between "modern growth" and "traditional stagnation." It is a question of finding the right path of development, the Middle Way between materialist heedlessness and traditionalist immobility, in short, of finding "Right Livelihood."

The American Testament

Second Week – First Day

The Declaration of Independence

The Constitution of the United States

*The Constitution of
the Confederate States of America*
(Preamble)

Abraham Lincoln, *The Gettysburg Address*

The Declaration of Independence

In CONGRESS, July 4, 1776

*The unanimous Declaration of the thirteen united
States of America*

WHEN in the Course of human events it becomes necessary for one people to dissolve the political bands which have connected them with another, and to assume among the powers of the earth, the separate and equal station to which the Laws of Nature and of Nature's God entitle them, a decent respect to the opinions of mankind requires that they should declare the causes which impel them to the separation.

We hold these truths to be self-evident, that all men are created equal, that they are endowed by their Creator with certain unalienable Rights, that among these are Life, Liberty and the pursuit of Happiness. —That to secure these rights, Governments are instituted among Men, deriving their just powers from the consent of the governed, —That whenever any Form of Government becomes destructive of these ends, it is the Right of the People to alter or to abolish it, and to institute new Government, laying its foundation on such principles and organizing its powers in such form, as to them shall seem most likely to effect their Safety and Happiness. Prudence, indeed, will dictate that Governments long established should not be changed for light and transient causes; and accordingly all experience hath shewn that mankind are more disposed to suffer, while evils are sufferable, than to right themselves by abolishing the forms to which they are accustomed. But when a long train of abuses and usurpations, pursuing invariably the same Object evinces a design to reduce them under absolute Despotism, it is their right, it is their duty, to throw off such Government, and to provide new Guards for their future security. —Such has been the patient sufferance of these Colonies; and such is now the necessity which constrains them to alter their former Systems of Government. The history of the present King of Great Britain is a history of repeated injuries and usurpations, all having in direct object the establishment of an absolute Tyranny over these States. To prove this, let Facts be submitted to a candid world.

He has refused his Assent to Laws, the most wholesome and necessary for the public good.

He has forbidden his Governors to pass Laws of immediate and pressing importance, unless suspended in their operation till his Assent should be obtained; and when so suspended, he has utterly neglected to attend to them.

He has refused to pass other Laws for the accommodation of large districts of people, unless those people would relinquish the right of Representation in the Legislature, a right inestimable to them and formidable to tyrants only.

He has called together legislative bodies at places unusual, uncomfortable, and distant from the depository of their Public Records, for the sole purpose of fatiguing them into compliance with his measures.

He has dissolved Representative Houses repeatedly, for opposing with manly firmness his invasions on the rights of the people.

He has refused for a long time, after such dissolutions, to cause others to be elected; whereby the Legislative Powers, incapable of Annihilation, have returned to the People at large for their exercise; the State remaining in the mean time exposed to all the dangers of invasion from without, and convulsions within.

He has endeavoured to prevent the population of these states; for that purpose obstructing the Laws for Naturalization of Foreigners; refusing to pass others to encourage their migrations hither, and raising the conditions of new Appropriations of Lands.

He has obstructed the Administration of Justice, by refusing his Assent to Laws for establishing Judiciary Powers.

He has made Judges dependent on his Will alone, for the tenure of their offices, and the amount and payment of their salaries.

He has erected a multitude of New Offices, and sent hither swarms of Officers to harass our people, and eat out their substance.

He has kept among us, in times of peace, Standing Armies without the Consent of our legislatures.

He has affected to render the Military independent of and superior to the Civil Power.

He has combined with others to subject us to a jurisdiction foreign to our constitution, and unacknowledged by our laws; giving his Assent to their Acts of pretended Legislation:

For quartering large bodies of armed troops among us:

For protecting them, by a mock Trial, from punishment for any Murders which they should commit on the Inhabitants of these States:

For cutting off our Trade with all parts of the world:

For imposing Taxes on us without our Consent:

For depriving us in many cases, of the benefits of Trial by Jury:

For transporting us beyond Seas to be tried for pretended offences:

For abolishing the free System of English Laws in a neighbouring

Province, establishing therein an Arbitrary government, and enlarging its Boundaries so as to render it at once an example and fit instrument for introducing the same absolute rule into these Colonies:

For taking away our Charters, abolishing our most valuable Laws and altering fundamentally the Forms of our Governments:

For suspending our own Legislatures, and declaring themselves invested with power to legislate for us in all cases whatsoever.

He has abdicated Government here, by declaring us out of his Protection and waging War against us.

He has plundered our seas, ravaged our Coasts, burnt our towns and destroyed the lives of our people.

He is at this time transporting large Armies of foreign Mercenaries to compleat the works of death, desolation and tyranny, already begun with circumstances of Cruelty & Perfidy scracely paralleled in the most barbarous ages, and totally unworthy the Head of a civilized nation.

He has constrained our fellow Citizens taken Captive on the high Seas to bear Arms against their Country, to become the executioners of their friends and Brethren, or to fall themselves by their Hands.

He has excited domestic insurrections amongst us, and has endeavoured to bring on the inhabitants of our frontiers, the merciless Indian Savages, whose known rule of warfare, is an undistinguished destruction of all ages, sexes and conditions.

In every stage of these Oppressions We have Petitioned for Redress in the most humble terms: Our repeated Petitions have been answered only by repeated injury. A Prince, whose character is thus marked by every act which may define a Tyrant, is unfit to be the ruler of a free people.

Nor have We been wanting in attentions to our Brittish brethren. We have warned them from time to time of attempts by their legislature to extend an unwarrantable jurisdiction over us. We have reminded them of the circumstances of our emigration and settlement here. We have appealed to their native justice and magnanimity, and we have conjured them by the ties of our common kindred to disavow these usurpations, which would inevitably interrupt our connections and correspondence. They too have been deaf to the voice of justice and of consanguinity. We must, therefore, acquiesce in the necessity, which denounces our Separation, and hold them, as we hold the rest of mankind, Enemies in War, in Peace Friends.

WE, THEREFORE, the Representatives of the UNITED STATES OF AMERICA, in General Congress, Assembled, appealing to the Supreme Judge of the world for the rectitude of our intentions, do, in the Name, and by Authority of the good People of these Colonies, solemnly publish and declare, That these United Colonies are, and of Right ought to be FREE AND INDEPENDENT STATES; that they are Absolved from all Allegiance to the British Crown, and that all political connection between them and the State of Great Britain, is and ought to be totally dissolved; and that as Free and Independent States, they have full Power to levy War, conclude

Peace, contract Alliances, establish Commerce, and to do all other Acts and Things which Independent States may of right do.—And for the support of this Declaration, with a firm reliance on the protection of Divine Providence, we mutually pledge to each other our Lives, our Fortunes and our sacred Honor.

JOHN HANCOCK

New Hampshire.
Josiah Bartlett,
Wm. Whipple,
Matthew Thronton.

Rhode Island.
Step. Hopkins,
William Ellery,

Connecticut.
Roger Sherman,
Sam'el Huntington,
Wm. Williams,
Oliver Wolcott.

New York.
Wm. Floyd,
Phil. Livingston,
Frans. Lewis,
Lewis Morris.

New Jersey.
Richd. Stockton,
Jno. Witherspoon,
Fras. Hopkinson,
John Hart,
Abra. Clark.

Pennsylvania.
Robt. Morris,
Benjamin Rush,
Benj. Franklin,
John Morton,
Geo. Clymer,
Jas. Smith,
Geo. Taylor,
James Wilson,
Geo. Ross.

Massachusetts-Bay.
Saml. Adams,
John Adams,
Robt. Treat Paine,
Elbridge Gerry.

Delaware.
Caesar Rodney,
Geo. Read,
Tho. M'Kean.

Maryland.
Samuel Chase,
Wm. Paca,
Thos. Stone,
Charles Carroll of Carrollton.

Virginia.
George Wythe,
Richard Henry Lee,
Th. Jefferson,
Benj. Harrison,
Ths. Nelson, Jr.,
Francis Lightfoot Lee,
Carter Braxton.

North Carolina.
Wm. Hooper,
Joseph Hewes,
John Penn.

South Carolina.
Edward Rutledge,
Thos. Heyward, Junr.,
Thomas Lynch, Junr.,
Arthur Middleton.

Georgia.
Button Gwinnett,
Lyman Hall,
Geo. Walton.

IN CONGRESS
January, 18, 1777.

Ordered:

That an authenticated copy of the Declaration of Independency, with the names of the Members of Congress subscribing the same, be sent to each of the United States, and that they be desired to have the same put on record.

By order of Congress.

Attest, CHAS. THOMSON, *Secy.*   A true copy. JOHN HANCOCK, *Presidt.*

The Constitution of the United States

$\mathbf{W}$E the People of the United States, in Order to form a more perfect Union, establish Justice, insure domestic Tranquility, provide for the common defence, promote the general Welfare,and secure the Blessings of Liberty to ourselves and our Posterity, do ordain and establish this Constitution for the United States of America.

Article I

Section 1. All legislative Powers herein granted shall be vested in a Congress of the United States, which shall consist of a Senate and House of Representatives.

Section 2. The House of Representatives shall be composed of Members chosen every second Year by the People of the several States, and the Electors in each State shall have the Qualifications requisite for Electors of the most numerous Branch of the State Legislature.

No Person shall be a Representative who shall not have attained to the Age of twenty five Years, and been seven Years a Citizen of the United States, and who shall not, when elected, be an Inhabitant of that State in which he shall be chosen.

Representatives and direct Taxes shall be apportioned among the several States which may be included within this Union, according to their respective Numbers, which shall be determined by adding to the whole Number of free Persons, including those bound to Service for a Term of Years, and excluding Indians not taxed, three fifths of all other Persons. The actual Enumeration shall be made within three Years after the first Meeting of the Congress of the United States, and within every subsequent Term of ten Years, in such Manner as they shall by Law direct. The Number of Representatives shall not exceed one for every thirty Thousand, but each State shall have at Least one Representative; and until such enumeration shall be made, the State of New Hampshire shall be entitled to chuse three, Massachusetts eight, Rhode-Island and Providence Plantations one, Connecticut five, New-York six, New Jersey four, Pennsylvania eight, Delaware one, Maryland six, Virginia ten, North Carolina five, South Carolina five, and Georgia three.

When vacancies happen in the Representation from any State, the Executive Authority thereof shall issue Writs of Election to fill such Vacancies.

The House of Representatives shall chuse their speaker and other Officers; and shall have the sole Power of Impeachment.

Section 3.   The Senate of the United States shall be composed of two Senators from each State, chosen by the Legislature thereof, for six Years; and each Senator shall have one Vote.

Immediately after they shall be assembled in Consequence of the first Election, they shall be divided as equally as may be into three Classes. The Seats of the Senators of the first Class shall be vacated at the Expiration of the second Year, of the second Class at the Expiration of the fourth Year, and of the third Class at the Expiration of the sixth Year, so that one third may be chosen every second Year; and if Vacancies happen by Resignation, or otherwise, during the Recess of the Legislature of any State, the Executive thereof may make temporary Appointments until the next Meeting of the Legislature, which shall then fill such Vacancies.

No Person shall be a Senator who shall not have attained to the Age of thirty Years, and been nine Years a Citizen of the United States, and who shall not, when elected, be an Inhabitant of that State for which he shall be chosen.

The Vice President of the United States shall be President of the Senate, but shall have no Vote, unless they be equally divided.

The Senate shall chuse their other Officers, and also a President pro tempore, in the Absence of the Vice President, or when he shall exercise the Office of President of the United States.

The Senate shall have the sole Power to try all Impeachments. When sitting for that Purpose, they shall be on Oath or Affirmation. When the President of the United States is tried, the Chief Justice shall preside: And no Person shall be convicted without the Concurrence of two thirds of the Members present.

Judgment in Cases of Impeachment shall not extend further than to removal from Office, and disqualification to hold and enjoy any Office of honor, Trust or Profit under the United States: but the Party convicted shall nevertheless be liable and subject to Indictment, Trial, Judgment and Punishment, according to law.

Section 4.   The Times, Places and Manner of holding Elections for Senators and Representatives, shall be prescribed in each State by the Legislature thereof; but the Congress may at any time by Law make or alter such Regulations, except as to the Places of chusing Senators.

The Congress shall assemble at least once in every Year, and such Meeting shall be on the first Monday in December, unless they shall by Law appoint a different Day.

Section 5. Each House shall be the Judge of the Elections, Returns and Qualifications of its own Members, and a Majority of each shall constitute a Quorum to do Business; but a smaller Number may adjourn from day to day, and may be authorized to compel the Attendance of absent Members, in such Manner, and under such Penalties as each House may provide.

Each House may determine the Rules of its Proceedings, punish its Members for disorderly Behaviour, and, with the Concurrence of two thirds, expel a Member.

Each House shall keep a Journal of its Proceedings, and from time to time publish the same, excepting such Parts as may in their Judgment require Secrecy; and the Yeas and Nays of the Members of either House on any question shall, at the Desire of one fifth of those Present, be entered on the Journal.

Neither House, during the Session of Congress, shall, without the Consent of the other, adjourn for more than three days, nor to any other place than that in which the two Houses shall be sitting.

Section 6. The Senators and Representatives shall receive a Compensation for their Services, to be ascertained by Law, and paid out of the Treasury of the United States. They shall in all Cases, except Treason, Felony and Breach of the Peace, be privileged from Arrest during their Attendance at the Session of their respective Houses, and in going to and returning from the same; and for any Speech or Debate in either House, they shall not be questioned in any other Place.

No Senator or Representative shall, during the Time for which he was elected, be appointed to any civil Office under the Authority of the United States, which shall have been created, or the Emoluments whereof shall have been encreased during such time; and no Person holding any Office under the United States, shall be a Member of either House during his Continuance in Office.

Section 7. All Bills for raising Revenue shall originate in the House of Representatives; but the Senate may propose or concur with Amendments as on other Bills.

Every Bill which shall have passed the House of Representatives and the Senate, shall, before it become a Law, be presented to the President of the United States; If he approve he shall sign it, but if not he shall return it, with his Objections to that House in which it shall have originated, who shall enter the Objections at large on their Journal, and proceed to reconsider it. If after such Reconsideration two thirds of that House shall agree to pass the Bill, it shall be sent, together with the Objections, to the other House, by which it shall likewise be reconsidered, and if approved by two thirds of that House, it shall become a Law. But in all such Cases the Votes of both Houses shall be determined by Yeas and Nays, and the Names of the Persons voting for and against the Bill shall be entered on the Journal of each House respectively. If any Bill shall not be returned by the President within ten Days (Sundays excepted) after it shall have been presented to him, the Same shall be a Law, in like Manner as if he had signed it, unless the Congress by their Adjournment prevent its Return, in which Case it shall not be a Law.

Every Order, Resolution, or Vote to which the Concurrence of the Senate and House of Representatives may be necessary (except on a question of Adjournment) shall be presented to the President of the United States; and before the Same shall take Effect, shall be approved by him, or being disapproved by him, shall be repassed by two thirds of the Senate and House of Representatives, according to the Rules and Limitations prescribed in the Case of a Bill.

Section 8. The Congress shall have Power to lay and collect Taxes, Duties, Imposts and Excises, to pay the Debts and provide for the common Defence and general Welfare of the United States; but all Duties, Imposts and Excises shall be uniform throughout the United States;

To borrow Money on the Credit of the United States;

To regulate Commerce with foreign Nations, and among the several States, and with the Indian Tribes;

To establish an uniform Rule of Naturalization, and uniform Laws on the subject of Bankruptcies throughout the United States;

To coin Money, regulate the Value thereof, and of foreign Coin, and fix the Standard of Weights and Measures;

To provide for the Punishment of counterfeiting the Securities and current Coin of the United States;

To establish Post Offices and post Roads;

To promote the Progress of Science and useful Arts, by securing for limited Times to Authors and Inventors the exclusive Right to their respective Writings and Discoveries;

To constitute Tribunals inferior to the supreme Court;

To define and punish Piracies and Felonies committed on the high Seas, and Offences against the Law of Nations;

To declare War, grant Letters of Marque and Reprisal, and make Rules concerning Captures on Land and Water;

To raise and support Armies, but no Appropriation of Money to that Use shall be for a longer Term than two Years;

To provide and maintain a Navy;

To make Rules for the Government and Regulation of the land and naval Forces;

To provide for calling forth the Militia to execute the Laws of the Union, suppress Insurrections and repel Invasions;

To provide for organizing, arming, and disciplining the Militia, and for governing such Part of them as may be employed in the Service of the United States, reserving to the States respectively, the Appointment of the Officers, and the Authority of training the Militia according to the discipline prescribed by Congress;

To exercise exclusive Legislation in all Cases whatsoever, over such District (not exceeding ten Miles square), as may, by Cession of particular States, and the Acceptance of Congress, become the Seat of the Government of the United States, and to exercise like Authority over all Places purchased by the Consent of the Legislature of the State in which the Same shall be for the Erection of Forts, Magazines, Arsenals, dock-Yards, and other needful Buildings; — And

To make all Laws which shall be necessary and proper for carrying into Execution the foregoing Powers, and all other Powers vested by this Constitution in the Government of the United States, or in any Department or Officer thereof.

Section 9. The Migration or Importation of such Persons as any of the States now existing shall think proper to admit, shall not be prohibited by the Congress prior to the Year one thousand eight hundred and eight, but a Tax or duty may be imposed on such Importation, not exceeding ten dollars for each Person.

The Privilege of the Writ of Habeas Corpus shall not be suspended, unless when in Cases of Rebellion or Invasion the public Safety may require it.

No Bill of Attainder or ex post facto Law shall be passed.

No capitation, or other direct, Tax shall be laid, unless in Proportion to the Census or Enumeration herein before directed to be taken.

No Tax or Duty shall be laid on Articles exported from any State.

No Preference shall be given by any Regulation of Commerce or Revenue to the Ports of one State over those of another: nor shall Vessels bound to, or from, one State, be obliged to enter, clear, or pay Duties in another.

No money shall be drawn from the Treasury, but in Consequence of Appropriations made by Law; and a regular Statement and Account of the Receipts AND Expenditures of all public Money shall be published from time to time.

No title of Nobility shall be granted by the United States: And no Person holding any Office of Profit or Trust under them, shall, without the Consent of the Congress, accept of any present, Emolument, Office, or Title, of any kind whatever, from any King, Prince, or foreign State.

Section 10. No State shall enter into any Treaty, Alliance, or Confederation; grant Letters of Marque and Reprisal; coin Money; emit Bills of Credit; make any Thing but gold and silver Coin a Tender in Payment of Debts; pass any Bill of Attainder, ex post facto Law, or Law impairing the Obligation of Contracts, or grant any Title of Nobility.

No State shall, without the Consent of the Congress, lay any Imposts or Duties on Imports or Exports, except what may be absolutely necessary for executing its inspection Laws: and the net Produce of all Duties and Imposts, laid by any State on Imports or Exports, shall be for the Use of the Treasury of the United States; and all such Laws shall be subject to the Revision and Controul of the Congress.

No State shall, without the Consent of Congress, lay any Duty of Tonnage, keep Troops, or Ships of War in time of Peace, enter into any Agreement or Compact with another State, or with a foreign Power, or engage in War, unless actually invaded, or in such imminent Danger as will not admit of delay.

Article II

Section 1.   The executive Power shall be vested in a President of the United States of America. He shall hold his Office during the Term of four Years, and, together with the Vice President, chosen for the same term, be elected, as follows

Each State shall appoint, in such Manner as the Legislature thereof may direct, a Number of Electors, equal to the whole Number of Senators and Representatives to which the State may be entitled in the Congress: but no Senator or Representative, or Person holding an Office of Trust or Profit under the United States, shall be appointed an Elector.

The Electors shall meet in their respective States, and vote by Ballot for two Persons, of whom one at least shall not be an Inhabitant of the same State with themselves. And they shall make a List of all the Persons voted for, and of the Number of Votes for each; which List they shall sign and certify, and transmit sealed to the Seat of the Government of the United States, directed to the President of the Senate. The President of the Senate shall, in the Presence of the Senate and House of Representatives, open all the Certificates, and the Votes shall then be counted. The Person having the greatest Number of Votes shall be the President, if such Number be a Majority of the whole Number of Electors appointed; and if there be more than one who have such Majority, and have an equal Number of Votes, then the House of Representatives shall immediately chuse by Ballot one of them for President: and if no Person have a Majority, then from the five highest on the List the said House shall in like Manner chuse the President. But in chusing the President, the Votes shall be taken by States, the Representation from each State having one Vote; A quorum for this Purpose shall consist of a Member or Members from two thirds of the States, and a Majority of all the States shall be necessary to a Choice. In every Case, after the Choice of the President, the Person having the greatest Number of Votes of the Electors shall be the Vice President. But if there should remain two or more who have equal Votes, the Senate shall chuse from them by Ballot the Vice President.

The Congress may determine the Time of chusing the Electors, and the Day on which they shall give their Votes; which Day shall be the same throughout the United States.

No Person except a natural born Citizen, or a Citizen of the United States, at the time of the Adoption of this Constitution, shall be eligible to the Office of President; neither shall any Person be eligible to that Office who shall not have attained to the Age of thirty five Years, and been fourteen Years a Resident within the United States.

In Case of the Removal of the President from Office, or of his Death, Resignation, or Inability to discharge the Powers and Duties of the said Office, the Same shall devolve on the Vice President, and the Congress may by Law provide for the Case of Removal, Death, Resignation or Inability, both of the President and Vice President, declaring what Officer shall then act as President, and such Officer shall act accordingly, until the

Disability be removed, or a President shall be elected.

The President shall, at stated Times, receive for his Services, a Compensation, which shall neither be encreased nor diminished during the Period for which he shall have been elected, and he shall not receive within that Period any other Emolument from the United States, or any of them.

Before he enter on the Execution of his Office, he shall take the following Oath or Affirmation: — "I do solemnly swear (or affirm) that I will faithfully execute the Office of President of the United States, and will to the best of my Ability, preserve, protect and defend the Constitution of the United States."

Section 2.   The President shall be Commander in Chief of the Army and Navy of the United States, and of the Militia of the several States, when called into the actual Service of the United States; he may require the Opinion, in writing, of the principal Officer in each of the executive Departments, upon any Subject relating to the Duties of their respective Offices, and he shall have Power to grant Reprieves and Pardons for Offences against the United States, except in Cases of Impeachment.

He shall have Power, by and with the Advice and Consent of the Senate, to make Treaties, provided two thirds of the Senators present concur; and he shall nominate, and by and with the Advice and Consent of the Senate, shall appoint Ambassadors, other public Ministers and Consuls, Judges of the supreme Court, and all other Officers of the United States, whose Appointments are not herein otherwise provided for, and which shall be established by Law; but the Congress may by Law vest the Appointment of such inferior Officers, as they think proper, in the President alone, in the Courts of Law, or in the Heads of Departments.

The President shall have Power to fill up all Vacancies that may happen during the Recess of the Senate, by granting Commissions which shall expire at the End of their next Session.

Section 3.   He shall from time to time give to the Congress Information of the State of the Union, and recommend to their Consideration such Measures as he shall judge necessary and expedient; he may, on extraordinary Occasions, convene both Houses, or either of them, and in Case of Disagreement between them, with Respect to the Time of Adjournment, he may adjourn them to such Time as he shall think proper; he shall receive Ambassadors and other public Ministers; he shall take Care that the Laws be faithfully executed, and shall Commission all the Officers of the United States.

Article III

Section 1.   The judicial Power of the United States, shall be vested in one supreme Court, and in such inferior Courts as the Congress may from time to time ordain and establish. The Judges, both of the supreme and inferior Courts, shall hold their Offices during good Behaviour, and shall, at stated Times, receive for their Services, a Compensation, which shall not be diminished during their Continuance in Office.

Section 2. The judicial Power shall extend to all Cases, in Law and Equity, arising under this Constitution, the Laws of the United States, and Treaties made, or which shall be made, under their Authority; — to all Cases affecting Ambassadors, other public Ministers and Consuls; — to all Cases of admiralty and maritime Jurisdiction; — to Controversies to which the United States shall be a Party; — to Controversies between two or more States; between a State and Citizens of another State; — between Citizens of different States; — between Citizens of the same State claiming Lands under Grants of different States, and between a State, or the Citizens thereof, and foreign States, Citizens or Subjects.

In all Cases affecting Ambassadors, other public Ministers and Consuls, and those in which a State shall be a Party, the supreme Court shall have original Jurisdiction. In all other Cases before mentioned, the supreme Court shall have appellate Jurisdiction, both as to Law and Fact, with such exceptions, and under such Regulations as the Congress shall make.

The Trial of all Crimes, except in Cases of Impeachment, shall be by Jury; and such Trial shall be held in the State where the said Crimes shall have been committed; but when not committed within any State, the Trial shall be at such Place or Places as the Congress may by Law have directed.

Section 3. Treason against the United States, shall consist only in levying War against them, or in adhering to their Enemies, giving them Aid and Comfort. No Person shall be convicted of Treason unless on the Testimony of two Witnesses to the same overt Act, or on Confession in open Court.

The Congress shall have Power to declare the Punishment of Treason, but no Attainder of Treason shall work Corruption of Blood, or Forfeiture except during the Life of the Person attainted.

Article IV

Section 1. Full Faith and Credit shall be given in each State to the public Acts, Records, and judicial Proceedings of every other State. And the Congress may by general Laws prescribe the Manner in which such Acts, Records and Proceedings shall be proved, and the Effect thereof.

Section 2. The Citizens of each State shall be entitled to all Privileges and Immunities of Citizens in the several States.

A Person charged in any State with Treason, Felony, or other Crime, who shall flee from Justice, and be found in another State, shall on Demand of the executive Authority of the State from which he fled, be delivered up, to be removed to the State having Jurisdiction of the Crime.

No person held to Service or Labour in one State, under the Laws thereof, escaping into another, shall, in Consequence of any Law or Regulation therein, be discharged from such Service or Labour, but shall be delivered up on Claim of the Party to whom such Service or Labour may be due.

Section 3. New States may be admitted by the Congress into this Union; but no new State shall be formed or erected within the Jurisdiction of any other State; nor any State be formed by the Junction of two or more

States, or Parts of States, without the Consent of the Legislatures of the States concerned as well as of the Congress.

The Congress shall have Power to dispose of and make all needful Rules and Regulations respecting the Territory or other Property belonging to the United States; and nothing in this Constitution shall be so construed as to Prejudice any Claims of the United States, or of any particular State.

Section 4.   The United States shall guarantee to every State in this Union a Republican Form of Government, and shall protect each of them against Invasion; and on Application of the Legislature, or of the Executive (when the Legislature cannot be convened) against domestic Violence.

Article V

The Congress, whenever two thirds of both Houses shall deem it necessary, shall propose Amendments to this Constitution, or, on the Application of the Legislatures of two thirds of the several States, shall call a Convention for proposing Amendments, which, in either Case, shall be valid to all Intents and Purposes, as Part of this Constitution, when ratified by the Legislatures of three fourths of the several States, or by Conventions in three fourths thereof, as the one or the other Mode of Ratification may be proposed by the Congress; Provided that no Amendment which may be made prior to the Year One thousand eight hundred and eight hundred and eight shall in any Manner affect the first and fourth Clauses in the Ninth Section of the first Article; and that no State, without its Consent, shall be deprived of its equal Suffrage in the Senate.

Article VI

All Debts contracted and Engagements entered into, before the Adoption of this Constitution, shall be as valid against the United States under this Constitution, as under the Confederation.

This Constitution, and the Laws of the United States which shall be made in Pursuance thereof; and all Treaties made, or which shall be made, under the Authority of the United States, shall be the supreme Law of the Land; and the Judges in every State shall be bound thereby, any Thing in the Constitution or Laws of any State to the Contrary notwithstanding.

Article VII

The Ratification of the Conventions of nine States shall be sufficient for the establishment of this Constitution between the States so ratifying the Same.

Done in Convention by the Unanimous Consent of the States
present the Seventeenth Day of September in the Year of our
Lord one thousand seven hundred and Eighty seven and
of the Independence of the United States of America the Twelfth
IN WITNESS whereof We have hereunto subscribed our Names,

Geo. Washington — President and deputy from Virginia
(and 38 others from 12 States)

Amendments

(The first 10 Amendments were ratified December 15, 1791, and form what is known as the "Bill of Rights.")

Amendment 1   Congress shall make no law respecting an establishment of religion, or prohibiting the free exercise thereof; or abridging the freedom of speech, or of the press; or the right of the people peaceably to assemble, and to petition the Government for a redress of grievances.

Amendment 2   A well regulated Militia, being necessary to the security of a free State, the right of the people to keep and bear arms, shall not be infringed.

Amendment 3   No Soldier shall, in time of peace, be quartered in any house, without the consent of the Owner, nor in time of war, but in a manner to be prescribed by law.

Amendment 4   The right of the people to be secure in their persons, houses, papers, and effects, against unreasonable searches and seizures, shall not be violated, and no Warrants shall issue, but upon probable cause, supported by Oath or affirmation, and particularly describing the place to be searched, and the persons or things to be seized.

Amendment 5   No person shall be held to answer for a capital, or otherwise infamous crime, unless on a presentment or indictment of a Grand Jury, except in cases arising in the land or naval forces, or in the Militia, when in actual service in time of War or public danger; nor shall any person be subject for the same offence to be twice put in jeopardy of life or limb; nor shall be compelled in any criminal case to be a witness against himself, nor be deprived of life, liberty, or property, without due process of law; nor shall private property be taken for public use, without just compensation.

Amendment 6   In all criminal prosecutions, the accused shall enjoy the right to a speedy and public trial, by an impartial jury of the State and district wherein the crime shall have been committed, which district shall have been previously ascertained by law, and to be informed of the nature and cause of the accusation; to be confronted with the witnesses against him; to have compulsory process for obtaining witnesses in his favor, and to have the Assistance of Counsel for his defence.

Amendment 7   In Suits at common law, where the value in controversy shall exceed twenty dollars, the right of trial by jury shall be preserved, and no fact tried by a jury, shall be otherwise re-examined in any Court of the United States, than according to the rules of the common law.

Amendment 8 Excessive bail shall not be required, nor excessive fines imposed, nor cruel and unusual punishments inflicted.

Amendment 9 The enumeration in the Constitution, of certain rights, shall not be construed to deny or disparage others retained by the people.

Amendment 10 The powers not delegated to the United States by the Constitution, nor prohibited by it to the States, are reserved to the States respectively, or to the people.

Amendment 11 *(Ratified February 7, 1795)* The Judicial power of the United States shall not be construed to extend to any suit in law or equity, commenced or prosecuted against one of the United States by Citizens of another State, or by Citizens or Subjects of any Foreign State.

Amendment 12 *(Ratified July 27, 1804)* The Electors shall meet in their respective states and vote by ballot for President and Vice-President, one of whom, at least, shall not be an inhabitant of the same state with themselves; they shall name in their ballots the person voted for as President, and in distinct ballots the person voted for as Vice-President, and they shall make distinct lists of all persons voted for as President, and of all persons voted for as Vice-President, and of the number of votes for each, which lists they shall sign and certify, and transmit sealed to the seat of the government of the United States, directed to the President of the Senate; — The President of the Senate shall, in the presence of the Senate and House of Representatives, open all the certificates and the votes shall then be counted; — The person having the greatest number of votes for President, shall be the President, if such number be a majority of the whole number of Electors appointed; and if no person have such majority, then from the persons having the highest numbers not exceeding three on the list of those voted for as President, the House of Representatives shall choose immediately, by ballot, the President. But in choosing the President, the votes shall be taken by states, the representation from each state having one vote; a quorum for this purpose shall consist of a member or members from two-thirds of the states, and a majority of all the states shall be necessary to a choice. And if the House of Representatives shall not choose a President whenever the right of choice shall devolve upon them, before the fourth day of March next following, then the Vice-President shall act as President, as in the case of the death or other constitutional disability of the President. — The person having the greatest number of votes as Vice-President, shall be the Vice-President, if such number be a majority of the whole number of Electors appointed, and if no person have a majority, then from the two highest numbers on the list, the Senate shall choose a Vice-President; a quorum for the purpose shall consist of two-thirds of the whole number of Senators, and a majority of the whole number shall be necessary to a choice. But no person constitutionally ineligible to the office of President shall be eligible to that of Vice-President of the United States.

Amendment 13 *(Ratified December 6, 1865)   Section 1.*   Neither slavery nor involuntary servitude, except as a punishment for crime whereof the party shall have been duly convicted, shall exist within the United States, or any place subject to their jurisdiction.   *Section 2.*   Congress shall have power to enforce this article by appropriate legislation.

Amendment 14 *(Ratified July 9, 1868)   Section 1.*   All persons born or naturalized in the United States, and subject to the jurisdiction thereof, are citizens of the United States and of the State wherein they reside. No State shall make or enforce any law which shall abridge the privileges or immunities of citizens of the United States; nor shall any State deprive any person of life, liberty, or property, without due process of law; nor deny to any person within its jurisdiction the equal protection of the laws.   *Section 2.*   Representatives shall be apportioned among the several States according to their respective numbers, counting the whole number of persons in each State, excluding Indians not taxed. But when the right to vote at any election for the choice of electors for President and Vice President of the United States, Representatives in Congress, the Executive and Judicial officers of a State, or the members of the Legislature thereof, is denied to any of the male inhabitants of such State, being twenty-one years of age, and citizens of the United States, or in any way abridged except for participation in rebellion, or other crime, the basis of representation therein shall be reduced in the proportion which the number of such male citizens shall bear to the whole number of male citizens twenty-one years of age in such State.   *Section 3.*   No person shall be a Senator or Representative in Congress, or elector of President and Vice President, or hold any office, civil or military, under the United States, or under any State, who, having previously taken an oath, as a member of Congres, or as an officer of the United States, or as a member of any State legislature, or as an executive or judicial officer of any State, to support the Constitution of the United States, shall have engaged in insurrection or rebellion against the same, or given aid or comfort to the enemies thereof. But Congress may by a vote of two-thirds of each House, remove such disability.   *Section 4.*   The validity of the public debt of the United States, authorized by law, including debts incurred for payment of pensions and bounties for services in suppressing insurrection or rebellion, shall not be questioned. But neither the United States nor any State shall assume or pay any debt or obligation incurred in aid of insurrection or rebellion against the United States, or any claim for the loss or emancipation of any slave; but all such debts, obligations and claims shall be held illegal and void.   *Section 5.*   The Congress shall have power to enforce, by appropriate legislation, the provisions of this article.

Amendment 15 *(Ratified February 3, 1870)   Section 1.*   The right of citizens of the United States to vote shall not be denied or abridged by the United States or by any State on account of race, color, or previous condition of servitude.   *Section 2.*   The Congress shall have power to enforce this article by appropriate legislation.

Amendment 16 (Ratified February 3, 1913) The Congress shall have power to lay and collect taxes on income, from whatever source derived, without apportionment among the several States, and without regard to any census or enumeration.

Amendment 17 (Ratified April 8, 1913) The Senate of the United States shall be composed of two Senators from each State, elected by the people thereof for six years; and each Senator shall have one vote. The electors in each State shall have the qualifications requisite for electors of the most numerous branch of the State legislatures. When vacancies hapen in the representation of any State in the Senate, the executive authority of such State shall issue writs of election to fill such vacancies; PROVIDED, That the legislature of any State may empower the executive thereof to make temporary appointments until the people fill the vacancies by election as the legislature may direct. This amendment shall not be so construed as to affect the election or term of any Senator chosen before it becomes valid as part of the Constitution.

Amendment 18 (Ratified January 16, 1919) Section 1. After one year from the ratification of this article the manufacture, sale, or transportation of intoxicating liquors within, the importation thereof into, or the exportation thereof from the United States and all territory subject to the jurisdiction thereof for beverage purposes is hereby prohibited. *Section 2.* The Congress and the several States shall have concurrent power to enforce this article by appropriate legislation. *Section 3.* This article shall be inoperative unless it shall have been ratified as an amendment to the Constitution by the legislatures of the several States as provided in the Constitution, within seven years from the date of the submission hereof to the States by the Congress.

Amendment 19 (Ratified August 18, 1920) The right of citizens of the United States to vote shall not be denied or abridged by the United States or by any State on account of sex. Congress shall have power to enforce this article by appropriate legislation.

Amendment 20 (Ratified January 23, 1933) Section 1. The terms of the President and Vice President shall end at noon on the 20th day of January, and the terms of Senators and Representatives at noon on the 3rd day of January, of the years in which such terms would have ended if this article had not been ratified; and the terms of their successors shall then begin. *Section 2.* The Congress shall assemble at least once in every year, and such meeting shall begin at noon on the 3rd day of January, unless they shall by law appoint a different day. *Section 3.* If, at the time fixed for the beginning of the term of the President, the President-elect shall have died, the Vice President-elect shall become President. If a President shall not have been chosen before the time fixed for the beginning of his term, or if the President-elect shall have failed to qualify, then the Vice President-elect shall act as President until a President shall have qualified; and the Congress may by law provide for the case wherein neither a President-elect nor a Vice President-elect shall have qualified, declaring who shall then act as President, or the manner in which one who is to act shall be selected, and such person shall act accordingly until a President or Vice President shall have qualified. *Section 4.* The Congress may by law provide for the case of the death of any of the persons from whom the House of Representatives may choose a President whenever the right of choice shall have developed upon them, and for the case of the death of any of the persons from whom the Senate may choose a Vice President whenever the right of choice shall have devolved upon them. *Section 5.* Sections 1 and 2 shall take effect on the 15th day of October following the ratification of this article. *Section 6.* This article shall be inoperative unless it shall have been ratified as an amendment to the Constitution by the legislatures of three-fourths of the several States within seven years from the date of its submission.

Amendment 21 (Ratified December 5, 1933) Section 1. The eighteenth article of amendment to the Constitution of the United States is hereby repealed. *Section 2.* The transportation or importation into any State, Territory, or possession of the United States for delivery or use therein of intoxicating liquors, in violation of the laws thereof, is hereby prohibited. *Section 3.* This article shall be inoperative unless it shall have been ratified as an amendment to the Constitution by conventions in the several States, as provided in the Constitution, within seven years from the date of the submission hereof to the States by the Congress.

Amendment 22 (Ratified February 27, 1951) Section 1. No person shall be elected to the office of the President more than twice, and no person who has held the office of President, or acted as President, for more than two years of a term to which some other person was elected President shall be elected to the office of the President more than once. But this Article shall not apply to any person holding the office of President when this Article was proposed by the Congress, and shall not prevent any person who may be holding the office of President, or acting as President, during the term within which this Article becomes operative from holding the office of President or acting as President during the remainder of such term. *Section 2.* This article shall be inoperative unless it shall have been ratified as an amendment to the Constitution by the legislatures of three-fourths of the several States within seven years from the date of its submission to the States by the Congress.

Amendment 23 (Ratified March 29, 1961) Section 1. The District constituting the seat of Government of the United States shall appoint in such manner as the Congress may direct: A number of electors of President and Vice President equal to the whole number of Senators and Representatives in Congress to which the District would be entitled if it were a

State, but in no event more than the least populous State; they shall be in addition to those appointed by the States, but they shall be considered, for the purposes of the election of President and Vice President, to be electors appointed by a State; and they shall meet in the District and perform such duties as provided by the twelfth article of amendment.   *Section 2.*   The Congress shall have power to enforce this article by appropriate legislation.

Amendment 24 *(Ratified January 23, 1964)   Section 1.*   The right of citizens of the United States to vote in any primary or other election for President or Vice President, for electors for President or Vice President, or for Senator or Representative in Congress, shall not be denied or abridged by the United States or any State by reason of failure to pay any poll tax or other tax.   *Section 2.*   The Congress shall have power to enforce this article by appropriate legislation.

Amendment 25 *(Ratified February 10, 1967)   Section 1.*   In case of the removal of the President from office or of his death or resignation, the Vice President shall become President.   *Section 2.*   Whenever there is a vacancy in the office of the Vice President, the President shall nominate a Vice President who shall take office upon confirmation by a majority vote of both Houses of Congress.   *Section 3.*   Whenever the President transmits to the President pro tempore of the Senate and the Speaker of the House of Representatives his written declaration that he is unable to discharge the powers and duties of his office, and until he transmits to them a written declaration to the contrary, such powers and duties shall be discharged by the Vice President as Acting President.   *Section 4.*   Whenever the Vice President and a majority of either the principal officers of the executive departments or of such other body as Congress may be law provide, transmit to the President pro tempore of the Senate and the Speaker of the House of Representatives their written declaration that the President is unable to discharge the powers and duties of his office, the Vice President shall immediately assume the powers and duties of the office as Acting President.   Thereafter, when the President transmits to the President pro tempore of the Senate and the Speaker of the House of Representatives his written declaration that no inability exists, he shall resume the powers and duties of his office unless the Vice President and a majority of either the principal officers of the executive department or of such other body as Congress may by law provide, transmit within four days to the President pro tempore of the Senate and the Speaker of the House of Representatives their written declaration that the President is unable to discharge the powers and duties of his office. Thereupon Congress shall decide the issue, assembling within forty-eight hours for that purpose if not in session. If the Congress, within twenty-one days after receipt of the latter written declaration, or, if Congress is not in session, within twenty-one days after Congress is required to assemble, determines by two-thirds vote of both Houses that the President is unable to discharge the powers and duties of his office, the Vice President shall continue to discharge the same as Acting President;

otherwise, the President shall resume the powers and duties of his office.

Amendment 26 *(Ratified July 1, 1971)   Section 1.*   The right of citizens of the United States, who are eighteen years of age or older, to vote shall not be denied or abridged by the United States or by any State on account of age.   *Section 2.*   The Congress shall have power to enforce this article by appropriate legislation.

The Constitution of the Confederate States of America

Preamble

WE, the people of the Confederate States, each State acting in its sovereign and independent character, in order to form a permanent federal government, establish iustice, insure domestic tranquillity, and secure the blessings of liberty to ourselves and our posterity—invoking the favor and guidance of Almighty God—do ordain and establish this Constitution for the Confederate States of America.

The Gettysburg Address

by Abraham Lincoln

FOUR score and seven years ago our fathers brought forth on this continent a new nation, conceived in liberty and dedicated to the proposition that all men are created equal.

Now we are engaged in a great civil war, testing whether that nation or any nation so conceived and so dedicated can long endure. We are met on a great battlefield of that war. We have come to dedicate a portion of that field as a final resting place for those who here gave their lives that that nation might live. It is altogether fitting and proper that we should do this.

But, in a larger sense, we cannot dedicate—we cannot consecrate—we cannot hallow—this ground. The brave men, living and dead, who struggled here have consecrated it far above our poor power to add or detract. The world will little note nor long remember what we say here, but it can never forget what they did here. It is for us, the living, rather, to be dedicated here to the unfinished work which they who fought here have thus far so nobly advanced.

It is rather for us to be here dedicated to the great task remaining before us—that from these honored dead we take increased devotion to that cause for which they gave the last full measure of devotion; that we here highly resolve that these dead shall not have died in vain; that this nation, under God, shall have a new birth of freedom; and that government of the people, by the people, for the people shall not perish from the earth.

Agreement, Consensus, and Limits of Dissent

Second Week — Second Day

The Federalist Papers, Number 10

Alexis de Tocqueville,
Democracy in America, First Book, Chapter 15
and Conclusion (selection)

John Stuart Mill,
Representative Government, Chapter 8

Ch. Anwar Sani,
Address to the United Nations
General Assembly (selection)

The Federalist Papers

Number 10

AMONG the numerous advantages promised by a well-constructed Union, none deserves to be more accurately developed than its tendency to break and control the violence of faction. The friend of popular governments never finds himself so much alarmed for their character and fate as when he contemplates their propensity to this dangerous vice. He will not fail, therefore, to set a due value on any plan which, without violating the principles to which he is attached, provides a proper cure for it. The instability, injustice, and confusion introduced into the public councils, have, in truth, been the mortal diseases under which popular governments have everywhere perished; as they continue to be the favourite and fruitful topics from which the adversaries to liberty derive their most specious declamations. The valuable improvements made by the American constitutions on the popular models, both ancient and modern, cannot certainly be too much admired; but it would be an unwarrantable partiality, to contend that they have as effectually obviated the danger on this side, as was wished and expected. Complaints are everywhere heard from our most considerate and virtuous citizens, equally the friends of public and private faith, and of public and personal liberty, that our governments are too unstable, that the public good is disregarded in the conflicts of rival parties, and that measures are too often decided, not according to the rules of justice and the rights of the minor party, but by the superior force of an interested and overbearing majority. However anxiously we may wish that these complaints had no foundation, the evidence of known facts will not permit us to deny that they are in some degree true. It will be found, indeed, on a candid review of our situation, that some of the distresses under which we labour have been erroneously charged on the operation of our governments; but it will be found, at the same time, that other causes will not alone account for many of our heaviest misfortunes; and, particularly, for that prevailing and increasing distrust of public engagements, and alarm for private rights, which are echoed from one end of the continent to the other. These must be chiefly, if not wholly, effects of the unsteadiness and injustice with which a factious spirit has tainted our public administrations.

By a faction, I understand a number of citizens, whether amounting to a majority or minority of the whole, who are united and actuated by some common impulse of passion, or of interest, adverse to the rights of other citizens, or to the permanent and aggregate interests of the community.

There are two methods of curing the mischiefs of faction: the one, by removing its causes; the other, by controlling its effects.

There are again two methods of removing the causes of faction: the one, by destroying the liberty which is essential to its existence; the other, by giving to every citizen the same opinions, the same passions, and the same interests.

It could never be more truly said than of the first remedy, that it was worse than the disease. Liberty is to faction what air is to fire, an ailment without which it instantly expires. But it could not be less folly to abolish liberty, which is essential to political life, because it nourishes faction, than it would be to wish the annihilation of air, which is essential to animal life, because it imparts to fire its destructive agency.

The second expedient is as impracticable as the first would be unwise. As long as the reason of man continues fallible, and he is at liberty to exercise it, different opinions will be formed. As long as the connection subsists between his reason and his self-love, his opinions and his passions will have a reciprocal influence on each other; and the former will be objects to which the latter will attach themselves. The diversity in the faculties of men, from which the rights of property originate, is not less an insuperable obstacle to a uniformity of interests. The protection of these faculties is the first object of government. From the protection of different and unequal faculties of acquiring property, the possession of different degrees and kinds of property immediately results; and from the influence of these on the sentiments and views of the respective proprietors, ensues a division of the society into different interests and parties.

The latent causes of faction are thus sown in the nature of man; and we see them everywhere brought into different degrees of activity, according to the different circumstances of civil society. A zeal for different opinions concerning religion, concerning government, and many other points, as well of speculation as of practice; an attachment of different leaders ambitiously contending for pre-eminence and power; or to persons of other descriptions whose fortunes have been interesting to the human passions, have, in turn, divided mankind into parties, inflamed them with mutual animosity, and rendered them much more disposed to vex and oppress each other than to cooperate for their common good. So strong is this propensity of mankind to fall into mutual animosities, that where no substantial occasion presents itself, the most frivolous and fanciful distinctions have been sufficient to kindle their unfriendly passions and excite their most violent conflicts. But the most common and durable source of factions has been the various and unequal distribution of property. Those who hold and those who are without property have ever formed distinct interests in society. Those who are creditors, and those who are debtors, fall under a like discrimination. A landed interest, a manufacturing interest, a mercantile interest, with many lesser interests, grow up of necessity in civilised nations, and divide them into different classes, actuated by different sentiments and views. The regulation of these various and interfering interests forms the principal task of modern legislation, and involves the spirit of party and faction in the necessary and ordinary operations of the government.

No man is allowed to be a judge in his own cause, because his interest would certainly bias his judgment, and, not improbably, corrupt his integrity. With equal, nay, with greater reason, a body of men are unfit to be both judges and parties at the same time; yet what are many of the most important acts of legislation but so many judicial determinations, not indeed concerning the rights of single persons, but concerning the rights of large bodies of citizens? And what are the different classes of legislators but advocates and parties to the causes which they determine? Is a law proposed concerning private debts? It is a question to which the creditors are parties on one side and the debtors on the other. Justice ought to hold the balance between them. Yet the parties are, and must be, themselves the judges; and the most numerous party, or, in other words, the most powerful faction must be expected to prevail. Shall domestic manufactures be encouraged, and in what degree, by restrictions on foreign manufactures? are questions which would be differently decided by the landed and the manufacturing classes, and probably by neither with a sole regard to justice and the public good. The apportionment of taxes on the various descriptions of property is an act which seems to require the most exact impartiality; yet there is, perhaps, no legislative act in which greater opportunity and temptation are given to a predominant party to trample on the rules of justice. Every shilling with which they overburden the inferior number is a shilling saved to their own pockets.

It is in vain to say that enlightened statesmen will be able to adjust these clashing interests, and render them all subservient to the public good. Enlightened statesmen will not always be at the helm. Nor, in many cases, can such an adjustment be made at all without taking into view indirect and remote considerations, which will rarely prevail over the immediate interest which one party may find in disregarding the rights of another or the good of the whole.

The inference to which we are brought is, that the *causes* of faction cannot be removed, and that relief is only to be sought in the means of controlling its *effects*.

If a faction consists of less than a majority, relief is supplied by the republican principle, which enables the majority to defeat its sinister views by regular vote. It may clog the administration, it may convulse the society; but it will be unable to execute and mask its violence under the forms of the Constitution. When a majority is included in a faction, the form of popular government, on the other hand, enables it to sacrifice to its ruling passion or interest both the public good and the rights of other citizens. To secure the public good and private rights against the danger of such a faction, and at the same time to preserve the spirit and the form of popular government, is then the great object to which our inquiries are directed. Let me add that it is the great desideratum by which this form of government can be rescued from the opprobrium under which it has so long laboured, and be recommended to the esteem and adoption of mankind.

By what means is this object obtainable? Evidently by one of two only. Either the existence of the same passion or interest in a majority at the same time must be prevented, or the majority, having such co-existent passion or interest, must be rendered, by their number and local situation, unable to concert and carry into effect schemes of oppression. If the impulse and the opportunity be suffered to coincide, we well know that neither moral nor religious motives can be relied on as an adequate control. They are not found to be such on the injustice and violence of individuals, and lose their efficacy in proportion to the number combined together, that is, in proportion as their efficacy becomes needful.

From this point of view of the subject it may be concluded that a pure democracy, by which I mean a society consisting of a small number of citizens, who assemble and administer the government in person, can admit of no cure for the mischiefs of faction. A common passion or interest will, in almost every case, be felt by a majority of the whole; a communication and concert result from the form of government itself; and there is nothing to check the inducements to sacrifice the weaker party or an obnoxious individual. Hence it is that such democracies have ever been spectacles of turbulence and contention; have ever been found incompatible with personal security or the rights of property; and have in general been as short in their lives as they have been violent in their deaths. Theoretic politicians, who have patronised this species of government, have erroneously supposed that by reducing mankind to a perfect equality in their political rights, they would, at the same time, be perfectly equalised and assimilated in their possessions, their opinions, and their passions.

A republic, by which I mean a government in which the scheme of representation takes place, opens a different prospect, and promises the cure for which we are seeking. Let us examine the points in which it varies from pure democracy, and we shall comprehend both the nature of the cure and the efficacy which it must derive from the Union.

The two great points of difference between a democracy and a republic are: first, the delegation of the government, in the latter, to a small number of citizens elected by the rest; secondly, the greater number of citizens, and greater sphere of country, over which the latter may be extended.

The effect of the first difference is, on the one hand, to refine and enlarge the public views, by passing them through the medium of a chosen body of citizens, whose wisdom may best discern the true interest of their country, and whose patriotism and love of justice will be least likely to sacrifice it to temporary or partial considerations. Under such a regulation, it may well happen that the public voice, pronounced by the representatives of the people, will be more consonant to the public good than if pronounced by the people themselves, convened for the purpose. On the other hand, the effect may be inverted. Men of factious tempers, of local prejudices, or of sinister designs, may, by intrigue, by corruption, or by other means, first obtain the suffrages, and then betray the interests, of the people. The question resulting is, whether small or extensive republics are more favourable to the election of proper guardians of the public weal; and it is clearly decided in favour of the latter by two obvious considerations:

In the first place, it is to be remarked that, however small the republic may be, the representatives must be raised to a certain number, in order to guard against the cabals of a few; and that, however large it may be, they must be limited to a certain number, in order to guard against the confusion of a multitude. Hence the number of representatives in the two cases not being in proportion to that of the two constituents, and being proportionally greater in the small republic, it follows that, if the proportion of fit characters be not less in the large than in the small republic, the former will present a greater option, and consequently a greater probability of a fit choice.

In the next place, as each representative will be chosen by a greater number of citizens in the large than in the small republic, it will be more difficult for unworthy candidates to practise with success the vicious arts by which elections are too often carried; and the suffrages of the people being more free, will be more likely to centre in men who possess the most attractive merit and the most diffusive and established character.

It must be confessed that in this, as in most other cases, there is a mean, on both sides of which inconveniences will be found to lie. By enlarging too much the number of electors, you render the representative too little acquainted with all their local circumstances and lesser interests; as by reducing it too much, you render him unduly attached to these, and too little fit to comprehend and pursue great and national objects. The federal Constitution forms a happy combination in this respect; the great and aggregate interests being referred to the national, the local and particularly to the State legislatures.

The other point of difference is, the greater number of citizens and extent of territory which may be brought within the compass of republican than of democratic government; and it is this circumstance principally which renders factious combinations less to be dreaded in the former than in the latter. The smaller the society, the fewer probably will be the distinct parties and interests composing it; the fewer the distinct parties and interests, the more frequently will a majority be found of the same party; and the smaller the number of individuals composing a majority, and the smaller the compass within which they are placed, the more easily will they concert and execute their plans of oppression. Extend the sphere, and you take in a greater variety of parties and interests; you make it less probable that a majority of the whole will have a common motive to invade the rights of other citizens; or if such a common motive exists, it will be more difficult for all who feel it to discover their own strength, and to act in unison with each other. Besides other impediments, it may be remarked that, where there is a consciousness of unjust or dishonourable purposes, communication is always checked by distrust in proportion to the number whose concurrence is necessary.

Hence, it clearly appears, that the same advantage which a republic has over a democracy, in controlling the effects of faction, is enjoyed by a large over a small republic—is enjoyed by the Union over the States composing it. Does the advantage consist in the substitution of representatives whose enlightened views and virtuous sentiments render them superior to local prejudices and to schemes of injustice? It will not be denied that the representation of the Union will be most likely to possess these requisite endowments. Does it consist in the greater security afforded by a greater variety of parties, against the event of any one party being able to outnumber and oppress the rest? In an equal degree does the increased variety of parties comprised within the Union increase this security? Does it, in fine, consist in the greater obstacles opposed to the concert and accomplishment of the secret wishes of an unjust and interest majority? Here, again, the extent of the Union gives it the most palpable advantage.

The influence of factious leaders may kindle a flame within their particular States, but will be unable to spread a general conflagration through the other States. A religious sect may degenerate into a political faction in a part of the Confederacy; but the variety of sects dispersed over the entire face of it must secure the national councils against any danger from that source. A rage for paper money, for an abolition of debts, for an equal division of property, or for any other improper or wicked project, will be less apt to pervade the whole body of the Union than a particular member of it; in the same proportion as such a malady is more likely to taint a particular county or district, than an entire State.

In the extent and proper structure of the Union, therefore, we behold a republican remedy for the diseases most incident to republican government. And according to the degree of pleasure and pride we feel in being republicans, ought to be our zeal in cherishing the spirit and supporting the character of Federalists.

Publius

Democracy in America

by Alexis de Tocqueville

First Book — Chapter XV
Unlimited Power of the Majority in the United States
and its Consequences

...I HOLD it to be an impious and detestable maxim that, politically speaking, the people have a right to do anything; and yet I have asserted that all authority originates in the will of the majority. Am I, then, in contradiction with myself?

A general law, which bears the name of justice, has been made and sanctioned, not only by a majority of this or that people, but by a majority of mankind. The rights of every people are therefore confined within the limits of what is just. A nation may be considered as a jury which is empowered to represent society at large and to apply justice, which is its law. Ought such a jury, which represents society, to have more power than the society itself, whose laws it executes?

When I refuse to obey an unjust law, I do not contest the right of the majority to command, but I simply appeal from the sovereignty of the people to the sovereignty of mankind. Some have not feared to assert that a people can never outstep the boundaries of justice and reason in those affairs which are peculiarly its own and that, consequently, full power may be given to the majority by which they are represented. But this is the language of a slave.

A majority taken collectively is only an individual, whose opinions, and frequently whose interests, are opposed to those of another individual, who is styled a minority. If it be admitted that a man possessing absolute power may misuse that power by wronging his adversaries, why should not a majority be liable to the same reproach? Men do not change their characters by uniting with each other; nor does their patience in the presence of obstacles increase with their strength. For my own part, I cannot believe it; the power to do everything, which I should refuse to one of my equals, I will never grant to any number of them.

I do not think that, for the sake of preserving liberty, it is possible to combine several principles in the same government so as really to oppose them to one another. The form of government which is usually termed *mixed* has always appeared to me a mere chimera. Accurately speaking, there is no such thing as a *mixed government,* in the sense usually given to that word, because, in all communities, some one principle of action may be discovered which preponderates over the others. England, in the last century—which has been especially cited as an example of this sort of government—was essentially an aristocratic state, although it comprised some great elements of democracy; for the laws and customs of the country were such that the aristocracy could not but preponderate in the long run and direct public affairs according to its own will. The error arose from seeing the interests of the nobles perpetually contending with those of the people, without considering the issue of the contest, which was really the important point. When a community actually has a mixed government —that is to say, when it is equally divided between adverse principles—it must either experience a revolution or fall into anarchy.

I am therefore of opinion that social power superior to all others must always be placed somewhere; but I think that liberty is endangered when this power finds no obstacle which can retard its course and give it time to moderate its own vehemence.

Unlimited power is in itself a bad and dangerous thing. Human beings are not competent to exercise it with discretion. God alone can be omnipotent, because his wisdom and his justice are always equal to his power. There is no power on earth so worthy of honor in itself, or clothed with rights so sacred, that I would admit its uncontrolled and all-predominant authority. When I see that the right and the means of absolute command are conferred on any power whatever, be it called a people or a king, an aristocracy or a democracy, a monarchy or a republic, I say there is the germ of tyranny, and I seek to live elsewhere, under other laws.

In my opinion, the main evil of the present democratic institutions of the United States does not arise, as is often asserted in Europe, from their weakness but from their irresistible strength. I am not so much alarmed at the excessive liberty which reigns in that country as at the inadequate securities which one finds there against tyranny. . . .

Effects of the Omnipotence of the Majority upon the Arbitrary Authority of American Public Officers

A *distinction* must be drawn between tyranny and arbitrary power. Tyranny may be exercised by means of the law itself, and in that case it is not arbitrary; arbitrary power may be exercised for the public good, in which case it is not tyrannical. Tyranny usually employs arbitrary means, but, if necessary, it can do without them.

In the United States the omnipotence of the majority, which is favorable to the legal despotism of the legislature, likewise favors the arbitrary authority of the magistrate. The majority has absolute watch over its execution; and as it has equal authority over those who are in power, and the community at large, it considers public officers as its passive agents and readily confides to them the task of carrying out its designs. The details of their office, and the privileges which they are to enjoy, are rarely defined beforehand. It treats them as a master does his servants, since they are always at work in his sight, and he can direct or reprimand them at any instant. . . .

Power Exercised by the Majority in America upon Opinion

. . . I know of no country in which there is so little independence of mind and real freedom of discussion as in America. In any constitutional state in Europe, every sort of religious and political theory may be freely preached and disseminated; for there is no country in Europe so subdued by any single authority as not to protect the man who raises his voice in the cause of truth from the consequences of his hardihood. If he is unfortunate enough to live under an absolute government, the people are often upon his side; if he inhabits a free country, he can, if necessary, find a shelter behind the throne. The aristocratic part of society supports him in some countries, and the democracy in others. But in a nation where democratic institutions exist, organized like those of the United States, there is but one authority, one element of strength and success, with nothing beyond it.

In America the majority raises formidable barriers around the liberty of opinion; within these barriers, an author may write what he pleases, but woe to him if he goes beyond them. Not that he is in danger of an *auto da fé*, but he is exposed to continued obloquy and persecution. His political career is closed forever, since he has offended the only authority which is able to open it. Every sort of compensation, even that of celebrity, is refused to him. Before publishing his opinions, he imagined that he held them in common with others; but no sooner has he declared them than he is loudly censured by his opponents, whilst those who think like him, without having the courage to speak out, abandon him in silence. He yields at length, overcome by the daily effort which he has to make, and subsides into silence, as if he felt remorse for having spoken the truth. . . .

The Greatest Dangers of the American Republics Proceed from the Omnipotence of the Majority

Governments usually perish from impotence or from tyranny. In the former case, their power escapes from them; it is wrested from their grasp in the latter. Many observers who have witnessed the anarchy of democratic states have imagined that the government of those states was naturally weak and impotent. The truth is that, when war is once begun between parties, the government loses its control over society. But I do not think that a democratic power is naturally without force or resources; say, rather, that it is almost always by the abuse of its force, and the misemployment of its resources, that it becomes a failure. Anarchy is almost always produced by its tyranny or its mistakes but not by its want of strength.

It is important not to confound stability with force, or the greatness of a thing with its duration. In democratic republics the power which directs society is not stable, for it often changes hands and assumes a new direction. But, whichever way it turns, its force is almost irresistible. The governments of the American republics appear to me to be as much centralized as those of the absolute monarchies of Europe and more energetic than they are. I do not, therefore, imagine that they will perish from weakness.

If ever the free institutions of America are destroyed, that event may be attributed to the omnipotence of the majority, which may at some future time urge the minorities to desperation, and oblige them to have recourse to physical force. Anarchy will then be the result, but it will have been brought about by despotism. . . .

Conclusion to First Book
The United States and Russia

. . . Today there are two great peoples who, starting from different points, seem to approach the same destiny; they are the Russians and the Anglo-Americans. Both of them have grown in obscurity, and, while men were looking the other way, they suddenly reach the first rank of nations. At almost the same time the world became aware of their birth and of their greatness.

All other peoples seem to have nearly reached the limits of their potentialities, and to have nothing left to do but to maintain their present status. But these two people are growing; all others have stopped or progress only with the greatest effort; these alone follow with ease and celerity a course whose limit the eye cannot yet detect.

The American battles the obstacles of nature; the Russian, those of man. The former combats the wilderness and savagery, the latter, civilization with all its weapons. American conquests are won with the laborer's plowshare; Russian triumphs, with the soldier's sword. To attain its ends, the American relies upon personal interest and allows free scope to the unguided energy and common sense of individuals. The Russian somehow concentrates the power of society in one man. The method of the former is freedom; of the latter, servitude.

Their starting-point is different, their ways are diverse, yet each of them seems called by the secret design of Providence to control, some day, the destinies of half the world.

Representative Government

by John Stuart Mill

Chapter 8
Of the Extension of the Suffrage

SUCH a representative democracy as has now been sketched, representative of all, and not solely of the majority—in which the interests, the opinions, the grades of intellect which are outnumbered would nevertheless be heard, and would have a chance of obtaining by weight of character and strength of argument an influence which would not belong to their numerical force—this democracy, which is alone equal, alone impartial, alone the government of all by all, the only true type of democracy—would be free from the greatest evils of the falsely-called democracies which now prevail, and from which the current idea of democracy is exclusively derived. But even in this democracy, absolute power, if they chose to exercise it, would rest with the numerical majority; and these would be composed exclusively of a single class, alike in biasses, prepossessions, and general modes of thinking, and a class, to say no more, not the most highly cultivated. The constitution would therefore still be liable to the characteristic evils of class government: in a far less degree, assuredly, than that exclusive government by a class, which new usurps the name of democracy; but still, under no effective restraint, except what might be found in the good sense, moderation, and forbearance of the class itself. If checks of this description are sufficient, the philosophy of constitutional government is but solemn trifling. All trust in constitutions is grounded on the assurance they may afford, not that the depositaries of power will not, but that they cannot, misemploy it. Democracy is not the ideally best form of government unless this weak side of it can be strengthened; unless it can be so organised that no class, not even the most numerous, shall be able to reduce all but itself to political insignificance, and direct the course of legislation and administration

307

by its exclusive class interest. The problem is, to find the means of preventing this abuse, without sacrificing the characteristic advantages of popular government.

These twofold requisites are not fulfilled by the expedient of a limitation of the suffrage, involving the compulsory exclusion of any portion of the citizens from a voice in the representation. Among the foremost benefits of free government is that education of the intelligence and of the sentiments which is carried down to the very lowest ranks of the people when they are called to take a part in acts which directly affect the great interests of their country. On this topic I have already dwelt so emphatically that I only return to it because there are few who seem to attach to this effect of popular institutions all the importance to which it is entitled. People think it fanciful to expect so much from what seems so slight a cause—to recognise a potent instrument of mental improvement in the exercise of political franchises by manual labourers. Yet unless substantial mental cultivation in the mass of mankind is to be a mere vision, this is the road by which it must come. If any one supposes that this road will not bring it, I call to witness the entire contents of M. de Tocqueville's great work; and especially his estimate of the Americans. Almost all travellers are struck by the fact that every American is in some sense both a patriot, and a person of cultivated intelligence; and M. de Tocqueville has shown how close the connection is between these qualities and their democratic institutions. No such wide diffusion of the ideas, taste, and sentiments of educated minds has ever been seen elsewhere, or even conceived as attainable.[1]

Yet this is nothing to what we might look for in a government equally democratic in its unexclusiveness, but better organised in other important points. For political life is indeed in America a most valuable school, but it is a school from which the ablest teachers are excluded; the first minds in the country being as effectually shut out from the national representation, and from public functions generally, as if they were under a formal disqualification. The Demos, too, being in America the one source of power, all the selfish ambition of the country gravitates towards it, as it does in despotic countries towards the monarch: the people, like the despot, is pursued with adulation and sycophancy, and the corrupting effects of power fully keep pace with its improving and ennobling influences. If, even with this alloy, democratic institutions produce so marked a superiority of mental development in the lowest class of Americans, compared with the corresponding classes in England and elsewhere, what would it be if the good portion of the influence could be retained without the bad? And this, to a certain extent, may be done; but not by excluding that portion of the people who have fewest intellectual stimuli of other kinds from so inestimable an introduction to large, distant, and complicated interests as is afforded by the attention they may be induced to bestow on political affairs. It is by political discussion that the manual labourer, whose employment is a routine, and whose way of life brings him in contact with no variety of impressions, circumstances, or ideas, is taught that remote causes, and events which take place far off, have a most sensible effect even on his personal interests; and it is from political discussion, and collective political action, that one whose daily occupations concentrate his interests in a small circle round himself, learns to feel for and with his fellow citizens, and becomes consciously a member of a great community. But political discussions fly over the heads of those who have no votes, and are not endeavouring to acquire them. Their position, in comparison with the electors, is that of the audience in a court of justice, compared with the twelve men in the jury-box. It is not *their* suffrages that are asked, it is not their opinion that is sought to be influenced; the appeals are made, the arguments addressed, to others than them; nothing depends on the decision they may arrive at, and there is no necessity and very little inducement to them to come to any. Whoever, in an otherwise popular government, has no vote, and no prospect of obtaining it, will either be a permanent malcontent, or will feel as one whom the general affairs of society do not concern; for whom they are to be managed by others; who "has no business with the laws except to obey them," nor with public interests and concerns except as a looker-on. What he will know or care about them from this position may partly be measured by what an average woman of the middle class knows and cares about politics, compared with her husband or brothers.

Independently of all these considerations, it is a personal injustice to withhold from anyone, unless for the prevention of greater evils, the ordinary privilege of having his voice reckoned in the disposal of affairs in which he has the same interest as other people. If he is compelled to pay, if he may be compelled to fight, if he is required implicitly to obey, he should be legally entitled to be told what for; to have his consent asked, and his opinion counted at its worth, though not at more than its worth. There ought to be no pariahs in a full-grown and civilised nation; no persons disqualified, except through their own default. Every one is degraded, whether aware of it or not, when other people, without consulting him, take upon themselves unlimited power to regulate his destiny. And even in a much more improved state than the human mind has ever yet reached, it is not in nature that they who are thus disposed of should meet with as fair play as those who have a voice. Rulers and ruling classes are under a necessity of considering the interests and wishes of those who have the suffrage; but of those who are excluded, it is in their option whether they will do so or not, and, however honestly disposed, they are in general too fully occupied with things which they *must* attend to, to have much room in their thoughts for anything which they can with impunity disregard. No arrangement of the suffrage, therefore, can be permanently satisfactory in which any person or class is peremptorily excluded; in which the electoral privilege is not open to all persons of full age who desire to obtain it.

There are, however, certain exclusions, required by positive reasons, which do not conflict with this principle, and which, though an evil in themselves, are only to be got rid of by the cessation of the state of things which requires them. I regard it as wholly inadmissible that any person should participate in the suffrage without being able to read, write, and, I will add, perform the common operations of arithmetic. Justice demands, even when the suffrage does not depend on it, that the means of attaining these elementary acquirements should be within the reach of every person, either gratuitously, or at an expense not exceeding what the poorest who earn their own living can afford. If this were really the case, people would no more think of giving the suffrage to a man who could not read, than of giving it to a child who could not speak; and it would not be society that would exclude him, but his own laziness. When society has not performed its duty, by rendering this amount of instruction accessible to all, there is some hardship in the case, but it is a hardship that ought to be borne. If society has neglected to discharge two solemn obligations, the more important and more fundamental of the two must be fulfilled first: universal teaching must precede universal enfranchisement. No one but those in whom an *a priori* theory has silenced common sense will maintain that power over others, over the whole community, should be imparted to people who have not acquired the commonest and most essential requisites for taking care of themselves; for pursuing intelligently their own interests, and those of the persons most nearly allied to them. This argument, doubtless, might be pressed further, and made to prove much more. It would be eminently desirable that other things besides reading, writing, and arithmetic could be made necessary to the suffrage; that some knowledge of the conformation of the earth, its natural and political divisions, the elements of general history, and of the history and institutions of their own country, could be required from all electors. But these kinds of knowledge, however indispensable to an intelligent use of the suffrage, are not, in this country, nor probably anywhere save in the Northern United States, accessible to the whole people; nor does there exist any trustworthy machinery for ascertaining whether they have been acquired or not. The attempt, at present, would lead to partiality, chicanery, and every kind of fraud. It is better that the suffrage should be conferred indiscriminately, or even withheld indiscriminately, than that it should be given to one and withheld from another at the discretion of a public officer. In regard, however, to reading, writing, and calculating, there need be no difficulty. It would be easy to require from every one who presented himself for registry that he should, in the presence of the registrar, copy a sentence from an English book, and perform a sum in the rule of three; and to secure, by fixed rules and complete publicity, the honest application of so very simple a test. This condition, therefore, should in all cases accompany universal suffrage; and it would, after a few years, exclude none but those who cared so little for the privilege, that their vote, if given, would not in general be an indication of any real political opinion.

It is also important, that the assembly which votes the taxes, either general or local, should be elected exclusively by those who pay something towards the taxes imposed. Those who pay no taxes, disposing by their votes of other people's money, have every motive to be lavish and none to economise. As far as money matters are concerned, any power of voting possessed by them is a violation of the fundamental principle of free government; a severance of the power of control from the interest in its beneficial exercise. It amounts to allowing them to put their hands into other people's pockets for any purpose which they think fit to call a public one; which in some of the great towns of the United States is known to have produced a scale of local taxation onerous beyond example, and wholly borne by the wealthier classes. That representation should be coextensive with taxation, not stopping short of it, but also not going beyond it, is in accordance with the theory of British institutions. But to reconcile this, as a condition annexed to the representation, with universality, it is essential, as it is on many other accounts desirable, that taxation, in a visible shape, should descend to the poorest class. In this country, and in most others, there is probably no labouring family which does not contribute to the indirect taxes, by the purchse of tea, coffee, sugar, not to mention narcotics or stimulants. But this mode of defraying a share of the public expenses is hardly felt: the payer, unless a person of education and reflection, does not identify his interest with a low scale of public expenditure as closely as when money for its support is demanded directly from himself; and even supposing him to do so, he would doubtless take care that, however lavish an expenditure he might, by his vote, assist in imposing upon the government, it should not be defrayed by any additional taxes on the articles which he himself consumes. It would be better that a direct tax, in the simple form of a capitation, should be levied on every grown person in the community; or that every such person should be admitted an elector on allowing himself to be rated *extra ordinem* to the assessed taxes; or that a small annual payment rising and falling with the gross expenditure of the country should be required from every registered elector; that so everyone might feel that the money which he assisted in voting was partly his own, and that he was interested in keeping down its amount.

However this may be, I regard it as required by first principles, that the receipt of parish relief should be a peremptory disqualification for the franchise. He who cannot by his labour suffice for his own support has no claim to the privilege of helping himself to the money of others. By becoming dependent on the remaining members of the community for actual subsistence, he abdicates his claim to equal rights with them in other respects. Those to whom he is indebted for the continuance of his very existence may justly claim the exclusive management of those common concerns, to which he now brings nothing, or less than he takes away. As a condition of the franchise, a term should be fixed, say five years previous to the registry, during which the applicant's name has not been on the parish books as a recipient of relief. To be an uncertified bankrupt, or to have taken the benefit of the Insolvent Act, should disqualify for the franchise until the person has paid his debts, or at least proved that he is not now, and has not for some long period been, dependent on eleemosynary support. Non-payment of taxes, when so long persisted in that it cannot have arisen from inadvertence, should disqualify while it lasts. These exclusions are not in their nature permanent. They exact such conditions only as all are able, or ought to be able, to fulfil if they choose. They leave the suffrage accessible to all who are in the normal condition of a human being: and if any one has to forego it, he either does not care sufficiently for it to do for its sake what he is already bound to do, or he is in a general condition of depression and degradation in which this slight addition, necessary for the security of others, would be unfelt, and on emerging from which, this mark of inferiority would disappear with the rest.

In the long run, therefore (supposing no restrictions to exist but those of which we have now treated), we might expect that all, except that (it is to be hoped) progressively diminishing class, the recipients of parish relief, would be in possession of votes, so that the suffrage would be, with that slight abatement, universal. That it should be thus widely expanded is, as we have seen, absolutely necessary to an enlarged and elevated conception of good government. Yet in this state of things, the great majority of voters, in most countries, and emphatically in this, would be manual labourers; and the twofold danger, that of too low a standard of political intelligence, and that of class legislation, would still exist in a very perilous degree. It remains to be seen whether any means exist by which these evils can be obviated.

They are capable of being obviated, if men sincerely wish it; not by any artificial contrivance, but by carrying out the natural order of human life, which recommends itself to every one in things in which he has no interest or traditional opinion running counter to it. In all human affairs, every person directly interested, and not under positive tutelage, has an admitted claim to a voice, and when his exercise of it is not inconsistent with the safety of the whole, cannot justly be excluded from it. But though every one ought to have a voice—that every one should have an equal voice is a totally different proposition. When two persons who have a joint interest in any business differ in opinion, does justice require that both opinions should be held of exactly equal value? If, with equal virtue, one is superior to the other in knowledge and intelligence—or if, with equal intelligence, one excels the other in virtue—the opinion, the judgment, of the higher moral or intellectual being is worth more than that of the inferior: and if the institutions of the country virtually assert that they are of the same value, they assert a thing which is not. One of the two, as the wiser or better man, has a claim to superior weight: the difficulty is in ascertaining which of the two it is; a thing impossible as between individuals, but, taking men in bodies and in numbers, it can be done with a certain approach to accuracy. There would be no pretence for applying this doctrine to any case which could with reason be considered as one of individual and private right. In an affair which concerns only one of two persons, that one is entitled to follow his own opinion, however much wiser the other may be than himself. But we are speaking of things which equally concern them both; where, if the more ignorant does not yield his share of the matter to the guidance of the wiser man, the wiser man must resign his to that of the more ignorant. Which of these modes of getting over the difficulty is most for the interest of both, and most conformable to the general fitness of things? If it be deemed unjust that either should have to give way, which injustice is greatest? that the better judgment should give way to the worse, or the worse to the better?

Now, national affairs are exactly such a joint concern, with the difference, that no one needs ever be called upon for a complete sacrifice of his own opinion. It can always be taken into the calculation, and counted at a certain figure, a higher figure being assigned to the suffrages of those whose opinion is entitled to greater weight. There is not, in this arrangement, anything necessarily invidious to those to whom it assigns the lower degrees of influence. Entire exclusion from a voice in the common concerns is one thing: the concession to others of a more potential voice, on the ground of greater capacity for the management of the joint interests, is another. The two things are not merely different, they are incommensurable. Every one has a right to feel insulted by being made a nobody, and stamped as of no account at all. No one but a fool, and only a fool of a peculiar description, feels offended by the acknowledgment that there are others whose opinion, and even whose wish, is entitled to a greater amount of consideration than his. To have no voice in what are partly his own concerns is a thing which nobody willingly submits to; but when what is partly his concern is also partly another's, and he feels the other to understand the subject better than himself, that the other's opinion should be counted for more than his own accords with his expectations, and with the course of things which in all other affairs of life he is accustomed to acquiesce in. It is only necessary that this superior influence should be assigned on grounds which he can comprehend, and of which he is able to perceive the justice.

I hasten to say that I consider it entirely inadmissible, unless as a temporary makeshift, that the superiority of influence should be conferred in consideration of property. I do not deny that property is a kind of test; education in most countries, though anything but proportional to riches, is on the average better in the richer half of society than in the poorer. But the criterion is so imperfect; accident has so much more to do than merit with enabling men to rise in the world; and it is so impossible for any one, by acquiring any amount of instruction, to make sure of the corresponding rise in station, that this foundation of electoral privilege is always, and will continue to be, supremely odious. To connect plurality of votes with any pecuniary qualification would be not only objectionable in itself, but a sure mode of discrediting the principle, and making its permanent maintenance impracticable. The Democracy, at least of this country, are not at present jealous of personal superiority, but they are naturally and must justly so of that which is grounded on mere pecuniary circumstances. The only thing which can justify reckoning one person's opinion as equivalent to more than one is individual mental superiority; and what is wanted is some approximate means of ascertaining that. If there existed such a thing as a really national education or a trustworthy system of general examination, education might be tested directly. In the absence of these, the nature of a person's occupation is some test. An employer of labour is on the average more intelligent than a labourer; for he must labour with his head, and not solely with his hands. A foreman is generally more intelligent than an ordinary labourer, and a labourer in the skilled trades than in the unskilled. A banker, merchant, or manufacturer is likely to be more intelligent than a tradesman, because he has larger and more complicated interests to manage.

In all these cases it is not the having merely undertaken the superior function, but the successful performance of it, that tests the qualifications; for which reason, as well as to prevent persons from engaging nominally in an occupation for the sake of the vote, it would be proper to require that the occupation should have been persevered in for some length of time (say three years). Subject to some such condition, two or more votes might be allowed to every person who exercises any of these superior functions. The liberal professions, when really and not nominally practised, imply, of course, a still higher degree of instruction; and wherever a sufficient examination, or any serious conditions of education, are required before entering on a profession, its members could be admitted at once to a plurality of votes. The same rule might be applied to graduates of universities; and even to those who bring satisfactory certificates of having passed through the course of study required by any school at which the higher branches of knowledge are taught, under proper securities that the teaching is real, and not a mere pretence. The "local" or "middle class" examination for the degree of Associate, so laudably and public-spiritedly established by the Universities of Oxford and Cambridge, and any similar ones which may be instituted by other competent bodies (provided they are fairly open to all comers), afford a ground on which plurality of votes might with great advantage be accorded to those who have passed the test. All these suggestions are open to much discussion in the detail, and to objections which it is of no use to anticipate. The time is not come for giving to such plans a practical shape, nor should I wish to be bound by the particular proposals which I have made. But it is to me evident, that in this direction lies the true ideal of representative government; and that to work towards it, by the best practical contrivances which can be found, is the path of real political improvement.

If it be asked to what length the principle admits of being carried, or how many votes might be accorded to an individual on the ground of superior qualifications, I answer, that this is not in itself very material, provided the distinctions and gradations are not made arbitrarily, but are such as can be understood and accepted by the general conscience and understanding. But it is an absolute condition not to overpass the limit prescribed by the fundamental principle laid down in a former chapter as the condition of excellence in the constitution of a representative system. The plurality of votes must on no account be carried so far that those who are privileged by it, or the class (if any) to which they mainly belong, shall outweigh by means of it all the rest of the community. The distinction in favour of education, right in itself, is further and strongly recommended by its preserving the educated from the class legislation of the uneducated; but it must stop short of enabling them to practise class legislation on their own account. Let me add, that I consider it an absolutely necessary part of the plurality scheme that it be open to the poorest individual in the community to claim its privileges, if he can prove that, in spite of all difficulties and obstacles, he is, in point of intelligence, entitled to them. There ought to be voluntary examinations at which any person whatever might present himself, might prove that he came up to the standard of knowledge and ability laid down as sufficient, and be admitted, in consequence, to the plurality of votes. A privilege which is not refused to any one who can show that he has realised the conditions on which in theory and principle it is dependent would not necessarily be repugnant to any one's sentiment of justice: but it would certainly be so, if, while conferred on general presumptions not always infallible, it were denied to direct proof.

Plural voting, though practised in vestry elections and those of poor-law guardians, is so unfamiliar in elections to Parliament that it is not likely to be soon or willingly adopted: but as the time will certainly arrive when the only choice will be between this and equal universal suffrage, whoever does not desire the last, cannot too soon begin to reconcile himself to the former. In the meantime, though the suggestion, for the present, may not be a practical one, it will serve to mark what is best in principle, and enable us to judge of the eligibility of any indirect means, either existing or capable of being adopted, which may promote in a less perfect manner the same end. A person may have a double vote by other means than that of tendering two votes at the same hustings; he may have a vote in each of two different constituencies: and though this exceptional privilege at present belongs rather to superiority of means than of intelligence, I would not abolish it where it exists, since until a truer test of education is adopted it would be unwise to dispense with even so imperfect a one as is afforded by pecuniary circumstances. Means might be found of giving a further extension to the privilege, which would connect it in a more direct manner with superior education. In any future Reform Bill which lowers greatly the pecuniary conditions of the suffrage, it might be a wise provision to allow all graduates of universities, all persons who have passed creditably through the higher schools, all members of the liberal professions, and perhaps some others, to be registered specifically in those characters, and to give their votes as such in any constituency in which they choose to register; retaining, in addition, their votes as simple citizens in the localities in which they reside.

Until there shall have been devised, and until opinion is willing to accept, some mode of plural voting which may assign to education, as such, the degree of superior influence due to it, and sufficient as a counterpoise to the numerical weight of the least educated class; for so long the benefits of completely universal suffrage cannot be obtained without bringing with them, as it appears to me, a chance of more than equivalent evils. It is possible, indeed (and this is perhaps one of the transitions through which we may have to pass in our progress to a really good representative system), that the barriers which restrict the suffrage might be entirely levelled in some particular constituencies, whose members, consequently, would be returned principally by manual labourers; the existing electoral qualification being maintained elsewhere, or any alteration in it being accompanied by such a grouping of the constituencies as to prevent the labouring class from becoming preponderant in Parliament. By such a compromise, the anomalies in the representation would not only be retained, but augmented: this however is not a conclusive objection; for if the country does not choose to pursue the right ends by a regular system directly leading to them, it must be content with an irregular makeshift, as being greatly preferable to a system free from irregularities, but regularly adapted to wrong ends, or in which some ends equally necessary with the others have been left out. It is a far graver objection, that this adjustment is incompatible with the intercommunity of local constituencies which Mr. Hare's plan requires; that under it every voter would remain imprisoned within the one or more constituencies in which his name is registered, and unless willing to be represented by one of the candidates for those localities, would not be represented at all.

So much importance do I attach to the emancipation of those who already have votes, but whose votes are useless, because always outnumbered; so much should I hope from the natural influence of truth and reason, if only secured a hearing and a competent advocacy—that I should not despair of the operation even of equal and universal suffrage, if made real by the proportional representation of all minorities, on Mr. Hare's principle. But if the best hopes which can be formed on this subject were certainties, I should still contend for the principle of plural voting. I do not propose the plurality as a thing in itself undesirable, which, like the exclusion of part of the community from the suffrage, may be temporarily tolerated while necessary to prevent greater evils. I do not look upon equal voting as among the things which are good in themselves, provided they can be guarded against inconveniences. I look upon it as only relatively good; less objectionable than inequality of privilege grounded on irrelevant or adventitious circumstances, but in principle wrong, because recognising a wrong standard, and exercising a bad influence on the voter's mind. It is not useful, but hurtful, that the constitution of the country should declare ignorance to be entitled to as much political power as knowledge. The national institutions should place all things that they are concerned with before the mind of the citizen in the light in which it is for his good that he should regard them: and as it is for his good that he should think that every one is entitled to some influence, but the better and wiser to more than others, it is important that this conviction should be professed by the State, and embodied in the national institutions. Such things constitute the *spirit* of the institutions of a country: that portion of their influence which is least regarded by common, and especially by English, thinkers; though the institutions of every country, not under great positive oppression, produce more effect by their spirit than by any of their direct provisions, since by it they shape the national character. The American institutions have imprinted strongly on the American mind that any one man (with a white skin) is as good as any other; and it is felt that this false creed is nearly connected with some of the more unfavourable points in American character. It is not a small mischief that the constitution of any country should sanction this creed; for the belief in it, whether express or tacit, is almost as detrimental to moral and intellectual excellence as any effect which most forms of government can produce.

It may, perhaps, be said, that a constitution which gives equal influence, man for man, to the most and to the least instructed, is nevertheless conducive to progress, because the appeals constantly made to the less instructed classes, the exercise given to their mental powers, and the exertions which the more instructed are obliged to make for enlightening their judgment and ridding them of errors and prejudices, are powerful stimulants to their advance in intelligence. That this most desirable effect really attends the admission of the less educated classes to some, and even to a large share of power, I admit, and have already strenuously maintained. But theory and experience alike prove that a counter current sets in when they are made the possessors of all power. Those who are supreme over everything, whether they be One, or Few, or Many, have no longer need of the arms of reason: they can make their mere will prevail; and those who cannot be resisted are usually far too well satisfied with their own opinions to be willing to change them, or listen without impatience to any one who tells them that they are in the wrong. The position which gives the strongest stimulus to the growth of intelligence is that of rising into power, not that of having achieved it; and of all resting-points, temporary or permanent, in the way to ascendancy, the one which develops the best and highest qualities is the position of those who are strong enough to make reason prevail, but not strong enough to prevail against reason. This is the position in which, according to the principles we have laid down, the rich and the poor, the much and the little educated, and all the other classes and denominations which divide society between them, ought as far as practicable to be placed. And by combining this principle with the otherwise just one of allowing superiority of weight to superiority of mental qualities, a political constitution would realise that kind of relative perfection which is alone compatible with the complicated nature of human affairs.

In the preceding argument for universal, but graduated suffrage, I have taken no account of difference of sex. I consider it to be as entirely irrelevant to political rights as difference in height or in the colour of the hair. All human beings have the same interest in good government; the welfare of all is alike affected by it, and they have equal need of a voice in it to secure their share of its benefits. If there be any difference, women require it more than men, since, being physically weaker, they are more dependent on law and society for protection. Mankind have long since abandoned the only premises which will support the conclusion that women ought not to have votes. No one now holds that women should be in personal servitude; that they should have no thought, wish, or occupation, but to be the domestic drudges of husbands, fathers, or brothers. It is allowed to unmarried, and wants but little of being conceded to married women, to hold property, and have pecuniary and business interests, in the same manner as men. It is considered suitable and proper that women should think, and write, and be teachers. As soon as these things are admitted, the political disqualification has no principle to rest on. The whole mode of thought of the modern world is with increasing emphasis pronouncing against the claim of society to decide for individuals what they are and are not fit for, and what they shall and shall not be allowed to attempt. If the principles of modern politics and political economy are good for anything, it is for proving that these points can only be rightly judged of by the individuals themselves; and that, under complete freedom of choice, wherever there are real diversities of aptitude, the great number will apply themselves to the things for which they are on the average fittest, and the exceptional course will only be taken by the exceptions. Either the whole tendency of modern social improvements has been wrong, or it ought to be carried out to the total abolition of all exclusions and disabilities which close any honest employment to a human being.

But it is not even necessary to maintain so much in order to prove that women should have the suffrage. Were it as right, as it is wrong, that they should be a subordinate class, confined to domestic occupations and subject to domestic authority, they would not the less require the protection of the suffrage to secure them from the abuse of that authority. Men, as well as women, do not need political rights in order that they may govern, but in order that they may not be misgoverned. The majority of the male sex are, and will be all their lives, nothing else than labourers in cornfields or manufactories; but this does not render the suffrage less desirable for them, nor their claim to it less irresistible, when not likely to make a bad use of it. Nobody pretends to think that woman would make a bad use of the suffrage. The worst that is said is that they would vote as mere dependents, at the bidding of their male relations. If it be so, so let it be. If they think for themselves, great good will be done, and if they do not, no harm. It is a benefit to human beings to take off their fetters, even if they do not desire to walk. It would already be a great improvement in the moral position of women to be no longer declared by law incapable of an opinion, and not entitled to a preference, respecting the most important concerns of humanity. There would be some benefit to them individually in having something to bestow which their male relatives cannot exact, and are yet desirous to have. It would also be no small benefit that the husband would necessarily discuss the matter with his wife, and that the vote would not be his exclusive affair, but a joint concern. People do not sufficiently consider how markedly the fact that she is able to have some action on the outward world independently of him raises her dignity and value in a vulgar man's eyes, and makes her the object of a respect which no personal qualities would ever obtain for one whose social existence he can entirely appropriate.

The vote itself, too, would be improved in quality. The man would often be obliged to find honest reasons for his vote, such as might induce a more upright and impartial character to serve with him under the same banner. The wife's influence would often keep him true to his own sincere opinion. Often, indeed, it would be used, not on the side of public principle, but of the personal interest or worldly vanity of the family. But wherever this would be the tendency of the wife's influence, it is exerted to the full already in that bad direction; and with the more certainty, since under the present law and custom she is generally too utter a stranger to politics in any sense in which they involve principle to be able to realise to herself that there is a point of honour in them, and most people have as little sympathy in the point of honour of others, when their own is not placed in the same thing, as they have in the religious feelings of those whose religion differs from theirs. Give the woman a vote, and she comes under the operation of the political point of honour. She learns to look on politics as a thing on which she is allowed to have an opinion, and in which if one has an opinion it ought to be acted upon; she acquires a sense of personal accountability in the matter, and will no longer feel, as she does at present, that whatever amount of bad influence she may exercise, if the man can but be persuaded, all is right, and his responsibility covers all. It is only by being herself encouraged to form an opinion, and obtain an intelligent comprehension of the reasons which ought to prevail with the conscience against the temptations of personal or family interest, that she can ever cease to act as a disturbing force on the political conscience of the man. Her indirect agency can only be prevented from being politically mischievous by being exchanged for direct.

I have supposed the right of suffrage to depend, as in a good state of things it would, on personal conditions. Where it depends, as in this and most other countries, on conditions of property, the contradiction is even more flagrant. There is something more than ordinarily irrational in the fact that when a woman can give all the guarantees required from a male elector, independent circumstances, the position of a householder and head of a family, payment of taxes, or whatever may be the conditions imposed, the very principle and system of a representation based on property is set aside, and an exceptionally personal disqualification is created for the mere purpose of excluding her. When it is added that in the country where this is done a woman now reigns, and that the most glorious ruler whom that country ever had was a woman, the picture of unreason, and scarcely disguised injustice, is complete. Let us hope that as the work proceeds of pulling down, one after another, the remains of the mouldering fabric of monopoly and tyranny, this one will not be the last to disappear; that the opinion of Bentham, of Mr. Samuel Bailey, of Mr. Hare, and many other of the most powerful political thinkers of this age and country (not to speak of others), will make its way to all minds not rendered obdurate by selfishness or inveterate prejudice; and that, before the lapse of another generation, the accident of sex, no more than the accident of skin, will be deemed a sufficient justification for depriving its possessor of the equal protection and just privileges of a citizen.

---

[1] The following "extract from the Report of the English Commissioner to the New York Exhibition," which I quote from Mr. Carey's *Principles of Social Science*, bears striking testimony to one part, at least, of the assertion in the text: —

"We have a few great engineers and mechanics, and a large body of clever workmen; but the Americans seem likely to become a whole nation of such people. Already, their rivers swarm with steamboats; their valleys are becoming crowded with factories; their towns, surpassing those of every state of Europe, except Belgium, Holland, and England, are the abodes of all the skill which now distinguishes a town population; and there is scarcely an art in Europe not carried on in America with equal or greater skill than in Europe, though it has been here cultivated and improved through ages. A whole nation of Franklins, Stephensons, and Watts in prospect, is something wonderful for other nations to contemplate. In contrast with the comparative inertness and ignorance of the bulk of the people of Europe, whatever may be the superiority of a few well-instructed and gifted persons, the great intelligence of the whole people of America is the circumstance most worthy of public attention."

Address
to the United Nations
General Assembly

by Ch. Anwar Sani

IN the more abstract sense as to the substance of the remarks on how a majority should behave, independently of whether they do or do not apply to actual developments as we see them today in the United Nations, we who are considered or consider ourselves as belonging to the so-called majority would do well to study them. We should not make the same mistakes as were made in the past by today's so-called minority who were then the majority and had in fact the capacity to implement the decisions of the United Nations, but who apparently were not in a position to do very much.

On the other hand, the so-called minority needs to exercise some serious introspection and self-criticism. As I said, at one time this same so-called minority was itself a majority, a real majority, numerically as well as in terms of capacity to support this Organization and implement its decisions. What was their role during those years when they constituted the majority with regard to those problems with which we are still confronted today? What has been their role in the Middle East conflict? What have they done, all-powerful as they were, to make South Africa respect United Nations decisions? What has been their role in the process of decolonization? What have they effectively contributed to bridge the widening prosperity gap between them, as the rich industrialized states, and the poor developing nations which they have exploited for hundreds of years? These are the questions which in the first place they should try to answer in all frankness to themselves before painting a picture in the way they did of the behaviour of the so-called mechanical majority which they claim to exist today in the United Nations. Perhaps they will be able then to understand better why the so-called majority acts in the way it is doing and to exercise more restraint in reacting to the recent developments which my delegation understands indeed cannot be expected to be to their liking.

Indonesia is a country which has a tradition of decision-making through a process of what we called *musyawarah* and *mufakat*, consultations and consensus. Most of our countries have at one stage or another known that method. But most of us have traded it for a decision-making process based upon the contention that half plus one should be right. In the Indonesian national process of decision-making the majority has the obligation to try, in accordance with their responsibility to the entire people, to accommodate the minority as much as possible in order to reach a consensus; the process may be lengthy, cumbersome, sometimes exasperating; but we are much better off than during the period immediately after our independence when we experimented with the "half plus one is right" approach. Perhaps it is easier to do so in the national context, where the point of departure and concrete aims are firmly established in the constitution and the differences mainly concern the methods of achieving them. Indonesia has a tradition of respect for minority views, of trying to accommodate them as far as we can. Of course it is expected that the minority will also do their utmost to arrive at an accommodation with the majority. This is also the approach that governs the participation of the Indonesian delegation in the work of the United Nations. My delegation would not like to see the United Nations turn into an arena of confrontation between majority and minority, even if that minority does not in fact represent a practical majority, in terms of capacity to support this Organization and implement its decisions, as claimed by the representative of the United States. We do not see in the United Nations a factory to turn out resolutions, but a forum for the combined and concerted efforts of all the countries in the world to find concrete solutions for concrete problems affecting the whole of mankind.

Second Week — Third Day

Henry David Thoreau, *On Civil Disobedience*

Mohandas K. Gandhi, *Indian Home Rule*
(selection)

Martin Luther King, Jr.
Letter from Birmingham City Jail

Eldridge Cleaver, *Soul On Ice*,
"Domestic Law and International Order"

Afternoon session:
Group reading of Sophocles' *Antigone*

On Civil Disobedience

by Henry David Thoreau

I HEARTILY accept the motto, "That government is best which governs least"; and I should like to see it acted up to more rapidly and systematically. Carried out, it finally amounts to this, which also I believe: "That government is best which governs not at all"; and, when men are prepared for it, that will be the kind of government which they will have. Government is at best but an expedient; but most governments are usually, and all governments are sometimes, inexpedient. The objections which have been brought against a standing army, and they are many and weighty, and deserve to prevail, may also at last be brought against a standing government. The standing army is only an arm of the standing government. The government itself, which is only the mode which the people have chosen to execute their will, is equally liable to be abused and perverted before the people can act through it. Witness the present Mexican War, the work of comparatively a few individuals using the standing government as their tool, for, in the outset, the people would not have consented to this measure.

This American government—what is it but a tradition, though a recent one, endeavoring to transmit itself unimpaired to posterity, but each instant losing some of its integrity? It has not the vitality and force of a single living man, for a single man can bend it to his will. It is a sort of wooden gun to the people themselves; and, if ever they should use it in earnest as a real one against each other, it will surely split. But it is not the less necessary for this, for the people must have some complicated machinery or other, and hear its din, to satisfy that idea of government which they have. Governments show thus how successfully men can be imposed on, even impose on themselves, for their own advantage. It is excellent, we must all allow; yet this government never of itself furthered any enterprise but by the alacrity with which it got out of its way. *It* does not keep the country free. *It* does not settle the West. *It* does not educate. The charcter inherent in the American people has done all that has been accomplished, and it would have done somewhat more if the government had not sometimes got in its way. For government is an expedient by which men would fain succeed in letting one another alone; and, as has been said, when it is most expedient, the governed are most let alone by it. Trade and commerce, if they were not made of India rubber, would never manage to bounce over the obstacles which legislators are continually putting in their way; and, if one were to judge these men wholly by the effects of their actions, and not partly by their intentions, they would deserve to be classed and punished with those mischievous persons who put obstructions on the railroads.

But, to speak practically and as a citizen, unlike those who call themselves no-government men, I ask for, not at once no government, but *at once* a better government. Let every man make known what kind of government would command his respect, and that will be one step toward obtaining it.

After all, the practical reason why, when the power is once in the hands of the people, a majority are permitted, and for a long period continue, to rule, is not because they are most likely to be in the right, nor because this seems fairest to the minority, but because they are physically the strongest. But a government in which the majority rule in all cases cannot be based on justice, even as far as men understand it. Can there not be a government in which majorities do not virtually decide right and wrong, but conscience?— in which majorities decide only those questions to which the rule of expediency is applicable? Must the citizen ever for a moment, or in the least degree, resign his conscience to the legislator? Why has every man a conscience, then? I think that we should be men first and subjects afterward. It is not desirable to cultivate a respect for the law so much as for the right. The only obligation which I have a right to assume is to do at any time what I think right. It is truly enough said that a corporation has no conscience, but a corporation of conscientious men is a corporation *with* a conscience. Law never made men a whit more just; and, by means of their respect for it, even the well-disposed are daily made the agents of injustice. A common and natural result of an undue respect for law is that you may see a file of soldiers, colonel, captain, corporal, privates, powder-monkeys and all, marching in admirable order over hill and dale to the wars, against their wills, aye, against their common sense and consciences, which makes it very steep marching indeed and produces a palpitation of the heart. They have no doubt that it is a damnable business in which they are concerned; they are all peaceably inclined. Now, what are they? Men at all? or small movable forts and magazines, at the service of some unscrupulous man in power? Visit the Navy Yard, and behold a marine, such a man as an American government can make, or such as it can make a man with its black arts, a mere shadow and reminiscence of humanity, a man laid out alive and standing, and already, as one may say, buried under arms with funeral accompaniments, though it may be

> Not a drum was heard, nor a funeral note,
>   As his corpse to the ramparts we hurried;

> Not a soldier discharged his farewell shot
> O'er the grave where our hero we buried.

The mass of men serve the state thus, not as men mainly, but as machines, with their bodies. They are the standing army, and the militia, jailers, constables, *posse comitatus*, etc. In most cases there is no free exercise whatever of the judgment or of the moral sense; but they put themselves on a level with wood and earth and stones; and wooden men can perhaps be manufactured that will serve the purpose as well. Such command no more respect than men of straw or a lump of dirt. They have the same sort of worth only as horses and dogs. Yet such as these even are commonly esteemed good citizens. Others, as most legislators, politicians, lawyers, ministers, and office-holders, serve the state chiefly with their heads; and, as they rarely make any moral distinctions, they are as likely to serve the devil, without intending it, as God. A very few, as heroes, patriots, martyrs, reformers in the great sense, and *men*, serve the state with their consciences also, and so necessarily resist it for the most part; and they are commonly treated by it as enemies. A wise man will only be useful as a man and will not submit to be "clay" and "stop a hole to keep the wind away" but leave that office to his dust at least—

> I am too high-born to be propertied,
> To be a secondary at control,
> Or useful serving-man and instrument
> To any sovereign state throughout the world.

He who gives himself entirely to his fellow-men appears to them useless and selfish; but he who gives himself partially to them is pronounced a benefactor and philanthropist.

How does it become a man to behave toward this American government today? I answer that he cannot without disgrace be associated with it. I cannot for an instant recognize that political organization as *my* government which is the *slave's* government also.

All men recognize the right of revolution, that is, the right to refuse allegiance to and to resist the government, when its tyranny or its inefficiency are great and unendurable. But almost all say that such is not the case now. But such was the case, they think, in the Revolution of '75. If one were to tell me that this was a bad government because it taxed certain foreign commodities brought to its ports, it is most probable that I should not make an ado about it, for I can do without them; all machines have their friction, and possibly this does enough good to counterbalance the evil. At any rate, it is a great evil to make a stir about it. But when the friction comes to have its machine, and oppression and robbery are organized, I say, let us not have such a machine any longer. In other words, when a sixth of the population of a nation which has undertaken to be the refuge of liberty are slaves, and a whole country is unjustly overrun and conquered by a foreign army, and subjected to military law, I think that it is not too soon for honest men to rebel and revolutionize. What makes this duty the more urgent is the fact that the country so overrun is not our own but ours is the invading army.

Paley, a common authority with many on moral questions, in his chapter on the "Duty of Submission to Civil Government," resolves all civil obligation into expediency; and he proceeds to say that "so long as the interest of the whole society requires it, that is, so long as the established government cannot be resisted or changed without public inconveniency, it is the will of God that the established government be obeyed, and no longer. . . . This principle being admitted, the justice of every particular case of resistance is reduced to a computation of the quantity of the danger and grievance on the one side, and of the probability and expense of redressing it on the other." Of this, he says, every man shall judge for himself. But Paley appears never to have contemplated those cases to which the rule of expediency does not apply, in which a people, as well as an individual, must do justice, cost what it may. If I have unjustly wrested a plank from a drowning man, I must restore it to him though I drown myself. This, according to Paley, would be inconvenient. But he that would save his life, in such a case, shall lose it. This people must cease to hold slaves, and to make war on Mexico, though it cost them their existence as a people.

In their practice, nations agree with Paley; but does anyone think that Massachusetts does exactly what is right at the present crisis?

> A drab of state, a cloth-o'-silver slut,
> To have her train borne up, and her soul trail in the dirt.

Practically speaking, the opponents to a reform in Massachusetts are not a hundred thousand politicians at the South, but a hundred thousand merchants and farmers here, who are more interested in commerce and agriculture than they are in humanity and are not prepared to do justice to the slave and to Mexico, *cost what it may.* I quarrel not with far-off foes but with those who, near at home, co-operate with and do the bidding of those far away, and without whom the latter would be harmless. We are accustomed to say that the mass of men are unprepared; but improvement is slow, because the few are not materially wiser or better than the many. It is not so important that many should be as good as you as that there be some absolute goodness somewhere, for that will leaven the whole lump. There are thousands who are *in opinion* opposed to slavery and to the war, who yet in effect do nothing to put an end to them; who, esteeming themselves children of Washington and Franklin, sit down with their hands in their pockets and say that they know not what to do, and do nothing; who even postpone the question of freedom to the question of free trade and quietly read the prices-current along with the latest advices from Mexico, after dinner, and, it may be, fall asleep over them both. What is the price-current of an honest man and patriot today? They hesitate, and they regret, and sometimes they petition; but they do nothing in earnest and with effect. They will wait, well disposed, for others to remedy the evil that they may no longer have it to regret. At most, they give only a cheap vote, and a feeble countenance and Godspeed, to the right, as it goes by them. There are nine hundred and ninety-nine patrons of virtue to one virtuous man; but it is easier to deal with the real possessor of a thing than with the temporary guardian of it.

All voting is a sort of gaming, like checkers or backgammon, with a slight moral tinge to it, a playing with right and wrong, with moral questions; and betting naturally accompanies it. The character of the voters is not staked. I cast my vote, perchance, as I think right; but I am not vitally concerned that that right should prevail. I am willing to leave it to the majority. Its obligation, therefore, never exceeds that of expediency. Even voting *for the right* is *doing* nothing for it. It is only expressing to men feebly your desire that it should prevail. A wise man will not leave the right to the mercy of chance nor wish it to prevail through the power of the majority. There is but little virtue in the action of masses of men. When the majority shall at length vote for the abolition of slavery, it will be because they are indifferent to slavery, or because there is but little slavery left to be abolished by their vote. *They* will then be the only slaves. Only *his* vote can hasten the abolition of slavery who asserts his own freedom by his vote.

I hear of a convention to be held at Baltimore, or elsewhere, for the selection of a candidate for the presidency, made up chiefly of editors and men who are politicians by profession; but I think, what is it to any independent, intelligent, and respectable man what decision they may come to; shall we not have the advantage of his wisdom and honesty, nevertheless? Can we not count upon some independent votes? Are there not many individuals in the country who do not attend conventions? But, no; I find that the respectable man, so called, has immediately drifted from his position, and despairs of his country, when his country has more reason to despair of him. He forthwith adopts one of the candidates thus selected as the only *available* one, thus proving that he is himself *available* for any purposes of the demagogue. His vote is of no more worth than that of any unprincipled foreigner or hireling native who may have been bought. Oh, for a man who is a *man* and, as my neighbor says, has a bone in his back which you cannot pass your hand through! Our statistics are at fault; the population has been returned too large. How many *men* are there to a square thousand miles in this country? Hardly one. Does not America offer any inducement for men to settle here? The American has dwindled into an Odd Fellow—one who may be known by the development of his organ of gregariousness, and a manifest lack of intellect and cheerful self-reliance; whose first and chief concern, on coming into the world, is to see that the almshouses are in good repair; and, before yet he has lawfully donned the virile garb, to collect a fund for the support of the widows and orphans that may be; who, in short, ventures to live only by the aid of the mutual insurance company, which has promised to bury him decently.

It is not a man's duty, as a matter of course, to devote himself to the eradication of any, even the most enormous, wrong; he may still properly have other concerns to engage him; but it is his duty, at least, to wash his hands of it and, if he gives it no thought longer, not to give it practically his support. If I devote myself to other pursuits and contemplations, I must first see, at least, that I do not pursue them sitting upon another man's shoulders. I must get off him first that he may pursue his contemplations too. See what gross inconsistency is tolerated. I have heard some of my townsmen say, "I should like to have them order me out to help put down an insurrection of the slaves, or to march to Mexico—see if I would go"; and yet these very men have each, directly by their allegiance, and so indirectly, at least, by their money, furnished a substitute. The soldier is applauded who refuses to serve in an unjust war by those who do not refuse to sustain the unjust government which makes the war; is applauded by those whose own act and authority he disregards and sets at naught; as if the state were penitent to that degree that it hired one to scourge it while it sinned but not to that degree that it left off sinning for a moment. Thus, under the name of order and civil government, we are all made at last to pay homage to and support our own meanness. After the first blush of sin comes its indifference; and from immoral it becomes, as it were, *unmoral* and not quite unnecessary to that life which we have made.

The broadest and most prevalent error requires the most disinterested virtue to sustain it. The slight reproach to which the virtue of patriotism is commonly liable, the noble are most likely to incur. Those who, while they disapprove of the character and measures of a government, yield to it their allegiance and support are undoubtedly its most conscientious supporters and so frequently the most serious obstacles to reform. Some are petitioning the state to dissolve the Union, to disregard the requisitions of the President. Why do they not dissolve it themselves—the union between themselves and the state—and refuse to pay their quota into its treasury? Do not they stand in the same relation to the state that the state does to the Union? And have not the same reasons prevented the state from resisting the Union which have prevented them from resisting the state?

How can a man be satisfied to entertain an opinion merely and enjoy *it?* Is there any enjoyment in it if his opinion is that he is aggrieved? If you are cheated out of a single dollar by your neighbor, you do not rest satisfied with knowing that you are cheated, or with saying that you are cheated, or even with petitioning him to pay you your due; but you take effectual steps at once to obtain the full amount and see that you are never cheated again. Action from principle—the perception and the performance of right —changes things and relations; it is essentially revolutionary and does not consist wholly with anything which was. It not only divides states and churches; it divides families; aye, it divides the *individual,* separating the diabolical in him from the divine.

Unjust laws exist; shall we be content to obey them, or shall we endeavor to amend them, and obey them until we have succeeded, or shall we transgress them at once? Men generally, under such a government as this, think that they ought to wait until they have persuaded the majority to alter them. They think that, if they should resist, the remedy would be worse than the evil. But it is the fault of the government itself that the remedy *is* worse than the evil. *It* makes it worse. Why is it not more apt to anticipate and provide for reform? Why does it not cherish its wise minority? Why does it cry and resist before it is hurt? Why does it not encourage its citizens to be on the alert to point out its faults and *do* better than it would have them? Why does it always crucify Christ and excommunicate Copernicus and Luther and pronounce Washington and Franklin rebels?

One would think that a deliberate and practical denial of its authority was the only offense never contemplated by government; else, why has it not assigned its definite, its suitable and proportionate penalty? If a man who has no property refuses but once to earn nine shillings for the state, he is put in prison for a period unlimited by any law that I know and determined only by the discretion of those who placed him there; but if he should steal ninety times nine shillings from the state, he is soon permitted to go at large again.

If the injustice is part of the necessary friction of the machine of government, let it go, let it go; perchance it will wear smooth—certainly the machine will wear out. If the injustice has a spring, or a pulley, or a rope, or a crank, exclusively for itself, then perhaps you may consider whether the remedy will not be worse than the evil; but if it is of such a nature that it requires you to be the agent of injustice to another, then, I say, break the law. Let your life be a counterfriction to stop the machine. What I have to do is to see, at any rate, that I do not lend myself to the wrong which I condemn.

As for adopting the ways which the state has provided for remedying the evil, I know not of such ways. They take too much time, and a man's life will be gone. I have other affairs to attend to. I came into this world, not chiefly to make this a good place to live in, but to live in it, be it good or bad. A man has not everything to do but something; and, because he cannot do *everything*, it is not necessary that he should do *something* wrong. It is not my business to be petitioning the governor or the legislature any more than it is theirs to petition me; and, if they should not hear my petition, what should I do then? But in this case the state has provided no way; its very constitution is the evil. This may seem to be harsh and stubborn and unconciliatory; but it is to treat with the utmost kindness and consideration the only spirit that can appreciate or deserve it. So is all change for the better, like birth and death which convulse the body.

I do not hesitate to say that those who call themselves abolitionists should at once effectually withdraw their support, both in person and property, from the government of Massachusetts and not wait till they constitute a majority of one before they suffer the right to prevail through them. I think that it is enough if they have God on their side, without waiting for that other one. Moreover, any man more right than his neighbors constitutes a majority of one alredy.

I meet this American government, or its representative the state government, directly, and face to face, once a year, no more, in the person of its tax-gatherer; this is the only mode in which a man situated as I am necessarily meets it; and it then says distinctly, "Recognize me"; and the simplest, the most effectual, and, in the present posture of affairs, the indispensablest mode of treating with it on this head, of expressing your little satisfaction with and love for it, is to deny it then. My civil neighbor, the tax-gatherer, is the very man I have to deal with—for it is, after all, with men and not with parchment that I quarrel—and he has voluntarily chosen to be an agent of the government. How shall he ever know well what he is and does as an officer of the government, or as a man, until he is obliged to consider whether he shall treat me, his neighbor, for whom he has respect, as a neighbor and well-disposed man, or as a maniac and disturber of the peace, and see if he can get over this obstruction to his neighborliness without a ruder and more impetuous thought or speech corresponding with his action? I know this well, that if one thousand, if one hundred, if ten men whom I could name—if ten *honest* men only—aye, if *one* honest man, in this state of Massachusetts, *ceasing to hold slaves,* were actually to withdraw from this co-partnership, and be locked up in the county jail therefor, it would be the abolition of slavery in America. For it matters not how small the beginning may seem to be; what is once well done is done forever. But we love better to talk about it; that, we say, is our mission. Reform keeps many scores of newspapers in its service but not one man. If my esteemed neighbor, the state's ambassador, who will devote his days to the settlement of the question of human rights in the Council Chamber, instead of being threatened with the prisons of Carolina, were to sit down the prisoner of Massachusetts, that state which is so anxious to foist the sin of slavery upon her sister—though at present she can discover only an act of inhospitality to be the ground of a quarrel with her—the legislature would not wholly waive the subject the following winter.

Under a government which imprisons any unjustly, the true place for a just man is also a prison. The proper place today, the only place which Massachusetts has provided for her freer and less desponding spirits, is in her prisons, to be put out and locked out of the state by her own act, as they have already put themselves out by their principles. It is there that the fugitive slave, and the Mexican prisoner on parole, and the Indian come to plead the wrongs of his race, should find them; on that separate, but more free and honorable ground, where the state places those who are not *with* her but *against* her—the only house in a slave state in which a free man can abide with honor. If any think that their influence would be lost there, and their voices no longer afflict the ear of the state, that they would not be as an enemy within its walls; they do not know by how much truth is stronger than error, nor how much more eloquently and effectively he can combat injustice who has experienced a little in his own person. Cast your whole vote, not a strip of paper merely, but your whole influence. A minority is powerless while it conforms to the majority; it is not even a minority then; but it is irresistible when it clogs by its whole weight. If the alternative is to keep all just men in prison, or give up war and slavery, the state will not hesitate which to choose. If a thousand men were not to pay their tax bills this year, that would not be a violent and bloody measure, as it would be to pay them, and enable the state to commit violence and shed innocent blood. This is, in fact, the definition of a peaceable revolution, if any such is possible. If the tax-gatherer, or any other public officer, asks me, as one has done, "But what shall I do?" my answer is, "If you really wish to do anything, resign your office." When the subject has refused allegiance, and the officer has resigned his office, then the revolution is accomplished. But even suppose blood should flow. Is there not a sort of blood shed when the conscience is wounded? Through this wound a man's real manhood and immortality flow out, and he bleeds to an everlasting death. I see this blood flowing now.

I have contemplated the imprisonment of the offender, rather than the seizure of his goods—though both will serve the same purpose—because they who assert the purest right, and consequently are most dangerous to a corrupt state, commonly have not spent much time in accumulating property. To such the state renders comparatively small service, and a slight tax is wont to appear exorbitant, particularly if they are obliged to earn it by special labor with their hands. If there were one who lived wholly without the use of money, the state itself would hesitate to demand it of him. But the rich man—not to make any individious comparison—is always sold to the institution which makes him rich. Absolutely speaking, the more money, the less virtue; for money comes between a man and his objects and obtains them for him; and it was certainly no great virtue to obtain it. It puts to rest many questions which he would otherwise be taxed to answer; while the only new question which it puts is the hard but superfluous one, how to spend it. Thus his moral ground is taken from under his feet. The opportunities of living are diminished in proportion as what are called the "means" are increased. The best thing a man can do for his culture when he is rich is to endeavor to carry out those schemes which he entertained when he was poor. Christ answered the Herodians according to their condition. "Show me the tribute money," said he—and one took a penny out of his pocket. If you use money which has the image of Caesar on it, and which he has made current and valuable, that is, *if you are men of the state*, and gladly enjoy the advantages of Caesar's government, then pay him back some of his own when he demands it; "Render therefore to Caesar that which is Caesar's, and to God those things which are God's"—leaving them no wiser than before as to which was which; for they did not wish to know.

When I converse with the freest of my neighbors, I perceive that, whatever they may say about the magnitude and seriousness of the question, and their regard for the public tranquillity, the long and the short of the matter is that they cannot spare the protection of the existing government, and they dread the consequences of disobedience to it to their property and families. For my own part, I should not like to think that I ever rely on the protection of the state. But, if I deny the authority of the state when it presents its tax bill, it will soon take and waste all my property, and so harass me and my children without end. This is hard. This makes it impossible for a man to live honestly and at the same time comfortably in outward respects. It will not be worth the while to accumulate property; that would be sure to go again. You must hire or squat somewhere, and raise but a small crop, and eat that soon. You must live within yourself and depend upon yourself, always tucked up and ready for a start, and not have many affairs.

A man may grow rich in Turkey even, if he will be in all respects a good subject of the Turkish government. Confucius said: "If a state is governed by the principles of reason, poverty and misery are subjects of shame; if a state is not governed by the principles of reason, riches and honors are the subjects of shame." No; until I want the protection of Massachusetts to be extended to me in some distant southern port, where my liberty is endangered, or until I am bent solely on building up an estate at home by peaceful enterprise, I can afford to refuse allegiance to Massachusetts and her right to my property and life. It costs me less in every sense to incur the penalty of disobedience to the state than it would to obey. I should feel as if I were worth less in that case.

Some years ago the state met me in behalf of the church and commanded me to pay a certain sum toward the support of a clergyman whose preaching my father attended but never I myself. "Pay it," it said, "or be locked up in the jail." I declined to pay. But, unfortunately, another man saw fit to pay it. I did not see why the schoolmaster shuld be taxed to support the priest, and not the priest the schoolmaster; for I was not the state's schoolmaster, but I supported myself by voluntary subscription. I did not see why the lyceum should not present its tax bill, and have the state to back its demand, as well as the church. However, at the request of the selectmen, I condescended to make some such statement as this in writing: "Know all men by these presents, that I, Henry Thoreau, do not wish to be regarded as a member of any incorporated society which I have not joined." This I gave to the town clerk; and he has it. The state, having thus learned that I did not wish to be regarded as a member of that church, has never made a like demand on me since, though it said that it must adhere to its original presumption that time. If I had known how to name them, I should then have signed off in detail from all the societies which I never signed on to; but I did not know where to find a complete list.

I have paid no poll tax for six years. I was put into a jail once on this account, for one night; and, as I stood considering the walls of solid stone, two or three feet thick, the door of wood and iron, a foot thick, and the iron grating which strained the light, I could not help being struck with the foolishness of that institution which treated me as if I were mere flesh and blood and bones to be locked up. I wondered that it should have concluded at length that this was the best use it could put me to and had never thought to avail itself of my services in some way. I saw that, if there was a wall of stone between me and my townsmen, there was a still more difficult one to climb or break through before they could get to be as free as I was. I did not for a moment feel confined, and the walls seemed a great waste of stone and mortar. I felt as if I alone of all my townsmen had paid my tax. They plainly did not know how to treat me but behaved like persons who are underbred. In every threat and in every compliment there was a blunder, for they thought that my chief desire was to stand the other side of that stone wall. I could not but smile to see how industriously they locked the door on my meditations, which followed them out again without let or hinderance, and *they* were really all that was dangerous. As they could not reach me, they had resolved to punish my body; just as boys, if they cannot come at some person against whom they have a spite, will abuse his dog. I saw that the state was half-witted, that it was timid as a lone woman with her silver spoons, and that it did not know its friends from its foes, and I lost all my remaining respect for it and pitied it.

Thus the state never intentionally confronts a man's sense, intellectual or moral, but only his body, his senses. It is not armed with superior wit or honesty but with superior physical strength. I was not born to be forced. I will breathe after my own fashion. Let us see who is the strongest. What force has a multitude? They only can force me who obey a higher law than I. They force me to become like themselves. I do not hear of *men* being *forced* to live this way or that by masses of men. What sort of life were that to live? When I meet a government which says to me, "Your money or your life," why should I be in haste to give it my money? It may be in a great strait and not know what to do; I cannot help that. It must help itself; do as I do. It is not worth the while to snivel about it. I am not responsible for the successful working of the machinery of society. I am not the son of the engineer. I perceive that, when an acorn and a chestnut fall side by side, the one does not remain inert to make way for the other, but both obey their own laws, and spring and grow and flourish as best they can, till one, perchance, over-shadows and destroys the other. If a plant cannot live according to its nature, it dies; and so a man.

The night in prison was novel and interesting enough. The prisoners in their shirt sleeves were enjoying a chat and the evening air in the doorway when I entered. But the jailer said, "Come, boys, it is time to lock up"; and so they dispersed, and I heard the sound of their steps returning into the hollow apartments. My room mate was introduced to me by the jailer as "a first-rate fellow and a clever man." When the door was locked, he showed me where to hang my hat, and how he managed matters there. The rooms were whitewashed once a month; and this one, at least, was the whitest, most simply furnished, and probably the neatest apartment in the town. He naturally wanted to know where I came from and what brought me there; and, when I had told him, I asked him in my turn how he came there, presuming him to be an honest man, of course; and, as the world goes, I believe he was. "Why," said he, "they accuse me of burning a barn; but I never did it." As near as I could discover, he had probably gone to bed in a barn when drunk, and smoked his pipe there; and so a barn was burned. He had the reputation of being a clever man, had been there some three months waiting for his trial to come on, and would have to wait as much longer; but he was quite domesticated and contented, since he got his board for nothing and thought that he was well treated.

He occupied one window, and I the other; and I saw, that, if one stayed there long, his principal business would be to look out the window. I had soon read all the tracts that were left there and examined where former prisoners had broken out, and where a grate had been sawed off, and heard the history of the various occupants of that room; for I found that even here there was a history and a gossip which never circulated beyond the walls of the jail. Probably this is the only house in the town where verses are composed, which are afterward printed in a circular form, but not published. I was shown quite a long list of verses which were composed by some young men who had been detected in an attempt to escape who avenged themselves by singing them.

I pumped my fellow-prisoner as dry as I could, for fear I should never see him again; but at length he showed me which was my bed and left me to blow out the lamp.

It was like traveling into a far country, such as I had never expected to behold, to lie there for one night. It seemed to me that I never had heard the town clock strike before, nor the evening sounds of the village; for we slept with the windows open, which were inside the grating. It was to see my native village in the light of the Middle Ages, and our Concord was turned into a Rhine stream, and visions of knights and castles passed before me. They were the voices of old burghers that I heard in the streets. I was an involuntary spectator and auditor of whatever was done and said in the kitchen of the adjacent village inn—a wholly new and rare experience to me. It was a closer view of my native town. I was fairly inside of it. I never had seen its institutions before. This is one of its peculiar institutions, for it is a shire town. I began to comprehend what its inhabitants were about.

In the morning our breakfasts were put through the hole in the door, in small oblong-square tin pans, made to fit, and holding a pint of chocolate, with brown bread, and an iron spoon. When they called for the vessels again, I was green enough to return what bread I had left; but my comrade seized it and said that I should lay that up for lunch or dinner. Soon after, he was let out to work at haying in a neighboring field, whither he went every day; so he bade me goodday, saying that he doubted if he should see me again.

When I came out of prison—for someone interfered and paid the tax—I did not perceive that great changes had taken place on the common, such as he observed who went in a youth and emerged a tottering and gray-headed man; and yet a change had to my eyes come over the scene—the town, and state, and country—greater than any that mere time could effect. I saw yet more distinctly the state in which I lived. I saw to what extent the people among whom I lived could be trusted as good neighbors and friends; that their friendship was for summer weather only; that they did not greatly purpose to do right; that they were a distinct race from me by their prejudices and superstitions, as the Chinamen and Malays are; that, in their sacrifices to humanity, they ran no risks, not even to their property; that, after all, they were not so noble but they treated the thief as he had treated them, and hoped, by a certain outward observance and a few prayers, and by walking in a particular straight though useless path from time to time, to save their souls. This may be to judge my neighbors harshly; for I believe that most of them are not aware that they have such an institution as the jail in their village.

It was formerly the custom in our village, when a poor debtor came out of jail, for his acquaintances to salute him looking through their fingers, which were crossed to represent the grating of a jail window, "How do ye do?" My neighbors did not thus salute me but first looked at me, and then at one another, as if I had returned from a long journey. I was put into jail as I was going to the shoemaker's to get a shoe which was mended. When I was let out the next morning, I proceeded to finish my errand, and, having put on my mended shoe, joined a huckleberry party, who were impatient to put themselves under my conduct; and in half an hour—for the horse was soon tackled—was in the midst of a huckleberry field, on one of our highest hills, two miles off; and then the state was nowhere to be seen.

This is the whole history of "My Prisons."

I have never declined paying the highway tax, because I am as desirous of being a good neighbor as I am of being a bad subject; and, as for supporting schools, I am doing my part to educate my fellow-countrymen now. It is for no particular item in the tax bill that I refuse to pay it. I simply wish to refuse allegiance to the state, to withdraw and stand aloof from it effectually. I do not care to trace the course of my dollar, if I could, till it buys a man, or a musket to shoot one with—the dollar is innocent—but I am concerned to trace the effects of my allegiance. In fact, I quietly declare war with the state, after my fashion, though I will still make what use and get what adventure of her I can, as is usual in such cases.

If others pay the tax which is demanded of me, from a sympathy with the state, they do but what they have already done in their own case, or rather they abet injustice to a greater extent than the state requires. If they pay the tax from a mistaken interest in the individual taxed, to save his property or prevent his going to jail, it is because they have not considered wisely how far they let their private feelings interfere with the public good.

This, then, is my position at present. But one cannot be too much on his guard in such a case, lest his action be biased by obstinacy or an undue regard for the opinions of men. Let him see that he does only what belongs to himself and to the hour.

I think sometimes: Why, this people mean well; they are only ignorant; they would do better if they knew how; why give your neighbors this pain to treat you as they are not inclined to? But I think, again, this is no reason why I should do as they do or permit others to suffer much greater pain of a different kind. Again, I sometimes say to myself: When many millions of men, without heat, without ill-will, without personal feeling of any kind, demand of you a few shillings only, without the possibility, such is their constitution, of retracting or altering their present demand, and without the possibility, on your side, of appeal to any other millions, why expose yourself to this overwhelming brute force? You do not resist cold and hunger, the winds and the waves, thus obstinately; you quietly submit to a thousand similar necessities. You do not put your head into the fire. But just in proportion as I regard this as not wholly a brute force, but partly a human force, and consider that I have relations to those millions as to so many millions of men, and not of mere brute or inanimate things, I see that appeal is possible, first and instantaneously, from them to the Maker of them, and secondly, from them to themselves. But, if I put my head deliberately into the fire, there is no appeal to fire or to the Maker of fire, and I have only myself to blame. If I could convince myself that I have any right to be satisfied with men as they are, and to treat them accordingly, and not according, in some respects, to my requisitions and expectations of what they and I ought to be, then, like a good Mussulman and fatalist, I should endeavor to be satisfied with things as they are, and say it is the will of God. And, above all, there is this difference between resisting this and a purely brute or natural force—that I can resist this with some effect; but I cannot expect, like Orpheus, to change the nature of the rocks and trees and beasts.

I do not wish to quarrel with any man or nation. I do not wish to split hairs, to make fine distinctions, or set myself up as better than my neighbors. I seek rather, I may say, even an excuse for conforming to the laws of the land. I am but too ready to conform to them. Indeed, I have reason to suspect myself on this head; and each year, as the tax-gatherer comes round, I find myself disposed to review the acts and position of the general and state governments, and the spirit of the people, to discover a pretext for conformity. I believe that the state will soon be able to take all my work of this sort out of my hands, and then I shall be no better a patriot than my fellow-countrymen. Seen from a lower point of view, the Constitution, with all its faults, is very good; the law and the courts are very respectable; even this state and this American government are, in many respects, very admirable and rare things, to be thankful for, such as a great many have described them; but seen from a point of view a little higher, they are what I have described them; seen from a higher still, and the highest, who shall say what they are, or that they are worth looking at or thinking of at all?

However, the government does not concern me much, and I shall bestow the fewest possible thoughts on it. It is not many moments that I live under a government, even in this world. If a man is thought-free, fancy-free, imagination-free, that which *is not* never for a long time appearing *to be* to him, unwise rulers or reformers cannot fatally interrupt him.

I know that most men think differently from myself; but those whose lives are by profession devoted to the study of these or kindred subjects content me as little as any. Statesmen and legislators, standing so completely within the institution, never distinctly and nakedly behold it. They speak of moving society but have no resting-place without it. They may be men of a certain experience and discrimination, and have no doubt invented ingenious and even useful systems, for which we sincerely thank them; but all their wit and usefulness lie within certain not very wide limits. They are wont to forget that the world is not governed by policy and expediency. Webster never goes behind government and so cannot speak with authority about it. His words are wisdom to those legislators who contemplate no essential reform in the existing government; but for thinkers, and those who legislate for all time, he never once glances at the subject. I know of those whose serene and wise speculations on this theme would soon reveal the limits of his mind's range and hospitality. Yet, compared with the cheap professions of most reformers, and the still cheaper wisdom and eloquence of politicians in general, his are almost the only sensible and valuable words, and we thank Heaven for him. Comparatively, he is always strong, original, and, above all, practical. Still his quality is not wisdom but prudence. The lawyer's truth is not Truth, but consistency, or a consistent expediency. Truth is always in harmony with herself and is not concerned chiefly to reveal the justice that may consist with wrongdoing. He well deserves to be called, as he has been called, the Defender of the Constitution. There are really no blows to be given by him but defensive ones. He is not a leader but a follower. His leaders are the men of '87. "I have never made an effort," he says, "and never propose to make an effort; I have never countenanced an effort, and never mean to countenance an effort, to disturb the arrangement as originally made, by which the various states came into the Union." Still thinking of the sanction which the Constitution gives to slavery, he says, "Because it was a part of the original compact—let it stand." Notwithstanding his special acuteness and ability, he is unable to take a fact out of its merely political relations and behold it as it lies absolutely to be disposed of by the intellect—what, for instance, it behooves a man to do here in America today with regard to slavery, but ventures, or is driven, to make some such desperate answer as the following, while professing to speak absolutely, and as a private man—from which what new and singular code of social duties might be inferred? "The manner," says he, "in which the government of those states where slavery exists are to regulate it is for their own consideration, under their responsibility to their constituents, to the general laws of propriety, humanity, and justice, and to God. Associations formed elsewhere, springing from a feeling of humanity, or any other cause, have nothing whatever to do with it. They have never received any encouragement from me, and they never will."

They who know of no purer sources of truth, who have traced up its stream no higher, stand, and wisely stand, by the Bible and the Constitution, and drink at it there with reverence and humility; but they who behold where it comes trickling into this lake or that pool gird up their loins once more and continue their pilgrimage toward its fountainhead.

No man with a genius for legislation has appeared in America. They are rare in the history of the world. There are orators, politicians, and eloquent men by the thousand; but the speaker has not yet opened his mouth to speak who is capable of settling the much-vexed questions of the day. We love eloquence for its own sake and not for any truth which it may utter or any heroism it may inspire. Our legislators have not yet learned the comparative value of free trade and of freedom, of union, and of rectitude, to a nation. They have no genius or talent for comparatively humble questions of taxation and finance, commerce and manufactures and agriculture. If we were left solely to the wordy wit of legislators in Congress for our guidance, uncorrected by the seasonable experience and the effectual complaints of the people, America would not long retain her rank among the nations. For eighteen hundred years, though perchance I have no right to say it, the New Testament has been written; yet where is the legislator who has wisdom and practical talent enough to avail himself of the light which it sheds on the science of legislation?

The authority of government, even such as I am willing to submit to— for I will cheerfully obey those who know and can do better than I, and in many things even those who neither know nor can do so well—is still an impure one; to be strictly just, it must have the sanction and consent of the governed. It can have no pure right over my person and property but what I concede to it. The progress from an absolute to a limited monarchy, from a limited monarchy to a democracy, is a progress toward a true respect for the individual. Is a democracy, such as we know it, the last improvement possible in government? Is it not possible to take a step further toward recognizing and organizing the rights of man? There will never be a really free and enlightened state, until the state comes to recognize the individual as a higher and independent power, from which all its own power and authority are derived, and treats him accordingly. I please myself with imagining a state at last which can afford to be just to all men and to treat the individual with respect as a neighbor, which even would not think it inconsistent with its own repose if a few were to live aloof from it, not meddling with it, nor embraced by it, who fulfilled all the duties of neighbors and fellowmen. A state which bore this kind of fruit, and suffered it to drop off as fast as it ripened, would prepare the way for a still more perfect and glorious state, which also I have imagined, but not yet anywhere seen.

Indian Home Rule

by Mohandas K. Gandhi

READER: I cannot follow this. There seems little doubt that we shall have to expel the English by force of arms. So long as they are in the country we cannot rest. . . .

Editor: . . . I believe that you want the millions of India to be happy, not that you [merely] want the reins of government in your hands. If that be so, we have to consider only one thing: how can the millions obtain self-rule? You will admit that people under several Indian princes are being ground down. The latter mercilessly crush them. Their tyranny is greater than that of the English, and if you want such tyranny in India, then we shall never agree. My patriotism does not teach me that I am to allow people to be crushed under the heel of Indian princes if only the English retire. If I have power, I should resist the tyranny of Indian princes just as much as that of the English. By patriotism I mean the welfare of the whole people, and if I could secure it at the hands of the English, I should bow down my head to them. If any Englishman dedicated his life to securing the freedom of India, resisting tyranny, and serving the land, I should welcome that Englishman as an Indian.

Again [you say that] India can fight. . . only when she has arms. You have not considered this problem at all. The English are splendidly armed; that does not frighten me, but it is clear that, to pit ourselves against them in arms, thousands of Indians must be armed. If such a thing be possible, how many years will it take? Moreover, to arm India on a large scale is to Europeanize it. Then her condition will be just as pitiable as that of Europe. This means, in short, that India must accept European civilization, and if that is what we want, the best thing is that we have among us those who are so well trained in that civilization. We will then fight for a few rights, will get what we can and so pass our days. But the fact is that the Indian nation will not adopt arms, and it is well that it does not.

Introducing the concept of "soul-force" or "passive resistance," Gandhi argued that it was the only method by which home rule could be regained.

Thousands, indeed tens of thousands, depend for their existence on a very active working of this force. Little quarrels of millions of families in their daily lives disappear before the exercise of this force. Hundreds of nations live in peace. History does not and cannot take note of this fact. History is really a record of every interruption of the even working of the force of love or of the soul. Two brothers quarrel; one of them repents and reawakens the love that was lying dormant in him; the two again begin to live in peace; nobody takes note of this. But if the two brothers, through the intervention of solicitors or some other reason, take up arms or go to law—which is another form of the exhibition of brute force—their doings would be immediately noticed in the press, they would be the talk of their neighbors and would probably go down to history. And what is true of families and communities is true of nations. There is no reason to believe that there is one law for families and another for nations. History, then, is a record of an interruption of the course of nature. Soul-force, being natural, is not noted in history.

Reader: According to what you say, it is plain that instances of this kind of passive resistance are not to be found in history. It is necessary to understand this passive resistance more fully. It will be better, therefore, if you enlarge upon it.

Editor: Passive resistance is a method of securing rights by personal suffering; it is the reverse of resistance by arms. When I refuse to do a thing that is repugnant to my conscience, I use soul-force. For instance, the government of the day has passed a law which is applicable to me. I do not like it. If by using violence I force the government to repeal the law, I am employing what may be termed body-force. If I do not obey the law and accept the penalty for its breach, I use soul-force. It involves sacrifice of self.

Everybody admits that sacrifice of self is infinitely superior to sacrifice of others. Moreover, if this kind of force is used in a cause that is unjust, only the person using it suffers. He does not make others suffer for his mistakes. Men have before now done many things which were subsequently found to have been wrong. No man can claim that he is absolutely in the right or that a particular thing is wrong because he thinks so, but it is wrong for him so long as that is his deliberate judgment. It is therefore meet that he should not do that which he knows to be wrong, and suffer the consequence whatever it may be. This is the key to the use of soul-force.

Reader: You would then disregard laws—this is rank disloyalty. We have always been considered a law-abiding nation. You seem to be going even beyond the extremists. They say that we must obey the laws that have been passed, but that if the laws be bad, we must drive out the lawgivers even by force.

Editor: Whether I go beyond them or whether I do not is a matter of no consequence to either of us. We simply want to find out what is right and to act accordingly. The real meaning of the statement that we are a law-abiding nation is that we are passive resisters. When we do not like certain laws, we do not break the heads of law-givers but we suffer and do not submit to the laws. That we should obey laws whether good or bad is a new-fangled notion. There was no such thing in former days. The people disregarded those laws they did not like and suffered the penalties for their breach. It is contrary to our manhood if we obey laws repugnant to our conscience. Such teaching is opposed to religion and means slavery. If the government were to ask us to go about without any clothing, should we do so? If I were a passive resister, I would say to them that I would have nothing to do with their law. But we have so forgotten ourselves and become so compliant that we do not mind any degrading law.

A man who has realized his manhood, who fears only God, will fear no one else. Man-made laws are not necessarily binding on him. Even the government does not expect any such thing from us. They do not say: "You must do such and such a thing," but they say: "If you do not do it, we will punish you." We are sunk so low that we fancy that it is our duty and our religion to do what the law lays down. If man will only realize that it is unmanly to obey laws that are unjust, no man's tyranny will enslave him. This is the key to self-rule or home-rule.

It is a superstition and ungodly thing to believe that an act of a majority binds a minority. Many examples can be given in which acts of majorities will be found to have been wrong and those of minorities to have been right. All reforms owe their origin to the initiation of minorities in opposition to majorities. If among a band of robbers a knowledge of robbing is obligatory, is a pious man to accept the obligation? So long as the superstition that men should obey unjust laws exists, so long will their slavery exist. And a passive resister alone can remove such a superstition.

To use brute-force, to use gun-powder, is contrary to passive resistance, for it means that we want our opponent to do by force that which we desire but he does not. And if such a use of force is justifiable, surely he is entitled to do likewise by us. And so we should never come to an agreement. We may simply fancy, like the blind horse moving in a circle round a mill, that we are making progress. Those who believe that they are not bound to obey laws which are repugnant to their conscience have only the remedy of passive resistance open to them. Any other must lead to disaster.

Reader: From what you say I deduce that passive resistance is a splendid weapon of the weak, but that when they are strong they may take up arms.

Editor: This is gross ignorance. Passive resistance, that is, soul-force, is matchless. It is superior to the force of arms. How, then, can it be considered only a weapon of the weak? Physical-force men are strangers to the courage that is requisite in a passive resister. Do you believe that a coward can ever disobey a law that he dislikes? Extremists are considered to be advocates of brute force. Why do they, then, talk about obeying laws? I do not blame them. They can say nothing else. When they succeed in driving out the English and they themselves become governors, they will want you and me to obey their laws. And that is a fitting thing for their constitution.

But a passive resister will say he will not obey a law that is against his conscience, even though he may be blown to pieces at the mouth of a cannon.

What do you think? Wherein is courage required—in blowing others to pieces from behind a cannon, or with a smiling face to approach a cannon and be blown to pieces? Who is the true warrior—he who keeps death always as a bosom-friend, or he who controls the death of others? Believe me that a man devoid of courage and manhood can never be a passive resister.

This, however, I will admit: that even a man weak in body is capable of offering this resistance. One man can offer it just as well as millions. Both men and women can indulge in it. It does not require the training of an army; it needs no jiu-jitsu. Control over the mind is alone necessary, and when that is attained, man is free like the king of the forest and his very glance withers the enemy.

Passive resistance is an all-sided sword, it can be used anyhow; it blesses him who uses it and him against whom it is used. Without drawing a drop of blood it produces far-reaching results. It never rusts and cannot be stolen. Competition between passive resisters does not exhaust. The sword of passive resistance does not require a scabbard. It is strange indeed that you should consider such a weapon to be a weapon merely of the weak.

Reader: You have said that passive resistance is a specialty of India. Have cannons never been used in India?

Editor: Evidently, in your opinion, India means its few princes. To me it means its teeming millions on whom depends the existence of its princes and our own.

Kings will always use their kingly weapons. To use force is bred in them. They want to command, but those who have to obey commands do not want guns: and these are in a majority throughout the world. They have to learn either body-force or soul-force. Where they learn the former, both the rulers and the ruled become like so many madmen; but where they learn soul-force, the commands of the rulers do not go beyond the point of their swords, for true men disregard unjust commands. Peasants have never been subdued by the sword, and never will be. They do not know the use of the sword, and they are not frightened by the use of it by others. That nation is great which rests its head upon death as its pillow. Those who defy death are free from all fear. For those who are laboring under the delusive charms of brute-force, this picture is not overdrawn. The fact is that, in India, the nation at large has generally used passive resistance in all departments of life. We cease to cooperate with our rulers when they displease us. This is passive resistance.

I remember an instance when, in a small principality, the villagers were offended by some command issued by the prince. The former immediately began vacating the village. The prince became nervous, apologized to his subjects, and withdrew his command. Many such instances can be found in India. Real Home Rule is possible only where passive resistance is the guiding force of the people. Any other rule is foreign rule.

Reader: Then you will say that it is not at all necessary for us to train the body?

Editor: I will certainly not say any such thing. It is difficult to become a passive resister unless the body is trained. As a rule, the mind, residing in a body that has become weakened by pampering, is also weak, and where there is no strength of mind there can be no strength of soul. We shall have to improve our physique by getting rid of infant marriages and luxurious living. If I were to ask a man with a shattered body to face a cannon's mouth I should make a laughing-stock of myself.

Reader: From what you say, then, it would appear that it is not a small thing to become a passive resister, and, if that is so, I should like you to explain how a man may become one.

Reader: To become a passive resister is easy enough but it is also equally difficult. I have known a lad of fourteen years become a passive resister; I have known also sick people to do likewise; and I have also known physically strong and otherwise happy people unable to take up passive resistance. After a great deal of experience it seems to me that those who want to be passive resisters for the service of the country have to observe perfect chastity, adopt poverty, follow truth, and cultivate fearlessness.

Chastity is one of the greatest disciplines without which the mind cannot attain requisite firmness. A man who is unchaste loses stamina, becomes emasculated and cowardly. He whose mind is given over to animal passions is not capable of any great effort. This can be proved by innumerable instances. What, then, is a married person to do is the question that arises naturally; and yet it need not. When a husband and wife gratify the passions, it is less an animal indulgence on that account. Such an indulgence, except for perpetuating the race, is strictly prohibited. But a passive resister has to avoid even that very limited indulgence because he can have no desire for progeny. A married man, therefore, can observe perfect chastity. This subject is not capable of being treated at greater length. Several questions arise: How is one to carry one's wife with one? what are her rights? and other similar questions. Yet those who wish to take part in a great work are bound to solve these puzzles.

Just as there is necessity for chastity, so is there for poverty. Pecuniary ambition and passive resistance cannot well go together. Those who have money are not expected to throw it away, but they *are* expected to be indifferent about it. They must be prepared to lose every penny rather than give up passive resistance.

Passive resistance has been described in the course of our discussion as truth-force. Truth, therefore, has necessarily to be followed and that at any cost. In this connection, academic questions such as whether a man may not lie in order to save a life, etc., arise, but these questions occur only to those who wish to justify living. Those who want to follow truth every time are not placed in such a quandry; and if they are, they are still saved from a false position.

Passive resistance cannot proceed a step without fearlessness. Those alone can follow the path of passive resistance who are free from fear, whether as to their possessions, false honor, their relatives, the government, bodily injuries or death.

These observances are not to be abandoned in the belief that they are difficult. Nature has implanted in the human breast ability to cope with any difficulty or suffering that may come to man unprovoked. These qualities are worth having, even for those who do not wish to serve the country. Let there be no mistake, as those who want to train themselves in the use of arms are also obliged to have these qualities more or less. Everybody does not become a warrior for the wish. A would-be warrior will have to observe chastity and to be satisfied with poverty as his lot. A warrior without fearlessness cannot be conceived of. It may be thought that he would not need to be exactly truthful, but that quality follows real fearlessness. When a man abandons truth, he does so owing to fear in some shape or form. The above four attributes, then, need not frighten anyone. It may be as well here to note that a physical-force man has to have many other useless qualities which a passive resister never needs. And you will find that whatever extra effort a swordsman needs is due to lack of fearlessness. If he is an embodiment of the latter, the sword will drop from his hand that very moment. He does not need its support. One who is free from hatred requires no sword. A man with a stick suddenly came face to face with a lion and instinctively raised his weapon in self-defense. The man saw that he had only prated about fearlessness when there was none in him. That moment he dropped the stick and found himself free from all fear.

In the manner of a lawyer summing up his brief, Gandhi reduced his argument to its essentials in this final portion of Hind Swaraj. *After his prophetic last sentence, he appended a list of twenty authoritative books, eighteen of them by Europeans, and eight testimonies to the superiority of Indian civilization, all of them by Englishmen.*

Reader: What, then, would you say to the English?

Editor: To them I would respectfully say: "I admit you are my rulers. It is not necessary to debate the question whether you hold India by the sword or by my consent. I have no objection to your remaining in my country, but although you are the rulers, you will have to remain as servants of the people. It is not we who have to do as you wish, but it is you who have to do as we wish. You may keep the riches that you have drained away from this land, but you may not drain riches henceforth. Your function will be, if you so wish, to police India; you must abandon the idea of deriving any commercial benefit from us. We hold the civilization that you support to be the reverse of civilization. We consider our civilization to be far superior to yours. If you realize this truth, it will be to your advantage and, if you do not, according to your own proverb, you should only live in our country in the same manner as we do. You must not do anything that is contrary to our religions. It is your duty as rulers that for the sake of the Hindus you should eschew beef, and for the sake of Mahomedans you should avoid bacon and ham. We have hitherto said nothing because we have been cowed down, but you need not consider that you have not hurt our feelings by your conduct. We are not expressing our sentiments either through base selfishness or fear, but because it is our duty now to speak out boldly. We consider your schools and law courts to be useless. We want our own ancient schools and courts to be restored. The common language of India is not English but Hindi. You should, therefore, learn it. We can hold communication with you only in our national language.

"We cannot tolerate the idea of your spending money on railways and the military. We see no occasion for either. You may fear Russia;[1] we do not. When she comes we shall look after her. If you are with us, we may then receive her jointly. We do not need any European cloth. We shall manage with articles produced and manufactured at home. You may not keep one eye on Manchester and the other on India. We can work together only if our interests are identical.

"This has not been said to you in arrogance. You have great military resources. Your naval power is matchless. If we wanted to fight with you on your own ground, we should be unable to do so, but if the above submissions be not acceptable to you, we cease to play the part of the ruled. You may, if you like, cut us to pieces. You may shatter us at the cannon's mouth. If you act contrary to our will, we shall not help you; and without our help, we know that you cannot move one step forward.

"It is likely that you will laugh at all this in the intoxication of your power. We may not be able to disillusion you at once; but if there be any manliness in us, you will see shortly that your intoxication is suicidal and that your laugh at our expense is an aberration of intellect. We believe that at heart you belong to a religious nation. We are living in a land which is the source of religions. How we came together need not be considered, but we can make mutual good use of our relations.

"You English who have come to India are not good specimens of the English nation, nor can we, almost half-Anglicized Indians, be considered good specimens of the real Indian nation. If the English nation were to know all you have done, it would oppose many of your actions. The mass of the Indians have had few dealings with you. If you will abandon your so-called civilization and search into your own scriptures, you will find that our demands are just. Only on condition of our demands being fully satisfied may you remain in India; and if you remain under those conditions, we shall learn several things from you and you will learn many from us. So doing we shall benefit each other and the world. But that will happen only when the root of our relationship is sunk in a religious soil."

Reader: What will you say to the nation?

Editor: Who is the nation?

Reader: For our purposes it is the nation that you and I have been thinking of, that is, those of us who are affected by European civilization, and who are eager to have Home Rule.

Editor: To these I would say: "It is only those Indians who are imbued with real love who will be able to speak to the English in the above strain without being frightened, and only those can be said to be so imbued who conscientiously believe that Indian civilization is the best and that the European is a nine-days' wonder. Such ephemeral civilizations have often come and gone and will continue to do so. Those only can be considered to be so imbued who, having experienced the force of the soul within themselves, will not cower before brute-force, and will not, on any account, desire to use brute-force. Those only can be considered to have been so imbued who are intensely dissatisfied with the prsent pitiable condition, having already drunk the cup of poison.

If there be only one such Indian, he will speak as above to the English and the English will have to listen to him."

Reader: This is a large order. When will all carry it out?

Editor: You make a mistake. You and I have nothing to do with the others. Let each do his duty. If I do my duty, that is, serve myself, I shall be able to serve others. Before I leave you, I will take the liberty of repeating:

1. Real home rule is self-rule or self-control.

2. The way to it is passive resistance: that is soul-force or love-force.

3. In order to exert this force, Swadeshi in every sense is necessary.

4. What we want to do should be done, not because we object to the English or because we want to retaliate, but because it is our duty to do so. Thus, supposing that the English remove the salt-tax, restore our money, give the highest posts to Indians, withdraw the English troops, we shall certainly not use their machine-made goods, nor use the English language, nor many of their industries. It is worth noting that these things are, in their nature, harmful; hence we do not want them. I bear no enmity towards the English but I do towards their civilization.

In my opinion, we have used the term *Swaraj* without understanding its real significance. I have endeavored to explain it as I understand it, and my conscience testifies that my life henceforth is dedicated to its attainment.

---

[1] Russia's conquest of Central Asia in the latter half of the nineteenth century had alarmed the British, who feared a possible invasion of India through Afghanistan.

Letter From Birmingham City Jail

by Martin Luther King, Jr.

The following is the public statement directed to Martin Luther King, Jr., by eight Alabama clergymen.

WE the undersigned clergymen are among those who, in January, issued "An Appeal for Law and Order and Common Sense," in dealing with racial problems in Alabama. We expressed understanding that honest convictions in racial matters could properly be pursued in the courts, but urged that decisions of those courts should in the meantime be peacefully obeyed.

Since that time there had been some evidence of increased forbearance and a willingness to face facts. Responsible citizens have undertaken to work on various problems which cause racial friction and unrest. In Birmingham, recent public events have given indication that we all have opportunity for a new constructive and realistic approach to racial problems.

However, we are now confronted by a series of demonstrations by some of our Negro citizens, directed and led in part by outsiders. We recognize the natural impatience of people who feel that their hopes are slow in being realized. But we are convinced that these demonstrations are unwise and untimely.

We agree rather with certain local Negro leadership which has called for honest and open negotiation of racial issues in our area. And we believe this kind of facing of issues can best be accomplished by citizens of our own metropolitan area, white and Negro, meeting with their knowledge and experience of the local situation. All of us need to face that responsibility and find proper channels for its accomplishment.

Just as we formerly pointed out that "hatred and violence have no sanction in our religious and political traditions," we also point out that such actions as incite to hatred and violence, however technically peaceful those actions may be, have not contributed to the resolution of our local problems. We do not believe that these days of new hope are days when extreme measures are justified in Birmingham.

We commend the community as a whole, and the local news media and law enforcement officials in particular, on the calm manner in which these demonstrations have been handled. We urge the public to continue to show restraint should the demonstrations continue, and the law enforcement officials to remain calm and continue to protect our city from violence.

We further strongly urge our own Negro community to withdraw support from these demonstrations, and to unite locally in working peacefully for a better Birmingham. When rights are consistently denied, a cause should be pressed in the courts and in negotiations among local leaders, and not in the streets. We appeal to both our white and Negro citizenry to observe the principles of law and order and common sense.

> *Bishop C. C. J. Carpenter, Bishop Joseph A. Durick, Rabbi Milton L. Grafman, Bishop Paul Hardin, Bishop Nolan B. Harmon, Rev. George M. Murray, Rev. Edward V. Ramage, Rev. Earl Stallings.*

April 12, 1963

MY dear Fellow Clergymen,

While confined here in the Birmingham City Jail, I came across your recent statement calling our present activities "unwise and untimely." Seldom, if ever, do I pause to answer criticism of my work and ideas. If I sought to answer all of the criticisms that cross my desk, my secretaries would be engaged in little else in the course of the day, and I would have no time for constructive work. But since I feel that you are men of genuine goodwill and your criticisms are sincerely set forth, I would like to answer your statement in what I hope will be patient and reasonable terms.

I think I should give the reason for my being in Birmingham, since you have been influenced by the argument of "outsiders coming in." I have the honor of serving as president of the Southern Christian Leadership Conference, an organization operating in every Southern state, with headquarters in Atlanta, Georgia. We have some eighty-five affiliate organizations all across the South—one being the Alabama Christian Movement for Human Rights. Whenever necessary and possible we share staff, educational and financial resources with our affiliates. Several months ago our local affiliate here in Birmingham invited us to be on call to engage in a nonviolent direct action program if such were deemed necessary. We readily consented and when the hour came we lived up to our promises. So I am here, along with several members of my staff, because we were invited here. I am here because I have basic organizational ties here.

Beyond this, I am in Birmingham because injustice is here. Just as the eighth century prophets left their little villages and carried their "thus saith the Lord" far beyond the boundaries of their home towns; and just as the Apostle Paul left his little village of Tarsus and carried the gospel of Jesus Christ to practically every hamlet and city of the Graeco-Roman world, I too am compelled to carry the gospel of freedom beyond my particular home town. Like Paul, I must constantly respond to the Macedonian call for aid.

Moreover, I am cognizant of the interrelatedness of all communities and states. I cannot sit idly by in Atlanta and not be concerned about what happens in Birmingham. Injustice anywhere is a threat to justice everywhere. We are caught in an inescapable network of mutuality, tied in a single garment of destiny. Whatever affects one directly affects all indirectly. Never again can we afford to live with the narrow, provincial "outside agitator" idea. Anyone who lives inside the United States can never be considered an outsider anywhere in this country.

You deplore the demonstrations that are presently taking place in Birmingham. But I am sorry that your statement did not express a similar concern for the conditions that brought the demonstrations into being. I am sure that each of you would want to go beyond the superficial social analyst who looks merely at effects, and does not grapple with underlying causes. I would not hesitate to say that it is unfortunate that so-called demonstrations are taking place in Birmingham at this time, but I would say in even more emphatic terms that it is even more unfortunate that the white power structure of this city left the Negro community with no other alternative.

In any nonviolent campaign there are four basic steps: 1) Collection of the facts to determine whether injustices are alive. 2) Negotiation. 3) Self-purification and 4) Direct Action. We have gone through all of these steps in Birmingham. There can be no gainsaying of the fact that racial injustice engulfs this community.

Birmingham is probably the most thoroughly segregated city in the United States. Its ugly record of police brutality is known in every section of this country. Its unjust treatment of Negroes in the courts is a notorious reality. There have been more unsolved bombings of Negro homes and churches in Birmingham than any city in this nation. These are the hard, brutal and unbelievable facts. On the basis of these conditions Negro leaders sought to negotiate with the city fathers. But the political leaders consistently refused to engage in good faith negotiation.

Then came the opportunity last September to talk with some of the leaders of the economic community. In these negotiating sessions certain promises were made by the merchants—such as the promise to remove the humiliating racial signs from the stores. On the basis of these promises Rev. Shuttlesworth and the leaders of the Alabama Christian Movement for Human Rights agreed to call a moratorium on any type of demonstration. As the weeks and months unfolded we realized that we were the victims of a broken promise. The signs remained. Like so many experiences of the past we were confronted with blasted hopes, and the dark shadow of a deep disappointment settled upon us. So we had no alternative except that of preparing for direct action, whereby we would present our very bodies as a means of laying our case before the conscience of the local and national community. We were not unmindful of the difficulties involved. So we decided to go through a process of self-purification. We started having workshops on nonviolence and repeatedly asked ourselves the questions, "Are you able to accept blows without retaliating?" "Are you able to endure the ordeals of jail?" We decided to set our direct action program around the Easter season, realizing that with the exception of Christmas, this was the largest shopping period of the year. Knowing that a strong economic withdrawal program would be the by-product of direct action, we felt that this was the best time to bring pressure on the merchants for the needed changes. Then it occurred to us that the March election was ahead and so we speedily decided to postpone action until after election day. When we discovered that Mr. Connor was in the run-off, we decided again to postpone action so that the demonstrations could not be used to cloud the issues. At this time we agreed to begin our nonviolent witness the day after the run-off.

This reveals that we did not move irresponsibly into direct action. We too wanted to see Mr. Connor defeated; so we went through postponement after postponement to aid in this community need. After this we felt that direct action could be delayed no longer.

Creative Tension

You may well ask, "Why direct action? Why sit-ins, marches, etc.? Isn't negotiation a better path?" You are exactly right in your call for negotiation. Indeed, this is the purpose of direct action. Nonviolent direct action seeks to create such a crisis and establish such creative tension that a community that has constantly refused to negotiate is forced to confront the issue. It seeks so to dramatize the issue that it can no longer be ignored. I just referred to the creation of tension as a part of the work of the nonviolent resister. This may sound rather shocking. But I must confess that I am not afraid of the word tension. I have earnestly worked and preached against violent tension, but there is a type of constructive nonviolent tension that is necessary for growth. Just as Socrates felt that it was necessary to create a tension in the mind so that individuals could rise from the bondage of myths and half-truths to the unfettered realm of creative analysis and objective appraisal, we must see the need of having nonviolent gadflies to create the kind of tension in society that will help men to rise from the dark depths of prejudice and racism to the majestic heights of understanding and brotherhood. So the purpose of the direct action is to create a situation so crisis-packed that it will inevitably open the door to negotiation. We, therefore, concur with you in your call for negotiation. Too long has our beloved Southland been bogged down in the tragic attempt to live in monologue rather than dialogue.

One of the basic points in your statement is that our acts are untimely. Some have asked, "Why didn't you give the new administration time to act?" The only answer that I can give to this inquiry is that the new administration must be prodded about as much as the outgoing one before it acts.

We will be sadly mistaken if we feel that the election of Mr. Boutwell will bring the millennium to Birmingham. While Mr. Boutwell is much more articulate and gentle than Mr. Connor, they are both segregationists, dedicated to the task of maintaining the status quo. The hope I see in Mr. Boutwell is that he will be reasonable enough to see the futility of massive resistance to desegregation. But he will not see this without pressure from the devotees of civil rights. My friends, I must say to you that we have not made a single gain in civil rights without determined legal and nonviolent pressure. History is the long and tragic story of the fact that privileged groups seldom give up their privileges voluntarily. Individuals may see the moral light and voluntarily give up their unjust posture; but as Reinhold Niebuhr has reminded us, groups are more immoral than individuals.

We know through painful experience that freedom is never voluntarily given by the oppressor; it must be demanded by the oppressed. Frankly, I have never yet engaged in a direct action movement that was "well timed," according to the timetable of those who have not suffered unduly from the disease of segregation. For years now I have heard the words "Wait!" It rings in the ear of every Negro with a piercing familiarity. This "Wait" has almost always meant "Never." It has been a tranquilizing thalidomide, relieving the emotional stress for a moment, only to give birth to an ill-formed infant of frustration. We must come to see with the distinguished jurist of yesterday that "justice too long delayed is justice denied." We have waited for more than three hundred and forty years for our constitutional and God-given rights. The nations of Asia and Africa are moving with jet-like speed toward the goal of political independence, and we still creep at horse and buggy pace toward the gaining of a cup of coffee at a lunch counter. I guess it is easy for those who have never felt the stinging darts of segregation to say, "Wait." But when you have seen vicious mobs lynch your mothers and fathers at will and drown your sisters and brothers at whim; when you have seen hate-filled policemen curse, kick, brutalize and even kill your black brothers and sisters with impunity; when you see the vast majority of your twenty million Negro brothers smothering in an airtight cage of poverty in the midst of an affluent society; when you suddenly find your tongue twisted and your speech stammering as you seek to explain to your six-year-old daughter why she can't go to the public amusement park that has just been advertised on television, and see tears welling up in her little eyes when she is told that Funtown is closed to colored children, and see the depressing clouds of inferiority begin to form in her little mental sky, and see her begin to distort her little personality by unconsciously developing a bitterness toward white people; when you have to concoct an answer for a five-year-old son asking in agonizing pathos: "Daddy, why do white people treat colored people so mean?"; when you take a cross country drive and find it necessary to sleep night after night in the uncomfortable corners of your automobile because no motel will accept you; when you are humiliated day in and day out by nagging signs reading "white" and "colored"; when your first name becomes "nigger" and your middle name becomes "boy" (however old you are) and your last name becomes "John," and when your wife and mother are never given the respected title "Mrs."; when you are harried by day and haunted at night by the fact that you are a Negro, living constantly at tip-toe stance never quite knowing what to expect next, and plagued with inner fears and outer resentments; when you are forever fighting a degenerating sense of "nobodiness"; then you will understand why we find it difficult to wait. There comes a time when the cup of endurance runs over, and men are no longer willing to be plunged into an abyss of injustice where they experience the blackness of corroding despair. I hope, sirs, you can understand our legitimate and unavoidable impatience.

Breaking the Law

You express a great deal of anxiety over our willingness to break laws. This is certainly a legitimate concern. Since we so diligently urge people to obey the Supreme Court's decision of 1954 outlawing segregation in the public schools, it is rather strange and paradoxical to find us consciously breaking laws. One may well ask, "how can you advocate breaking some laws and obeying others?" The answer is found in the fact that there are two types of laws: There are *just* and there are *unjust* laws. I would agree with Saint Augustine that "An unjust law is no law at all."

Now what is the difference between the two? How does one determine when a law is just or unjust? A just law is a man-made code that squares with the moral law or the law of God. An unjust law is a code that is out of harmony with the moral law. To put it in the terms of Saint Thomas Aquinas, an unjust law is a human law that is not rooted in eternal and natural law. Any law that uplifts human personality is just. Any law that degrades human personality is unjust. All segregation statutes are unjust because segregation distorts the soul and damages the personality. It gives the segregator a false sense of superiority, and the segregated a false sense of inferiority. To use the words of Martin Buber, the great Jewish philosopher, segregation substitutes an "I-it" relationship for the "I-thou" relationship, and ends up relegating persons to the status of things. So segregation is not only politically, economically and sociologically unsound, but it is morally wrong and sinful. Paul Tillich has said that sin is separation. Isn't segregation an existential expression of man's tragic separation, an expression of his awful estrangement, his terrible sinfulness? So I can urge men to disobey segregation ordinances because they are morally wrong.

Let us turn to a more concrete example of just and unjust laws. An unjust law is a code that a majority inflicts on a minority that is not binding on itself. This is difference made legal. On the other hand a just law is a code that a majority compels a minority to follow that it is willing to follow itself. This is sameness made legal.

Let me give another explanation. An unjust law is a code inflicted upon a minority which that minority had no part in enacting or creating because they did not have the unhampered right to vote. Who can say that the legislature of Alabama which set up the segregation laws was democratically elected? Throughout the state of Alabama all types of conniving methods are used to prevent Negroes from becoming registered voters and there are some counties without a single Negro registered to vote despite the fact that the Negro constitutes a majority of the population. Can any law set up in such a state be considered democratically structured?

These are just a few examples of unjust and just laws. There are some instances when a law is just on its face and unjust in its application. For instance, I was arrested Friday on a charge of parading without a permit. Now there is nothing wrong with an ordinance which requires a permit for a parade, but when the ordinance is used to preserve segregation and to deny citizens the First Amendment privilege of peaceful assembly and peaceful protest, then it becomes unjust.

I hope you can see the distinction I am trying to point out. In no sense do I advocate evading or defying the law as the rabid segregationist would do. This would lead to anarchy. One who breaks an unjust law must do it *openly, lovingly* (not hatefully as the white mothers did in New Orleans when they were seen on television screaming "nigger, nigger, nigger"), and with a willingness to accept the penalty. I submit that an individual who breaks a law that conscience tells him is unjust, and willingly accepts the penalty by staying in jail to arouse the conscience of the community over its injustice, is in reality expressing the very highest respect for law.

Of course, there is nothing new about this kind of civil disobedience. It was seen sublimely in the refusal of Shadrach, Meshach and Abednego to obey the laws of Nebuchadnezzar because a higher moral law was involved. It was practiced superbly by the early Christians who were willing to face hungry lions and the excruciating pain of chopping blocks, before submitting to certain unjust laws of the Roman empire. To a degree academic freedom is a reality today because Socrates practiced civil disobedience.

The White Moderate

We can never forget that everything Hitler did in German was "legal" and everything the Hungarian freedom fighters did in Hungary was "illegal." It was "illegal" to aid and comfort a Jew in Hitler's Germany. But I am sure that if I had lived in Germany during that time I would have aided and comforted my Jewish brothers even though it was illegal. If I lived in a Communist country today where certain principles dear to the Christian faith are suppressed, I believe I would openly advocate disobeying these anti-religious laws. I must make two honest confessions to you, my Christian and Jewish brothers. First, I must confess that over the last few years I have been gravely disappointed with the white moderate. I have almost reached the regrettable conclusion that the Negro's great stumbling block in the stride toward freedom is not the White Citizen's Council-er or the Ku Klux Klanner, but the white moderate who is more devoted to "order" than to justice; who prefers a negative peace which is the absence of tension to a positive peace which is the presence of justice; who constantly says "I agree with you in the goal you seek, but I can't agree with your methods of direct action"; who paternalistically feels that he can set the timetable for another man's freedom; who lives by the myth of time and who constantly advises the Negro to wait until a "more convenient season."

Shallow understanding from people of goodwill is more frustrating than absolute misunderstanding from people of ill will. Lukewarm acceptance is much more bewildering than outright rejection.

I had hoped that the white moderate would understand that law and order exist for the purpose of establishing justice, and that when they fail to do this they become dangerously structured dams that block the flow of social progress. I had hoped that the white moderate would understand that the present tension in the South is merely a necessary phase of the transition from an obnoxious negative peace, where the Negro passively accepted his unjust plight, to a substance-filled positive peace, where all men will respect the dignity and worth of human personality. Actually, we who engage in non-violent direct action are not the creators of tension. We merely bring to the surface the hidden tension that is already alive. We bring it out in the open where it can be seen and dealt with. Like a boil that can never be cured as long as it is covered up but must be opened with all its pus-flowing ugliness to the natural medicines of air and light, injustice must likewise be exposed, with all of the tension its exposing creates, to the light of human conscience and the air of national opinion before it can be cured.

In your statement you asserted that our actions, even though peaceful, must be condemned because they precipitate violence. But can this assertion be logically made? Isn't this like condemning the robbed man because his possession of money precipitated the evil act of robbery? Isn't this like condemning Socrates because his unswerving commitment to truth and his philosophical delvings precipitated the misguided popular mind to make him drink the hemlock? Isn't this like condemning Jesus because His unique God-Consciousness and never-ceasing devotion to His will precipitated the evil act of crucifixion? We must come to see, as federal courts have consistently affirmed, that it is immoral to urge an individual to withdraw his efforts to gain his basic constitutional rights because the quest precipitates violence. Society must protect the robbed and punish the robber.

I had also hoped that the white moderate would reject the myth of time. I received a letter this morning from a white brother in Texas which said: "All Christians know that the colored people will receive equal rights eventually, but it is possible that you are in too great of a religious hurry. It has taken Christianity almost 2000 years to accomplish what it has. The teachings of Christ take time to come to earth." All that is said here grows out of a tragic misconception of time. It is the strangely irrational notion that there is something in the very flow of time that will inevitably cure all ills. Actually time is neutral. It can be used either destructively or constructively. I am coming to feel that the people of ill-will have used time much more effectively than the people of good will. We will have to repent in this generation not merely for the vitriolic words and actions of the bad people, but for the appalling silence of the good people. We must come to see that human progress never rolls in on wheels of inevitability. It comes through the tireless efforts and persistent work of men willing to be co-workers with God, and without this hard work time itself becomes an ally of the forces of social stagnation. We must use time creatively, and forever realize that the time is always ripe to do right. Now is the time to make real the promise of democracy, and transform our pending national elegy into a creative psalm of brotherhood. Now is the time to lift our national policy from the quicksand of racial injustice to the solid rock of human dignity.

You spoke of our activity in Birmingham as extreme. At first I was rather disappointed that fellow clergymen would see my nonviolent efforts as those of the extremist. I started thinking about the fact that I stand in the middle of two opposing forces in the Negro community. One is a force of complacency made up of Negroes who, as a result of long years of oppression, have been so completely drained of self-respect and a sense of "somebodiness" that they have adjusted to segregation, and of a few Negroes in the middle class who, because of a degree of academic and economic security, and because at points they profit by segregation, have unconsciously become insensitive to the problems of the masses. The other force is one of bitterness and hatred and comes perilously close to advocating violence. It is expressed in the various black nationalist groups that are springing up over the nation, the largest and best known being Elijah Muhammad's Muslim movement. This movement is nourished by the contemporary frustration over the continued existence of racial discrimination. It is made up of people who have lost faith in America, who have absolutely repudiated Christianity, and who have concluded that the white man is an incurable "devil." I have tried to stand between these two forces saying that we need not follow the "do-nothingism" of the complacent or the hatred and despair of the black nationalist. There is the more excellent way of love and nonviolent protest. I'm grateful to God that, through the Negro church, the dimension of nonviolence entered our struggle. If this philosophy had not emerged, I am convinced that by now many streets of the South would be flowing with floods of blood. And I am further convinced that if our white brothers dismiss as "rabble rousers" and "outside agitators" those of us who are working through the channels of nonviolent direct action and refuse to support our nonviolent efforts, millions of Negroes, out of frustration and despair, will seek solace and security in black nationalist ideologies, a development that will lead inevitably to a frightening racial nightmare.

Oppressed people cannot remain oppressed forever. The urge for freedom will eventually come. This is what happened to the American Negro. Something within has reminded him of his birthright of freedom; something without has reminded him that he can gain it. Consciously and unconsciously, he has been swept in by what the Germans call the *Zeitgeist*, and with his black brothers of Africa, and his brown and yellow brothers of Asia, South America and the Caribbean, he is moving with a sense of cosmic urgency toward the promised land of racial justice. Recognizing this vital urge that has engulfed the Negro community, one should readily understand public demonstrations. The Negro has many pent up resentments and latent frustrations. He has to get them out. So let him march sometime; let him have his prayer pilgrimages to the city hall; understand why he must have sit-ins and freedom rides. If his repressed emotions do not come out in these nonviolent ways, they will come out in ominous expressions of violence. This is not a threat; it is a fact of history. So I have not said to my people "get rid of your discontent." But I have tried to say that this normal and healthy discontent can be channelized through the creative outlet of nonviolent direct action. Now this approach is being dismissed as extremist. I must admit that I was initially disappointed in being so categorized.

Extremists for Love

But as I continued to think about the matter I gradually gained a bit of satisfaction from being considered an extremist. Was not Jesus an extremist in love—"Love your enemies, bless them that curse you, pray for them that despitefully use you." Was not Amos an extremist for justice—"Let justice roll down like waters and righteousness like a mighty stream." Was not Paul an extremist for the gospel of Jesus Christ—"I bear in my body the marks of the Lord Jesus." Was not Martin Luther an extremist—"Here I stand; I can do none other so help me God." Was not John Bunyan an extremist— "I will stay in jail to the end of my days before I make a butchery of my conscience." Was not Abraham Lincoln an extremist—"This nation cannot survive half slave and half free." Was not Thomas Jefferson an extremist— "We hold these truths to be self-evident, that all men are created equal." So the question is not whether we will be extremist but what kind of extremist will we be. Will we be extremists for hate or will we be extremists for love? Will we be extremists for the preservation of injustice—or will we be extremists for the cause of justice? In that dramatic scene on Calvary's hill, three men were crucified. We must not forget that all three were crucified for the same crime—the crime of extremism. Two were extremists for immorality, and thusly fell below their environment. The other, Jesus Christ, was an extremist for love, truth, and goodness, and thereby rose above his environment. So, after all, maybe the South, the nation and the world are in dire need of creative extremists.

I had hoped that the white moderate would see this. Maybe I was too optimistic. Maybe I expected too much. I guess I should have realized that few members of a race that has oppressed another race can understand or appreciate the deep groans and passionate yearnings of those that have been oppressed and still fewer have the vision to see that injustice must be rooted out by strong, persistent and determined action. I am thankful, however, that some of our white brothers have grasped the meaning of this social revolution and committed themselves to it. They are still all too small in quantity, but they are big in quality. Some like Ralph McGill, Lillian Smith, Harry Golden and James Dabbs have written about our struggle in eloquent, prophetic and understanding terms. Others have marched with us down nameless streets of the South. They have languished in filthy roach-infested jails, suffering the abuse and brutality of angry policemen who see them as "dirty nigger lovers." They, unlike so many of their moderate brothers and sisters, have recognized the urgency of the moment and sensed the need for powerful "action" antidotes to combat the disease of segregation.

The White Church

Let me rush on to mention my other disappointment. I have been so greatly disappointed with the white church and its leadership. Of course, there are some notable exceptions. I am not unmindful of the fact that each of you has taken some significant stands on this issue. I commend you, Rev. Stallings, for your Christian stand on this past Sunday, in welcoming Negroes to your worship service on a non-segregated basis. I commend the Catholic leaders of this state for integrating Springhill College several years ago.

But despite these notable exceptions I must honestly reiterate that I have been disappointed with the church. I do not say that as one of the negative critics who can always find something wrong with the church. I say it as a minister of the gospel, who loves the church; who was nurtured in its bosom; who has been sustained by its spiritual blessings and who will remain true to it as long as the cord of life shall lengthen.

I had the strange feeling when I was suddenly catapulted into the leadership of the bus protest in Montgomery several years ago that we would have the support of the white church. I felt that the white ministers, priests and rabbis of the South would be some of our strongest allies. Instead, some have been outright opponents, refusing to understand the freedom movement and misrepresenting its leaders; all too many others have been more cautious than courageous and have remained silent behind the anesthetizing security of the stained-glass windows.

In spite of my shattered dreams of the past, I came to Birmingham with the hope that the white religious leadership of this community would see the justice of our cause, and with deep moral concern, serve as the channel through which our just grievances would get to the power structure. I had hoped that each of you would understand. But again I have been disappointed. I have heard numerous religious leaders of the South call upon their worshippers to comply with a desegregation decision because it is the *law*, but I have longed to hear white ministers say, "follow this decree because integration is morally *right* and the Negro is your brother." In the midst of blatant injustices inflicted upon the Negro, I have watched white churches stand on the sideline and merely mouth pious irrelevancies and sanctimonious trivialities. In the midst of a mighty struggle to rid our nation of racial and economic injustice, I have heard so many ministers say, "those are social issues with which the gospel has no real concern," and I have watched so many churches commit themselves to a completely other-worldly religion which made a strange distinction between body and soul, the sacred and the secular.

So here we are moving toward the exit of the twentieth century with a religious community largely adjusted to the status quo, standing as a tail-light behind other community agencies rather than a headlight leading men to higher levels of justice.

I have travelled the length and breadth of Alabama, Mississippi and all the other southern states. On sweltering summer days and crisp autumn mornings I have looked at her beautiful churches with their lofty spires pointing heavenward. I have beheld the impressive outlay of her massive religious education buildings. Over and over again I have found myself asking: "What kind of people worship here? Who is their God? Where were their voices when the lips of Governor Barnett dripped with words of interposition and nullification? Where were they when Governor Wallace gave the clarion call for defiance and hatred? Where were their voices of support when tired, bruised and weary Negro men and women decided to rise from the dark dungeons of complacency to the bright hills of creative protest?"

Yes, these questions are still in my mind. In deep disappointment, I have wept over the laxity of the church. But be assured that my tears have been tears of love. There can be no deep disappointment where there is not deep love. Yes, I love the church; I love her sacred walls. How could I do otherwise? I am in the rather unique position of being the son, the grandson and the great-grandson of preachers. Yes, I see the church as the body of Christ. But, oh! How we have blemished and scarred that body through social neglect and fear of being nonconformists.

Disturbers of the Peace

There was a time when the church was very powerful. It was during that period when the early Christians rejoiced when they were deemed worthy to suffer for what they believed. In those days the church was not merely a thermometer that recorded the ideas and principles of popular opinion; it was a thermostat that transformed the mores of society. Whereever the early Christians entered a town the power structure got disturbed and immediately sought to convict them for being "disturbers of the peace" and "outside agitators." But they went on with the conviction that they were "a colony of heaven," and had to obey God rather than man. They were small in number but big in commitment. They were too God-intoxicated to be "astronomically intimidated." They brought an end to such ancient evils as infanticide and gladiatorial contests.

Things are different now. The contemporary church is often a weak, ineffectual voice with an uncertain sound. It is so often the arch supporter of the status quo. Far from being disturbed by the presence of the church, the power structure of the average community is consoled by the church's silent and often vocal sanction of things as they are.

But the judgment of God is upon the church as never before. If the church of today does not recapture the sacrificial spirit of the early church, it will lose its authentic ring, forfeit the loyalty of millions, and be dismissed as an irrelevant social club with no meaning for the twentieth century. I am meeting young people every day whose disappointment with the church has risen to outright disgust.

Maybe again, I have been too optimistic. Is organized religion too inextricably bound to status-quo to save our nation and the world? Maybe I must turn my faith to the inner spiritual church, the church within the church, as the true *ecclesia* and the hope of the world. But again I am thankful to God that some noble souls from the ranks of organized religion have broken loose from the paralyzing chains of conformity and joined us as active partners in the struggle for freedom. They have left their secure congregations and walked the streets of Albany, Georgia, with us. They have gone through the highways of the South on tortuous rides for freedom. Yes, they have gone to jail with us. Some have been kicked out of their churches, and lost support of their bishops and fellow ministers. But they have gone with the faith that right defeated is stronger than evil triumphant. These men have been the leaven in the lump of the race. Their witness has been the spiritual salt that has preserved the true meaning of the Gospel in these troubled times. They have carved a tunnel of hope through the dark mountain of disappointment.

I hope the church as a whole will meet the challenge of this decisive hour. But even if the church does not come to the aid of justice, I have no despair about the future. I have no fear about the outcome of our struggle in Birmingham, even if our motives are presently misunderstood. We will reach the goal of freedom in Birmingham and all over the nation, because the goal of America is freedom. Abused and scorned though we may be, our destiny is tied up with the destiny of America. Before the pilgrims landed at Plymouth we were here. Before the pen of Jefferson etched across the pages of history the majestic words of the Declaration of Independence, we were here. For more than two centuries our fore-parents labored in this country without wages; they made cotton king; and they built the homes of their masters in the midst of brutal injustice and shameful humiliation—and yet out of a bottomless vitality they continued to thrive and develop. If the inexpressible cruelties of slavery could not stop us, the opposition we now face will surely fail. We will win our freedom because the sacred heritage of our nation and the eternal will of God are embodied in our echoing demands.

Bull Connor's Police

I must close now. But before closing I am impelled to mention one other point in your statement that troubled me profoundly. You warmly commended the Birmingham police force for keeping "order" and "preventing violence." I don't believe you would have so warmly commended the police force if you had seen its angry violent dogs literally biting six unarmed, nonviolent Negroes. I don't believe you would so quickly commend the policemen if you would observe their ugly and inhuman treatment of Negroes here in the city jail; if you would watch them push and curse old Negro women and young Negro girls; if you would see them slap and kick old Negro men and young boys; if you will observe them, as they did on two occasions, refuse to give us food because we wanted to sing our grace together. I'm sorry that I can't join you in your praise for the police department.

It is true that they have been rather disciplined in their public handling of the demonstrators. In this sense they have been rather publicly "nonviolent." But for what purpose? To preserve the evil system of segregation. Over the last few years I have consistently preached that nonviolence demands that the means we use must be as pure as the ends we seek. So I have tried to make it clear that it is wrong to use immoral means to attain moral ends. But now I must affirm that it is just as wrong, or even more so, to use moral means to preserve immoral ends. Maybe Mr. Connor and his policemen have been rather publicly nonviolent, as Chief Pritchett was in Albany, Georgia, but they have used the moral means of nonviolence to maintain the immoral end of flagrant racial injustice. T. S. Eliot has said that there is no greater treason than to do the right deed for the wrong reason.

I wish you had commended the Negro sit-inners and demonstrators of Birmingham for their sublime courage, their willingness to suffer and their amazing discipline in the midst of the most inhuman provocation. One day the South will recognize its real heroes. They will be the James Merediths, courageously and with a majestic sense of purpose facing jeering and hostile mobs and the agonizing loneliness that characterizes the life of the pioneer. They will be old oppressed, battered Negro women, symbolized in a seventy-two-year-old woman of Montgomery, Alabama, who rose up with a sense of dignity and with her people decided not to ride the segregated buses, and responded to one who inquired about her tiredness with ungrammatical profundity: "My feet is tired, but my soul is rested." They will be the young high school and college students, young ministers of the gospel and a host of their elders courageously and nonviolently sitting-in at lunch counters and willingly going to jail for conscience's sake. One day the South will know that when these disinherited children of God sat down at lunch counters they were in reality standing up for the best in the American dream and the most sacred values in our Judeo-Christian heritage, and thusly, carrying our whole nation back to those great wells of democracy which were dug deep by the founding fathers in the formulation of the Constitution and the Declaration of Independence.

Never before have I written a letter this long (or should I say a book?). I'm afraid that it is much too long to take your precious time. I can assure you that it would have been much shorter if I had been writing from a comfortable desk, but what else is there to do when you are alone for days in the dull monotony of a narrow jail cell other than write long letters, think strange thoughts, and pray long prayers?

If I have said anything in this letter that is an overstatement of the truth and is indicative of an unreasonable impatience, I beg you to forgive me. If I have said anything in this letter that is an understatement of the truth and is indicative of my having a patience that makes me patient with anything less than brotherhood, I beg God to forgive me.

I hope this letter finds you strong in the faith. I also hope that circumstances will soon make it possible for me to meet each of you, not as an integrationist or a civil rights leader, but as a fellow clergyman and a Christian brother. Let us all hope that the dark clouds of racial prejudice will soon pass away and the deep fog of misunderstanding will be lifted from our fear-drenched communities and in some not too distant tomorrow the radiant stars of love and brotherhood will shine over our great nation with all of their scintillating beauty.

Yours for the cause of Peace and Brotherhood
Martin Luther King, Jr.

Soul On Ice

by Eldridge Cleaver

Domestic Law and International Order

THE POLICE department and the armed forces are the two arms of the power structure, the muscles of control and enforcement. They have deadly weapons with which to inflict pain on the human body. They know how to bring about horrible deaths. They have clubs with which to beat the body and the head. They have bullets and guns with which to tear holes in the flesh, to smash bones, to disable and kill. They use force, to make you do what the deciders have decided you must do.

Every country on earth has these agencies of force. The people everywhere fear this terror and force. To them it is like a snarling wild beast which can put an end to one's dreams. They punish. They have cells and prisons to lock you up in. They pass out sentences. They won't let you go when you want to. You have to stay put until they give the word. If your mother is dying, you can't go to her bedside to say goodbye or to her graveside to see her lowered into the earth, to see her, for the last time, swallowed up by that black hole.

The techniques of the enforcers are many: firing squads, gas chambers, electric chairs, torture chambers, the garrote, the guillotine, the tightening rope around your throat. It has been found that the death penalty is necessary to back up the law, to make it easier to enforce, to deter transgressions against the penal code. That everybody doesn't believe in the same laws is beside the point.

Which laws get enforced depends on who is in power. If the capitalists are in power, they enforce laws designed to protect their system, their way of life. They have a particular abhorrence for crimes against property, but are prepared to be liberal and show a modicum of compassion for crimes against the person—unless, of course, an instance of the latter is combined

363

with an instance of the former. In such cases, nothing can stop them from throwing the whole book at the offender. For instance, armed robbery with violence, to a capitalist, is the very epitome of evil. Ask any banker what he thinks of it.

If Communists are in power, they enforce laws designed to protect their system, their way of life. To them, the horror of horrors is the speculator, that man of magic who has mastered the art of getting something with nothing and who in America would be a member in good standing of his local Chamber of Commerce.

"The people," however, are nowhere consulted, although everywhere everything is done always in their name and ostensibly for their betterment, while their real-life problems go unsolved. "The people" are a rubber stamp for the crafty and sly. And no problem can be solved without taking the police department and the armed forces into account. Both kings and bookies understand this, as do first ladies and common prostitutes.

The police do on the domestic level what the armed forces do on the international level: protect the way of life of those in power. The police patrol the city, cordon off communities, blockade neighborhoods, invade homes, search for that which is hidden. The armed forces patrol the world, invade countries and continents, cordon off nations, blockade islands and whole peoples; they will also overrun villages, neighborhoods, enter homes, huts, caves, searching for that which is hidden. The policeman and the soldier will violate your person, smoke you out with various gases. Each will shoot you, beat your head and body with sticks and clubs, with rifle butts, run you through with bayonets, shoot holes in your flesh, kill you. They each have unlimited firepower. They will use all that is necessary to bring you to your knees. They won't take no for an answer. If you resist their sticks, they draw their guns. If you resist their guns, they call for reinforcements with bigger guns. Eventually they will come in tanks, in jets, in ships. They will not rest until you surrender or are killed. The policeman and the soldier will have the last word.

Both police and the armed forces follow orders. Orders. Orders flow from the top down. Up there, behind closed doors, in antechambers, in conference rooms, gavels bang on the tables, the tinkling of silver decanters can be heard as icewater is poured by well-fed, conservatively dressed men in hornrimmed glasses, fashionably dressed American widows with rejuvenated faces and tinted hair, the air permeated with the square humor of Bob Hope jokes. Here all the talking is done, all the thinking, all the deciding. Gray rabbits of men scurry forth from the conference room to spread the decisions throughout the city, as News. Carrying out orders is a job, a way of meeting the payments on the house, a way of providing for one's kiddies. In the armed forces it is also a duty, patriotism. Not to do so is treason.

Every city has its police department. No city would be complete without one. It would be sheer madness to try operating an American city without the heat, the fuzz, the man. Americans are too far gone, or else they haven't arrived yet; the center does not exist, only the extremes. Take away the cops and Americans would have a coast-to-coast free-for-all. There are, of course, a few citizens who carry their own private cops around with them, built into their souls. But there is robbery in the land, and larceny, murder, rape, burglary, theft, swindles, all brands of crime, profit, rent, interest— and these blasé descendants of Pilgrims are at each other's throats. To complicate matters, there are also rich people and poor people in America. There are Negroes and whites, Indians, Puerto Ricans, Mexicans, Jews, Chinese, Arabs, Japanese—all with equal rights but unequal possessions. Some are haves and some are have-nots. All have been taught to worship at the shrine of General Motors. The whites are on top in America and they want to stay there, up there. They are also on top in the world, on the international level, and they want to stay up there, too. Everywhere there are those who want to smash this precious toy clock of a system, they want ever so much to change it, to rearrange things, to pull the whites down off their high horse and make them equal. Everywhere the whites are fighting to prolong their status, to retard the erosion of their position. In America, when everything else fails, they call out the police. On the international level, when everything else fails, they call out the armed forces.

A strange thing happened in Watts, in 1965, August. The blacks, who in this land of private property have all private and no property, got excited into an uproar because they noticed a cop before he had a chance to wash the blood off his hands. Usually the police department can handle such flare-ups. But this time it was different. Things got out of hand. The blacks were running amok, burning, shooting, breaking. The police department was powerless to control them; the chief called for reinforcements. Out came the National Guard, that ambiguous hybrid from the twilight zone where the domestic army merges with the international; that hypocritical force poised within America and capable of action on either level, capable of backing up either the police or the armed forces. Unleashing their formidable firepower, they crushed the blacks. But things will never be the same again. Too many people saw that those who turned the other cheek in Watts got their whole head blown off. At the same time, heads were being blown off in Vietnam. America was embarrassed, not by the quality of her deeds but by the surplus of publicity focused upon her negative selling points, and a little frightened because of what all those dead bodies, on two fronts, implied. Those corpses spoke eloquently of potential allies and alliances. A community of interest began to emerge, dripping with blood, out of the ashes of Watts. The blacks in Watts and all over America could now see the Viet Cong's point: both were on the receiving end of what the armed forces were dishing out.

So now the blacks, stung by the new knowledge they have unearthed, cry out: *"POLICE BRUTALITY!"* From one end of the country to the other, the new war cry is raised. The youth, those nodes of compulsive energy who are all fuel and muscle, race their motors, itch to do something. The Uncle Toms, no longer willing to get down on their knees to lick boots, do so from a squatting position. The black bourgeoisie call for Citizens' Review Boards, to assert civilian control over the activity of the police. In back rooms, in dark stinking corners of the ghettos, self-conscious black men curse their own cowardice and stare at their rifles and pistols and shotguns laid out on tables before them, trembling as they wish for a manly impulse to course through their bodies and send them screaming mad into the streets shooting from the hip. Black women look at their men as if they are bugs, curious growths of flesh playing an inscrutable waiting game. Violence becomes a homing pigeon floating through the ghettos seeking a black brain in which to roost for a season.

In their rage against the police, against police brutality, the blacks lose sight of the fundamental reality: that the police are only an instrument for the implementation of the policies of those who make the decisions. Police brutality is only one facet of the crystal of terror and oppression. Behind police brutality there is social brutality, economic brutality, and political brutality. From the perspective of the ghetto, this is not easy to discern: the TV newscaster and the radio announcer and the editorialists of the newspapers are wizards of the smoke screen and the snow job.

What is true on the international level is true also at home; except that the ace up the sleeve is easier to detect in the international arena. Who would maintain that American soldiers are in Vietnam on their own motion? They were conscripted into the armed forces and taught the wisdom of obeying orders. They were sent to Vietnam by orders of the generals in the Pentagon, who receive them from the Secretary of Defense, who receives them from the President, who is shrouded in mystery. The soldier in the field in Vietnam, the man who lies in the grass and squeezes the trigger when a little half-starved, trembling Vitnamese peasant crosses his sights, is only following orders, carrying out a policy and a plan. He hardly knows what it is all about. They have him wired-up tight with the slogans of TV and the World Series. All he knows is that he has been assigned to carry out a certain ritual of duties. He is well trained and does the best he can. He does a good job. He may want to please those above him with the quality of his performance. He may want to make sergeant, or better. This man is from some hicky farm in Shit Creek, Georgia. He only knew whom to kill after passing through boot camp. He could just as well come out ready to kill Swedes. He will kill a Swede dead, if he is ordered to do so.

Same for the policeman in Watts. He is not there on his own. They have all been assigned. They have been told what to do and what not to do. They have also been told what they better not do. So when they continually do something, in every filthy ghetto in this shitty land, it means only that they are following orders.

It's no secret that in America the blacks are in total rebellion against the System. They want to get their nuts out of the sand. They don't like the way America is run, from top to bottom. In America, everything is owned. Everything is held as private property. Someone has a brand on everything. There is nothing left over. Until recently, the blacks themselves were counted as part of somebody's private property, along with the chickens and the goats. The blacks have not forgotten this, principally because they are still treated as if they are part of someone's inventory of assets— or perhaps, in this day of rage against the costs of welfare, blacks are listed among the nation's liabilities. On any account, however, blacks are in no position to respect or help maintain the institution of private property. What they want is to figure out a way to get some of that property for themselves, to divert it to their own needs. This is what it is all about, and this is the real brutality involved. This is the source of all brutality.

The police are the armed guardians of the social order. The blacks are the chief domestic victims of the American social order. A conflict of interest exists, therefore, between the blacks and the police. It is not solely a matter of trigger-happy cops, of brutal cops who love to crack black heads. Mostly it's a job to them. It pays good. And there are numerous fringe benefits. The real problem is a trigger-happy social order.

The Utopians speak of a day when there will be no police. There will be nothing for them to do. Every man will do his duty, will respect the rights of his neighbor, will not disturb the peace. The needs of all will be taken care of. Everyone will have sympathy for his fellow man. There will be no such thing as crime. There will be, of course, no prisons. No electric chairs, no gas chambers. The hangman's rope will be the thing of the past. The entire earth will be a land of plenty. there will be no crimes against property, no speculation.

It is easy to see that we are not on the verge of entering Utopia: there are cops everywhere. North and South, the Negroes are the have-nots. They see property all around them, property that is owned by whites. In this regard, the black bourgeoisie has become nothing but a ridiculous nuisance. Having waged a battle for entrance into the American mainstream continually for fifty years, all of the black bourgeoisie's defenses are directed outward, against the whites. They have no defenses against the blacks and no time to erect any. The black masses can handle them any time they choose, with one mighty blow. But the white bourgeoisie presents a bigger problem, those whites who own everything. With many shackled by unemployment, hatred in black hearts for this system of private property increases daily. The sanctity surrounding property is being called into question. The mystique of the deed of ownership is melting away. In other parts of the world, peasants rise up and expropriate the land from the former owners. Blacks in America see that the deed is not eternal, that it is not signed by God, and that new deeds, making blacks the owners, can be drawn up.

The Black Muslims raised the cry, *'WE MUST HAVE SOME LAND!"* *"SOME LAND OF OUR OWN OR ELSE!"* Blacks in America shrink from the colossus of General Motors. They can't see how to wade through that thicket of common stocks, preferred stocks, bonds and debentures. They only know that General Motors is huge, that it has billions of dollars under its control, that it owns land, that its subsidiaries are legion, that it is a respository of vast powers. The blacks want to crack the nut of General Motors. They are meditating on it. Meanwhile, they must learn that the police take orders from General Motors. And that the Bank of America has something to do with them even though they don't have a righteous penny in the bank. They have no bank accounts, only bills to pay. The only way they know of making withdrawals from the bank is at the point of a gun. The shiny fronts of skyscrapers intimidate them. They do not own them. They feel alienated from the very sidewalks on which they walk. This white man's country, this white man's world. Overflowing with men of color. An economy consecrated to the succor of the whites. Blàcks are incidental. The war on poverty, that monstrous insult to the rippling muscles in a black man's arms, is an index of how men actually sit down and plot each other's deaths, actually sit down with slide rules and calculate how to hide bread from the hungry. And the black bourgeoisie greedily sopping up what crumbs are tossed into their dark corner.

There are 20,000,000 of these blacks in America, probably more. Today they repeat, in awe, this magic number to themselves: there are 20,000,000 of us! They shout this to each other in humiliated astonishment. No one need tell them that there is vast power latent in their mass. They know that 20,000,000 of anything is enough to get some recognition and consideration. They know also that they must harness their number and hone it into a sword with a sharp cutting edge. White General Motors also knows that the unity of these 20,000,000 ragamuffins will spell the death of the system of its being. At all costs, then, they will seek to keep these blacks from uniting, from becoming bold and revolutionary. These white property owners know that they must keep the blacks cowardly and intimidated. By a complex communications system of hints and signals, certain orders are given to the chief of police and the sheriff, who pass them on to their men, the footsoldiers in the trenches of the ghetto.

We experience this system of control as madness. So that Leonard Deadwyler, one of these 20,000,000 blacks, is rushing his pregnant wife to the hospital and is shot dead by a policeman. An accident. That the sun rises in the east and sets in the west is also an accident, by design. The blacks are up in arms. From one end of America to the other, blacks are outraged at this accident, this latest evidence of what an accident-prone people they are, of the cruelty and pain of their lives, these blacks at the mercy of trigger-happy Yankees and Rebs in coalition against their skin. They want the policeman's blood as a sign that the Viet Cong is not the only answer. A sign to save them from the deaths they must die, and inflict. The power structure, without so much as blinking an eye, wouldn't mind tossing Bova to the mob, to restore law and order, but it knows in the vaults of its strength that at all cost the blacks must be kept at bay, that it must uphold the police department, its Guardian. Nothing must be allowed to threaten the set-up. Justice is secondary. Security is the byword.

Meanwhile, blacks are looking on and asking tactical questions. They are asked to die for the System in Vietnam. In Watts they are killed by it. Now—NOW!—they are asking each other, in dead earnest: Why not die right here in Babylon fighting for a better life, like the Viet Cong? If those little cats can do it, what's wrong with big studs like us?

A mood sets in, spreads across America, across the face of Babylon, jells in black hearts everywhere.

Participation and Power:
The Modern Corporation and Society

Second Week — Fourth Day

Franklin D. Roosevelt,
1944 State of the Union Message (selection)

Harlan Cleveland,
The Future Executive, Chapter 4 (selection)

Louis K. Liggett Co. v. Lee.
288 U.S. 517, 548-567. (1933).
Mr. Justice Brandeis, dissenting in part.

Arthur M. Okun, *Equality and Efficiency*,
Chapter 4 (selection)

Peter F. Drucker, *The Unseen Revolution*,
Chapter 1 (selection), 5

1944
State of the Union
Message

by Franklin D. Roosevelt

A New Bill of Rights

IN this war we have been compelled to learn how interdependent upon each other are all groups and sections of the population of America.

Increased food costs, for example, will bring new demands for wage increases from all war workers, which will in turn raise all prices of all things, including those things which the farmers themselves have to buy. Increased wages or prices will each in turn produce the same results. They all have a particularly disastrous result on all fixed income groups.

And I hope you will remember that all of us in this government represent the fixed-income group just as much as we represent business owners, workers, and farmers. This group of fixed-income people includes teachers, clergy, policemen, firemen, widows, and minors on fixed incomes, wives and dependents of our soldiers and sailors, and old-age pensioners. They and their families add up to one-quarter of our 130 million people. They have few or no high-pressure representatives at the Capitol. In a period of gross inflation they would be the worst sufferers.

If ever there was a time to subordinate individual or group selfishness to the national good that time is now. Disunity at home—bickerings, self-seeking partisanship, stoppages of work, inflation, business as usual, politics as usual, luxury as usual—these are the influences which can undermine the morale of the brave men ready to die at the front for us nere.

Those who are doing most of the complaining are not deliberately striving to sabotage the national war effort. They are laboring under the delusion that the time is past when we must make prodigious sacrifices—that the war is already won and we can begin to slacken off. But the dangerous folly of that point of view can be measured by the distance that separates our troops from their ultimate objectives in Berlin and Tokyo—and by the sum of all the perils that lie along the way.

Overconfidence and complacency are among our deadliest enemies. Last spring—after notable victories at Stalingrad and in Tunisia and against the U-boats on the high seas—overconfidence became so pronounced that war production fell off. In two months, June and July 1943, more than a thousand airplanes that could have been made and should have been made were not made. Those who failed to make them were not on strike. They were merely saying, "The war's in the bag—so let's relax." That attitude on the part of anyone—government or management or labor—can lengthen this war. It can kill American boys.

Let us remember the lessons of 1918. In the summer of that year the tide turned in favor of the Allies. But this government did not relax. In fact, our national effort was stepped up. In August 1918, the draft-age limits were broadened from 21-31 to 18-45. The President called for "force to the utmost," and his call was heeded. And in November, only three months later, Germany surrendered.

That is the way to fight and win a war—all-out—and not with half an eye on the battlefronts abroad and the other eye and a half on personal, selfish, or political interests here at home.

Therefore, in order to concentrate all our energies and resources on winning the war, and to maintain a fair and stable economy at home, I recommend that the Congress adopt:

1. A realistic tax law—which will tax all unreasonable profits, both individual and corporate, and reduce the ultimate cost of the war to our sons and daughters. The tax bill now under consideration by the Congress does not begin to meet this test.

2. A continuation of the law for the renegotiation of war contracts—which will prevent exorbitant profits and assure fair prices to the government. For two long years I have pleaded with the Congress to take undue profits out of war.

3. A cost-of-food law—which will enable the government (a) to place a reasonable floor under the prices the farmer may expect for his production; and (b) to place a ceiling on the prices a consumer will have to pay for the food he buys. This should apply to necessities only, and will require public funds to carry out. It will cost in appropriations about 1 per cent of the present annual cost of the war.

4. Early reenactment of the stabilization statute of October 1942. This expires June 30, 1944, and if it is not extended well in advance, the country might just as well expect price chaos by summer. We cannot have stabilization by wishful thinking. We must take positive action to maintain the integrity of the American dollar.

5. A national service law—which, for the duration of the war, will prevent strikes and, with certain appropriate exceptions, will make available for war production or for any other essential services every able-bodied adult in this nation.

These five measures together form a just and equitable whole. I would not recommend a national service law unless the other laws were passed to keep down the cost of living, to share equitably the burdens of taxation, to hold the stabilization line, and to prevent undue profits. The federal government already has the basic power to draft capital and property of all kinds for war purposes on a basis of just compensation.

As you know, I have for three years hesitated to recommend a national service act. Today, however, I am convinced of its necessity. Although I believe that we and our allies can win the war without such a measure, I am certain that nothing less than total mobilization of all our resources of manpower and capital will guarantee an earlier victory and reduce the toll of suffering and sorrow and blood.

I have received a joint recommendation for this law from the heads of the War Department, the Navy Department, and the Maritime Commission. These are the men who bear responsibility for the procurement of the necessary arms and equipment, and for the successful prosecution of the war in the field. They say:

> When the very life of the nation is in peril the responsibility for service is common to all men and women. In such a time there can be no discrimination between the men and women who are assigned by the government to its defense at the battlefield and the men and women assigned to producing the vital military operations. A prompt enactment of a national service law would be merely an expression of the universality of this responsibility.

I believe the country will agree that those statements are the solemn truth.

National service is the most democratic way to wage a war. Like selective service for the armed forces, it rests on the obligation of each citizen to serve his nation to his utmost where he is best qualified. It does not mean reduction in wages. It does not mean loss of retirement and seniority rights and benefits. It does not mean that any substantial numbers of war workers will be disturbed in their present jobs. Let these facts be wholly clear. . . .

Our soldiers and sailors and marines know that the overwhelming majority of them will be deprived of the opportunity to vote if the voting machinery is left exclusively to the states under existing state laws—and that there is no likelihood of these laws being changed in time to enable them to vote at the next election. The Army and Navy have reported that it will be impossible effectively to administer forty-eight different soldier-voting laws. It is the duty of the Congress to remove this unjustifiable discrimination against the men and women in our armed forces—and to do it as quickly as possible.

It is our duty now to begin to lay the plans and determine the strategy for the winning of a lasting peace and the establishment of an American standard of living higher than ever before known. We cannot be content, no matter how high that general standard of living may be, if some fraction of our people—whether it be one-third or one-fifth or one-tenth—is ill-fed, ill-clothed, ill-housed, and insecure.

This republic had its beginning, and grew to its present strength, under the protection of certain inalienable political rights—among them the right of free speech, free press, free worship, trial by jury, freedom from unreasonable searches and seizures. They were our rights to life and liberty. As our nation has grown in size and stature, however—as our industrial economy expanded—these political rights proved inadequate to assure us equality in the pursuit of happiness.

We have come to a clear realization of the fact that true individual freedom cannot exist without economic security and independence. "Necessitous men are not freemen." People who are hungry and out of a job are the stuff of which dictatorships are made. In our day these economic truths have become accepted as self-evident. We have accepted, so to speak, a second Bill of Rights under which a new basis of security and prosperity can be established for all—regardless of station, race, or creed.

Among these are:

The right to a useful and remunerative job in the industries or shops or farms or mines of the nation;

The right to earn enough to provide adequate food and clothing and recreation;

The right of every farmer to raise and sell his products at a return which will give him and his family a decent living;

The right of every businessman, large and small, to trade in an atmosphere of freedom from unfair competition and domination by monopolies at home or abroad;

The right of every family to a decent home;

The right to adequate medical care and the opportunity to achieve and enjoy good health;

The right to adequate protection from the economic fears of old age, sickness, accident, and unemployment;

The right to a good education.

All of these rights spell security. And after this war is won, we must be prepared to move forward, in the implementation of these rights, to new goals of human happiness and well-being. America's own rightful place in the world depends in large part upon how fully these and similar rights have been carried into practice for our citizens. For unless there is security here at home there cannot be lasting peace in the world. . . .

I ask the Congress to explore the means for implementing this economic bill of rights—for it is definitely the responsibility of the Congress so to do. Many of these problems are already before committees of the Congress in the form of proposed legislation. I shall from time to time communicate with the Congress with respect to these and further proposals. In the event that no adequate program of progress is evolved, I am certain that our nation will be conscious of the fact.

Our fighting men abroad—and their families at home—expect such a program and have the right to insist upon it. It is to their demands that this government should pay heed rather than to the whining demands of selfish pressure groups who seek to feather their nests while young Americans are dying. . . .

Each and every one of us has a solemn obligation under God to serve this nation in its most critical hour—to keep this nation great—to make this nation greater in a better world.

The Future Executive

by Harlan Cleveland

Chapter 4
The Blurring of "Public" and "Private"

EVEN COMPARED to a generation ago, our private enterprise system is just as enterprising but not nearly so private. The growing sense of public responsibility in American business—verbalized at inspirational lunches but also increasingly in evidence during office hours—can be seen as the search for legitimacy by managers of properties whose "ownership" is no longer the key to executive responsibility.

It is now commonplace to observe that the diffusion of property divorces ownership from control of the economic system. Managers of productive enterprises, and managers of pension funds, mutual trusts, bank-held trusts and funds, and other large-scale forms of organized "private property," are each year harder put to say to whom they are effectively responsible. If the question is "Who owns General Motors or AT&T?" the honest answer is so vague an entity ("the public") that it leaves the collective leadership of managers in control of what is owned. To the more operational question, "Who is responsible for the actions of General Motors or AT&T?" the answer is clear enough: a large and growing number of their executives. But to whom are they responsible?

The issue about identity illustrated by these simple questions is paralleled in large-scale philanthropy and nonprofit enterprise. In a Ford Foundation or an American Cancer Society or a private university, as in most large corporations and financial institutions, some effort is usually made to separate powers between a legislative board of directors, or trustees, and a group of executive managers. But what the muckrakers of a generation ago used to call "interlocking directorates" are now more the rule than the exception—that is, the board of directors will be heavy with corporate vice presidents, major clients, alumni, contractors, benefactors, and others who can be expected to share the general orientation of the managerial group. Taking board members and top managers together, they often operate as a self-perpetuating oligarchy. As such they are responsible to each other and themselves—and therefore ultimately to people-in-general, which is to say to their own collective guess as to when public acquiescence will give way to public outrage.

People-in-general are not, however, very helpful in deciding questions of ethics and policy—how much profit to reinvest, when to build new plants, whether to merge with the competition, what prices are fair, how much to raise wages, what causes to promote through bank loans or foundation grants. These decisions are made by sovereign individuals, their ethical responsibility obscured from outsiders (and sometimes from themselves) by complex committee work, what the Communists call "collective leadership."

What induces the Public Executives in private organizations to operate within acceptable boundaries (as measured by public outrage and consequent government intervention) is a double sanction—personal conscience, modified by external expectations about executive behavior. What tugs at the conscience, or outrages the relevant publics, is different in different places and even at different times in the same place. Twenty years ago most American businessmen felt no active responsibility for investing in black industry or training youngsters from the ghetto. Now many of them do, partly because they have come to feel some moral obligation to help solve a national problem that can no longer be ignored, and partly because they fear the social and corporate consequences if they fail to do their part. Ten years ago industries could dump waste in the rivers and oil in the oceans; but now a whole generation of converts to ecology are asking with Ralph Nader why, if individuals are forbidden by ordinance from relieving themselves in the nearest stream, this sensible antipollution rule should not apply to industries as well. I recently listened to a gas company executive describe all the antipollution equipment and procedures he was building into the specifications for a new refinery. "Ten years ago they would have thrown me out of the stockholders' meeting if I had suggested spending this kind of money to protect the public interest," he remarked. "Today they would throw me out if I *didn't* recommend all this public-interest spending."

For the responsible executive, the difference between working in a nominally private or an overtly public agency lies not so much in the kinds of ethical issues that arise as in the procedures available for judging whether they have been resolved to the public's taste. Executives in both environments have to unlock the same mysteries, imply in their decisions the same kinds of answers to ultimate questions: how to reconcile efficiency with humanity, how to promote full employment without undue inflation, how much is "sufficiency," what prices to charge and pay, what costs to incur now for what benefits later on, how hard to press toward undefinable goals, how fast to grow, which direction is up.

In a public agency questions like these which touch the organization's ultimate purposes are no less pressing, no less inherent in day-to-day decisions, no less difficult to answer than are the analogous enigmas in private business. But they do not create the same sense of moral crisis because there is a legitimate, agreed-upon *procedure* for answering them. The opinion of people-in-general is ultimately consulted (sometimes much too late, to be sure) by counting votes in a general election or in a legislature which for the manager's purpose is defined as "representative" no matter how unrepresentative it may in practice be. But in private enterprise, profit and nonprofit, the public interest is not authoritatively determined. The public interest is what the managers think it is—unless they so outrage their relevant publics that they bring government regulation on themselves.

People-in-general exercise their ultimate power most decisively by making private managers responsible to the government, in a single act which both justifies and monitors the managers' power over large organizations affected with the public interest. Such decisions stretch in a long line from the nationalization of the Post Office and the public utility holding company acts, through the Federal Communications Act and the efforts to bring labor unions under governmental regulation, down to the fights to enforce fair-employment practices and destroy racial discrimination in education and housing. Government participation in higher education, through subsidies for research and training, has made private universities think hard about their dependence on what voters and elected officials may do to their autonomy if aroused.

Even private philanthropy, which long had the greatest autonomy, has now fallen afoul of adverse reaction by people-in-general, acting mostly through the power to tax and to exempt from taxes. It started seriously in 1961, when Congressman B. Carroll Reece conducted an unfriendly investigation of some of the big foundations, arguing that tax "exemptions are acts of grace by the Federal Government. . .the Federal Government permits the equivalent of public moneys to be used by these foundations. Accordingly, it is justifed in applying. . .such conditions on the exemptions as may be calculated to prevent abuse of the privilege and to prevent the use of the exempted funds against the public interest."

The foundations were eloquent in describing the good things they were doing, but they never really found a persuasive counterdoctrine. The best they could do was to invoke a vague constitutional protection and then argue that their own "high duty of public responsibility" was as effective a safeguard against abuse as any conceivable form of government regulation.

The 1960s saw a spectacular growth in the number and resources of private foundations, including many which were patently tax dodges and a few which were obviously meddling in elective politics. The Ford Foundation's rather casual decision to give research grants to several

Kennedy Administration alumni touched off an effort to include in a tax reform bill provisions to control the amounts spent by tax-exempt foundations and proscribe some categories of spending. The issue became so complicated that the central moral and political issue—if foundations are responsible to the public, how does the public monitor the exercise of that responsibility?—ran out into the sands of legal technicality. But the issue remains, sharpening the foundations' self-questions about each action they take in the public's name.

To avoid the embarrassment of undue restrictions on their freedom of action, the Public Executives in American corporate enterprise and private nonprofit organizations are reacting in ways that further blur the distinction between "public" and "private."

First, the managers intensify the practice of "collective leadership." As we have seen, this is necessary for technological reasons anyway; growing bigness, growing complexity of relations, and more specialization of function multiply the interrelated decisions to be made and diffuse the power to make them. Major decisions are typically made by an executive committee, often in tandem with a finance committee or other groups of executives. This obscures the personal accountability for major decisions which, because they are of interest to the public, are likely to be controversial. It is, for example, rare to find a price increase announced personally by a top official of a modern corporation.

Second, the managers maintain a curtain of public relations, with an increasing emphasis on "institutional advertising" to build an image of a good-guy corporation taking the public's quite legitimate interests full into account. Those who do not show forth their interest in conservation, ecology, safety, economy, planning, beauty, and culture risk regulation to enforce it.

In a third response to the "public" imperative, the executives in private organizations are arranging to bring the government into their affairs as a risk-taking partner. This trend is so familiar that it scracely needs to be spelled out here. Atomic energy, aerospace, communications, housing and urban redevelopment, health delivery, soil conservation, the savings bank business, foreign investment guarantees, research and development in nearly every field—the list could be indefinitely extended. For the private side of the bargain, it is a profitable but perilous partnership; government aims and policies can shift suddenly. The fate of a regional industry may hang on a few votes in one House of Congress, as the debates over antiballistic missile systems and supersonic aircraft illustrated in 1970 and 1971. A change in direction—cutbacks in the space program and the decline of military procurement for Vietnam are recent examples—can blight whole industries; the largest companies are developing quotas of government business to protect them from fluctuations in public policy. In higher education a major financial crisis occurs whenever the Department of Defense cuts back on R & D funds, or the National Institutes of Health have their appropriation reduced.

Because public policy is thus an element in business planning, the managers of American corporations find it logical to intervene more frequently and more deeply in the processes by which governments make up their multiple minds. If business executives are responsible not only for running their own businesses but for preventing depressions, competing with the European Common Market, and defending the U.S. against the Soviet Union, then they must participate in setting interest rates, controlling government spending, allocating government subsidies to the right interests, planning defense production, and managing U.S. foreign policy. If business firms are going to be held responsible for progress in their own urban communities, their managers had better interest themselves in the honesty of local government and the rehabilitation of "downtown." If the state legislatures are going to regulate the insurance business, the managers of insurance companies had better try even harder to regulate the state legislatures.

The process is ill described by the old-fashioned word "lobbying," which to most people means influencing legislators. Since most important legislation is now written in the executive departments of government, the power of new-style lobbies can be most accurately measured by the strength of their "representatives" within the *executive* bureaucracy.

The blurring of "public" and "private" makes it hard to draft a law or write a rule against conflict of interest that applies to any but the minor cases of corruption in office. The big interests of industry and government are not even seen to be in conflict. (It was not Charles Wilson's first statement—"What's good for the country is good for General Motors"—that got him into trouble, but the fact that he added, "...and vice versa.") It is considered normal and natural for a steel man to lubricate with government contracts the growth of steel production; for a housing man to get more housing built by having the government absorb as much of the risk as possible; for a farmers' representative to promote aid for farmers from inside the Department of Agriculture; for a labor organizer temporarily in the government to promote the right of labor to organize. We have institutionalized the inside track.

Louis K. Liggett Co. v. Lee

by Mr. Justice Brandeis

dissenting in part

---

288 U.S. 517, 548-567, 53 S. Ct. 481,
490;497, 77 L.Ed. 929, 944-955,
85 A.L.R. 699, 714-725 (1933).

THE prevalence of the corporation in America has led men of this generation to act, at times, as if the privilege of doing business in corporate form were inherent in the citizen; and has led them to accept the evils attendant upon the free and unrestricted use of the corporate mechanism as if these evils were the inescapable price of civilized life, and, hence, to be borne with resignation. Throughout the greater part of our history a different view prevailed. Although the value of this instrumentality in commerce and industry was fully recognized, incorporation for business was commonly denied long after it had been freely granted for religious, educational, and charitable purposes. It was denied because of fear. Fear of encroachment upon the liberties and opportunities of the individual. Fear of the subjection of labor to capital. Fear of monopoly. Fear that the absorption of capital by corporations, and their perpetual life, might bring evils similar to those which attended mortmain. There was a sense of some insidious menace inherent in large aggregations of capital, particularly when held by corporations. So at first the corporate privilege was granted sparingly; and only when the grant seemed necessary in order to procure for the community some specific benefit otherwise unattainable. The later enactment of general incorporation laws does not signify that the apprehension of corporate domination had been overcome. The desire for business expansion created an irresistible demand for more charters; and it was believed that under general laws embodying safeguards of universal application the scandals and favoritism incident to special incorporation could be avoided. The general laws, which long

385

embodied severe restrictions upon size and upon the scope of corporate activity, were, in part, an expression of the desire for equality of opportunity.[1]

(a) Limitation upon the amount of the authorized capital of business corporations was long universal. The maximum limit frequently varied with the kinds of business to be carried on, being dependent apparently upon the supposed requirements of the efficient unit. Although the statutory limits were changed from time to time, this principle of limitation was long retained. Thus in New York the limit was at first $100,000 for some businesses and as little as $50,000 for others. Until 1881 the maximum for business corporations in New York was $2,000,000; and until 1890, $5,000,000. In Massachusetts the limit was at first $200,000 for some businesses and as little as $5,000 for others. Until 1871 the maximum for mechanical and manufacturing corporations was $500,000; and until 1899 $1,000,000. The limit of $1,000,000 was retained for some businesses until 1903.

In many other states, including the leading ones in some industries, the removal of the limitations upon size was more recent. Pennsylvania did not remove the limits until 1905. Its first general act not having contained a maximum limit, that of $500,000 was soon imposed. Later, it was raised to $1,000,000; and, for iron and steel companies, to $5,000,000. Vermont limited the maximum to $1,000,000 until 1911, when no amount over $10,000,000 was authorized if, in the opinion of a judge of the Supreme Court, such a capitalization would tend "to create a monopoly or result in restraining competition in trade." Maryland limited until 1918 the capital of mining companies to $3,000,000; and prohibited them from holding more than 500 acres of land (except in Allegany County, where 1,000 acres was allowed). New Hampshire did not remove the maximum limit until 1919. It had been $1,000,000 until 1907, when it was increased to $5,000,000. Michigan did not remove the maximum limit until 1921. The maximum, at first $100,000, had been gradually increased until in 1903 it became $10,000,000 for some corporations and $25,000,000 for others; and in 1917 became $50,000,000. Indiana did not remove until 1921 the maximum limit of $2,000,000 for petroleum and natural gas corporations. Missouri did not remove its maximum limit until 1927. Texas still has such a limit for certain corporations.

(b) Limitations upon the scope of a business corporation's powers and activity were also long universal. At first, corporations could be formed under the general laws only for a limited number of purposes— usually those which required a relatively large fixed capital, like transportation, banking, and insurance, and mechanical, mining, and manufacturing enterprises. Permission to incorporate for "any lawful purpose" was not common until 1875; and until that time the duration of corporate franchises was generally limited to a period of 20, 30, or 50 years. All, or a majority, of the incorporators or directors, or both, were required to be residents of the incorporating state. The powers which the corporation might exercise in carrying out its purposes were sparingly conferred and strictly construed.

Severe limitations were imposed on the amount of indebtedness, bonded or otherwise. The power to hold stock in other corporations was not conferred or implied. The holding company was impossible.

(c) The removal by the leading industrial states of the limitations upon the size and powers of business corporations appears to have been due, not to their conviction that maintenance of the restrictions was undesirable in itself, but to the conviction that it was futile to insist upon them; because local restriction would be circumvented by foreign incorporation. Indeed, local restriction seemed worse than futile. Lesser states, eager for the revenue derived from the traffic in charters, had removed safeguards from their own incorporation laws.[2] Companies were early formed to provide charters for corporations in states where the cost was lowest and the laws least restrictive. The states joined in advertising their wares.[3] The race was one not of diligence but of laxity.[4] Incorporation under such laws was possible; and the great industrial States yielded in order not to lose wholly the prospect of the revenue and the control incident to domestic incorporation.

The history of the changes made by New York is illustrative. The New York revision of 1890, which eliminated the maximum limitation on authorized capital, and permitted intercorporate stockholding in a limited class of cases, was passed after a migration of incorporation from New York, attracted by the more liberal incorporation laws of New Jersey. But the changes made by New York in 1890 were not sufficient to stem the tide. In 1892, the Governor of New York approved a special charter for the General Electric Company, modelled upon the New Jersey act, on the ground that otherwise the enterprise would secure a New Jersey charter. Later in the same year the New York corporation law was again revised, allowing the holding of stock in other corporations. But the New Jersey law still continued to be more attractive to incorporators. By specifically providing that corporations might be formed in New Jersey to do all their business elsewhere, the state made its policy unmistakably clear. Of the seven largest trusts existing in 1904, with an aggregate capitalization of over two and a half billion dollars, all were organized under New Jersey law; and three of these were formed in 1899. During the first seven months of that year, 1336 corporations were organized under the laws of New Jersey, with an aggregate authorized capital of over two billion dollars. The Comptroller of New York, in his annual report for 1899, complained that "our tax list reflects little of the great wave of organization that has swept over the country during the past year and to which, this state contributed more capital than any other state in the Union." "It is time," he declared, "that great corporations having their actual headquarters in this State and a nominal office elsewhere, doing nearly all of their business within our borders, should be brought within the jurisdiction of this State not only as to matters of taxation but in respect to other and equally important affairs." In 1901 the New York corporation law was again revised.

The history in other states was similar. Thus the Massachusetts revision of 1903 was precipitated by the fact that "the possibilities of incorporation in other states have become well known, and have been availed of to the detriment of this Commonwealth."

Able, discerning scholars[5] have pictured for us the economic and social results of thus removing all limitations upon the size and activities of business corporations and of vesting in their managers vast powers once exercised by stockholders—results not designed by the states and long unsuspected. They show that size alone gives to giant corporations a social significance not attached ordinarily to smaller units of private enterprise. Through size, corporations, once merely an efficient tool employed by individuals in the conduct of private business, have become an institution— an institution which has brought such concentration of economic power that so-called private corporations are sometimes able to dominate the state. The typical business corporation of the last century, owned by a small group of individuals, managed by their owners, and limited in size by their personal wealth, is being supplanted by huge concerns in which the lives of tens or hundreds of thousands of employees and the property of tens or hundreds of thousands of investors are subjected, through the corporate mechanism, to the control of a few men. Ownership has been separated from control; and this separation has removed many of the checks which formerly operated to curb the misuse of wealth and power. And, as ownership of the shares is becoming continually more dispersed, the power which formerly accompanied ownership is becoming increasingly concentrated in the hands of a few. The changes thereby wrought in the lives of the workers, of the owners and of the general public, are so fundamental and far-reaching as to lead these scholars to compare the evolving "corporate system" with the feudal system; and to lead other men of insight and experience to assert that this "master institution of civilised life" is committing it to the rule of a plutocracy.[6]

The data submitted in support of these conclusions indicate that in the United States the process of absorption has already advanced so far that perhaps two-thirds of our industrial wealth has passed from individual possession to the ownership of large corporations whose shares are dealt in on the stock exchange;[7] that 200 nonbanking corporations, each with assets in excess of $90,000,000, control directly about one-fourth of all our national wealth, and that their influence extends far beyond the assets under their direct control;[8] that these 200 corporations, while nominally controlled by about 2,000 directors, are actually dominated by a few hundred persons[9]—the negation of industrial democracy. Other writers have shown that, coincident with the growth of these giant corporations, there has occurred a marked concentration of individual wealth;[10] and that the resulting disparity in incomes is a major cause of the existing depression.[11] Such is the Frankenstein monster which states have created by their corporation laws.[12]

---

[1] That the desire for equality and the dread of special privilege were largely responsible for the general incorporation laws is indicated by the fact that many states included in their constitutions a prohibition of the grant of special charters. The first constitutional provision requiring incorporation under general laws seems to be that in the New York Constitution of 1846, article 8, § 1 (except where objects of incorporations were not thus attainable). Other states followed in later years.

[2] The traffic in charters quickly became widespread. In 1894 Cook on Stock and Stockholders (3d Ed.) Vol. II, pp. 1604, 1605, thus described the situation: "New Jersey is a favorite state for incorporations. Her laws seem to be framed with a special view to attracting incorporation fees and business fees from her sister states and especially from New York, across the river. She has largely succeeded in doing so, and now runs the state government very largely on revenues derived from New York enterprises.

Maine formerly was a resort for incorporators, but a recent decision of its highest court holding stockholders liable on stock which has been issued for property, where the court thought the property was not worth the par value of the stock, makes Maine too dangerous a state to incorporate in, especially where millions of dollars of stock are to be issued for mines, patents and other choice assortments of property.

[3] Thus, in an official pamphlet containing the corporation laws of Delaware (1901), the secretary of state wrote in the preface: "It is believed that no state has on its statute books more complete and liberal laws than these"; and the outstanding advantages were then enumerated.

[4] A change in the policy of New Jersey was urged by Woodrow Wilson in his inaugural address as Governor. In 1913 the so-called "Seven-Sisters" Acts were passed by New Jersey, forbidding, among other things, intercorporate stockholding. Laws 1913, c. 18. These, in turn, were repealed in 1917. Laws 1917, c. 195.

[5] Adolf A. Berle, Jr., and Gardiner C. Means, The Modern Corporation and Private Property (1932). Compare William Z. Ripley, Main Street and Wall Street (1927).

[6] Thorstein Veblen, Absentee Ownership and Business Enterprise (1923) p. 86: Walter Rathenu, Die Neue Wirstschaft (1918) pp. 78-81.

[7] Berle and Means, The Modern Corporation and Private Property, Preface, p. vii.

[8] Id., pp. 31, 32. Compare H. W. Laidler, Concentration of Control in American Industry (1931).

[9] Berle and Means, p. 46, n. 34.

[10] Federal Trade Commission, National Wealth and Income (1926); George L. Knapp pointed out that in 1929, 504 persons had $1,185,135,300 taxable net income whereas the aggregate gross market value of all the cotton and all the wheat grown in the United States in 1930 by the 2,332,000 cotton and wheath farmers was only $1,191,451,000 (see Labor, March 31, 1931, p. 4; Id., May 19, 1931, p. 4; Id., November 29, 1932, p. 4); and that the estimate of the aggregate dividends and interest paid in the United States in 1932 was $1,642,000,000, whereas that of factory wages was $903,000,000. See Labor, February 14, 1933, p. 4.

[11] Compare J.A. Hobson, Poverty in Plenty (1931) cc. 2, 4.

[12] Compare I. Maurice Wormser, Frankenstein, Incorporated (1931).

Equality and Efficiency

by Arthur M. Okun

Chapter 4

ON what terms is the nation willing to trade equality for efficiency? Anyone who has passed a course in elementary economics can spout the right formal rule: promote equality up to the point where the added benefits of more equality are just matched by the added costs of greater inefficiency. As is so often the case with the rules that are taught in basic courses, this one provides insight but is hard to apply to the real world. The consequences of most redistributive measures on both equality and efficiency are uncertain and debatable. Confronted with a proposed tax or welfare equalization, no legislator or voter can assess how much the program would add to equality or subtract from efficiency. Thus decision-makers do not get opportunities in the real world to test neatly their priorities between the two competing objectives. But the author of a book can create a hypothetical world that suits him. And so I can propose an experiment by which you can test your attitudes toward the tradeoff.

The Leaky-Bucket Experiment

First, consider the American families who make up the bottom 20 percent of the income distribution. Their after-tax incomes in 1974 were less than $7,000, averaging about $5,000. Now consider the top 5 percent of families in the income pyramid; they had after-tax incomes ranging upward from about $28,000, and averaging about $45,000. A proposal is made to levy an added tax averaging $4,000 (about 9 percent) on the income of the affluent families in an effort to aid the low-income families.[1] Since the low-income group I selected has four times as many families as the affluent group, that should, in principle, finance a $1,000 grant for the average low-income family. However, the program has an unsolved technological problem: the money must be carried from the rich to the poor in a leaky bucket. Some of it will simply disappear in transit, so the poor will not receive all the money that is taken from the rich. The average poor family will get less than $1,000, while the average rich family gives up $4,000.

I shall not try to measure the leak now, because I want you to decide how much leakage you would accept and still support the Tax-and-Transfer Equalization Act. Suppose 10 percent leaks out; that would leave $900 for the average poor family instead of the potential $1,000. Should society still make the switch? If 50 percent leaks out? 75 percent? Even if 99 percent leaks out, the poor get a little benefit; the $4,000 taken from the rich family will yield $10 for each poor family. Where would you draw the line? Your answer cannot be right or wrong—any more than your favorite flavor of ice cream is right or wrong.

Of course, the leak represents an inefficiency. The inefficiencies of real-world redistribution include the adverse effects on the economic incentives of the rich and the poor, and the administrative costs of tax-collection and transfer programs. The opponent of redistribution might argue that my experiment obscures the dynamics of the incentive effects. He might contend that any success in equalization today is likely to be transitory, as the adverse impact on work and investment incentives mounts over time and ultimately harms even the poor. What leaks out, he might insist, is the water needed to irrigate the next crop. In addition, anyone who views market-determined incomes as ethically ideal rewards for contribution would oppose the switch, regardless of the size of the leak.

On the other hand, some would keep switching from rich to poor as long as anything at all remains in the bucket. That is the import of John Rawls' difference principle, which insists that "all social values...are to be distributed equally unless an unequal distribution of any...is to everyone's advantage"—in particular, to the advantage of the typical person in the least-advantaged group.[2]

Rawls has a clear, crisp answer: Give priority to equality. And, as he always does, Milton Friedman has a clear, crisp answer: Give priority to efficiency.[3] My answer isn't neat. My answers rarely are, and that is one trouble I generally encounter in such ideological debates. Here, as elsewhere, I compromise. I cannot accept Rawls' egalitarian difference principle. It is supposed to emerge as a consensus of people in the "original position," when they develop social rules without knowing where their own future incomes will lie on the pyramid. But, as other economists have noted,[4] that difference principle would appeal only to people who hate to take any risk whatsoever. That is the implication of the view that no inequality is tolerable unless it raises the lowest income of the society. According to this "maximin" criterion, society is worse off if the lowest-income family loses one dollar, no matter how much everybody else in the society gains. For example, a framer of the social constitution would embrace the difference principle only if he preferred a society that guaranteed every family $14,000 a year—no more and no less—over one that provided 99 percent of all families with $20,000 and 1 percent with $13,000. Put the American people in an "original position," and I certainly would not expect them to act that way.[5]

If I were in Rawls' original position, I would argue that the social constitution should not seek to settle forever the precise weighting of inequality. It should instruct the society to weight equality heavily, but it should rely on the democratic political process it establishes to select reasonable weights on specific issues as they arise.

Unlike Friedman, I would make the switch in the leaky-bucket experiment with enthusiasm if the leakage were 10 or 20 percent. Unlike Rawls, I would stop short of the 99 percent leak. Since I feel obliged to play the far-fetched games that I make up, I will report that I would stop at a leakage of 60 percent in this particular example.

If your answer, like mine, lay somewhere between 1 and 99 percent, presumably the exact figure reflected some judgment of how much the poor needed the extra income and how much the rich would be pinched by the extra taxes. If the proposed tax were to be imposed only on the handful of wealthiest American families with annual incomes above $1 million, you might well support the equalization up to a much bigger leakage. In fact, some people would wish to take money away from the super-rich even if not one cent reached the poor. And those avid redistributors are not necessarily either mean or radical. Some think such a levy might help to curb the political and social power of the Hugheses and Gettys—an argument about which I expressed my skepticism in Chapter 1. Others see it as a symbolic kind of environmental program; they feel that the villas, yachts, and jets of the super-rich poison our land, water, and air. Still others are frankly envious. For any of these reasons, many would go even farther than would John Rawls.

I shall now carry that leaky bucket on one final trip, in an effort to determine attitudes about various income levels. Consider two groups of families, one with after-tax incomes of $10,000 and the other with $18,000—figures that bracket the $14,000 national mean in 1974. Suppose the proposal is to raise taxes on the $18,000 group and aid the $10,000 families by reducing the taxes they now pay. How much of a leak would you accept and still support that transfer? These families are quite far apart on the totem pole: the $10,000 family is only about three-eighths of the way up, while the $18,000 family stands four-fifths of the way to the top. I see some value in that redistribution, but my enthusiasm is limited; a leakage of 15 percent would stop me.

Somehow, everyone seems to develop a sense of where deprivation and hardship begin along the income scale. Among economists and laymen alike, the subjective threshold of deprivation most often mentioned is half of the average income of American families.[6] If the average is taken as the mean, that would run about $7,000 in 1974 (half the median would be $6,000). Filling that gap seems far more important to many reformers than narrowing disparities above that level. That attitude has very important implications for policy. Additional doses of the old tax-and-transfer compound can essentially cure the deficiency below half of average income, as I shall argue below. But they would have only limited effects on the differentials between the $10,000 and $18,000 groups. To shrink those differentials significantly would call for alternative prescriptions. In particular, society would need to find ways for more people to climb the ladder from fair jobs to good jobs by choosing some combination of various proposals for expanded formal education, enhanced vocational and manpower training programs, subsidies to employers for promoting workers within their own ranks, or an induced narrowing of wage differentials between higher and lower job classifications. These issues intrigue me. But because the bottom end of the income scale is the top of my priority list, I shall concentrate largely on the tax-transfer options.

Inspecting the Leakages

Just how leaky is the bucket? I can offer a few clues to the answer by inspecting the various inefficiencies of the tax-transfer reshuffle—administrative costs, reduced or misplaced work effort, distorted saving and investment behavior, and possible changes in socioeconomic attitudes.

Administrative Costs

The federal government has to hire people and buy computers in order to collect taxes and to distribute transfer payments. In addition, the taxpayer bears some costs of complying with the laws, including the time spent filling out forms and the fees paid to lawyers and accountants. These are deadweight burdens of the system and they absorb resources that could be serving productive ends. But the resulting leakages are fairly small and can be reasonably quantified; only a few percent of the contents leak out in this form.

Work Effort

The impact of taxes and transfers on work effort is more difficult to assess. Suppose, as a result of increased income-tax rates, an individual takes more leisure and does less work than he would otherwise; then something leaks out of the real income and output available to all the citizens combined. In that case, to give poor Paul $1, the extra tax will cut Richard's spendable income by more than $1, by, say, inducing him to take an unpaid vacation that he would not otherwise want. The vacation must be worth something to Richard, but not as much as the income he would have chosen had it not been for the tax hike. Whether the net loss is viewed as a cut in the potential benefit to Paul or an extra burden on Richard, it is an inefficiency. In fact, dozens of researchers have plowed into this area.[7] They have uncovered virtually no significant effects of the present tax system on the amount of work effort of the affluent.[8] Some limited effects of transfer payments have been found on the work effort of secondary earners (that is, ones other than the family head) in low-income families, but virtually none on primary earners.

It does not take a research project, however, to identify misplaced—socially unproductive—efforts devoted to tax minimization. High tax rates are followed by attempts of ingenious men to beat them as surely as snow is followed by little boys on sleds. One form of misplaced effort is on-the-job luxury financed by tax-deductible business expenses. That inefficiency is evident in some uses of company airplanes and yachts, business conferences in Capri and the Caribbean, and expense-account meals in posh restaurants that thrive on soft before-tax dollars.[9] These cases seem more serious to me for their obscenity than their inefficiency. And they could be curbed significantly—although not entirely—by amendments to the Internal Revenue Code. Those amendments could tighten further the definition of an eligible deduction in the area of high living; or, instead of this stick, they could provide a carrot in the form of a standard deduction for firms that include no luxury-tainted outlays as business expenses.

At some high rate of income taxation, people might also shift their efforts toward more untaxed services of a do-it-yourself variety or switch into occupations that bestowed more untaxed rewards in the form of perquisites and amenities. But, so far as economists can see, that is not a great national trend.

Saving and Investment

The impact of high tax rates on the willingness to save and invest is the leakage cited most widely and confirmed least convincingly. If progressive taxation had had a massive and dominant effect on saving and investment, the evidence would be loud and clear in the aggregate data. In 1929, when all federal tax rates were low and barely progressive, the nation saved and invested 16 percent of GNP; in 1973, with all the allegedly onerous "soak the rich" taxes, it saved and invested the same 16 percent of GNP.[10] (And the evidence does not suggest that other forces, on balance, pushed up on the saving rate and hence might have offset some important downward pressures from the tax system.) Nonetheless, incessant warnings are sounded, as they have been for generations, that the next step toward greater progressivity will take saving and investment over a cliff. No doubt, the disincentive effects would become significant at some set of very high tax rates, but the terrain is a gentle slope rather than a cliff.

More fundamentally, the specter of depressed saving is not only empirically implausible but logically fake—as was the egalitarian argument of the thirties that redistribution was needed to cut saving and thus bolster consumption. Both are fakes because the nation can have the level of saving and investment it wants with more or less redistribution, so long as it is willing to twist some other dials. For example, any threat that greater progressivity would make saving inadequate could be offset by more federal saving through budget surpluses or more middle-class saving through special incentives. Similarly, investment demand could be bolstered by easing credit policies or strengthening investment tax incentives.[11]

Most fundamentally, the concern about the distortion of saving incentives through taxation implies that, with a properly "neutral" tax system, the marketplace would grind out an optimal level of saving and investment. But that is a fantasy. Collective decisionmaking—not the marketplace— controls the whole area of public capital formation for such diverse facilities as dams, post offices, highways, and hospitals. Moreover, investment in human capital is determined largely by public budgets for education.

The market rules investment decisions on private physical capital, but the conditions for optimality do not prevail. The market result can be optimal only if everyone faces the same interest rate, and hence can use the same scale to balance the productivity of extra investment against his time preferences for consuming more now rather than saving for later. As I emphasized in Chapter 3, that neat balance is a grand illusion when some face 8 percent interest rates, others pay 36 percent, and still others cannot borrow at any price. So long as such disparities persist, there is no way to find the right national target for saving and investment in the marketplace. Decisions on how much the current generation should curb its consumption in order to bequeath more capital to future generations belong on the agenda for collective choice as clearly as does national defense policy. The only hope for the proper participation of lower-income groups in such decisions lies in voting by ballots rather than by dollars.

Socioeconomic Leakages

Some of the concerns about leakages from tax-and-transfer redistribution focus on adverse effects on attitudes rather than losses of real GNP. They raise a different set of questions: Do high tax rates on the affluent jeopardize the motivating influence of the rags-to-riches dream? Do they imply an adverse ethical judgment on economic success that might make talented youths ashamed to strive for the jackpot prizes? With respect to the transfer recipients, do payments that are not linked to work harm pride in self-reliance or compromise the conviction that contributing is belonging?

At the same time, questions arise about potentially favorable attitudinal effects: Does equalizing help to broaden participation in the mainstream? Does it reduce the disruptive force of envy? Can a shared concern for the poor help to unite society?

The attitudinal impacts are associated with specific kinds of leakages; and, in light of them, some leaks may be particularly worrisome—even if they imply no major loss of real GNP. For example, a desire to hold open the route from rags to riches argues for some moderation in top-bracket rates on income and estates; a concern for self-reliance and the work ethic points to the development of transfer programs that promote wage-earning activity by the disadvantaged.[12]

---

[1] As the redistribution is described here, the abrupt termination of the tax just below the top 5 percent of the distribution as well as of the transfer just above the bottom 20 percent would imply inequitable "notches." Any real-world proposal would have to smooth these out, and also to determine the proper sharing of the tax burden and transfer benefits.

[2] John Rawls, A Theory of Justice (Harvard University Press, 1971), p. 62.

[3] This position is clearly implied by Friedman's discussion in Capitalism and Freedom (University of Chicago Press, 1962), pp. 161-66, although it obviously is not addressed to my particular experiment.

[4] See Kenneth J. Arrow, "Some Ordinalist-Utilitarian Notes on Rawls's Theory of Justice," Journal of Philosophy, Vol. 70 (May 10, 1973), pp. 245-63; and Sidney S. Alexander, "Social Evaluation Through Notional Choice," Quarterly Journal of Economics, Vol. 88 (November 1974), pp. 597-624.

[5] I do believe that risk aversion encourages preferences for equality. In my view, Rawls' original position provides a better framework for a behavioral interpretation of egalitarian preferences than previous attempts to derive them from interpersonal comparisons. Anyone who dislikes gambling to some degree and who doesn't know where he will land on the income pyramid would tend to prefer less inequality in the distribution of income. Moreover, I would expect civilized human beings to display some degree of risk aversion (although not an absolute aversion). I'm not convinced, however, that egalitarian social preferences must rest on personal risk aversion. Suppose a bunch of gamblers were forming a society from an original position; would they necessarily prefer a world in which the winner takes all or might they see some justice in a degree of equality?

[6] The criterion of half of average income is used in Victor R. Fuchs, "Toward a Theory of Poverty," in Task Force on Economic Growth and Opportunity, *The Concept of Poverty* (Chamber of Commerce of the United States, 1965). Lee Rainwater finds that the public's subjective attitudes correspond to this criterion. See *What Money Buys: Inequality and the Social Meanings of Income* (Basic Books, 1974), pp. 41-63, 110-17.

[7] See, for example, George F. Break, "Income Taxes and Incentives to Work; An Empirical Study," *American Economic Review*, Vol. 47 (September 1957), pp. 529-49; the literature is summarized by Break in "The Incidence and Economic Effects of Taxation," in *The Economics of Public Finance* (Brookings Institution, 1974), pp. 180-91.

[8] The absence of dramatic effects should not be surprising. It could reflect a standoff between "substitution effects" and "income effects"—the two distinct and opposite influences implied by economic theory. Higher income taxes make leisure cheaper, setting off the substitution effect of trading work for leisure. But meanwhile they induce people to work more in order to avoid a major cut in living standards, as they reduce take-home pay and hence exert an income effect.

[9] The one effort I know that seeks to document these practices is *President's Tax Message...*, Submitted by Secretary of the Treasury Douglas Dillon, at Hearings conducted by the House Committee on Ways and Means, 87 Cong. 1 sess. (1961), pp. 177-259.

[10] This reflects the operation of Denison's law, enunciated in Edward F. Denison, "A Note on Private Saving," *Review of Economics and Statistics*, Vol. 40 (August 1958), pp. 261-67. Paul A. David and John L. Scadding have recently confirmed its accuracy in "Private Savings: Ultrarationality, Aggregation, and 'Denison's Law,'" *Journal of Political Economy*, Vol. 82 (March/April 1974), Pt. 1, pp. 225-49.

[11] One egalitarian who faces up to these issues and opportunities is James E. Meade; see his *Efficiency, Equality and the Ownership of Property* (Harvard University Press, 1965), pp. 53, 59.

[12] My colleague Richard Nathan offered a particularly interesting personal reaction. Because he is most concerned about the dangers of a dependent class that has neither self-respect nor the respect of other citizens, he would support switches up to a much larger leakage in the leaky-bucket experiment if the leak involved mainly administrative costs and more leisure for the rich than if it were principally the result of diminished work effort by the poor.

The Unseen Revolution

by Peter F. Drucker

1. The Revolution No One Noticed

The Attainment of Pension Fund Socialism

IF "SOCIALISM" IS DEFINED as "ownership of the means of production by the workers"—and this is both the orthodox and the only rigorous definition—then the United States is the first truly "Socialist" country.

Through their pension funds, employees of American business today own at least 25 percent of its equity capital, which is more than enough for control. The pension funds of the self-employed, of the public employees, and of school and college teachers own at least another 10 percent, giving the workers of America ownership of more than one-third of the equity capital of American business. Within another ten years the pension funds will inevitably increase their holdings, and by 1985 (probably sooner), they will own at least 50—if not 60—percent of equity capital. Ten years later, or well before the turn of the century, their holding should exceed around two-thirds of the equity capital (that is, the common shares) plus a major portion—perhaps 40 percent—of the debt capital (bonds, debentures, and notes) of the American economy. Inflation can only speed up this process.

Even more important especially for Socialist theory, the largest employee pension funds, those of the 1,000-1,300 biggest companies plus the 35 industry-wide funds (those of the college teachers and the teamsters for instance) already own control[1] of practically every single one of the 1,000 largest industrial corporations in America. This includes control of companies with sales well below $100 million, by today's standards at best fair-sized companies, if not actually small; the pension funds also control the fifty largest companies in each of the "non-industrial" groups, that is, in banking, insurance, retail, communications, and transportation.[2] These are what Socialist theory calls the "command positions" of the economy;

whoever controls them is in command of the rest.

Indeed, aside from farming, a larger sector of the American economy is owned today by the American worker through his investment agent, the pension fund, than Allende in Chile had brought under government ownership to make Chile a "Socialist country," than Castro's Cuba has actually nationalized, or than had been nationalized in Hungary or Poland at the height of Stalinism.

In terms of Socialist theory, the employees of America are the only true "owners" of the means of production. Through their pension funds they are the only true "capitalists" around, owning, controlling, and directing the country's "capital fund." The "means of production," that is, the American economy—again with agriculture the only important exception— is being run for the benefit of the country's employees. Profits increasingly become retirement pensions, that is "deferred compensation" of the employees. There is no "surplus value"; business revenue goes into the "wage fund."

Other countries have been moving in similar directions. The first charge on big business in Japan is job and income security for its employees. This is what "lifetime employment" means in terms of economic structure. If employees cannot be fired except when a business is bankrupt, then maintaining employee jobs and employee income must be the overriding demand on business management; job security rather than profit becomes the firm's objective and the test of management performance. But there is no trace in the Japanese system of "employee ownership," let alone of ownership and control of the nation's "capital fund" by either the employees or their trustees.[3]

At the opposite end of the spectrum of modern economies is Yugoslavia. There the workers or their representatives control the enterprise in which they are employed, elect its management, serve as a review board for that management, and can remove individual managers (though they cannot abolish management, the management function, or even management positions). Yet the workers have no say whatever about the formation, supply, or allocation of capital, which remains a tightly controlled state monopoly. Yugoslav workers, unlike Japanese workers, manage the means of production. But they do not control them, nor are the means of production run for their benefit. On the contrary, the state exacts a very heavy "cost of capital"; what Marxists call "surplus value" accrues to a "state capitalist fund" rather than to the "wage fund." The workers get bonuses if the company does well. If it does poorly, on the other hand, they lose their jobs and have no guaranteed pension bought for them out of past company revenues.

Only in the United States do the employees both own and get the profits, in the form of pensions, as part of wage income. Only in the United States are the employees through their pension funds also becoming the legal owners, the suppliers of capital, and the controlling force in the capital market.

In terms of nineteenth-century political economy—and especially

Marxist theory—Yugoslavia is "state capitalism" rather than a form of "socialism," though its capitalism is tempered by a high degree of local worker autonomy and worker responsibility. Japan is a "finance capitalism," with privately owned and independently managed banks making the ultimate capital-allocation decisions, though this is a finance capitalism subject to stringent safeguards on workers' jobs and workers' income. The United States alone, in terms of economic structure, has made the final step to a genuine "socialism," in which (to use Marxist terminology) "labor" as the "source of all value" receives the "full fruits of the productive process."

In other words, without consciously trying, the United States has "socialized" the economy but not "nationalized" it. America still sees herself, and is seen elsewhere, as "capitalist"; but if terms like "socialism" or "capitalism" have any meaning at all, the American system has actually become the "decentralized market socialism" which all the Marxist church fathers, saints, and apostles before Lenin had been preaching and promising, from Engels to Bebel and Kautsky, from Viktor Adler to Rosa Luxemburg, Jaures, and Eugene Debs.

Socialism came to America neither through the ballot box nor through the class struggle let alone a revolutionary uprising, neither as a result of "expropriating the expropriators" nor through a "crisis" brought on by the "contradictions of capitalism." Indeed, it was brought about by the most unlikely revolutionary of them all—the chief executive officer of America's largest manufacturing company, General Motors. Twenty-six years ago, in April 1950, Charles Wilson, then GM's president, proposed the establishment of a pension fund for GM workers to the United Automobile Workers Union. The UAW was at first far from enthusiastic, even though by that time pensions had become a priority demand of the American union movement. The union leaders saw clearly that Wilson's proposal aimed at making the pension system the business of the private sector. And the UAW—in common with most American unions—was in those years deeply committed to governmental social security. Wilson's proposal gave the union no role whatever in administering the General Motors pension fund. Instead, the company was to be responsible for the fund, which would be entrusted to professional "asset managers."

The union feared, with good reason as subsequent events have proven, that the pension fund would strengthen management and make the union members more dependent on it. Wilson's major innovation was a pension fund investing in the "American economy"—in other words, the free-enterprise system. And while this made financial sense to the union leaders, their strong preference until then had been for pension funds invested in government securities, that is, in the public sector. The union leadership was greatly concerned lest a company-financed and company-managed private pension plan—negotiated with the union and incorporated into the collective bargaining agreement—would open up a conflict within the union membership between older workers, interested in the largest possible pension payments, and younger workers, interested primarily in the cash in their weekly pay envelope. Above all, the union realized that one of the main reasons behind Wilson's proposal was a desire to blunt union militancy by making visible the workers' stake in company profits and company success. (One of the stalwarts in the GM department of the UAW proposed at that time, in all seriousness, that the union should lodge an unfair labor practices complaint against Wilson, since his pension proposal could have no purpose except to undermine the union.) But Wilson's offer was too tempting, especially to the rapidly growing number of older workers in the UAW. And so, in October, 1950, the GM Pension Fund began to operate.

5. New Alignments in American Politics

We have seen that pension fund socialism and the demographic changes underlying it will create new problems and demand new policies. They will create new issues and, predictably, make irrelevant many of the most visible issues of the last generation. They will fundamentally affect the temper, mood, values, and behavior of American society and, with it, of American politics.

We have also seen that pension fund socialism is in the process of creating a genuine new "interest group." And through the pension funds, it is creating the institutions around which this interest group can organize, institutions which represent the concerns and priorities of the new center of population and social gravity: older people on retirement and the older employees (past fifty or so) to whom retirement provisions are becoming increasingly important.

But will this new interest group lead to a realignment in American politics? It has all the qualifications to become a new political center. It is an interest group which cuts across existing lines. It contains whites and blacks, men and women, the middle class, the white-collar worker, and the blue-collar worker. It is thus capable of integrating people from all areas of American society and of mobilizing them for joint action in a common interest. It is a group with clearly definable interests; yet these are not divisive but integrating, interests—such as enable people, otherwise separated by their sectional concerns, to join in common effort. It could thus serve as a unifying focus, the center of American politics.

It is, further, a group with clearly defined self-interests. But they are not "selfish" interests. "What is good for the older people is good for America," may not be the "sexiest" slogan, but it is a plausible one. As an interest group, the new population center of gravity could therefore present itself as acting in the best interests of the entire society. After all, almost every adult member of this society—certainly the great majority who are employed and working—sees himself eventually as a member of the new group. What is good for it may not be good for him right away; but it is also not inimical to his own long-term interests. "Long-term" means, after all, only a few years for the large and growing segment of the working population that has already reached the age where its retirement support is a major concern, and the pension claim by far its largest asset and most valuable property.

An effective political faction requires common, identifiable "enemies," and the new group has such "enemies." There are three major issues on which the new interest group is held together by common opposition. These issues are, first, the interests of the "welfare society" of the retirement and pension system against the "welfare state"; second, the interest in productivity to redress its own inequality versus those egalitarian demands that threaten productivity; and third, the interest in a stable currency as one priority, if not the first priority, of economic policy. Beyond this, however, the new interest group has no "do's" or "don'ts." It is flexible and can work with anybody else. By and large, its imperatives do not put it into conflict with the traditional major interest groups of American society—whether labor, the farmer, business, or the employed middle class.

This new interest group has its own representative institution: the pension fund. Therefore, it has the means to organize itself for visibility, representation, and action. It has the organ through which it can make effective the controlling ownership in American business which it already holds. It has a "professional" representative in the "asset manager" and therefore access to the universities, the journalists, the opinion-makers, let alone the politicians. And the fact that this organ is quite different from the traditional organizations through which American interest groups have reached such opinion-makers and decision-makers may actually make it more effective and more powerful. The "asset manager," precisely because he is a professional, is not a lobbyist.

Finally, this new group is permanent. Both in numbers, that is, in absolute strength, and in the proportion of the adult population, that is, in relative strength, it will grow for a long time to come. The "youth generation" of the sixties was also a new "demographic center of gravity," to be sure. But at the very time when it became visible, vocal, and influential, it was already a transient, short-lived phenomenon and declining. And unlike "disadvantaged minority groups" the older people are not held together by a condition which either individual success or social action can change and make unimportant. The condition of the older people as well as their numerical weight are permanent, or at least "givens" for long decades to come.

These are almost the ideal, textbook qualifications for an interest group in America to become the center of political alignments. And pension fund socialism has emerged just at the time when the traditional alignments of American politics seem to be in utter confusion and disarray. Will this new interest group representing pension fund socialism bring about a major realignment in American politics? Will it become the new center, the new "majority"?

It certainly cannot be ruled out that pension fund socialism will lead to the emergence of a permanent majority—thought not the "silent majority" nor the "new majority" nor any of the other "majorities" which have been talked about these last few years. This permanent majority would comprise the employees over fifty or fifty-five, or that majority among them that is under employer pension plans; the self-employed with their own rapidly growing pension plans, which would include such potent groups as the lawyers, the physicians, the small businessmen, and the productive family farmers; the retired employees under pension plans; and the managements of institutions with private pension plans which, in addition to business, would include the health care institutions and a goodly part of the country's educational institutions, but also governments, especially local governments, whose solvency is threatened by inflationary pressures on pension plan funding.

This, in many ways, would be a reconstitution of the "old majority," that majority of farmer, skilled labor, and small business which Mark Hanna built in the 1890s and which dominated the country until the rise of mass production and giant corporations, the depression and the advent of the New Deal.

Mark Hanna's majority of 1896 is considered today to have been conservative, if not reactionary. This was not how his contemporaries saw it, including Samuel Gompers, the founder of the American Federation of Labor. Indeed, Mark Hanna's majority was basically a radical one. It put a new principle in the center and established it as foundation for the common interest. Mark Hanna no longer believed in the "invisible hand" of self-interest; but he still believed in an "invisible hand": productivity, tested in the market. It was productivity which established the common focus of interest for the major groups in Mark Hanna's America. It was productivity that drove Mark Hanna's economic engine. This was radical innovation in 1896. Indeed, the very word "productivity" was coined in Mark Hanna's circle, if not by Mark Hanna himself, as a manifesto to oust from power the old conservatives who had controlled the Republican Party ever since the Civil War, and whose majority was rapidly crumbling. But while Mark Hanna's new "invisible hand" established his new majority in power and gave it cohesion for more than a generation, it, in the last analysis, became his undoing during the Great Depression.[4]

A new permanent majority would have "a visible hand": the pension fund mechanism, which both symbolizes and makes effective the direct relationship between economic performance and economic welfare. This majority would have a great many internal conflicts—but so did Mark Hanna's majority of farmer, skilled worker, and small business. It would, however, also have major common interests, in economic performance, in equality based on efficiency, and in the stability of the currency. It would have what every permanent political grouping needs: common enemies— the "bureaucracy" and "transfer payments" to those not contributing from their earnings to the majority's pension funds and retirement monies but expecting to be supported by them. It would thus be able to develop both a political platform and an economic program.

This would not be a "conservative" majority. In fact, in many ways it would have a strong tendency toward radicalism, for example, in health care, housing, and equal rights for women. But the issues it would see as crucial—the emotions it feels, the things it considers important—would be very different from those which are seen, felt, and considered important today by "liberals" and "conservatives" alike. And the questions it will ask are almost certain to be totally different. In other words this alignment, if it comes, will be genuintely "new." It will no more bear resemblance to the conservative alignment of pre-New Deal days than to the liberal alignment of the last forty years.

Today such a majority might seem quite unlikely. But it is no more unlikely than Mark Hanna's "majority"—the majority that brought the Republican Party to power in 1896 and held together after that for thirty-five years—must have seemed to the conventional wisdom at the time of Cleveland, of Bryan, or of the traditional Republicans of the "GOP" of 1890. This new majority would require great political leadership. But it might also be brought together by the demagogue railing against "pointy-headed bureaucrats."

Predicting a new alignment for American politics is one of our oldest political sports. Since the earliest days of the Republic, every political alignment and every "majority" has appeared precarious, fragile, in disarray, on the point of unraveling. Yet such alignments, once established, have shown tremendous staying power in American politics. They have changed far less often than in any other country—perhaps because they are non-ideological and unashamedly interest-based. Existing political alignments in the United States are singularly resistant to political theory. Not only do they survive defeats; unlike most coalitions, whether political or military, American political alignments even survive their victories.

But realignments do occur. What tends to bring them about are fundamental changes in the population structure and in the center of population gravity. American political alignments change, as a rule, when new major institutions emerge as the result of fundamental shifts in the structure of ownership and in the control of major productive resources. What triggers realignment in American politics is thus precisely the kind of development which constitutes "the unseen revolution," the kind of development that brought pension fund socialism to America.

The emergence of the pension funds, therefore, offers the possibility—for the first time perhaps since the 1930s—of a genuine realignment in American politics, a realignment based on the realization that America has achieved her own distinct brand of "socialism."

---

[1] That is, they own at least one-third.

[2] The only exceptions are a few government-owned businesses, such as TVA; farmer-owned producer cooperatives like Sunkist Oranges; policy-holder-owned "mutual insurance companies," such as Prudential and most of the other very large life-insurance companies; and a shrinking group of smaller firms, in which the founders or their immediate descendants still either own the entire business or control it.

[3] On this, see my paper "Economic Realities and Enterprise Strategy," in *Modern Japanese Organization and Decision-Making,* edited by Ezra F. Vogel (Berkeley: University of California Press, 1975).

[4] Very few people seem to know that Mark Hanna not only founded the National Association of Manufacturers, but also played a crucial role in the formation of the American Federation of Labor (second perhaps only to Samuel Gompers) and was largely responsible for the development of "business unionism." It was this national interest in economic performance and high wages that Mark Hanna meant by the term "free enterprise," which he in all likelihood coined to distinguish the "American system" from "capitalism."

The Corporation and
Society in the 1970's

by Daniel Bell

OVER the last few years, there has been a notable change in public attitudes toward the corporation. Only twelve years ago, writing in Edward S. Mason's magisterial compendium on *The Corporation in Modern Society*, Eugene V. Rostow could comment:

> In reviewing the literature about the current development of [the large, publicly-held] corporations, and about possible programs for their reform, one is struck by the atmosphere of relative peace. There seems to be no general conviction abroad that reform is needed. The vehement feelings of the early thirties, expressing a sense of betrayal and frustration at a depression blamed on twelve years of business leadership, are almost entirely absent.

The reason for that tolerant and even benign attitude towards the corporation in the 1950's is not hard to find. Apart from the general sense of social peace induced by the Eisenhower administration (a peace maintained, in part, by the mobilization of the sentiments of society against an external enemy), a new and seemingly satisfactory conception of the role of the corporation in the society had arisen.

For 75 years, going back to 1890 when Congress passed the Sherman Antitrust Act, the corporation had been viewed with populist suspicion because of its size. Size, in the American lexicon, means power, and the bigness of business was perceived as both an economic and political threat to democracy. Economic size was equated with market power, or the ability to control (within limits) the price of products offered for sale. Large-scale assets were equated with undue influence, either in a local community or state, or in the nation itself.

But in the more than half century's experience with antitrust, a new economic sophistication had been developed. One was the important distinction between size and market control, and the realization that the two are not completely related. The two biggest manufacturing companies today are Standard Oil of New Jersey and General Motors, with $19.2 billion and $14.1 billion respectively in assets. GM has about 55 per cent of the United States' automotive production; but Standard Oil, though larger than GM, has only about 9 per cent of domestic oil refining and an even smaller percentage of production.

Size, clearly, is not a good predictor of market control. Market control is measured by "concentration ratios," i.e., the sales of the largest four companies, in a product line, as a percentage of total product sales. But it seems reasonably clear that, since the turn of the century, the concentration ratios have gone down considerably and that, in most industries, there is not increasing concentration but rather a ceaseless flux.[1]

But the more important shift was a change in ideology. The idea took hold that "size" was less relevant than "performance." Performance itself is an elusive criterion. It embraces the idea of receptivity to innovation; willingness to expand capacity (one of the chief charges by liberal economists in the 1940's against such "monopolistic" industries as aluminum and steel was that they were unwilling to expand capacity); the reflection of increased productivity in better quality, higher wages, and steady, if not lower, prices; and similar indices of responsiveness to the needs of the society.

The clearest mark of performance was growth. The fear of the 1930's, after all, was stagnation. Liberal economists such as Alvin Hansen had predicted, in fact, that the economy had achieved such a state of "maturity" that there was no longer the possibility of expansion. The facts belied these fears. New technological frontiers opened up after the war; and the large corporations took the initiative.

A vigorous, large company could present its case to the public that size was immaterial, so long as the corporation displayed those hallmarks of dynamism that added up to "performance." In fact, as J. K. Galbraith argued in his book *American Capitalism,* size was an asset because it enabled the large corporation to underwrite technological progress.

> It is admirably equipped for financing technical development. Its organization provides strong incentives for undertaking development and for putting it into use...The power that enables the firm to have some influence on price insures that the resulting gains will not be passed on to the public by imitators (who have stood none of the costs of development) before the outlay for development can be recouped. *In this way market power protects the incentive to technical development.* [Italics in the original.]

Here was a strong and sophisticated defense of bigness by the criterion of performance. And, to a considerable extent, the ideology of American business in the postwar years became its ability to perform. The justification of the corporation no longer lay primarily in the natural right of private property, but in its role as an instrument for providing more and more goods to the people. Because the corporation seemed to be performing this role adequately, criticism of it did, indeed, become muted, so that by the end of the 1950's the corporation had established a new legitimacy in American life.

The New Criticism

Today that legitimacy is being challenged, or at least the tolerant and benign attitude toward the corporation has receded. The paradox is that the ground of the new criticism is no longer size or bigness (though some old populist echoes persist), but performance itself. A feeling has begun to spread in the country that corporate performance has made the society uglier, dirtier, trashier, more polluted and noxious. The sense of identity between the self-interest of the corporation and the public interest has been replaced by a sense of incongruence.

Any issue that becomes ideological becomes distorted. The facts of spoliation of countryside and the reduction of various amenities are obvious; the reasons less so. One evident cause is the sheer increase of numbers of persons in the society and a change in social habits. Take, for example, the national parks: in 1930, the number of visitor-days (one person staying twelve hours) was 3 million in a population of 122 million; by 1960, it was 79 million, in a population of 179 million; and in 1968, there were 157 million visitor-days in a population of 200 million. The results are described vividly in an account in *The New York Times*:

> Yosemite, only a day's drive from San Francisco and Los Angeles, is generally considered the most overcrowded park. Congestion reaches its peak on major holidays and this Labor Day weekend was no exception. The constant roar in the background was not a water-fall but traffic. Transistor radios blared forth the latest rock tunes. Parking was at a premium. Dozens of children clambered over the rocks at the base of Yosemite Falls. Campsites, pounded into dust by incessant use, were more crowded than a ghetto. Even in remote areas, campers were seldom out of sight of each other. The whole experience was something like visiting Disneyland on a Sunday.

Moreover, if we take pollution of the air and water as the criterion of social ill, then clearly all sections of the society are at fault: The farmer who, by seeking to increase food production, uses more nitrate fertilizer and thus pollutes the rivers of the country; the individual automobile owner who, seeking greater mobility, spews noxious gas into the atmosphere; the Atomic Energy Commission which, in seeking to expand nuclear power, may be responsible for thermal pollution of the waters; and the corporation whose smokestacks emit smog-creating gases in the air, or whose waste products pollute the lakes.

But if one takes the attitude that everyone is to blame—and simply ends with the moral exhortation for each person to restrain his behavior— then one misses the important point. Such a situation itself points to the fact that the allocative mechanism of society, the proper distribution of costs and resources, is not working. In a free society, the socially optimal distribution of resources and goods exists where the market reflects the true economic cost of an item. But where private costs and social costs diverge, as A. C. Pigou pointed out 50 years ago, then the allocation of goods becomes skewed. When the owner of a factory has no incentive to take account of costs to others of the pollution he generates because these costs are not charged to him, factory output (or automobile mileage in the case of a car owner) will be at a higher level than is socially optimal.

The growing problem for modern society is this increasing divergence of private costs and social costs (what economists call technically an "externality," because such costs are not "internalized" by a firm in its own cost accounting). But along with this awareness there arises, too, the question whether the strict conception of costs—and return on investment—that is the rationale of the accounting procedures of the firm are at all adequate today. The question that then arises involves, not just the "social responsibility" of any particular corporation, but the "rightness" of the broader pattern of social organization and of the social goals of the society. And, to the extent that the corporation has been the institution integral to the existing pattern, it becomes the starting point of a new inquiry.

Perhaps we can see the quite radical difference between these two perspectives by setting up two modes, which I call the *economizing* mode and the *sociologizing* mode, as polar extremes within which the actions of the corporation can be estimated and judged.

The Economizing Mode

Beginning little more than 150 years ago, modern Western society was able to master a secret denied to all previous societies—a steady increase of wealth and a rising standard of living by peaceful means. Almost all previous societies had sought wealth by war, plunder, expropriation, tax-farming, or other means of extortion. Economic life, in the shorthand of game theory, was a zero-sum game; one group of winners could benefit only at the expense of another group of losers. The secret mastered by modern Western society was *productivity*, the ability to gain a more than proportional output from a given expenditure of capital, or a given exertion of labor; or, more simply, society could now get "more with less effort or less cost." Economic life could be a non-zero-sum game; everyone could end up a winner, though with differential gains.

In the popular view, productivity was made possible by the introduction of machinery or, more specifically, the discovery of new forms of power, mechanical or electrical, hitched to an engine. Clearly much of this view is true. But productivity, as a concept, became possible only through a new "supporting system" which dictated the placement of machines in a new way. To put the matter less abstractly, modern industrial society is a product of two "new men," the engineer and the economist, and of the concept which unites the two—the concept of efficiency. For the engineer, the design of a machine and its placement vis-a-vis other machines is a problem of finding the "one best way" to extract maximum output within a given physical layout. The economist introduces a calculus of monetary costs, within the framework of relative prices, as a means of finding the most appropriate mix of men and machines in the organization of production.

Modern industrial life, in contrast with traditional society, has been revolutionized by these innovations. The new sciences have introduced a distinctive mode of life. We can call it *economizing*. Economizing is the science of the best allocation of scarce resources among competing ends; it is the essential technique for the reduction of "waste"—as this is measured by the calculus stipulated by the regnant accounting technique. The conditions of economizing are a market mechanism as the arbiter of allocation, and a fluid price system which is responsive to the shifting patterns of supply and demand.

Economics itself, over the past 100 years, has developed a rigorous and elegant general system of theory to explain the relative prices of goods and services and of the factors in production, the allocation of those factors to various uses, the level of employment, and the level of prices. With economics comes a rational division of labor, specialization of function, complementarity of relations, the use of production functions (the best mix of capital and labor at relative prices), programming (the best ordering of scheduling of mixed batches in production or in transportation), etc. The words we associate with economizing are "maximization," "optimization," "least cost"—in short, the components of a conception of rationality. But this conception of rationality, it should be pointed out, was intended by its utilitarian founders as a rationality of *means,* a way of best satisfying a given *end.* The ends of life themselves were never given; they were seen as multiple or varied, to be chosen freely by the members of society. Economics would seek to satisfy these choices in the "best way," i.e., the most efficient means possible in order to "maximize" satisfaction.

For an understanding of the economizing mode, this distinction between rational means and a plurality of ends must be emphasized. Modern industrial society, being a liberal society, has never felt the need to define its ends or to establish priorities within some set of ends. It has always eschewed such collective decision-making. No conscious social decision ws made to "transform" society 200 years ago. No conclave met, as in a French constituent assembly or an American constitutional convention, to declare a new social order. Yet it is quite clear what the new goals of the new industrial society were to be—the ends that became "given" all involved the rising material output of goods. And other, traditional modes of life (the existence of artisan skills and crafts, the family hearth as a site of work) were sacrificed to the new system for the attainment of these economic ends.

Commonplace as this history may be, the singular fact needs to be emphasized. Unlike political change, no one "voted" for these decisions in some collective fashion, no one assessed (or could assess) the consequences of these changes. Yet a whole new way of life, based on the utilitarian calculus or the economizing mode, gradually began to transform the whole of society.

The Corporation: A New Social Invention

Productivity is a technique, steadily rising output of goods is an end; for the two to be realized they have to be institutionalized in some renewable system of organization. That institution was the corporation.

Much of economic history and some of economic theory has focused on the entrepreneur as the singularly important person who, sensing new opportunities, breaks the cake of custom and innovates new areas of economic life. Much of contemporary sociological theory has dealt with the manager as the faceless technocrat who runs a routinized operation. But to understand the corporation, one has to turn not to the entrepreneur (and the myths about him) or the manager (and the caricatures that are drawn of him), but to a figure historically and sociologically intermediate between the two—the organizer.

The church and the army have been the historic models of organizational life. The business corporation, which took its present shape in the first decades of the 20th century, was the one new social invention to be added to these historic forms. The men who created that form—Theodore N. Vail who put together AT&T, Walter Teagle of Standard Oil of New Jersey, Alfred P. Sloan of GM—designed an instrument which coordinates men, materials, and markets for the production of goods and services at least cost with the best possible return on capital investment. They did so by introducing the idea of functional rationality, of *economizing,* as a new mode of ordering social relations.

Of the three, only Alfred P. Sloan has put down directly the principles he employed. His account, *My Years With General Motors,* is fascinating, and one can take his sketch as prototypical of the corporate mode of mid-century America. The most striking aspect of Mr. Sloan's book is its language. Sloan's key terms are *concept, methodology,* and *rationality.* Throughout the book, Sloan uses these terms to explain the innovations he made in General Motors: "Durant had no systematic financial methodology. It was not his way of doing business." "The spacing of our product line of ten cars in seven lines in early 1921 reveals its irrationality." "In product variety only Buick and Cadillac had clear divisional concepts of their place in the market."

The language is not an accident or an affectation. It is surprising only to those who associate such language with the academy and not with the analytical necessities of organization. The language derives in part from Sloan's training as an engineer (he took a degree at MIT in 1895); but more, it derives directly from the revolution in organization that Sloan introduced: the initiation of detailed planning, of statistical methods and of financial controls. In explaining why he relied on market research and forecasting rather than salesmen's intuition, he remarked: ". . . In the automobile industry you cannot operate without programming and planning. It is a matter of respecting figures on the future as a guide."

The reasons for the success of General Motors can be attributed, in simplified fashion, to two elements: A market strategy based on a "clear concept" of product lines and an organizational form which combined decentralization of operations with coordination of policy.[2] The organizational structure of General Motors is commonplace now, and has been widely copied by most large corporations. At the time of its innovation, it was a novelty. Stated most simply, the principle of organization is to have a complete breakdown of the costs of each unit, and to exercise control of operating divisions through stringent budgets. Before the system was instituted, divisions in GM sold their parts to other divisions (e.g., a battery division to a car division) on the basis of cost plus a predetermined percentage. But the corporation at the top did not know which units were profitable and which not. "It was natural for the divisions to compete for investment funds," Sloan wrote, "but it was irrational for the general officers of the company not to know where to place the money to best advantage."

What Sloan did was to treat each division as a separate company, with the corporate group at the top acting as a "holding company," and to measure the performance of each division by the rate of return on investment consistent with attainable volume. The rate of return is thus a measure of performance and a means of ranking each division, not on the basis of its absolute profit alone, but on the rate of return on capital invested. The measure, in short, is the margin of profit multiplied by the rate of turnover of invested capital. Through these measures, the corporate group at the top could determine how to allocate the corporation's money in order to achieve a maximum return for the whole.

All aspects of corporate policy became subordinated to that end. In specifying the corporation's philosophy, Sloan was explicit:

> To this end [he writes] we made the assumptions of the business process explicit. We presumed that the first purpose in making a capital investment is the establishment of a business that will pay satisfactory dividends and preserve and increase its capital value. The primary object of the corporation, therefore, we declared, was to make money not just motor cars. Positive statements like this have a flavor that has gone out of fashion; but I still think that the ABC's of business have merit for reaching policy conclusions.

The economizing system of each corporation locks with each other to create a social system. Earnings per share of common stock becomes the balance wheel around which the system turns. If the earnings of a firm drop, it may find it difficult to attract capital, or may have to pay more for capital vis-a-vis other firms. Thus, the allocation of capital in the economy follows the same principle as it does within the corporation. Locked thus into competition, the degree of freedom of any single corporation to break away from this measuring rod—the rate of return on investment—is limited. Any change in the system has to be a change in the entire system. Profitability and productivity, thus, are the indices of corporate success. They are the tests of meeting the demands of the marketplace and the demand for the efficient distribution of resources within the firm and between members of the society. This is the rationale for the *economizing* mode for the corporation, as for the economy.

Limits of The Economizing Mode

The theoretical virtue of the market is that it coordinates human interdependence in some optimal fashion, in accordance with the expressed preferences of buyers and sellers (within any given distribution of income). But what ultimately provides direction for the economy, as Veblen pointed out long ago, is not the price system but *the value system of the culture* in which the economy is embedded. The price system is only a mechanism for the relative allocation of goods and services within the framework of *the kinds of demand* generated. Accordingly, economic guidance can only be as efficacious as the cultural value system which shapes it.

The value system of industrial society (communist as well as capitalist) has been centered around the desirability of economic growth; and the cultural value of Western society, particularly American society, has been the increase of private-consumption economic goods. There are, however, three drawbacks (at least) to this system.

The most important consideration is that it measures only *economic* goods. But as E. J. Mishan has pointed out, and as a once popular refrain had it, "the best things in life are free." Clean air, beautiful scenery, pure water, sunshine, to say nothing of the imponderables such as ease of meeting friends, satisfaction in work, etc.—they are "free goods" either because they are so abundant that there is little or no cost, or because they are not appropriable and saleable. Such free goods contribute greatly to our total welfare. But in our present accounting schemes, priced at zero, they add nothing to the economist's measure of wealth. Nor, when they disappear, do they show up as subtractions from wealth.

The second consideration is that growth, as measured by our present economic accounting, tends to generate more and more "spillovers" which become costs borne directly by other private parties or distributed among the society as a whole. These are what economists call "externalities." Externalities (or "external costs"), as economists define the term, are the unintended or unplanned impact, the "fallout" on Third Part C (and often D, E, and F, as well), of a private transaction between parties A and B. The result is a social cost (though frequently a social benefit, too). The most obvious example of a social cost is air pollution—the result, in part, of the increasing number of private cars in the society. In every elementary economics textbook, air was once the classic illustration of the "free good." Yet the irony is that in the next 30 years one of the most scarce resources we may have (in the sense of proportionately sharply rising costs) will be clean air. The costs of automobile disposal are not charged to the automobile owner; similarly, the costs of salvaging a depressed coal mining community are not charged to the companies selling the competing fuels which may have driven coal off the market.

The third problem with the economizing mode is that the value system of American society emphasizes, as the primary consideration, the satisfaction of individual private consumption; the result is an imbalance between public goods and private goods. In the popular psychology, taxes are not considered as the necessary purchase of public services that an individual cannot purchase for himself, but as money "taken away from *me* by *them.*" Taxes, thus, are not considered as an addition to welfare, but as subtractions from it. This is reinforced by politicians who claim that taxes are too "high" (but by what standard?) rather than asking: Are there needs which can be met only by public goods, and what are the taxes buying?

Thus, if one is trying to assess welfare (or the quality of life) in some optimal fashion, the problem is not only the simple commitment to economic growth, but the nature of the accounting and costing system of the economizing mode which has served to mask many of its deficiencies. Our fascination with Gross National Product is a good illustration.

GNP, Private Costs, and Social Costs

Conventionally we measure economic welfare primarily through the figures of Gross National Product. GNP was a marvelous economic concept. Developed largely by Simon Kuznets and his colleagues at the National Bureau of Economic Research in the late 1930's, it first came into government use in 1945 and is the basis of the framework of the United States National Economic Accounts. These accounts allow us to sketch the macroeconomic levels of activity in the society, and through them to measure economic shortfalls, the potentials of full employment revenues and the like, as a means of deciding on economic policy. But there are several drawbacks as well, particularly if we are concerned not only with wealth but the welfare of society.

GNP measures the value of goods and services bought and sold in the market. But the measure itself is only "additive." It does not discriminate between a genuine addition to welfare and what, in effect, may be a subtraction but is counted as an economic plus. Thus, in the conventional example, the output of a steel mill is a value added to GNP. But if the steel mill pollutes a lake, and then uses additional resources to clean up the lake, the new expenditure is also added to GNP. Similarly an increase in environmental deterioration over time would not show up as a decline in real output because the flow of benefits from the environment is not counted as an output to begin with (e.g., the usability of a lake or river for swimming). But expenditures designed to reduce environmental deterioration would show up as increased real output.

More important, however, is the fact that in assessing *public* services we do not have a means of estimating actual benefits or values. In items that are sold in the market, such as automobiles or clothing, we have market prices as the value individuals place on the products. But how do we value publicly provided services such as health, or education, or protection? Our accounting system does so only by the "input" costs, not by the output values. Thus the "output" of police services is measured by salaries paid to members of the Police Department, the costs of police cars, etc., not by the social and economic value of crimes prevented or violators apprehended; the value of health services is measured by the costs of doctor's fees and drugs, not by the reduction of time lost on account of illness; the value of education is measured by the cost of teachers' salaries, equipment, etc., not by the value imputable to the gain in pupil knowledge.

This is a central problem in the question of how much money should be spent on "public goods." People grumble over taxes, but there is no way, at present, of showing that the benefits received for these services may be far greater than the costs. And while there is no way of knowing, it is likely that public services of this kind are "undervalued," and therefore less appreciated.

The second limitation of the accounting system, which derives from the growing existence of externalities, is the divergence between private and social costs. The idea of social costs is an old one, going back 150 years to the socialist economist Sismondi. But it was not until about 50 years ago, when A. C. Pigou wrote his *Economics of Welfare,* that the phenomenon of social costs was integrated into the conceptual system of neoclassical equilibrium economics. Pigou pointed out that the investment of additional resources may throw costs "upon people not directly concerned" such as the "uncompensated damage done to surrounding woods from railway engines."[3]

But for almost half a century, this idea of divergence between private cost and social cost was almost completely neglected. Now with the rising concern with environmental spoliation, the second-order consequences of technological change and the increase in "externalities," the problem has moved into the center of social policy. In the next decade one of the major social questions will be the determination of who is to pay the cost of such externalities, and how the amounts will be assessed. Which costs ought to be borne by the parties that generate the costs, and which, legitimately, should be borne by the society as a whole, will be one of the most difficult questions in the political economy of the future. What we have now is only the beginning awareness of the problem. What we lack is a genuine total cost matrix which, for particular instances, would be able to assess the costs and benefits of particular actions and policies.[4]

The Sociologizing Mode

Important as all these issues are, they do not go to the heart of the matter, which is that the economizing mode is based on the proposition that *individual* satisfaction is the unit in which costs and benefits are to be reckoned. This is an atomistic view of society and reflects the utilitarian fallacy that the sum total of individual decisions is equivalent to a social decision. Yet the aggregate of individual decisions has collective effects far beyond the power of any individual to manage, and which often vitiate the individual's desires. Thus, every individual may value the freedom and mobility which a personal automobile provides, yet the aggregate effect of so many autos on the roads at once can lead to clogged transportation. We might all accept, in the abstract, the principle that the automobile has become a vehicle of uglification; yet lacking a social decision about which alternative modes of transportation might best serve an area, I might have, willy-nilly, to go out and buy a car. Each of us, individually, may see the consequences of an individual action, but lacking a social mechanism to assess it, we become helpless, drift, and thereby accelerate it.

In effect, in contrast to the economizing mode of thought, one can specify—I apologize for the heavy-handed clumsiness—a sociologizing mode, or the effort to judge a society's needs in more conscious fashion,[5] and (to use an old-fashioned terminology) to do so on the basis of some explicit conception of the "public interest."

Two fundamental questions are involved.

First, the conscious establishment of social justice by the inclusion of all persons into the society. If the value system of a society is made more explicit as a means of guiding the allocative system (pricing) of a society, this value system must also establish, however roughly, the "right" distribution of income in the society, the minimum income available to all citizens, etc.

The second is the relative size of the public and the private sector. Economic goods, to put it in textbook fashion, are of two types, individual and social. Individual goods are "divisible"; each person buys the goods or services he wants—clothes, appliances, automobiles—on the basis of free consumer choice. Social goods are not "divisible" into individual items of possession, but are a communal service—national defense, police and fire protection, public parks, water resources, highways, and the like. These goods and services are not sold to individual consumers and are not adjusted to individual tastes. The nature and amounts of these goods must be set by a single decision, applicable jointly to all persons. Social goods are subject, therefore, to communal or political, rather than individual demand.

A man cannot ask for and individually buy in the market place his share of unpolluted air, even if he were willing to pay extra for it. These are actions that have to be taken in coordinated fashion through public channels. We can assign the costs of air pollution to its source, whether industrial, municipal, or individual, in order to force culprits to reduce the pollution, or we can use the money for remedial measures. In the same way, the laying out of roads, the planning of cities, the control of congestion, the organization of health care, the cleaning up of environmental pollution, the support of education—all these, necessarily, become matters of public policy, of public concern and often (though not necessarily) of public funding.

To say, in effect, that the public sector of the society has to be expanded, is not to assume, naively, that the failures of the market will now be remedied. Each arena has its own problems, and the beginning of political wisdom is to recognize the ineluctable difficulties in each. Public decision-making can easily be as irrational and counter-productive as private decision-making. The major sociological problem ahead will be the test of our ability to *foresee* the effects of social and technological change and to *construct alternative courses* in accordance with different valuations of ends, at different costs.

Varieties of Planning

A considerable amount of planning goes on already. Every major corporation today necessarily operates in accordance with a one-year fiscal plan and a five-year market strategy in order to meet competition or to expand its size. Each company plans singly and each introduces its own new technologies—yet no one monitors the collective effects. The same is true of the planning of various government agencies. In considering social effects, one finds this kind of planning unsatisfactory.

The first flaw is the fallacy inherent in single-purpose planning itself.[6] Most engineers, developers, industrialists, and government officials are single-purpose planners. The objective they have in mind is related almost solely to the immediate problem at hand—whether it be a power site, a highway, a canal, a river development—and even when cost-benefit analysis is used (as in the case of the Army Corps of Engineers) there is little awareness of, and almost no attempt to measure, the multiple consequences (i.e., the second-order and third-order effects) of the new system.

The second is the failure to make the necessary distinction between, as Veblen put it, the technological and institutional processes, or, in the terminology used by a panel of the National Academy of Sciences, between the "technologies" and "the supporting system." The automobile, the SST, pesticides, drugs—all these are technologies in the physical engineering sense of the term. The support system is the organization of production and distribution, or more generally the economic and legal matrix in which the technology is embedded. The simple point is that there is no "technological imperative," no exact one-to-one correspondence between a particular technology and a specific supporting system. As Jack Burnham pointed out in a pungent way: "When we buy an automobile we no longer buy an object in the old sense of the word, but instead we purchase a three-to-five year lease for participation in the state-recognized private transportation system, a highway system, a traffic safety system, an industrial parts-replacement system, a costly insurance system. . . ."[7]

One may therefore, depending on the problem, seek to change either the technology (the gasoline engine) or the support system (unrestricted private use of the roads). But what this allows us to do is to compare alternative modes, at alternative costs, and to design better systems to serve social needs. This, in turn, suggests a need for national "technology assessment."[8] With few exceptions, the decision about the future use of a technology today is made by the economic or institutional interests who will primarily benefit from it. But as the panel of the National Academy of Sciences argues: "Decisions concerning the development and application of new technologies must not be allowed to rest solely on their immediate utility to their sponsors and users. Timely consideration must be given to their long-term sacrifices entailed by their use and proliferation, and to potentially injurious effects upon sectors of society and the environment often quite remote from the places of production and application."

In rather inchoate fashion, assessment and decisional systems already exist in the federal government. The Federal Water Pollution Control Administration, the National Air Pollution Control Administration, and the Environmental Control Administration, all are empowered to make studies of consequences; but they have less power to establish controls. Some agencies, such as the Atomic Energy Commission, both promote new technology (e.g., nuclear power) and assess the consequences. But what may be needed are *independent* boards to make assessment and propose remedial actions to the Executive or to Congress. Whatever the final structures may be, it is clear that some social decision mechanisms will have to emerge in the next few years to make such assessments of second-order effects of technological and social change. New and large powers will be vested in administrative boards. New and complex tasks will confront the Congress.

And for the private corporation, a new principle in the relation of corporations to public policy will soon be emerging. Just as it has been public policy to provide tax inducements to help corporations expand plant capacity (by investment credits, or more rapid depreciation allowances), so it will be public policy to provide tax penalties either to force corporations to bear the burdens of social costs generated by the firm, or to favor an alternative technology or supporting system if the social costs can be minimized by the alternative system or the social benefits enhanced. Given the collective effects of private decisions, this involvement of public policy in corporate policy is inescapable.

Just as we may be moving into technology assessment, so we shall have to cope with social assessments as well. For example, the social map of the United States was redrawn after World War II by the rapid expansion of the suburbs and the extraordinary rise in suburban home ownership. But all this was made possible only as a matter of public policy: by federal guarantee of mortgages; by low down payments by veterans (often as little as 10 per cent down on a purchase price) so that "owning" became cheaper than renting; and by the policy of permitting the deduction of interest payments on mortgages from income taxes. But no one questioned the existing "support system" of large numbers of small developers creating tracts of unattached houses in mechanical grid.

There can be, let us say, three alternative models of suburban development: one, a pattern of detached homes with private walkways and separate garages; the second, a set of "cluster houses" with the sharing of common auxiliary facilities (e.g., garaging); and third, high-rise apartment houses with large green spaces. Each of these developments has vastly different "social costs" which are borne by the community, not by the developer (the pattern of roads, auxiliary land use, the location of schools, etc.). Yet these social costs are rarely, if ever, taken into consideration. There is no "total cost matrix" to make a buyer aware of what the alternative styles could cost him in terms of the secondary costs he and the community would have to pay as a result of his choice. Nor has public policy ever sought to make such a determination.

Now, I am not arguing that consumers should be required to take one or another of the patterns. But intelligent public policy—because it is public monies that are facilitating this social change—should inquire into the alternative total cost matrices of the different patterns, and of the consequences of maintaining or changing existing institutional patterns of home building and development. It is not a matter of "interference" or "non-interference" in the society; *any* action (including non-action) is bound to strengthen or weaken one or another vested interest. It is a matter of making the choices and consequences explicit.

The Corporation as a Sociological Institution

In traditional corporate law, property is defined as things (res), but the major lesson which corporations have learned in the last 30 years is that a corporation, while producing things, is made up of people, and that one cannot treat people—at least managerial and white-collar personnel—as things.

Corporations are institutions for economizing; but they are also ways of life for their members. Until the early years of the 20th century, the life of most Americans was bounded by the isolated small town, the church, and the family. The small town has virtually disappeared; the church has lost much of its emotional hold on people; and the tight bond between family and occupation, which gave a unity to life—the family farm, the family business, or the family occupation which the son inherited—has been sundered. The breakup of that traditional way of life, and the consequent sense of uprootedness and disorientation, is the source of what sociologists call *anomie.*

Emile Durkheim, the French sociologist who coined that term, thought that for *anomie* to be resolved there must be a group which could provide a sense of kindredness and common purpose for its members. Political society, he thought, was too amorphous and too distant. The answer, he said, lay in the occupational group, the profession, which could provide a new ethic for society. One of Durkheim's chief expositors, Elton Mayo of the Harvard Business School, thought that this purpose could be most effectively realized in the business corporation.

For a significant number of persons, this has necessarily become the case. The "four wishes" which the late sociologist W. I. Thomas thought were basic to human experience—the wish for security, for new experience, for response, and for recognition—can for these men only be obtained within the corporate milieu. Much of this led, 20 years ago, to the creation of the derogatory expression "the organization man" as signifying a new kind of conformity. If the image were meant to suggest that previously men had been free and individualist and now were uniform and identical, the history was mythical and the irony was simply a new ideology. For life in the small town had been largely narrow and bigoted—one has only to recall Sinclair Lewis's *Main Street*—and the world of organizations offered an authentic, fresh challenge and opportunity. Corporations can be forces for conformity; and they can equally be arenas for personal initiative.

A business corporation, like a university, or a government agency, or a large hospital—each with its hierarchy and status system—is now a life-time experience for many of its members. Necessarily, therefore, it can no longer be an instrument satisfying a single end—in the case of the business corporation, only turning out its goods and services—but it has to be a satisfactory way of life for its members. It not only has to satisfy its customers; it has to be agreeable to its "self."

A business corporation, however, is subject to different constraints, and has a somewhat different ethos, from a university or a government agency or a hospital. Corporations, unlike the other three, are competitive and have to be profitable. (And the profits, moreover, are often a major support —through taxes—of the other three.) Even so, if we set up a continuum, with *economizing* at one end of the scale (in which all aspects of organization are single-mindedly reduced to becoming means to the goals of production and profit) and *sociologizing* at the other (in which all workers are guaranteed lifetime jobs, and the satisfaction of the work force becomes the primary levy on resources), then in the last 30 years the corporation has been moving steadily, for almost all its employees, towards the *sociologizing* end of the scale. One has only to note, in the rising percentage of "fringe benefit costs," the index of that shift—vacations, disability pay, health insurance, supplementary unemployment benefits, pensions, and the like.

All of this, historically, was inescapable. To the extent that the traditional sources of social support (the small town, church and family) have crumbled in society, new kinds of organizations, particularly the corporation, have taken their place; and these inevitably become the arenas in which the demands for security, justice, and esteem are made. To think of the business corporation, then, simply as an economic instrument is to fail totally to understand the meaning of the social changes of the last half century.

The Balance of Obligation

When one uses the phrase the "social responsibility" of the corporation, one is not indulging in rhetoric (though many corporate officials are), or thinking of *noblesse oblige* (which fewer corporate officials do), or assuming that some subversive doctrine is being smuggled into society (as some laissez-faire economists suggest), but simply accepting a cardinal sociopsychological fact about human attachments. Unless one assumes that loyalty and identification are simply monetary transactions, or that employment is simply a limited relation of service-for-payment, then the corporation is a social world, with social obligations to its members, as well as an economizing instrument competitively providing goods at least cost to an economic world of consumers.

But what is the balance of obligation, and how far can one go in either direction? Perhaps the best way of trying to deal with this question is to confront some questions which have already emerged or which may be emerging in the next decade.

1. *Satisfaction on the Job.* The trite observation from the "human relations" literature of 20 years ago was that a man more satisfied with his job was likely to have higher morale and be more productive. Thus, the mechanical layout of work, set down by the engineer, was modified to take into account the findings of industrial psychologists and sociologists. The

increase in costs could be justified by the more than proportional increase in productivity.

But what if a change in job patterns increases satisfaction but does *not* increase productivity? What is the corporation to do? The conventional answer is that the primary obligation of the corporation is to profits and that marginal increases in costs can only be justified by marginal increases in productivity. But let us take a variant of this problem. When a corporation hires more women, and these women ask for child-care centers to be paid for and maintained by the company, is it obligated to do so? The question is not just of treating such centers as a necessary cost to attract female labor when one has a tight labor market, but of a change in social values which would permit women who want to work to go back to work during the years when their children are young. A child-care center is a necessary component of job satisfaction for young women, even though it may add costs to a company far beyond the "gains" in productivity from such women. Does the conventional principle still hold?

2. *Minority Employment.* Does a corporation have a special obligation to take on a larger proportion of persons from minority groups which have suffered historical disadvantage—even if such persons are less able than a competitor for the job? And if the employment of such a person increases training costs and may lead to lower productivity? The problem, in principle, is no different from that of a university which may have to set aside a special quota and, sometimes, given the limited number of places, exclude "majority" group persons who on the formal criteria of merit (e.g., test scores, grades) may be more qualified. The question of merit versus social justice is, as most complex moral problems, a question of "right" versus "right," rather than right versus wrong. Where there is such a conflict of right, how does one balance one's obligations?

3. *Relative Pay.* How does one decide what a man is worth? A pure market principle, of competing supply and demand, only reflects relative scarcities, but relative scarcity is not identical with social justice. In most American industry, a distinction is still maintained between blue-collar work, wherein a man is paid by the piece or the hour, and white-collar work wherein a man is paid by the week or month. A few corporations—IBM, Texas Instruments—have abolished the distinction, but not many have followed that lead. What is the rationale for this invidious status distinction?

Within the corporation itself, the differential between the lowest paid (often the common labor rate) and the average of the top executive group may be about 25:1 or higher. On what basis is this spread justified? The original rationale was the market. But increasingly the market becomes less relevant for the determination of the relative differences between "grades" of labor and persons. Elliot Jaques, the English industrial psychologist, has sought to work out a principle of "equitable" pay on the basis of differential responsibility between jobs—as measured, for example, by the amount of independent time a man has to do a job and the degree of supervision. There may be other such "formal" systems. But because human beings want and need a clear rationale for the differences in reward among them, some principle of social justice for social distinctions will have to be articulated.

4. *Responsibility to a Community.* An old problem, but one which recurs as increasingly the corporation becomes the way of life for its members. Beyond the payment of taxes, what obligations does a corporation have to the local community where it locates its plants and headquarters? What are its responsibilities in creating amenities and a more satisfactory social and cultural environment?

5. *Responsibility for the Environment.* In the last few years, the corporation, along with the rest of the society, has learned that the environment cannot be treated as a "free good." How the costs are to be divided will be, as I have already indicated, one of the most difficult technical-political issues of the decade.

6. *The Confrontation with Moral Issues.* The corporation, like the university, has always pleaded that on moral questions it is "value-neutral." As a corporation, its obligation is to seek the best return on investment. But value neutrality is no longer so easily possible. The difficulty arising from American private investment in South Africa illustrates the problem. In the classic morality tale of 50 years ago, the example was one of the local churches which gained an income from properties on which brothels were located. The church could always claim a trade-off by arguing that it saved as many souls as it lost bodies. Such a calculus was never entirely convincing. A corporation's claim that it saves as many bodies as it loses souls is not likely to be more so.

What all this adds up to is that, on the continuum I have drawn of the *economizing* and *sociologizing* modes, the balance of attention shifts more and more to the latter. And, while on the particular questions I have cited which the corporation will face in the next decade, there are no exact answers or ready-made formulae, the standpoint from which the decisions will be considered will, more and more, be made from the sociological viewpoint.

The Turning Point for the Corporation

The question of "social responsibility" is, I believe, the crux of a debate that will become crucial in the next few years. One position has been put forth by Milton Friedman:

> What does it mean to say that the corporate executive has a "social responsibility" in his capacity to act as businessman? If this statement is not pure rhetoric, it must mean that he is to act in some way that is not in the interest of his employers. For example, that he is to refrain from increasing the price of the product in order to contribute to the social objective of preventing inflation, even though a price increase would be in the best interests of his corporation. Or that he is to make expenditures on reducing pollution beyond the amount that is in the best interests of the corporation or that is required by law in order to contribute to the social objective of improving the environment. Or that, at the expense of corporate

profits, he is to hire "hard-core" unemployed instead of better qualified available workmen to contribute to the social objective of reducing poverty. . . .

In a free-enterprise, private property system, a corporate executive is an employee of the owners of the business. He has direct responsibility to his employers. That responsibility is to conduct the business in accordance with their desires, which generally will be to make as much money as possible while conforming to the basic rules of the society, both those embodied in law and those embodied in ethical custom.[9]

There are two different kinds of answers to Friedman. Both were given recently by Alden Clausen, the new president and chief executive officer of the Bank of America, the biggest bank in the world.

For Clausen, one crucial question is: In what social context does the corporation operate today? As a recent article in *Fortune*, by John Davenport, reported: "To keep this giant money machine profitably growing is the first business of Alden Winshop (Tom) Clausen. . . It is of some significance that. . .his thoughts turn often to: how to alleviate if not cure the blight now spreading at Hunter's Point and south of Market Street [in San Francisco]; how to crack the city's hard-core unemployment; how to cope with student unrest at Berkeley or down the peninsula at Stanford."

In defending these objectives, Clausen confronted directly the views of Friedman. As the article in *Fortune* reported:

At the moment Clausen and his associates are less interested in modifying their bank's capital structure than in charting a course through a period when capitalism itself is under intense attack. . . .

Business, he argued, has to concern itself with nonbusiness problems today if it wants to be around tomorrow. The Friedman view is okay in the short pull. "But in the long pull, nobody can expect to make profits—or have any meaningful use for profits—if the whole fabric of society is being ripped to shreds."

There is, equally, a different question, apart from social expediency: Below the surface of this clash of views, there lies an important but seldomly explicitly confronted question about the nature of the corporation. Friedman sees the corporation as fundamentally an "artificial person" and the corporate manager as simply an agent of individual shareholders. Clausen sees the corporation as having a kind of life of its own, and hence having a certain freedom of choice in balancing its contribution to the long-range needs of the community against the immediate demands of owners.

And, as the writer John Davenport, himself a distinguished conservative, comments: There may be dangers lurking in Clausen's view of corporate autonomy, but there is surely something unrealistic in the view that society is just an atomized collection of individuals.[10]

The heart of the matter is the question of the nature of the corporation. Is the corporation primarily an instrument of "owners"—legally the stockholders—or is it an autonomous enterprise which, despite its particular history, has become—or should become—an instrument for service to society in a system of pluralist powers?

A classic debate on the question was initiated 40 years ago in the pages of the *Harvard Law Review* by A. A. Berle and Merrick Dodd. Berle held to the view, at the time (he later revised his views), that all corporate powers are powers in trust for the benefit of the stockholders. Dodd argued that legally such was the case, but the use of private property was deeply affected with a public interest and that the directors should be viewed as trustees for the enterprise as a whole—for the corporation viewed as an institution— and not merely as "attorneys for the stockholders." Berle responded that, since one could not offer "a clear and reasonably enforceable scheme of responsibilities to someone else," Dodd's proposal would place the control of the organization entirely in the hands of management. The problem, as he saw it, was: If there is not a prior legal statement of responsibility to the stockholders, how does one prevent management from exercising arbitrary social and political power, or from becoming overreaching and self-seeking?

This legal—and sociological—issue remains. Is the manager primarily a trustee for absentee investors? Or is the role of the manager, as Frank Abrams, when he was chairman of the board of Standard Oil of New Jersey, put it, to conduct his affairs "in such a way as to maintain an equitable and working balance among the claims of the various directly interested groups—stockholders, employees, customers and the public at large"?

Private Property or Private Enterprise?

The modern business corporation has lost many of the historic features of traditional capitalism, yet it has, for lack of a new rationale, retained the old ideology—and finds itself trapped by it.

Unhappy is a society that has run out of words to describe what is going on. So Thurman Arnold observed in connection with the language of private property—the myths and folklore of capitalism—which even 30 years ago was hopelessly out of date. *The point is that today ownership is simply a legal fiction.*

A stockholder is an owner because, in theory, he has put up equity capital and taken a risk. But only a minor proportion of corporate capital today is raised through the sale of equity capital. A more significant portion of capital comes through self-financing, by the success of the enterprise itself. In the last decade, more than 60 per cent of the capital investment of the nation's 1,000 largest manufacturing firms was financed internally. Retained capital is the basis of the ri : in net assets of large corporations. And the growth of retained capital is the product of managerial skill. (Equally, a large portion of new capital is raised by debentures, which become a fixed charge against earnings, rather than through floating equity or risk stock. Debentures hinge on the stability of the company and the prospect of repayment—again a managerial problem.)

If one were to follow the logic of Friedman's argument, as he does—it is his strength and weakness that he always follows the logic of his argument, to the very end—one would have to outlaw or at least discourage self-financing. Under the "pure" theory of market capitalism, a firm risks a stockholder's capital and then pays back any profits—in the form of dividends—to its legal owners, the stockholders. If it seeks to risk that money again, it should ask those stockholders to reinvest that money, rather than withhold it from them and reinvest it by managerial decision. Friedman argues that it is only the "double taxation" (through corporate and personal income tax) of dividends that prevents such a desirable state of affairs from emerging. But I should say that such a state of affairs is neither desirable nor possible. Given the pattern of stock ownership today—particularly with the growth of mutual funds, pension funds and trust funds—the stockholder is often an "in-and-out" person with little continuing interest in the enterprise. Such an in-and-out procedure may be a useful discipline for management and a measure of economic performance—but then it becomes a form of countervailing power, not ownership. True owners are involved directly and psychologically in the fate of an enterprise; and this description better fits the employees of the corporation, not its stockholders. For these employees, the corporation is a social institution which they inhabit. It is politically and morally unthinkable that their lives should be at the mercy of a financial speculator.

In other words, the corporation may be a *private enterprise* institution, but it is not really a *private property* institution. (If the assets of the enterprise are primarily the skill of its managerial employees, not machinery or things—and this is preeminently true in the science-based industries, in communications, and in the so-called "knowledge industries"—then property is anyway of lesser importance.) And if ownership is largely a legal fiction, then one ought to adopt a more realistic attitude to it. One can treat stockholders not as "owners" but as legitimate claimants to some fixed share of the profits of a corporation—and to nothing more.

The Meaning of "A Corporation"

What then is a corporation? If one goes back to the original meaning of the term, as a social invention of the late Middle Ages to meet some novel problems, a corporation was an instrument for self-governance for groups carrying on a common activity (artisan guilds, local boroughs, ecclesiastical bodies); it often had common economic assets, and its existence would persist beyond the lives of its individual members. Those who were "members" of the corporation were those directly responsible for its activities, those who were the legatees of the past members, and those chosen to carry on the work.

A business corporation today, like a university today, can be viewed in this original sociological conception of the term. Indeed, if one begins to look on the business corporation more and more on the model of the university, then the fallacy of ownership becomes more apparent. Who "owns" Harvard or the University of Chicago? Legally the "corporation," as composed by the overseers or the trustees. But in any sociological sense this is meaningless. The university is a self-selective ongoing enterprise of its members (administration, faculty, students, and alumni, with differential responsibilities and obligations) who seek to carry out its purposes with due regard to the interests of the particular community which constitutes the university—and also to the larger community that makes the university possible.

As a business institution, the "corporation" is the management and the board of directors, operating as trustees for members of the enterprise as a whole—not just stockholders, but workers and consumers too—and with due regard to the interests of society as a whole. But if this view is accepted, there is a significant logical corollary—that the constituencies which make up the corporation themselves have to be represented within the board of corporate power. Without that, there is no effective counter-vailing power to that of executive management. More important, without such representation, there would be a serious question about the "legiti-macy" of managerial power.

How such constituencies might be represented is a question to be explored. A dozen years ago, Bayless Manning, Jr., until recently the Dean of the Stanford Law School, sought to picture the corporation as if it were in law what it often is in fact, as a kind of "voting trust" wherein the stock-holder delegates all his rights, except that of collecting dividends, to the directors. In order to establish some check on the board of directors, he proposed a "second chamber," an "extrinsic body," which would review decisions of the board where conflicts of interest arose—such as compen-sation of officers, contributions to other enterprises (universities, community efforts, etc.) not directly related to a company's busines, clashes with a public interest, etc.

It is beyond the scope of this essay, and the competence of the author, to estimate the viability of these—or other—specific proposals. The problem is there; it is not going to go away; and discussion of possible resolutions is anything but premature.

From Bitterness to Banality

As a debate on these issues continues, one important consideration should be kept in mind—the bitterness of one generation is often the banality of another. Who, today, gives a second thought to Savings Bank Life Insurance? Yet this idea, authored by Louis D. Brandeis in Massachu-setts, was fought for five months in passage through the legislature and was marked by one of the bitterest fights ever witnessed on Beacon Hill. (One line of attack was that people would not voluntarily seek insurance, and that they would not take it out at all if the expensive system of soliciting by agents were done away with.) The issue gave Brandeis a national reputa-tion, and eventually brought Brandeis to the Supreme Court. The reputa-tion remained, but the issue itself soon faded.

The lesson, however, was not, and is still not, wholly learned—reforms will never be as sweeping in their effects as their proponents hope, and the results will rarely be as damaging and apocalyptic as the opponents fear. Workmen's compensation was an issue that inflamed a generation of radicals and was fought by industry on the ground that it would relieve the workman of "individual responsibility" for his actions; yet who today would deny that industrial safety is a legitimate cost of factory operations?

Such reforms are always an expression of a revision—implicit or explicit—in the American "public philosophy." This kind of "revisionism" is inevitable as men and societies change, and as the dominant values assume a new shape. The private enterprise system has been the primary institution of Western society not because of its coercive power but because its values— economizing and increasing output of material goods—were congruent with the major consumer values of the society. With all its obvious imperfections the system "worked." Today, however, those values are themselves being questioned, not in the way socialists and radicals questioned them a generation ago—that they were achieved at the cost of exploiting the worker —but at the very core, the creation of more private goods at the expense of other social values. I return to a point made earlier that unlike the polity, no one, meeting collectively, "voted in" our market economy. But now votes are being taken.

It seems clear to me that, today, we in America are moving away from a society based on a private-enterprise market system toward one in which the most important economic decisions will be made at the political level, in terms of consciously-defined "goals" and "priorities." The dangers inherent in such a shift are familiar enough to anyone acquainted with the liberal tradition. In the past, there was an "unspoken consensus," and the public philosophy did not need to be articulated. And this was a strength, for articulation often invites trials by force when implicit differences are made manifest. Today, however, there is a visible change from market to non-market political decision-making. The market disperses responsibility: the political center is visible, the question of who gains and who loses is clear, and government becomes a cockpit.

But to be hypnotized by such dangers is little less than frivolous. No social or economic order has a writ of immortality, and the consumer-oriented free-enterprise society no longer satisfies the citizenry, as once it did. So it will have to change, in order that something we still recognize as a liberal society might survive.

Whether such a change will represent "progress" is a nice metaphysical question that I, for one, do not know how to answer. This was a society "designed" by Locke and Smith and it rested on the premises of individualism and market rationality in which the varied ends desired by individuals would be maximized by free exchange. We now move to a communal ethic, without that community being, as yet, wholly defined. In a sense, the movement away from governance by political economy to governance by political philosophy—for that is the meaning of the shift—is a return to precapitalist modes of social thought. But whether this be progress or regress, it clearly makes it incumbent upon us to think more candidly and rigorously about our values, and about the kind of world we wish to live in.

[1] The stereotype that the big company has a big market share is obviously supported by many examples. Only it is refuted by even more. If one looks at the "symbolic" examples of concentration, it is quite clear that in no industry today is concentration at a comparable level with the period after the great wave of consolidations, from 1898 to 1902. As pointed out by Professor Segall of the University of Chicago: In 1900, International Harvester produced 85 per cent of the nation's harvesting machines. In 1902, National Biscuit controlled 70 per cent of the biscuit output. In 1901, American Can turned out 90 per cent of its industry's output. In 1902, Corn Products had 80 per cent of its industry's capacity. In 1902 U.S. Leather accounted for more than 60 per cent of leather output; Distillers Securities provided more than 60 per cent of whiskey output; International Paper produced 60 per cent of all newsprint. In 1900, American Sugar Refining refined virtually all the sugar in the country. For a comprehensive discussion of the contemporary degree of concentration see M. A. Adelman, "The Two Faces of Economic Concentration," *The Public Interest*, 21 (Fall 1970).

[2] This market strategy and organizational form allowed GM to come from behind to oust Ford, a genius at production techniques, from the leading position in the market. In 1921, Ford had 60 per cent of the car and truck market and almost complete control of the low-priced field. Chevrolet, GM's entry in the low-price field, had only 4 per cent of the market. To meet Ford head-on in price competition would have been suicidal. Sloan's strategy was not to undercut the Ford price but to *top* it somewhat, seeking to skim off that layer of buyers who would be willing to go to a higher price on the assumption they were getting a better car. By successive "upgrading" of items, largely through annual model changes, GM won the larger share. In effect, GM countered "style" to "utility" and won.

[3] In his book, Pigou gave dozens of examples of similar "disservices": the destruction of neighborhoods by the construction of factories in residential districts; the costs to the consumers of competitive advertising; the increase in expenditures for police and prisons because of the rising sale of liquor; the overrunning of a neighbor's land by rabbits originating from game preserves; the costs of diplomacy and armies because of the rise of foreign investments, etc.

In this country the theme was elaborated by John Maurice Clark of Columbia, who, in his *Economics of Overhead Costs* (1923), drew a distinction between social and market values and between social and market costs. For Clark, as Allan Gruchy points out, the business concept of cost excluded many important social costs such as communal health hazards, unemployment and other costs associated with business fluctuations. Clark's concern was to bring commercial efficiency closer to social efficiency, and with making the economic system account for social values, clean air, scenic beauty, etc., as well as market values.

[4] I do not minimize the technical and political difficulties of establishing such a matrix. Let me provide a "homely" example of a problem which, many years ago, first brought the social cost problem to my personal attention.

In New York City when I was a boy, snow was removed from the streets by the hiring of extra trucks which would cart mounds of it away and dump it in the river. Many years later, Paul Screvane, who was the Commissioner of Sanitation, ordered his men to push the snow into the middle of the streets, where it was churned into slush by passing cars. Perhaps he did it because the costs of hiring trucks had gone up exorbitantly, or because he wanted to demonstrate an outstanding record in office so that he could run for mayor. The sanitation department showed a commendable record of economy. But (as I figured out from the records of the Industry and Commerce Association), after each snowfall the cleaning and dyeing bills in the city went up substantially, because the passing cars would splatter the clothes of the innocent bystander.

Now, which was the "rational" solution? One could say that Screvane's method was highly irrational, because it passed the costs of snow removal onto the backs of the unfortunate pedestrians, and if the cleaning and dyeing bills were higher than the cost of hiring additional trucks, it was truly a misallocation of resources. Yet one could also say that if the trucks had been hired, direct city exenses would have been increased and taxes would have to go up, increasing the resentments of the taxpayers in the city, so that the system of "Russian roulette" whereby a random group of bystanders bore the costs might have a greater "political" rationality than economic cost-benefit analysis.

⁵ One can say, theoretically, that the price system could manage the problem, e.g., when the costs of individual congestion become high it would then become profitable for alternative modes of transportation to compete with the private car. But the price system, in this instance, relies on *trial and error* to assess the result. The difficulty is that such assessments, *after the fact*, are likely to be futile—an enormous amount of resources would have been misallocated, and a preemptive "system" of transportation will have been established. Under such a system, clogged highways will eventually result in the building of more highways.

⁶ For an elaboration of this point, see Harold Gilliam, "The Fallacy of Single-Purpose Planning," in the *Dœdalus* issue on America's Changing Environment (Fall 1967).

⁷ Jack Burnham, *Beyond Modern Sculpture* (New York, 1968). If one asks what a sculptor is doing discussing the automobile system, his argument is cast in the context of the disappearance of "objects" in contemporary society and their replacement by "systems."

⁸ The idea of "technology assessment" grew largely out of the studies of the House Science and Astronautics Committee under the leadership of Congressman Daddario. Two panels, one in the National Academy of Sciences and one in the National Academy of Engineering, were set up to test the feasibility of the idea. The National Academy of Sciences panel, under the direction of Harvey Brooks, agreed that assessment was possible and proposed a number of ways in which the process could be implemented in government. The Engineering panel undertook three studies—of subsonic aircraft noise, of computer-assisted instruction, and of multiphasic health screening—to further this idea. Both reports on Technology Assessment were published by the Morse Committee in July 1969.

⁹ From "The Social Responsibility of Business Is to Increase Its Profits," in *The Sunday Times Magazine*, September 13, 1970. The argument is elaborated in Friedman's book *Capitalism and Freedom*.

¹⁰ John Davenport, "Bank of America Is Not for Burning," *Fortune*, January 1971.

Business Civilization
in Decline

by Robert L. Heilbroner

Chapter 5

THE DEMISE of capitalism, in other words, does not hinge on its nuclear obliteration. It seems certain to occur even if, as all mankind must hope, international conflict is held to a manageable level.

What are the reasons for expecting its demise? I discern three, all associated with the internal effects of the cessation of growth within the long run of a century. The first internal effect is the constriction of the expansive drive that has been the specific characteristic of the business system, evidenced in our own day by the bursting of corporate production beyond its national territory. The increasingly severe constraints on industrial growth must bring to a halt the consuming passion of a business civilization for private expansion.

In itself, this exhaustion of the "spirit" of capitalism will spell a profound change in the values, the ambitions, the morale of a business system, of which we shall speak more later. More important, however, is that the end of corporate growth will bring about the progressive elimination of the profits that have been both the means and the end of the accumulation of private property. A business society, confined within the straitjacket of a more or less fixed volume of output, must expect a steady erosion of profits, as economists from Adam Smith to Marx and Keynes have long recognized. Corporations forced to operate in a fixed economic space will soon compete away each other's profits, or will suffer a fatal squeeze between the pressures of wage earners for larger shares of revenues and the inability to increase revenues by expanding output.

In the middle run, this squeeze on profits can perhaps be alleviated by shifting corporate activity into "service" industries, or by a continuing penetration of foreign markets. In the long run, however, the constraints on industrial production must exert an immense pressure against the profitability of corporate activity; and the possibilities for continued multinational expansion, in a world of scarcities, bitter hostilities, and intensified desires for national self-sufficiency, seem very unlikely to last more than another few decades.

The unavoidable curtailment of growth thus threatens the viability of capitalism by removing the primary source of the profits that have been the continuance of a business system. But suppose that profits are removed? Suppose that capitalism becomes, by degrees, a highly planned bureaucratic state in which corporations more and more resemble socialist trusts—according considerable privileges to their upper echelons, but no longer dependent on profits for survival?

Such a trustified, profitless, bureaucratic "capitalism" is certainly not unimaginable. But in the cessation of growth there still resides a serious—indeed, I think fatal—threat to the continuance of a business civilization. This threat lies in the removal of the safety valve by which the deep tension between the claims of labor and property has been lessened in the past.

Here we revert to our original discussion of capitalism as a system of privilege. For, however buried under ideology, there exists an inherent antagonism within a system where income is distributed by two entirely different principles—energy, intelligence, skill, and luck on the one hand, the brute claims of ownership on the other. This antagonism must be intensified when it becomes impossible to satisfy the claims of the working majority by granting it ever-larger absolute amounts of real income. The constraints on growth thus exert their most severe effect on the distribution of income. When output ceases to grow, the claims of the poor cannot be appeased by increments of income that do not come out of the pockets of the rich but out of larger total output. In a growthless economic system, the contest over incomes becomes a conflict over rights, and in this impending struggle I find it difficult to believe that the rights of property will not be ever more deeply invaded or ignored.

A second source of internal dissolution of the business system is allied with the first. It is the expansion of the planning apparatus whose roots and evolutionary course we have traced in previous chapters. As I have said before, planning is the inevitable next stage of capitalism, a stage that will assuredly attempt for a long time to preserve rather than destroy the structure of privilege central to a business civilization. But the inescapable rise of planning must also greatly strengthen the power of that congeries of technicians, scientists, and planners whose rise we have discussed as an aspect of the middle range of the future. The plannification of capitalism, in other words, however necessary for its survival in the middle run, is also a source of its extinction in the long run. For a hundred years hence, when the impact of environmental dangers is no longer a matter for speculation but for immediate alarm and control, planning requirements must far exceed anything that is compatible with either the prerogatives of property or the machinery of the market. In the face of extreme distributional tensions on the one hand and potentially lethal consequences of private economic activity on the other, the extension of public authority must reach into and displace private decision making, not only in the determination of incomes but in the choice and means of output.

Indeed, to the extent that the threats of the environment eventually force a dismantling of large-scale industrial processes, whether by foresighted planning or simply through localized disasters, political power is certain to be wielded without regard for any traditional criteria of a business system. Whether, in the long run, political authority will utilize "scientific" means of allocating resources and distributing incomes, or will simply impose a direct military discipline, we cannot foresee. But surely the claims of rents and interest and profits, the play of the market, or the right to conduct "private" enterprise will appear as archaic as the claims of royalty or nobility in the face of a democratic revolution.

These drastically changed aspects of the internal setting of capitalism—the end of business expansion and the extension of planning into every corner of economic life—offer two primary challenges to the continuation of capitalism, once the constraints of the long run begin to bear heavily on its operations. But they are attended by a third change that offers a threat of equal magnitude. This is the prospective erosion of the "spirit" of capitalism to which we have already referred.

Here we necessarily move even further into the realm of imponderables, and the possibility of ascribing a given time span disappears. Yet I do not think we should disregard the prospective decay of the value system of a business civilization because it is impossible to make hard and fast pronouncements with regard to the rate of its metastasis. So skeptical a social observer as Schumpeter was prepared, in the end, to pin his prediction of an end to capitalism on the change in its attitudes and outlooks. I suggest that we should also give due weight to the decay of business civilization from changes in its value structure.

Primary among these value changes I would place a waning belief in the ability of a business civilization to provide social morale. Traditionally, this morale has been pictured as arising spontaneously from the acknowledged capability of a business system to enhance the material well-being of its members. Few defenders of capitalism have tried to justify the system in terms of the nobility of its motivations or the spirituality of its aims. The defense of capitalism has always rested on the social contentment that was presumed to result from the release of mankind from its historic condition of material insufficiency.

This defense is already in doubt. For surely the business system has lived up to or exceeded the fondest hopes of its protagonists with respect to its productive virtuosity. What prodigies of material achievement the contemporary American enjoys as he drives over plains where his forebears trekked! What miracles of engineering does he not command to wash his clothes and his dishes, clean his teeth, shine his shoes, tell the time to the nearest tenth of a second, detect his incipient cancers, converse with friends in distant cities! Is he not only healthier and longer-lived than his forefathers, but better informed, better entertained—in a word, "better off" in nearly every measurable dimension?

But does not this recital reveal what has not been gained as well as what has been gained? Is the contemporary American a better as well as a richer citizen than his antecedents? Is he more at peace with his children, his parents, himself? Is he wiser as well as more informed; happier as well as more pampered; sturdier and more self-reliant as well as better fed, housed, clothed, transported? To ask these questions, rhetorical though they be, is, I think, to express a hollowness at the center of a business civilization— a hollowness from which the pursuit of material goods diverts our attention for a time, but that in the end insistently asserts itself.

What is the nature of this hollowness? I would trace it primarily to two aspects of the business civilization that undermine the gains that material advancement undoubtedly confer. The first is the tendency of a business civilization to substitute impersonal pecuniary values for personal nonpecuniary ones. Consider, for example, the conversion of sport—one of the oldest and most stirring rituals of mankind—into a commercial enterprise, in which athletes are no longer heroes but money makers, games no longer contests for glory but for cash, and the mercenary qualities of participants, which would have been a source of shame in a Greek or medieval festival, are trumpeted aloud as an admirable character trait.

Or consider advertising, perhaps the single most value-destroying activity of a business civilization. Schumpeter spoke of the cold rationality that was to prove the undoing of the system. He ignored the extraordinary subversive influence of the relentless effort to persuade people to change their lifeways, not out of any knowledge of, or deeply held convictions about, the "good life," but merely to sell whatever article or service is being pandered. I do not think we pay sufficient heed to the power of advertising in making cynics of us all: at a business forum I was once brash enough to say that I thought the main cultural effect of television advertising was to teach children that grown-ups told lies for money. How strong, deep or sustaining can be the values generated by a civilization that generates a ceaseless flow of half-truths and careful deceptions, in which it is common knowledge that only a fool is taken in by the charades and messages that supposedly tell us "the facts"?

Moreover, there is, I think, a second reason why the material achievements of a business civilization fail to generate the satisfactions we expect of it. This is the disregard of business for the value of work. A business civilization regards work as a means to an end, not as an end to itself. The end is profit, income, consumption, economic growth, or whatever; but the act of labor itself is regarded as nothing more than an unfortunate necessity to which we must submit to obtain this end.

Now, of course, labor *is* a necessity on which material survival depends. In an environment of scarcity, even under the most enlightened and democratic government, work must be performed, some of which can be justified only in terms of the end to which it is directed. But the business civiliza-

tion carries the disregard of work far beyond what is required by the objective necessities of survival even at a fairly high level of material enjoyment.
Perhaps this is ultimately a fault that capitalism shares with industrial
socialism—a fault whose roots lie in the machine process and the worship
of efficiency. But this subordination of the act of labor to the overriding
calculus of technology and efficiency is given a special blessing under a
business civilization, where the values of output are celebrated and those of
input merely calculated.

Here, too, along with the mindless commercialization of life, lies the
basis for that vitiation of the spirit that is sapping business civilization from
within. The way of life encouraged by the business process has proved dis-
appointing not only with regard to its rewards but also with respect to its
requirements. Thus at the very time that the mechanism of the business
system must prepare to undergo an unprecedented trial, the participants in
the system cannot be expected to rally to its defense with the enthusiasm of
their parents or grandparents. Patriotism—or better, nationalism—may well
be on the rise in our day, but economic patriotism is on the decline, especially for believers in the orthodox capitalist faith.

These considerations apply with particular force to the market mechanism that, along with private property, constitutes an essential characteristic
of capitalism. The market in conventional theory is the means by which
capitalism allocates its productive efforts and distributes its rewards without
recourse to the alternative methods of tradition or command. It is vaunted,
in the conventional textbooks, for its flexibility, its "efficiency," its capacity
for matching social desire with social effort.

But the market mechanism also contains profound weaknesses that
have been overlooked during the period of uninhibited capitalist expansion.
One of these is its tendency to create extremely skewed distributions of
income and property, a tendency that a straitjacketed economy will no
longer accept with the forbearance of an expanding one. Another weakness is the failure of the market to protect us against the socially deleterious
side effects of production, such as pollution, an aspect that becomes intolerable in a threatened environment. And a third weakness is the matter to
which we have just referred—the exclusive focus of the market on economic
activity conceived and measured in quantities of material output, not in
qualities of human input. The market celebrates private consumption and
ignores private production. This indifference to the experience of work
corrodes and corrupts much of the way of life in a business civilization.

These "civilizational" challenges of the long run are also intimately
associated with the prospect of a decline in, and finally a halt to, growth.
The cessation of growth removes the possibility of a ceaseless revindication
of the business spirit through its self-justification in material aggrandizement.
The values of acquisitiveness ill accord with the imperatives of material conservation. The sanctity of property will have to endure inescapable encroachments in the name of social survival. The prevailing system of
business values must contend with technical or statist attitudes that will bring
the commercial orientation of capitalism into disrespect or disregard. Is it

possible to imagine the world a century hence, seeking to avoid material breakdown, bending every element of its political power to the curbing and redirection of the economic process, still open to the siren songs of an advertising mentality?

I suspect, then, that the cessation of growth will finally and fatally undermine a spirit that is already on the wane. On the one hand, the driving force of capitalist entrepreneurs will have been replaced by the carefully supervised calculations of state planners. On the other hand, the appetite for material growth will have been forcibly suppressed. Both the legitimacy and the functional purposes of private property and the market mechanism will have lost their claims for popular support. Perhaps most important of all, we can expect that this period of growing internal and external tension and heightened concern for survival is likely to produce its own values— nationalistic, religious—that will provide a needed new system of beliefs required to replace an outmoded one.

After capitalism, what? Not, I think, a "revolution." The demise of the business system is likely to proceed by degrees, insensibly altering a civilization that can be called "capitalist" into one that, whatever its appellation, no longer bears sufficient resemblance to the system we know to enable us to call it by the same name. We project the image of a tightly controlled society where the traditional pillars of capitalism—the legitimacy of private property and the operation of the market mechanism—have been amended beyond recognition, if not wholly superseded by state property and state directives.

Is such a postcapitalist system to be described as "fascism"? As "socialism"? I suspect that these traditional terms have little applicability to the political or economic structures of societies that, whatever their history, will be struggling to adapt to stringent and demanding environmental change.

Here I can do no better than to repeat a prognosis that I have expounded elsewhere.[1] It is to liken our distant prospects to those that followed the "fall" of the Roman Empire—the century or so after the sack of Rome in which the established institutions of the Empire gradually lost their ability to cope with the orderly provision of the former Roman territories, and in which a deep and pervasive crisis of faith simultaneously destroyed the Empire from within.

The analogy leads me to the belief that, as in the case of the fall of Rome, the end of business civilization will not come about as a single dramatic event. Rome may have been sacked in 410 A.D., but a variety of semi-Roman political forms lingered on after that event: the Ostrogoth and Visigoth kingdoms, the colossus of Byzantium, the Carolingian "empire." In similar fashion, the decline of the business civilization may or may not be marked by some extraordinary event comparable to the pillage of Rome, but it is also likely to be followed by a number of variant social orders, some of which may for a long time exhibit businesslike institutions or even some business-oriented values. Nonetheless, just as the fall of Rome eventually resulted in the disappearance of its central institutions and its "classical" spirit, so the successors to the civilization of business will sooner or later drift in a direction that will no longer bear much resemblance to the present order.

Here another Roman analogy may have significance for our long-term prospects. A crucial element in the transformation of the Roman system into the wholly different medieval period was the influence of the new religion of Christianity, which at first undermined the old order and later provided the spirit and shaped the institutional forms of the new order. So, too, in our future, I suspect that a major force for the transformation of business civilization will be a new religious orientation, directed against the canons and precepts of our time, and oriented toward a wholly different conception of the meaning of life and a mode of social organization congenial to the encouragement of that life.

What sort of religious orientation might this be? From our prior argument, a high degree of political authority will be inescapable in the period of extreme exigency we can expect a hundred years hence. This augurs for the cultivation of nationalist, authoritarian attitudes, perhaps today foreshadowed by the kind of religious politicism we find in China. The deification of the state, whatever we may think of it from the standpoint of our still-cherished individualist philosophies, seems therefore the most likely replacement for the deification of materialism that is the unacknowledged religion of our business culture.

This statist attitude, I should add, need not be one of a blind identification of secular rulers and divinity, comparable to the worst of the Roman emperors. Science and technology will be necessary partners with the state in defining the pace and pattern of economic life; and the "religion" of statism may therefore well include an admiration for scientific attitudes. What is crucial in the statist "religion," as I foresee it, is the elevation of the collective and communal destiny of man to the forefront of public consciousness, and the absolute subordination of private interests to public requirements. Whether this will be consistent with or conducive to political and intellectual liberties in general it is difficult to say. In principle, there is no reason why freedom of expression could not flourish in a survival-minded community. In practice, the centralization and intensification of political authority make this seem doubtful.

At a further remove, it is possible to imagine—one cannot "foresee"—an eventual dissolution of centralized power and a turn to the small-scale communities, based on self-sufficient and ecologically safe practices that have marked those enduring primitive worlds of which we spoke earlier. That is, perhaps, the destination toward which the constraints of nature are pushing the evolution of the social organism. But this achievement of communal society cannot possibly occur until the present unified structures of industrial production have been disassembled; until the threat of nuclear obliteration has been overcome once and for all; until the administration of economic life has been successfully internalized and no longer needs external sanction. All this is possible, but it is not on the agenda of the coming century, at least not for the industrial nations of the world.

I do not think that historians of the future will lament the disappearance of the business civilization. Who deplores the decline of Greek slavery, the end of the feudal relations between serf and lord, or the collapse of Mandarin China? Who will regret the passing of the conception of the "private" ownership of wealth that is patently social in origin and impact, or the end of the market mechanism with its efficiency in the attainment of every purpose save that of human development? The era of capitalism, once it is past, will be the occasion for amazement, perhaps even for a certain grudging respect, as Marx himself acknowledged in the *Communist Manifesto*, for it was capitalism, after all, that broke the bond of material servitude for humanity, even though it fastened upon it other social bonds that hobbled its potentialities in new ways.

Yet just as Periclean Greece or feudal Europe or imperial China were more than just economic forms of social organization, historians will surely see in capitalism more than its economic achievements and exactions. Here the balance sheet will be much more difficult to sum up. On the one hand, there is the crassness of outlook, the self-centeredness of behavior, so inextricably mixed with the idea of a business culture. This attitude is not, of course, peculiar to capitalism, although it may be peculiar to all commercial relationships. But it is in the nature of capitalist society that it has celebrated and made a norm of social values that are least tolerated in other civilizations. No other civilization has permitted the calculus of selfishness so to dominate its lifeways, nor has any other civilization allowed this narrowest of all motivations to be elevated to the status of a near categorical imperative.

But it would be wrong to sum up business civilization solely in terms of the philistinism that is its ugliest aspect. Bourgeois culture has also brought into being, and permitted to survive, other aspects of the individualism that is implicit in its economic philosophy. The ideas of political equality and dissent, of intellectual adventure, of social nonconformity, however much hedged about or breached in practice, owe much of their development to a bourgeois thought. Thus there are assuredly glories to the civilization of capitalism as there were glories to slave Greece or feudal Europe or ancient China. The parliaments, the scientific explorations, the spirit of artistic innovation of the capitalist world are its acropoli, its cathedrals, its bronzes. The self-conscious intellectual, half within, half outside his bourgeois home, is perhaps its most important cultural figure. And of course the material creations of its business organizations are its inextinguishable mark. Much as we now inspect Chichén Itzá, the Great Wall, the pyramids, Machu Picchu, so we may some day visit and marvel at the ruins of the great steel works at Sparrows Point, the atomic complex at Hanford, the computer centers at Houston.

Of all these attainments, that which is most difficult to appraise in terms of the future is the cultivation of the individualism that is so much a part of bourgeois economics, politics, thought, and art. Here is the crucial issue with which "socialism"—I use the word to describe whatever forms of society succeed the business civilization—will have to come to grips. Assuming away all the difficulties of bureaucracy, technology, or stubborn remnants of business habits, the great question to which an enlightened and humane "socialism" will have to address itself is the degree to which the individual will be encouraged to develop his or her unique attributes, differences, eccentricities.

This is not a question for which easy answers are available. For socialism will find its *raison d'être* in the deliberate cultivation of an "organic" society, one that establishes norms of behavior, shared moral standards, a unifying vision of its destination. But what will then be the bounds for the expression of private preferences? What will be the liberties accorded to artistic statements, social or sexual habits, political utterances?

No doubt the answers will depend to a large degree on the stringency of the constraints with which "socialism" will have to contend. But this is not the only problem. Much will also hinge on the conception of the nature of man himself—on his depiction as an infinitely malleable and plastic social creature, or as a being whose individualism ultimately reflects the uniqueness or the final autonomy of each person. The philosophy of individualism, which the capitalist epoch has nurtured and expressed, albeit in the grossest form, takes its strength from the assertion that there exists such a uniqueness, a final autonomy, within each individual. Like all deep beliefs, this is an untestable proposition. Whether it will survive the demands of the future I do not know. I only know that when I take the measure of capitalism, it is for me the element that, if it does not redeem the whole, at least offers the deepest reason to hope that not all of its civilization will disappear along with the business system.

---

[1] See "Second Thoughts on the Human Prospect," in the third printing of *An Inquiry into the Human Prospect* (New York, W. W. Norton, 1975). This essay was originally presented at the Seminar on Technology and Social Values at Columbia University.

Interdependence

PART SEVEN

Second Week — Sixth Day

Lewis Thomas,
The Lives of a Cell, "The Lives of a Cell"

Henry Steele Commager,
"A Declaration of INTERdependence"

Teilhard de Chardin,
The Phenomenon of Man
Chapters 1, 3 (selection)

Lewis Thomas, *The Lives of a Cell*, "Ceti"

The Lives of a Cell

by Lewis Thomas

The Lives of a Cell

WE are told that the trouble with Modern Man is that he has been trying to detach himself from nature. He sits in the topmost tiers of polymer, glass, and steel, dangling his pulsing legs, surveying at a distance the writhing life of the planet. In this scenario, Man comes on as a stupendous lethal force, and the earth is pictured as something delicate, like rising bubbles at the surface of a country pond, or flights of fragile birds.

But it is illusion to think that there is anything fragile about the life of the earth; surely this is the toughest membrane imaginable in the universe, opaque to probability, impermeable to death. We are the delicate part, transient and vulnerable as cilia. Nor is it a new thing for man to invent an existence that he imagines to be above the rest of life; this has been his most consistent intellectual exertion down the millennia. As illusion, it has never worked out to his satisfaction in the past, any more than it does today. Man is embedded in nature.

The biologic science of recent years has been making this a more urgent fact of life. The new, hard problem will be to cope with the dawning, intensifying realization of just how interlocked we are. The old, clung-to notions most of us have held about our special lordship are being deeply undermined.

Item. A good case can be made for our nonexistence as entities. We are not made up, as we had always supposed, of successively enriched packets of our own parts. We are shared, rented, occupied. At the interior of our cells, driving them, providing the oxidative energy that sends us out for the improvement of each shining day, are the mitochondria, and in a strict sense they are not ours. They turn out to be little separate creatures, the colonial posterity of migrant prokaryocytes, probably primitive bacteria that

447

swam into ancestral precursors of our eukaryotic cells and stayed there. Ever since, they have maintained themselves and their ways, replicating in their own fashion, privately, with their own DNA and RNA quite different from ours. They are as much symbionts as the rhizobial bacteria in the roots of beans. Without them, we would not move a muscle, drum a finger, think a thought.

Mitochondria are stable and responsible lodgers, and I choose to trust them. But what of the other little animals, similarly established in my cells, sorting and balancing me, clustering me together? My centrioles, basal bodies, and probably a good many other more obscure tiny beings at work inside my cells, each with its own special genome, are as foreign, and as essential, as aphids in anthills. My cells are no longer the pure line entities I was raised with; they are ecosystems more complex than Jamaica Bay.

I like to think that they work in my interest, that each breath they draw for me, but perhaps it is they who walk through the local park in the early morning, sensing my senses, listening to my music, thinking my thoughts.

I am consoled, somewhat, by the thought that the green plants are in the same fix. They could not be plants, or green, without their chloroplasts, which run the photosynthetic enterprise and generate oxygen for the rest of us. As it turns out, chloroplasts are also separate creatures with their own genomes, speaking their own language.

We carry stores of DNA in our nuclei that may have come in, at one time or another, from the fusion of ancestral cells and the linking of ancestral organisms in symbiosis. Our genomes are catalogues of instructions from all kinds of sources in nature, filed for all kinds of contingencies. As for me, I am grateful for differentiation and speciation, but I cannot feel as separate an entity as I did a few years ago, before I was told these things, nor, I should think, can anyone else.

Item. The uniformity of the earth's life, more astonishing than its diversity, is accountable by the high probability that we derived, originally, from some single cell, fertilized in a bolt of lightning as the earth cooled. It is from the progeny of this parent cell that we take our looks; we still share genes around, and the resemblance of the enzymes of grasses to those of whales is a family resemblance.

The viruses, instead of being single-minded agents of disease and death, now begin to look more like mobile genes. Evolution is still an infinitely long and tedious biologic game, with only the winners staying at the table, but the rules are beginning to look more flexible. We live in a dancing matrix of viruses; they dart, rather like bees, from organism to organism, from plant to insect to mammal to me and back again, and into the sea, tugging along pieces of this genome, strings of genes from that, transplanting grafts of DNA, passing around heredity as though at a great party. They may be a mechanism for keeping new, mutant kinds of DNA in the widest circulation among us. If this is true, the odd virus disease, on which we must focus so much of our attention in medicine, may be looked on as an accident, something dropped.

Item. I have been trying to think of the earth as a kind of organism, but it is no go. I cannot think of it this way. It is too big, too complex, with too many working parts lacking visible connections. The other night, driving through a hilly, wooded part of southern New England, I wondered about this. If not like an organism, what is it like, what is it *most* like? Then, satisfactorily for that moment, it came to me: it is *most* like a single cell.

A Declaration of INTERdependence

by Henry Steele Commager

WHEN in the course of history the threat of extinction confronts mankind, it is necessary for the people of The United States to declare their interdependence with the people of all nations and to embrace those principles and build those institutions which will enable mankind to survive and civilization to flourish.

Two centuries ago our forefathers brought forth a new nation; now we must join with others to bring forth a new world order. On this historic occasion it is proper that the American people should reaffirm those principles on which the United States of America was founded, acknowledge the new crises which confront them, accept the new obligations which history imposes upon them, and set forth the causes which impel them to affirm before all peoples their commitment to a Declaration of Interdependence.

We hold these truths to be self-evident: that all men are created equal; that the inequalities and injustices which afflict so much of the human race are the product of history and society, not of God or nature; that people everywhere are entitled to the blessings of life and liberty, peace and security and the realization of their full potential; that they have an inescapable moral obligation to preserve those rights for posterity; and that to achieve these ends all the peoples and nations of the globe should acknowledge their interdependence and join together to dedicate their minds and their hearts to the solution of those problems which threaten their survival.

To establish a new world order of compassion, peace, justice and security, it is essential that mankind free itself from the limitations of national prejudice, and acknowledge that the forces that unite it are incomparably deeper than those that divide it—that all people are part of one global community, dependent on one body of resources, bound together by the ties of a common humanity and associated in a common adventure on the planet Earth.

Let us then join together to vindicate and realize this great truth that mankind is one, and as one will nobly save or irreparably lose the heritage of thousands of years of civilization. And let us set forth the principles which should animate and inspire us if our civilization is to survive.

WE AFFIRM that the resources of the globe are finite, not infinite, that they are the heritage of no one nation or generation, but of all peoples, nations and of posterity, and that our deepest obligation is to transmit to that posterity a planet richer in material bounty, in beauty and in delight than we found it. Narrow notions of national sovereignty must not be permitted to curtail that obligation.

WE AFFIRM that the exploitation of the poor by the rich and the weak by the strong violates our common humanity and denies to large segments of society the blessings of life, liberty and happiness. We recognize a moral obligation to strive for a more prudent and more equitable sharing of the resources of the earth in order to ameliorate poverty, hunger and disease.

WE AFFIRM that the resources of nature are sufficient to nourish and sustain all the present inhabitants of the globe and that there is an obligation on every society to distribute those resources equitably, along with a corollary obligation upon every society to assure that its population does not place upon Nature a burden heavier than it can bear.

WE AFFIRM our responsibility to help create conditions which will make for peace and security and to build more effective machinery for keeping peace among the nations. Because the insensate accumulation of nuclear, chemical and biological weapons threatens the survival of Mankind we call for the immediate reduction and eventual elimination of these weapons under international supervision. We deplore the reliance on force to settle disputes between nation states and between rival groups within such states.

WE AFFIRM that the oceans are the common property of mankind whose dependence on their incomparable resources of nourishment and strength will, in the next century, become crucial for human survival, and that their exploitation should be so regulated as to serve the interests of the entire globe, and of future generations.

WE AFFIRM that pollution flows with the waters and flies with the winds, that it recognizes no boundary lines and penetrates all defenses, that it works irreparable damage alike to Nature and to Mankind—threatening with extinction the life of the seas, the flora and fauna of the earth, the health of the people in cities and the countryside alike—and that it can be adequately controlled only through international cooperation.

WE AFFIRM that the exploration and utilization of outer space is a matter equally important to all the nations of the globe and that no nation can be permitted to exploit or develop the potentialities of the planetary system exclusively for its own benefit.

WE AFFIRM that the economy of all nations is a seamless web, and that no one nation can any longer effectively maintain its processes of production and monetary systems without recognizing the necessity for collaborative regulation by international authorities.

WE AFFIRM that in a civilized society, the institutions of science and the arts are never at war and call upon all nations to exempt these institutions from the claims of chauvinistic nationalism and to foster that great community of learning and creativity whose benign function it is to advance civilization and the health and happiness of mankind.

WE AFFIRM that a world without law is a world without order, and we call upon all nations to strengthen and to sustain the United Nations and its specialized agencies, and other institutions of world order, and to broaden the jurisdiction of the World Court, that these may preside over a reign of law that will not only end wars but end as well that mindless violence which terrorizes our society even in times of peace.

WE can no longer afford to make little plans, allow ourselves to be the captives of events and forces over which we have no control, consult our fears rather than our hopes. We call upon the American people, on the threshold of the third century of their national existence, to display once again that boldness, enterprise, magnanimity and vision which enabled the founders of our Republic to bring forth a new nation and inaugurate a new era in human history. The fate of humanity hangs in the balance. Throughout the globe, hearts and hopes wait upon us. We summon all Mankind to unite to meet the great challenge.

The Phenomenon of Man

by Teilhard de Chardin

Chapter 1

The Threshold of the Terrestrial Planet: the Noosphere

WHEN COMPARED to all the living verticils, the human phylum is not like any other. But because the specific orthogenesis of the primates (urging them towards increasing cerebralisation) coincides with the axial orthogenesis of organised matter (urging all living things towards a higher consciousness) man, appearing at the heart of the primates, flourishes on the leading shoot of zoological evolution. It was with this observation that we rounded off our remarks on the state of the Pliocene world.

It is easy to see what privileged value that unique situation will confer upon the transit to reflection.

'The biological change of state terminating in the awakening of thought does not represent merely a critical point that the individual or even the species must pass through. Vaster than that, it affects life itself in its organic totality, and consequently it marks a transformation affecting the state of the entire planet.'

Such is the evidence—born of all the other testimony we have gradually assembled and added together in the course of our inquiry—which imposes itself irresistibly on both our logic and observation.

We have been following the successive stages of the same grand progression from the fluid contours of the early earth. Beneath the pulsations of geo-chemistry, of geo-tectonics and geo-biology, we have detected one and the same fundamental process, always recognisable—the one which was given material form in the first cells and was continued in the construction of nervous systems. We saw geogenesis promoted to biogenesis, which turned out in the end to be nothing else than psychogenesis.

With and within the crisis of reflection, the next turn in the series manifests itself. Psychogenesis has led to man. Now it effaces itself, relieved or absorbed by another and a higher function—the engendering and subsequent development of all the stages of the mind, in one word *noogenesis*. When for the first time in a living creature instinct perceived itself in its own mirror, the whole world took a pace forward.

As regards the choices and responsibilities of our activity, the consequences of this discovery are enormous. As regards our understanding of the earth they are decisive.

Geologists have for long agreed in admitting the zonal composition of our planet. We have already spoken of the barysphere, central and metallic, surrounded by the rocky lithosphere that in turn is surrounded by the fluid layers of the hydrosphere and the atmosphere. Since Suess, science has rightly become accustomed to add another to these four concentric layers, the living membrane composed of the fauna and flora of the globe, the biosphere, so often mentioned in these pages, an envelope as definitely universal as the other 'spheres' and even more definitely individualised than them. For, instead of representing a more or less vague grouping, it forms a single piece, the very tissue of the genetic relations which delineate the tree of life.

The recognition and isolation of a new era in evolution, the era of noogenesis, obliges us to distinguish correlatively a support proportionate to the operation—that is to say yet another membrane in the majestic assembly of telluric layers. A glow ripples outward from the first spark of conscious reflection. The point of ignition grows larger. The fire spreads in ever widening circles till finally the whole planet is covered with incandescence. Only one interpretation, only one name can be found worthy of this grand phenomenon. Much more coherent and just as extensive as any ˜preceding layer, it is really a new layer, the "thinking layer,' which, since its germination at the end of the Tertiary period, has spread over and above the world of plants and animals. In other words, outside and above the biosphere there is the noosphere.

With that it bursts upon us how utterly warped is every classification of the living world (or, indirectly, every construction of the physical one) in which man only figures logically as a *genus* or a new family. This is an error of perspective which deforms and uncrowns the whole phenomenon of the universe. To give man his true place in nature it is not enough to find one more pigeon-hole in the edifice of our systematisation or even an additional order or branch. With hominisation, in spite of the insignificance of the anatomical leap, we have the beginning of a new age. The earth 'gets a new skin.' Better still, it finds its soul.

Thenceforward, given its place in reality in proper dimensions, the historic threshold of reflection is much more important than any zoological gap, whether it be the one marking the origin of the tetrapods or even that of the metazoa. Among all the stages successively crossed by evolution, the birth of thought comes directly after, and is the only thing comparable in order of grandeur to, the condensation of the terrestrial chemism or the advent of life itself.

The paradox of man resolves itself by passing beyond measure. Despite the relief and harmony it brings to things, this perspective is at first sight disconcerting, running counter as it does to the illusion and habits which incline us to measure events by their material face. It also seems to us extravagant because, steeped as we are in what is human like a fish in the sea, we have difficulty in emerging from it in our minds so as to appreciate its specificness and breadth. But let us look round us a little more carefully. This sudden deluge of cerebralisation, this biological invasion of a new animal type which gradually eliminates or subjects all forms of life that are not human, this irresistible tide of fields and factories, this immense and growing edifice of matter and ideas— all these signs that we look at, day in day out—seem to proclaim that there has been a change on the earth and a change of planetary magnitude.

There can indeed be no doubt that, to an imaginary geologist coming one day far in the future to inspect our globe in fossil form, the most astounding of the revolutions undergone by the earth would be that which took place at the beginning of what has so rightly been called the psychozoic era. And even today, to a Martian capable of analysing sidereal radiations psychically no less than physically, the first characteristic of our planet would be, not the blue of the seas or the green of the forests, but the phosphorescence of thought.

The greatest revelation open to science today is to perceive that everything precious, active, and progressive originally contained in that cosmic fragment from which our world emerged, is now concentrated in and crowned by the noosphere.

And what is so supremely instructive about the origins of this noosphere (if we know how to look) is to see how *insensibly*, by dint of being universally and lengthily prepared, the enormous event of man's birth took place.

Chapter Three
The Modern Earth

A Change of Age   In every epoch man has thought himself at a 'turning-point of history.' And to a certain extent, if he be thought to be on a mountain spiral, he has not been wrong. But there are moments when this impression of transformation becomes accentuated and is thus particularly justified. And we are certainly not exaggerating the importance of our contemporary existences in estimating that, pivoted upon them, a turn of profound importance is taking place in the world which may even crush them.

When did this turn begin? It is naturally impossible to say exactly. Like a great ship, the human mass only changes its course gradually, so much so that we can put far back—at least as far as the Renaissance— the first vibrations which indicate the change of route. It is clear, at any rate, that at the end of the eighteenth century the course had been changed in the West. Since then, in spite of our occasional obstinacy in pretending that we are the same, we have in fact enetered a different world.

Firstly, economic changes. Advanced as it was in many ways two centuries ago, our civilisation was still based fundamentally on the soil and its partition. The type of 'real' property, the nucleus of the family, the prototype of the state (and even the universe) was still, as in the earliest days of society, the arable field, the territorial basis. Then, little by little, as a result of the 'dynamisation' of money, property has evaporated into something fluid and impersonal, so mobile that already the wealth of nations themselves has almost nothing in common with their frontiers.

Secondly, industrial changes. Up to the eighteenth century, in spite of the many improvements made, there was still only one known source of chemical energy—fire. And there was only one sort of mechanical energy employed—muscle, human or animal, multipled by the machine.

Lastly, social changes and the awakening of the masses.

Merely from looking at these external signs we can hardly fail to suspect that the great unrest which has pervaded our life in the West ever since the storm of the French Revolution springs from a nobler and deeper cause than the difficulties of a world seeking to recover some ancient equilibrium that it has lost. There is no question of shipwreck. What we are up against is the heavy swell of an unknown sea which we are just entering from behind the cape that protected us. What is troubling us intellectually, politically and even spiritually is something quite simple. With his customary acute intuition, Henri Breuil said to me one day: 'We have only just cast off the last moorings which held us to the Neolithic age.' The formula is paradoxical but illuminating. In fact the more I have thought over these words, the more inclined I have been to think that Breuil was right.

We are, at this very moment, passing through an age of *transition*.

The age of industry; the age of oil, electricity and the atom; the age of the machine, of huge collectivities and of science—the future will decide what is the best name to describe the era we are entering. The word matters little. What does matter is that we should be told that, at the cost of what we are enduring, life is taking a step, and a decisive step, in us and in our environment. After the long maturation that has been steadily going on during the apparent immobility of the agricultural centuries, the hour has come at last, characterised by the birth pangs inevitable in another change of state. There were the first men—those who witnessed our origin. There are others who will witness the great scenes of the end. To us, in our brief span of life, falls the honour and good fortune of coinciding with a critical change of the noosphere.

In these confused and restless zones in which present blends with future in a world of upheaval, we stand face to face with all the grandeur, the unprecedented grandeur, of the phenomenon of man. Here if anywhere, now if ever, have we, more legitimately than any of our predecessors, the right to think that we can measure the importance and detect the direction of the process of hominisation. Let us look carefully and try to understand. And to do so let us probe beneath the surface and try to decipher the particular form of mind which is coming to birth in the womb of the earth today.

Our earth of factory chimneys and offices, seething with work and business, our earth with a hundred new radiations—this great organism lives, in final analysis, because of and for the sake of, a new soul. Beneath a change of age lies a change of thought. Where are we to look for it, where are we to situate this renovating and subtle alteration which, without appreciably changing our bodies, has made new creatures of us? In one place and one only—in a new intuition involving a total change in the physiognomy of the universe in which we move—in other words, in an awakening.

What has made us in four or five generations so different from our forebears (in spite of all that may be said), so ambitious too, and so worried, is not merely that we have discovered and mastered other forces of nature. In final analysis it is, if I am not mistaken, that we have become conscious of the movement which is carrying us along, and have thereby realised the formidable problems set us by this reflective exercise of the human effort.

THE DISCOVERY OF EVOLUTION

A. The Perception of Space-time[1] We have all forgotten the moment when, opening our eyes for the first time, we saw light and things around us all jumbled up in it and all on one single plane. It requires a great effort to imagine the time when we were unable to read or again to take our minds back to the time when for us the world extended no farther than the walls of our home and our family circle.

Similarly it seems to us incredible that men could have lived without suspecting that the stars are hung above us hundreds of light years away, or that the contours of life stretched out millions of years behind us to the limits of our horizon. Yet we have only to open any of those books with barely yellowing pages in which the authors of the sixteenth, or even as late as the eighteenth, century discoursed on the structure of worlds to be startled by the fact that our great-great-great-grandfathers felt perfectly at ease in a cubic space where the stars turned round the earth, and had been doing so for less than 6,000 years. In a cosmic atmosphere which would suffocate us from the first moment, and in perspectives in which it is physically impossible for us to enter, they breathed without any inconvenience, if not very deeply.

Between them and us what, then, has happened?

I know of no more moving story nor any more revealing of the biological reality of a noogenesis than that of intelligence struggling step by step from the beginning to overcome the encircling illusion of proximity.

In the course of this struggle to master the dimensions and the relief of the universe, space was the first to yield—naturally, because it was more tangible. In fact the first hurdle was taken in this field when long, long ago a man (some Greek, no doubt, before Aristotle), bending back on itself the apparent flatness of things, had an intuition that there were antipodes. From then onwards round the round earth the firmament itself rolled roundly. But the focus of the spheres was badly placed. By its situation it incurably paralysed the elasticity of the system. It was only really in the time of Galileo, through rupture with the ancient geocentric view, that the skies were made free for the boundless expansions which we have since detected in them. The earth became a mere speck of sidereal dust. Immensity became possible, and to balance it the infinitesimal sprang into existence.

For lack of apparent yardsticks, the depths of the past took much longer to be plumbed. The movement of stars, the shape of mountains, the chemical nature of bodies—indeed all matter seemed to express a continual present. The physics of the seventeenth century was incapable of opening Pascal's eyes to the abysses of the past. To discover the real age of the earth and then of the elements, it was necessary for man to become fortuitously interested in an object of moderate mobility, such as life, for instance, or even volcanoes. It was thus through a narrow crack (that of 'natural history,' then in its infancy) that from the eighteenth century onwards light began to seep down into the great depths beneath our feet. In these initial estimates, the time considered necessary for the formation of the world was still very modest. But at least the impetus had been given and the way out opened up. After the walls of space, shaken by the Renaissance, it was the floor (and consequently the ceiling) of time which, from Buffon onwards, became mobile. Since then, under the unceasing pressure of facts, the process has continually accelerated. Although the strain has been taken off for close on two hundred years, the spirals of the world have still not been relaxed. The distance between the turns in the spiral has seemed ever greater and there have always been further turns appearing deeper still.

Yet in these first stages in man's awakening to the immensities of the cosmos, space and time, however vast, still remained homogenous and independent of each other; they were two great containers, quite separate one from the other, extending infinitely no doubt, but in which things floated about or were packed together in ways owing nothing to the nature of their setting.

The two compartments had been enlarged beyond measure, but within each of them the objects seemed as freely transposable as before. It seemed as if they could be placed here or there, moved forward, pushed back, or even suppressed at will. If no-one ventured formally as far as this play of thought, at least there was still no clear idea why or to what extent it was impossible. This was a question which did not arise.

It was only in the middle of the nineteenth century, again under the influence of biology, that the light dawned at last, revealing the *irreversible coherence* of all that exists. First the concatenations of life and, soon after, those of matter. The least molecule is, in nature and in position, a function of the whole sidereal process, and the least of the protozoa is structurally so knit into the web of life that, such is the hypothesis, its existence cannot be annihilated without *ipso facto* undoing the whole network of the biosphere. The *distribution, succession and solidarity of objects are born from their concrescence in a common genesis.* Time and space are organically joined again so as to weave, together, the stuff of the universe. That is the point we have reached and how we perceive things today.

Psychologically what is hidden behind this initiation? One might well become impatient or lose heart at the sight of so many minds (and not mediocre ones either) remaining today still closed to the idea of evolution, if the whole of history were not there to pledge to us that a truth once seen, even by a single mind, always ends up by imposing itself on the totality of human consciousness. For many, evolution is still only transformism, and transformism is only an old Darwinian hypothesis as local and as dated as Laplace's conception of the solar system or Wegener's Theory of Continental Drift. Blind indeed are those who do not see the sweep of a movement whose orbit infinitely transcends the natural sciences and has successively invaded and conquered the surrounding territory—chemistry, physics, sociology and even mathematics and the history of religions. One after the other all the fields of human knowledge have been shaken and carried away by the same under-water current in the direction of the study of some *development*. Is evolution a theory, a system or a hypothesis? It is much more: it is a general condition to which all theories, all hypotheses, all systems must bow and which they must satisfy henceforward if they are to be thinkable and true. Evolution is a light illuminating all facts, a curve that all lines must follow.

In the last century and a half the most prodigious event, perhaps, ever recorded by history since the threshold of reflection has been taking place in our minds: the definitive access of consciousness to a *scale of new dimensions;* and in consequence the birth of an entirely renewed universe, without any change of line or feature by the simple transformation of its intimate substance.

Until that time the world seemed to rest, static and fragmentable, on the three axes of its geometry. Now it is a casting from a single mould.

What makes and classifies a 'modern' man (and a whole host of our contemporaries is not yet 'modern' in this sense) is having become capable of seeing in terms not of space and time alone, but also of duration, or—and it comes to the same thing—of biological space-time; and above all having become incapable of seeing anything otherwise—anything—*not even himself.*

This last step brings us to the heart of the metamorphosis.

B. The Envelopment in Duration Obviously man could not see evolution all around him without feeling to some extent carried along by it himself. Darwin has demonstrated this. Nevertheless, looking at the progress of transformist views in the last hundred years, we are surprised to see how naively naturalists and physicists were able at the early stages to imagine themselves to be standing outside the universal stream they had just discovered. Almost incurably subject and object tend to become separated from each other in the act of knowing. We are continually inclined to isolate ourselves from the things and events which surround us, as though we were looking at them from outside, from the shelter of an observatory into which they were unable to enter, as though we were spectators, not elements, in what goes on. That is why, when it was raised by the concatenations of life, the question of man's origins was for so long restricted to the purely somatic and bodily side. A long animal heredity might well have formed our limbs, but our mind was always above the play of the realities it enumerated. However materialistic they might be, it did not occur to the first evolutionists that their scientific intelligence had anything to do in itself with evolution.

At this stage they were only half-way to the truth that concerned them.

From the very first pages of this book, I have been relentlessly insisting on one thing: for invincible reasons of homogeneity and coherence, the fibres of cosmogenesis demand their prolongation in us in a way that goes far deeper than flesh and blood. We are not only set adrift and carried away in the current of life by the material surface of our being; but, like a subtle fluid, space-time first drowns our bodies and then penetrates to our soul; it fills it and impregnates it; it blends itself with the soul's potentialities to such an extent that soon the soul no longer knows how to distinguish space-time from its own thoughts. To those who can use their eyes nothing, not even the summit of our being, can escape this flux any longer, because it is only definable in accretions of consciousness. The very act by which the fine edge of our minds penetrates the absolute is a phenomenon, as it were, of *emergence*. In short, first recognized only at a single point, then perforce extended to the whole inorganic and organic volume of matter, evolution is now, whether we like it or not, gaining the psychic zones of the world and transferring to the spiritual constructions of life not only the cosmic stuff but also the cosmic 'primacy' hitherto reserved by science to the tangled whirlwind of the ancient 'ether.'

How indeed could we incorporate thought into the organic flux of space-time without being forced to grant it the first place in the process? How would we imagine a cosmogenesis reaching right up to mind without being thereby confronted with a noogenesis?

We are not only concerned with thought as participating in evolution as an anomaly or as an epiphenomenon; but evolution as so reducible to and identifiable with a progress towards thought that the movement of our souls expresses and measures the very stages of progress of evolution itself. Man discovers that *he is nothing else than evolution become conscious of itself,* to borrow Julian Huxley's concise expression. It seems to me that our modern minds (because and inasmuch as they are modern) will never find rest until they settle down to this view. On this summit and on this summit alone are repose and illumination waiting for us.

[¹ Cf. Collingwood, *Idea of Nature* (O.U.P. 1944) *passim.*]

The Lives of a Cell

by Lewis Thomas

Ceti

TAU CETI is a relatively nearby star that sufficiently resembles our sun to make its solar system a plausible candidate for the existence of life. We are, it appears, ready to begin getting in touch with Ceti, and with any other interested celestial body in more remote places, out to the edge. CETI is also, by intention, the acronym of the First International Conference on Communication with Extraterrestrial Intelligence, held in 1972 in Soviet Armenia under the joint sponsorship of the National Academy of Sciences of the United States and the Soviet Academy, which involved eminent physicists and astronomers from various countries, most of whom are convinced that the odds for the existence of life elsewhere are very high, with a reasonable probability that there are civilizations, one place or another, with technologic mastery matching or exceeding ours.

On this assumption, the conferees thought it likely that radioastronomy would be the generally accepted mode of interstellar communication, on grounds of speed and economy. They made a formal recommendation that we organize an international cooperative program, with new and immense radio telescopes, to probe the reaches of deep space for electromagnetic signals making sense. Eventually, we would plan to send out messages on our own and receive answers, but at the outset it seems more practical to begin by catching snatches of conversation between others.

So, the highest of all our complex technologies in the hardest of our sciences will soon be engaged, full scale, in what is essentially biologic research—and with some aspects of social science, at that.

The earth has become, just in the last decade, too small a place. We have the feeling of being confined—shut in; it is something like outgrowing a small town in a small county. The views of the dark, pocked surface of

465

Mars, still lifeless to judge from the latest photographs, do not seem to have extended our reach; instead, they bring closer, too close, another unsatisfactory feature of our local environment. The blue noonday sky, cloudless, has lost its old look of immensity. The word is out that the sky is not limitless; it is finite. It is, in truth, only a kind of local roof, a membrane under which we live, luminous but confusingly refractile when suffused with sunlight; we can sense its concave surface a few miles over our heads. We know that it is tough and thick enough so that when hard objects strike it from the outside they burst into flames. The color photographs of the earth are more amazing than anything outside: we live inside a blue chamber, a bubble of air blown by ourselves. The other sky beyond, absolutely black and appalling, is wide-open country, irresistible for exploration.

Here we go, then. An extraterrestrial embryologist, having a close look at us from time to time, would probably conclude that the morphogenesis of the earth is coming along well, with the beginnings of a nervous system and fair-sized ganglions in the form of cities, and now with specialized, dish-shaped sensory organs, miles across, ready to receive stimuli. He may well wonder, however, how we will go about responding. We are evolving into the situation of a Skinner pigeon in a Skinner box, peering about in all directions, trying to make connections, probing.

When the first word comes in from outer space, finally, we will probably be used to the idea. We can already provide a quite good explanation for the origin of life, here or elsewhere. Given a moist planet with methane, formaldehyde, ammonia, and some usable minerals, all of which abound, exposed to lightning or ultraviolet irradiation at the right temperature, life might start off almost anywhere. The tricky, unsolved thing is how to get the polymers to arrange in membranes and invent replication. The rest is clear going. If they follow our protocol, it will be anaerobic life at first, then photosynthesis and the first exhalation of oxygen, then respiring life and the great burst of variation, then speciation, and, finally, some kind of consciousness. It is easy, in the telling.

I suspect that when we have recovered from the first easy acceptance of signs of life from elsewhere, and finished nodding at each other, and finished smiling, we will be in shock. We have had it our way, relatively speaking, being unique all these years, and it will be hard to deal with the thought that the whole, infinitely huge, spinning, clocklike apparatus around us is itself animate, and can sprout life whenever the conditions are right. We will respond, beyond doubt, by making connections after the fashion of established life, floating out our filaments, extending pili, but we will end up feeling smaller than ever, as small as a single cell, with a quite new sense of continuity. It will take some getting used to.

The immediate problem, however, is a much more practical, down-to-earth matter, and must be giving insomnia to the CETI participants. Let us assume that there is, indeed, sentient life in one or another part of remote space, and that we will be successful in getting in touch with it. What on earth are we going to talk about? If, as seems likely, it is a hundred or more light years away, there are going to be some very long pauses. The barest amenities, on which we rely for opening conversations—Hello, are you there?, from us, followed by Yes, hello, from them—will take two hundred years at least. By the time we have our party we may have forgotten what we had in mind.

We could begin by gambling on the rightness of our technology and just send out news of ourselves, like a mimeographed Christmas letter, but we would have to choose our items carefully, with durability of meaning in mind. Whatever information we provide must still make sense to us two centuries later, and must still seem important, or the conversation will be an embarrassment to all concerned. In two hundred years it is, as we have found, easy to lose the thread.

Perhaps the safest thing to do at the outset, if technology permits, is to send music. This language may be the best we have for explaining what we are like to others in space, with least ambiguity. I would vote for Bach, all of Bach, streamed out into space, over and over again. We would be bragging, of course, but it is surely excusable for us to put the best possible face on at the beginning of such an acquaintance. We can tell the harder truths later. And, to do ourselves justice, music would give a fairer picture of what we are really like than some of the other things we might be sending, like *Time*, say, or a history of the U.N. or Presidential speeches. We could send out our science, of course, but just think of the wincing at this end when the polite comments arrive two hundred years from now. Whatever we offer as today's items of liveliest interest are bound to be out of date and irrelevant, maybe even ridiculous. I think we should stick to music.

Perhaps, if the technology can be adapted to it, we should send some paintings. Nothing would better describe what this place is like, to an outsider, than the Cézanne demonstrations that an apple is really part fruit, part earth.

What kinds of questions should we ask? The choices will be hard, and everyone will want his special question first. What are your smallest particles? Did you think yourselves unique? Do you have colds? Have you anything quicker than light? Do you always tell the truth? Do you cry? There is no end to the list.

Perhaps we should wait a while, until we are sure we know what we want to know, before we get down to detailed questions. After all, the main question will be the opener: Hello, are you there? If the reply should turn out to be Yes, hello, we might want to stop there and think about that, for quite a long time.

Aspen Institute for Humanistic Studies